REFERENCE SERIES

Air Force Bases

Volume II

Air Bases Outside the United States of America

Harry R. Fletcher

United States Air Force Historical Research Agency

CENTER FOR AIR FORCE HISTORY
UNITED STATES AIR FORCE
WASHINGTON, D.C., 1993

Library of Congress Cataloging-in-Publication Data

Fletcher, Harry R.
　　Air Force Bases.

　　(Reference series)
　　Includes bibliographical references.
　　Contents: v. 2. Air bases outside the United States of America.
　　1. Air bases—United States—Directories. I. United States. Air Force.
Center for Air Force History. II. Series: Reference series (United States. Air Force.
Center for Air Force History).
UG633.M68　　　　　　　358.4'17'02573　　　　　　88-600231

Foreword

This volume is the second in a series on active Air Force bases and a continuation of a recent line of works prepared for the Center for Air Force History under the Reference Series. These reference books contain specific information about a number of topics of interest to the United States Air Force and other arms of the Department of Defense. They are designed to present fundamental data about such diverse subjects as Air Force aircraft, combat action, unit lineage and honors, campaign medals and streamers, and air bases, for those who will write more extensive narrative accounts about Air Force activities and operations. Volume II in the *Air Force Bases* series provides important background information about overseas installations that are less well known than domestic stations.

The active installations included in this volume, to be sure, represent only a fraction of the overseas bases, fields, and stations operated by the United States Air Force and its predecessor organizations since the beginning of World War II. Nevertheless, many of the most significant and enduring air bases appear in these pages, some of which are essential to America's defense posture. This work represents a starting point for military students and staff officers involved in defense research or planning, and for scholars interested in serious research of air bases and the Air Force organizations that operated from them.

Richard P. Hallion
Air Force Historian

Preface

Several years ago the Center for Air Force History began a series of reference works designed to provide vital information concerning various aspects of Air Force history, from the lineage of individual units to the medals and campaign honors awarded by the United States Air Force to its personnel and organizations. Brief resumes of bases and stations of the Air Force appeared ideal for inclusion in the reference series because basic data about Air Force installations are infrequently found in published works that most often feature the exploits of combat flyers and organizations. All Air Force organizations and personnel have nevertheless been quartered and trained for operations at some base, field, or station; every aerial exploit began at one of them. Day-to-day aircraft repair and maintenance took place there, while the base host organization looked after buildings of all kinds; maintained roads, runways, taxiways, revetments and supply dumps; and furnished health services, security, messing, legal, and recreational facilities. Base operating units and their commanders have all too often been overlooked, even though they supported important tactical units and often dozens of off-base and detached installations.

This book, *Air Force Bases, Volume II*, contains fundamental data on forty-four major air bases located outside of the territorial limits of the United States in fifteen countries or territories overseas. All of these bases, stations, or airports were of vital national significance as America grappled with the challenges of the Cold War. Volume I, published previously, provided similar information about domestic United States Air Force bases.

These works do not offer definitive accounts of each base; they do offer data of value to those interested in the histories of these stations and provide a ready reference for others seeking immediate, pertinent information about them. The emphasis has been placed upon major primary bases, most of which host major operational units of the active Air Force. A few installations covered in this work are exceptions to this rule. They have been included because they have significant missions in support of defense alliances, such as the North Atlantic Treaty Organization (NATO), and possess impressive histories of their own. Installations in this category include Lindsey and San Vito dei Normanni Air Stations and RAF Chicksands. Camp New Amsterdam, on the other hand, hosts a combat unit of the USAF, but is itself an off-base installation of Hahn AB, a primary installation. Andersen, although an Air Force base, is located in an unincorporated territory outside the United States, and therefore is included in this volume. Many great bases of the past, bases discontinued or disposed of before 1982, provided important support for the worldwide mission of the Air Force. It is hoped that some of these may be included in future works on Air Force bases.

A number of people played important roles in the preparation of this volume. At the Air Force Historical Research Agency, Mr. Lloyd H. Cornett, Jr., then Director, provided overall direction, while Mr. R. Cargill Hall, then Chief of the Research Division, guided the research effort, provided counsel on details, and edited the final manuscript. Air Force Reserve individual mobilization augmentee Captain William T. Branum assisted in the identification of many unit commanders and indexed thousands of USAF Installation Characteristics Reports. In the Research Division, Mr. Robert Mueller, author of volume I of this series, completed important parts of the basic research for a number of the bases included in this volume. Mr. Gerald E. Hasselwander and Mr. Charles A. Ravenstein offered helpful advice concerning base operations and unit assignments, while Captain Barry J. Anderson and Master Sergeant Martin E. James provided information concerning specific bases in Europe. Ms. Pauline Tubbs, editorial assistant, typed the first part of this manuscript, while Mrs. Jacqueline Blamires, editorial assistant, rendered outstanding service in typing, editing, and proofreading the major part of this work. I also owe a debt of thanks to Mrs. Helen J. Weaver, historical research assistant, and, especially, to Mr. Jack C. Pettee, who assisted in the research and verification of units from over 30,000 Unit Data Cards and compiled lists of organizations assigned at the various bases and stations. Mr. Julius A. Augustus did yeoman service in completing the work begun by Mr. Pettee.

Special thanks are also owed Mr. W. Gurvis Lawson of the Cartographic Information Division, Air University Library, who quickly and accurately resolved problems connected with the precise location of installations and the state or territory of jurisdiction. Dr. Charles H. Hildreth, former Command Historian, United States Air Forces in Europe, and Dr. Robert J. Parks, Command Historian, Pacific Air Forces, generously provided brief narratives and additional information regarding bases assigned to their respective commands. Mr. John T. Bohn, Command Historian, Strategic Air Command; Mr. Robert M. Kipp, Command Historian, Air Force Space Command; Mr. Robert J. Smith, Command Historian, Tactical Air Command; Mr. Robert T. Cossaboom, Command Historian, United

States Air Forces in Europe; and Dr. James K. Matthews, Command Historian, Military Airlift Command, all rendered invaluable assistance to the project by disseminating drafts of individual base sections to the appropriate historians for their critical review, additions, and corrections. I am also indebted to the historians at the various overseas installations who diligently read the draft manuscript and constructively added their comments and suggestions thereby making this a more precise and useful work. Mr. Larry R. Benson, Palace Team Chief, Historian Civilian Career Program, offered the author several helpful suggestions about European bases; his study, *USAF Aircraft Basing in Europe, North Africa, and the Middle East, 1945–1980*, published by the United States Air Forces in Europe (USAFE) in 1981, was particularly beneficial in the preparation of this volume, especially with regard to the operational capability of the respective USAFE bases. Mrs. Barbara J. Spears and other members of the Air Force Reference Branch, National Personnel Records Center at St. Louis, Missouri, assisted Mr. Mueller in identifying base commanders and in securing orders not available in the holdings of the Air Force Historical Research Agency. The Real Property Division of the USAF Directorate of Engineering and Services at Bolling AFB, DC, generously placed its entire collection of Installation Characteristics Reports at the disposal of the Agency. Research for this book depended in great part, of course, on the countless squadron, group, wing, and command historians whose narrative histories and appendices on file at the Air Force Historical Research Agency contained well selected primary source documents. That we were able to find as much primary material about the many bases that appear here is due largely to the pioneer efforts of these field historians of the past. Needless to say, responsibility for this work, including whatever inadequacies or weaknesses it may still contain, is mine alone.

Harry R. Fletcher
Montgomery, Alabama

The Author

HARRY R. FLETCHER, before his retirement in 1990, was a historian in the Research Division, Air Force Historical Research Agency, Maxwell AFB, Alabama. Born in Platteville, Wisconsin, he served in the armed forces during World War II and the Korean conflict. After receiving a bachelor's degree in history at Wisconsin State University, Platteville, in 1955, he completed work for the MA in modern European history at the University of Wisconsin in 1961 and pursued further graduate work in British and European history at Louisiana State University and the University of Wisconsin. In 1963 Mr. Fletcher joined the Studies Branch of the USAF Historical Division, Aerospace Studies Institute, where he served until 1969 as Editor, German Air Force Historical Monograph Project. From October 1969 to October 1974 he was Assistant Professor of European history, Chairman of the Department of History and Social Sciences, and, for a time, Chairman of the Department of Criminal Justice, Troy State University in Montgomery, Alabama. He rejoined the Research Division of the Air Force Historical Research Agency in 1974. Mr. Fletcher edited six monographs of the German series, all published by Arno Press, New York. He is the author of several articles on German Air Force history and the disposition of captured German and related records held by the United States Air Force.

Contents

CONTENTS

Introduction

United States Air Force installations date only from the creation of the United States Air Force in September of 1947. Many present-day bases, stations, and airports, however, trace their origin to Army Airfields of World War II, and thence back to the Army Air Corps and Air Service. Few of the current overseas bases that appear in this work were activated prior to 1950, although some originated as British, German, or Japanese camps or flying fields during or prior to World War II. Clark Air Base in the Philippines and Howard Air Base in Panama are two exceptions having military aviation connections dating from the days of the Air Service and Army Air Corps.

Following World War II, the Army Air Forces possessed a massive complement of permanent, temporary, standby, leased, and confiscated air bases, stations, and airfields throughout the United States and beyond, bases scattered from the Caribbean to the Far East and Arctic, and from the Mediterranean basin through central Europe. Many of these were discontinued or inactivated in 1946–1947 in the postwar U.S. military demobilization. By 1948 the new United States Air Force still retained an impressive number of overseas bases, but many of them, such as Andersen, Tempelhof, Rhein-Main, Lajes, and Wheelus had become bases primarily for the support of air transport operations and for the logistical activity of U.S. occupation forces in Europe and Japan.

In 1948 some of the existing fields were suitable for expansion and renovation to meet the increasing global requirements of an Air Force primarily oriented for strategic warfare. Others, however, proved poorly situated, delimited by encroaching population, or otherwise unsuitable for further military purposes and were therefore discontinued. By this time the extension of U.S. tactical and strategic air power in the postwar world was clearly limited by the requirements for foreign basing. When the Cold War ensued, the Air Force increasingly needed operational bases in many overseas areas to ensure a rapid U.S. response to military threats from the Soviet Union. Since bases in the desired areas were frequently nonexistent or inadequate, except as standby installations, a number of new bases had to be constructed. The Berlin Airlift of 1948–49, followed soon afterward by the Korean conflict, underscored the critical requirement for first-class operational bases in many parts of the world.

In the early 1950s, following the National Security Council's plan for U.S. military expansion, the Air Force planned and constructed installations in the Far East, Spain, French Morocco, and Greenland, while bases in Libya, the Azores, and the central and western Pacific were improved to accommodate the largest U.S. military aircraft. Most of the building tasks were directed by the Corps of Engineers, U.S. Army, although in Korea and elsewhere in the Far East Air Force Engineer Aviation units took a direct hand in building bases. In Spain, the Navy Bureau of Yards and Docks supervised construction performed by local contractors and construction firms. Elsewhere in Europe, the major part of building and renovating was handled by British, German, Dutch, and French engineers and construction companies.

Building installations in the postwar world proved to be far more difficult and expensive a process than was true in World War II, since bases had to be larger and facilities constructed in a far more permanent way for high-performance jet aircraft. Moreover, the service encountered delays in securing leases and contracts and even more problems in basing certain types of aircraft—unsettling political issues that had previously been resolved quickly in the press of a world war. Changes in governments, international lease and rental expirations, and alterations in defense alignments modified USAF basing plans. In September 1961 the Berlin Crisis increased Cold War tensions and provoked new demands for a stronger military presence in Europe, but by June 1963 other international pressures compelled the Air Force to abandon its bases in Morocco. Three years later, French President Charles de Gaulle announced the withdrawal of France from NATO, obliging the United States to withdraw from French airfields on 1 April 1967. Shortly thereafter, Colonel Muammar el-Qaddafi's *coup d'etat* in Libya forced the USAF to abandon Wheelus Air Base, prompting a hasty and massive relocation of units and equipment to the European continent.

Changes in technology and strategic doctrine also affected the use and of various overseas bases in the postwar years. With the introduction of long-range turbojet transports, for example, Lajes Air Base in the Azores declined in use and was nearly inactivated in the early 1970s, until the 1973 "Yom Kippur" war and the denial of overflight rights in Europe forcefully reminded American policymakers of the vital strategic value of this Atlantic air base. Other shifts in basing occurred in the United Kingdom, Germany, and the Far East as a result of new acquisitions, contracting of new leases, expiration of old agreements, and the fortunes of war in Southeast Asia. The movement of key organizations, such as Headquarters

United States Air Forces in Europe, to new locations also entailed considerable base and base support modification.

In the 1960s the Air Force constructed numerous bases in South Vietnam, Thailand, and elsewhere within range of the Southeast Asia combat area. As the conflict took an unfavorable turn and began to wind down, however, many of these bases were quickly discontinued and, with the termination of direct U.S. participation in 1973, USAF basing in the Far East shrank to its present complement of installations. The changing complexion of conventional and nuclear threats in the 1970s produced new demands upon tactical units and their supporting bases. These changes required the building of specially hardened shelters and maintenance facilities, and improved base defenses to thwart guerrilla and terrorist attacks. Volume II of Air Force Bases provides a comprehensive survey of major existing Air Force installations overseas in the post-Vietnam era.

Explanatory Notes

The following notes explain the particular terms, format, and methodology used in presenting information concerning USAF overseas bases appearing in this volume.

Location. Refers to the distance and direction of the base from the nearest city or town, and the base's location in relationship to other well known cities or geographical reference points. At the time this volume was prepared, Germany was divided into the German Democratic Republic in the east and the Federal Republic of Germany in the west. Because the tension between East and West was, in many cases, the reason for the existence of bases in Germany, the locations for facilities in Germany indicate Federal Republic of Germany and West Berlin.

Name. A few overseas bases memorialize prominent individuals, primarily Air Force personalities. Most overseas installations, however, derive their names from those formerly used by the host country, usually the names of nearby cities or towns, or geographical features. Diacritical marks frequently have been ignored in names given to Air Force bases. Consequently, no diacritical marks were used in preparing this volume.

Date of Current Name. Date the installation officially received its present designation.

Previous Names. Only the official names designated by the Air Force, former names used by the U.S. Army, or names used by the host country that originally operated the base appear, together with pertinent dates if known. With the establishment of the Department of the Air Force and the United States Air Force in September 1947, Army Airfields and Army Air Bases became Air Force Bases or Air Force Stations, but overseas installations in the territory of another country became Air Bases or Air Stations.

Date of Establishment. Date on which a base began operations, or when the administrative unit of an establishment was activated or organized by either a military service or a major command.

Date Construction Began. Date actual construction commenced, as opposed to preliminary surveying, soil testing, and transport of construction equipment.

EXPLANATORY NOTES

Date of Beneficial Occupancy. Date of occupancy of an installation before completion, when the air arm occupant began its mission, or the initial base support unit assumed responsibility for the base. The chronological sequence of establishment, construction, and occupancy often varied greatly, with establishment frequently occurring prior to construction. When two dates appeared to be equally valid for any given action, both are cited with appropriate annotations. For example, two primary documents of equal authenticity might exist, one providing the date on which construction was supposed to begin or the date construction personnel arrived at the site, and another reporting the actual beginning of construction. Here, as elsewhere in this volume, primary sources were consulted whenever possible.

Base Operating Units. Identifies organization providing custodial and support functions for the installations. These were generally Army Air Force base units, which became Air Force base units after 1948 and subsequently became air base or combat support groups. They must not be confused with other support and combat units having a tactical or operational mission and assigned at the base, such as a field maintenance squadron or a bombardment wing. These latter units are shown under "Units Assigned." In some instances a combat wing operated the base. The date base operating units were stationed at a base does not always coincide with the activation, inactivation, or disposal dates of the base. During the early history of a base, the operating unit was sometimes a U.S. Army, U.S. Navy, or civilian organization that briefly performed custodial functions on a *pro tem* basis until the first operating unit of the air arm arrived.

Base Commanders. The rank shown for each commander is the highest rank held by that individual while serving as base commander. The first senior base officer, who supervised most of the initial construction, was usually called "project officer," but all such officers (if known) are shown in the list of base commanders. The term "temporary" describes commanders who served briefly until the arrival of the designated commander. In some instances, bases reduced to subbase or off-base installation status were commanded by the base commander of the controlling primary installation. Occasionally base commanders remained on site beyond the date of base inactivation in order to complete final transfer of property or equipment, while at other times they departed prior to the official base closure. Sometimes only an initial could be found for the commander's first name; at other times the identity of the commander could not be established at all. Whenever the name of a commander or his tenure at the base could not be determined, the gap is indicated by "unk" (unknown). Likewise, when only an approximate date could be found, a "c." (circa) is used.

Major Off-Base and Detached Installations. "Off-base," "detached," and "detached/leased" installations important to the mission of the base are cited in chronological order according to their activation date or date of transfer to the base's accountability. They are further cited in alphabetical order and in numerical order, so that "Airman Housing Annex #1" would precede "Airman Housing Annex #2" on the listing. Off-base installations are accountable and are assigned property of the primary base or installation. A detached or detached/leased installation may belong to another base or agency, but it either furnishes support to or receives support from the primary base. Those ancillary, unmanned support facilities, such as small electronic or radio communications and landing instrumentation sites, and facilities having no direct bearing upon the base's overall operational capability, have generally been excluded.

The date of assignment or transfer of jurisdiction to another USAF base, to another U.S. Government agency, or to a foreign government are cited when available to complete the dates of actual jurisdiction. Known activation, inactivation, and disposal dates are shown. "Disposed" signifies that a primary installation had been relieved of jurisdiction and property accountability for a given subinstallation. The term "inactive" signifies that property and operational responsibility and jurisdiction continued to remain with the primary installation.

Major Changes in Operational Capability. This section provides a brief summary of the base's major mission and activities, together with references to major renovations and expansion of existing facilities and construction of new buildings and structures.

Major Commands to Which Assigned. This section sets forth the chronological assignments of each base to a major command or branch of the U.S. Armed Forces. Some of the older bases may show assignments to commands that no longer exist, while a few may trace base assignments from the time the installation served as a foreign air base or military establishment. Changes of assignment signify a transfer of the base to another command, the discontinuance of the command itself with the installation and its components being absorbed by other commands or other parts of the U.S. Armed Forces, or its reversion to the control of a host country.

Major Changes in Status. Legal changes in the status of each base are shown whenever applicable and known. In a few cases, the term "none" is used to indicate that the base has remained active. Temporary or permanent periods of inactivation are listed, as are the dates showing transfers between military services, other agencies, and host countries; renewed activation (reactivation); annexation or transfer to host countries. Any changes from subbase to off-base to primary base status, or vice-versa, as well as from "under construction" to "active," or from "reduced operational" to "caretaker" status are also listed. An installation in caretaker status supports only those personnel and operations required for its physical upkeep, preceding or following a period of active status. A major command or service declares an installation "surplus" to government needs upon approval by the General Services Administration, after which it is designated "excess" and referred to an appropriate agency for disposal. In areas overseas, property is often leased or licensed by a host country and the property reverts back to that country upon expiration of the lease or license.

Other terms used in this section are "inactivation," "discontinuance," and "standby." The first indicates the inactivation or discontinuance of the base administrative unit, or an announcement of such action by the service. The term "standby" means the installation had ceased to be used as an operational site and had been placed on the inactive roll. Even though a caretaker unit might continue to be stationed there, the facility no longer had a mission in support of Air Force activities. In some instances, however, the installation is retained in anticipation of future needs. Other terms used under this heading are already explained under "Major Off-Base and Detached Installations."

Units Assigned. Assigned combat and support organizations from numbered flights upward appear chronologically by date of activation or assignment to the particular station. The activation/assignment date at a given base is listed first and the date of inactivation or transfer from that installation is listed second. If there is no closing date, a dash indicates that the unit is still active at that base. To determine all of the units on base in any given year, consult those assigned in earlier years. In compliance with military usage, all dates of assignment, activation/inactivation, or transfer appear by day, month, and year. Redesignated names of units appear in parentheses sequentially, beneath the original name. Brackets around words indicate that the words enclosed are a part of the unit's actual designation.

Numbered units precede named organizations, and are further aligned alphabetically in accordance with the precise designation of the unit as it would appear if spelled out rather than abbreviated. Only one entry is used for each continuous period of a unit's assignment at any installation. If a unit transferred and later that year returned to the base, however, two entries will appear, one for each period of assignment. Army units that never subsequently became a part of the Air Force, but may have been stationed at bases contained in this volume, have for the most part not been listed. Air National Guard units, except for those periods in which such units were serving on active federal assignments, are also excluded. Units briefly attached at a base while deployed from home bases are not usually shown among the list of units at the base of deployment.

As in the "Base Operating Units" section, unit prefixes and parenthesized suffixes identifying the specialty of the organization have been excluded. This and other unit information can be found in the lineage and honors of specific units contained in Air Force reference works on combat units, combat squadrons, and combat wings—all prepared by the USAF Historical Research Center and published through the Office of Air Force History. (See Maurer Maurer [ed.], *Air Force Combat Units of World War II* [1961; reprint ed., Office of Air Force History, 1985]; Maurer Maurer [ed.], *Combat Squadrons of the Air Force, World War II* [1969; reprint ed., Office of Air Force History, 1982]; and Charles A. Ravenstein, *Air Force Combat Wings: Lineage and Honors Histories 1947–1977* [Office of Air Force History, 1984].)

It is conceivable that a few, long-defunct organizations have been omitted that could not be located among the records of active, inactive, or disbanded units of the Air Force. Likewise, units assigned to off-base installations have been excluded, except in instances where the primary base itself was for a time an off-base installation.

Explanations of Air Force terms used in the volume may be found in the glossary in the back of this book. The abbreviations used are not always standard Air Force abbreviations, but have been designed for the understanding of the reading public at large.

Andersen Air Force Base

Location: Located 13 mi NE of Agana on NE tip of Guam.

Name: Named for Brig Gen James Roy Andersen (1904–1945). General Andersen graduated from the U.S. Military Academy in 1926, served at various Army installations, and obtained his wings at Kelly Fld, Texas, in 1936. During 1943–1944 he served on the War Department General Staff. In Jan 1945, General Andersen was assigned to HQ AAF, Pacific Ocean Area. He died on 26 Feb 1945 in an aircraft accident near Kwajalein Island, en route to Hawaii.

Date of Current Name: 7 Oct 1949.

Previous Names: North Fld, c. Dec 1944; North Fld AB Comd, 9 May 1946; North AAB, unk; North AFB, 1 Mar 1948; North Guam AFB, 22 Apr 1948; North Fld AFB, Guam, Feb 1949; North Guam AFB, Mar 1949.

Date of Establishment: 3 Feb 1945.

Date Construction Began: Dec 1944.

Date of Beneficial Occupancy: 3 Feb 1945.

Base Operating Units: 314th Bomb Wg, 17 Jan 1945; North Fld AB Comd (Prov), 15 Apr 1946; North AAB Comd (Prov), unk; North AFB Comd (Prov), Mar 1948; North Guam AFB Comd (Prov), 22 Apr 1948; 19th AB Gp, 17 Aug 1948; 6319th AB Wg, 1 Jun 1953; 3960th AB Wg, 1 Apr 1955 (rdsgd 3960th AB Gp, 1 Jul 1956; 3960th Cmbt Spt Gp, 1 Jul 1959; 3960th Strat Wg, 1 Nov 1963; 3960th Cmbt Spt Gp, 1 Aug 1964; 3960th Strat Wg, 1 Apr 1965); 43d Cmbt Spt Gp, 1 Jul 1970–.

Base Commanders: Col (later, Brig Gen) Thomas S. Power, 3 Feb 1945; Col Carl R. Storrie, 23 Jul 1945; Col Elbert D. Reynolds, Apr 1946; Col David Wade, 26 Apr 1947; Col Robert V. DeShazo, 4 Nov 1947; Lt Col Clarence G. Poff, Jul 1948; Lt Col Kenneth E. Turner, 17 Aug 1948; Lt Col Thomas H. Hollrook, Feb 1949; Lt Col Charles H. Haase, Apr 1949; Col Frederick E. Calhoun, Aug 1949; Lt Col George W. Webb, Jun 1950; Col John N. Ewbank Jr, Sep 1950; Lt Col George W. Webb, May 1951; Lt Col Lawrence A. Growden, Nov 1951; Lt Col John H. Stebbins, 30 May 1952; Col Leonard J. Rohrs, 28 Jul 1952; Col Corwin P. Vansant, 13 Jun 1954; Col Richard I. Dugan, 12 Jul 1954; Col William J. Wrigglesworth, 1 Apr 1955; Col Frank E. Marek, 1 Sep 1955; Col Gilbert F. Friederichs, 28

Jun 1957; Col John B. Carey Jr, 22 Jul 1958; Col George Pfeiffer Jr, 7 Jul 1960; Col James M. Bagley Jr, 21 Jul 1961; Col Dick F. Gibson, 21 Jun 1962; Col Henry F. Ledbetter, 31 Jul 1962; Col Edward C. Unger, 21 Apr 1964; Col Edward D. Gaitley Jr, 22 Jul 1964; Col Joseph J. Semanek, 10 Jul 1965; Col James M. Smith, 9 Jul 1967; Col Arthur G. Ray Jr, 1 Jul–c. 15 Nov 1970; Col Dwayne E. Kelley, 16 Nov 1970; Col John H. Vincent, 2 Oct 1972–22 Jan 1974; unk, 23 Jan–17 Mar 1974; Col Leo D. O'Halloran Jr, 18 Mar 1974; Col Joseph J. Gyulavics, 26 Aug 1975; Col David N. Gooch, 1 Aug 1977; Col James W. Lee, 6 Mar 1978; Col Keylor Chan, 15 Nov 1979; Col Adam Rech, 8 Jul 1981; Col James D. McCracken, 3 Aug 1982–.

Major Off-Base and Detached Installations:* Andersen/Agana Hsg Anx (rdsgd Agana Hsg Anx; Agana Fam Hsg Anx #3; Agana Hsg #3), 4 mi NE of Agana, Sep 1944 (actvd)–Dec 1949 (inactvd), unk (actvd)–30 Jun 1957 (dspd); Andersen Stor Anx (rdsgd Marbo Engr AF Stor Stn; Andersen Stor Anx; Andersen VOR Anx; Andersen/Marbo Engr Dep; Marbo Engr AF Stor Stn), 6 mi NE of Agana, 1 Sep 1944 (actvd)–17 Apr 1956 (inactvd), unk (actvd)–; Harmon AFB (rdsgd Andersen Quarry Anx), 5 mi NE of Agana, 23 Sep 1949 (asgnd)–; Northwest Fld, Guam, Jun 1950 (acquired through civil procedures)–; Andersen/Agana Water Sup Anx (rdsgd Agana GLOBECOM Anx; Andersen Comms Anx; Andersen Comms Anx #1), 6 mi NW of Agana, Apr 1951 (actvd)–; Andersen/Agana AVGAS Fuel Stor Anx (rdsgd Agana Fuel Stor Anx; Andersen POL Prods Stor Anx; Andersen POL Prods Stor Anx #1), 18 mi S of base, 28 Aug 1951 (asgnd)–; Andersen/Edusa Hsg Anx (rdsgd Edusa Hsg Anx; Andersen Fam Hsg #1), Agana, 7 Sep 1951 (asgnd)–17 Apr 1956 (inactvd), unk (actvd)–; Andersen/Marbo Admn Anx (rdsgd Marbo Admn Anx; Andersen Admn Anx), 8 mi ENE of Agana, 7 Sep 1951 (actvd)–; Harmon/Agana Crash Boat Anx (rdsgd Agana Crash Boat Anx; Andersen Dock Anx), 7 mi SW of Agana, Sep 1951 (actvd)–; Andersen/Marbo Hsg Anx (rdsgd Marbo Hsg Anx; Andersen Fam Hsg #2), 12 mi NE of Agana, 24 Apr 1959 (asgnd)–6 Jul 1964 (dspd); Andersen POL Prods Stor Anx #2, Agana, 1 Nov 1959 (asgnd)–; Andersen Comms Anx #2, Agana, 11 Oct 1962 (asgnd)–.

Major Changes in Operational Capability: At the end of World War II Andersen assumed responsibility for administering several active and semiactive bases in the Marianas; served as a training base for B–29 units from 1945 to 1950; served briefly from Jun 1950 to 1953 in administrative and logistic support capacity after deployment of 19th Bomb Gp to Kadena AB; hosted SAC B–29, B–36, KC–97, B–47 and B–52 rotational

---

*All installations are located on the island of Guam.

units 1953–1964; 1050-unit Capehart housing project completed 1958–1960; overall construction project (to repair damage by Typhoon Karen in 1962) 1963–1964; readiness crew facility, civil engineers industrial and operations complexes, and freight terminal building completed and updated 1963–1964; base facilities, installations, and utilities augmented to accommodate SEA B–52 combat missions, beginning 18 Jun 1965; construction Project Sunbath, in two phases, included dormitories, clinics, and other facilities, 1965–1967; runway and taxiway augmentation project completed Dec 1968; Typhoon Pamela wrought enormous destruction on 21 May 1971; newly constructed control tower, tallest structure on Guam, completed Oct 1971; overall upgrading and construction program, making base "typhoon proof," completed Oct 1980.

Major Commands to Which Assigned: Twentieth AF, 3 Feb 1945; FEAF, 15 May 1949; SAC, 1 Apr 1955–.

Major Changes in Status: None.

Units Assigned:

1944		[Prov]	19 Jun 47–1 Dec 47
31 Svc Gp		8089 Maint & Sup	
(31 Air Svc Gp)	28 Dec 44–24 Aug 48	Gp [Prov]	15 Aug 47–19 Dec 47
574 Mat Sq		HQ & Base Svcs Sq,	
(574 Air Mat Sq)	28 Dec 44–20 Aug 48	358 Air Svc Gp	47–24 Aug 48
1945		1948	
2 Cmbt Camera Unit	10 Jun 45–c. 1 Oct 45	19 AB Gp	17 Aug 48–1 Jun 53
6 Bomb Sq	17 Jan 45–20 May 46	19 AP Sq	17 Aug 48–1 Jun 53
19 Bomb Gp	16 Jan 45–5 Jul 50	19 Bomb Wg	17 Aug 48–1 Jun 53
28 Bomb Sq	16 Jan 45–5 Jul 50	19 Comms Sq	17 Aug 48–1 Jun 53
30 Bomb Sq	16 Jan 45–27 Jun 50	19 Food Svc Sq	17 Aug 48–1 Jun 53
62 Bomb Sq	18 Feb 45–16 Nov 45	19 Instls Sq	17 Aug 48–1 Jun 53
93 Bomb Sq	16 Jan 45–27 Jun 50	19 Maint & Sup Gp	17 Aug 48–1 Jun 53
1946		19 Maint Sq	17 Aug 48–1 Jun 53
4 Mess Sq, 20 AF		30 Bomb Sq	26 Mar 48–5 Jul 50
[Prov]	1 Oct 46–24 Apr 48	1949	
North Fld AB		13 VR Sq	
Comd [Prov]		(13 MV Rpr Sq)	1 Jul 49–8 Apr 55
(North Army AB		19 MV Sq	7 Oct 49–1 Jun 53
Comd [Prov];		1950	
North Guam AFB		1958 AACS Sq	
Comd [Prov])	15 May 46–24 Aug 48	(1958 Comms Sq)	10 Mar 50–1 Jul 76
1947		1951	
54 Recon Sq	7 Jul 47–15 Oct 47	3 Avn Fld Dep Sq	
310 Trnsp Sq [Prov]	2 Jun 47–19 Jun 47	(3 Avn Dep Sq;	
311 Guard Sq [Prov]	2 Jun 47–19 Jun 47	3 Mun Maint Sq)	24 May 51–30 Sep 72
312 Air Instls Sq		13 Ammo Sup	
[Prov]	2 Jun 47–19 Jun 47	Sq, Dep	12 Jan 51–8 Jul 54
560 Rpr Sq, Prov	2 Jun 47–19 Jun 47	54 Strat Recon Sq	
561 Shop Sq, Prov	2 Jun 47–19 Jun 47	(54 Wea Recon Sq)	21 Feb 51–18 Mar 60
654 Bomb Sq	7 Jul 47–15 Oct 47	1952	
8084 Comms Sq		9 Motor Trpt Sq	1 Apr 52–3 Dec 55
[Prov]	20 Oct 47–19 Dec 47	79 Air Rscu Sq	14 Nov 52–18 Sep 60
8085 Shop Sq, Prov	19 Jun 47–15 Aug 47	852 AC & W Sq	18 Apr 52–8 Jun 60
8087 Guard Sq [Prov]	19 Jun 47–19 Dec 47	1953	
8088 Air Instls Sq		1 Mat Recovery Sq	24 Mar 53–21 Dec 53

3

5 Mat Recovery Sq	15 May 53–1 Aug 53
24 Sup Sq, Sp	
(24 Sup Sq,	
Dep, Sp)	8 Dec 53–8 Mar 59
430 AP Sq	1 Jun 53–3 Dec 55
6319 AB Gp	1 Jun 53–1 Apr 55
6319 AB Wg	1 Jun 53–1 Apr 55
6319 Comms Sq	1 Jun 53–1 Apr 55
6319 Food Svc Sq	1 Jun 53–1 Apr 55
6319 Instls Sq	1 Jun 53–1 Apr 55
6319 Maint &	
Sup Gp	1 Jun 53–1 Apr 55
6319 Maint Sq	
(6319 Fld	
Maint Sq)	1 Jun 53–1 Apr 55
6319 Med Gp	
(6319 USAF Dispy)	1 Jun 53–1 Apr 55
6319 Sup Sq	1 Jun 53–1 Apr 55

1954

3 Air Div	18 Jun 54–1 Apr 70
27 Comms Sq, Div	
(27 Comms Sq,	
AF; 27 Comms	
Sq, Div;	
27 Comms Sq)	8 Oct 54–
92 Armnt & Elect	
Maint Sq	16 Oct 54–12 Jan 55
92 Bomb Wg	16 Oct 54–12 Jan 55
92 Fld Maint Sq	16 Oct 54–12 Jan 55
92 Prdc Maint Sq	16 Oct 54–12 Jan 55
325 Bomb Sq	16 Oct 54–12 Jan 55
326 Bomb Sq	16 Oct 54–12 Jan 55
393 Bomb Sq	10 Jul 54–8 Oct 54
508 Air Rflg Sq	20 Jul 54–11 Oct 54
509 Armnt & Elect	
Maint Sq	10 Jul 54–8 Oct 54
509 Bomb Wg	10 Jul 54–8 Oct 54
509 Fld Maint Sq	10 Jul 54–8 Oct 54
509 Prdc Maint Sq	10 Jul 54–8 Oct 54
715 Bomb Sq	10 Jul 54–8 Oct 54
830 Bomb Sq	10 Jul 54–8 Oct 54

1955

5 Armnt & Elect	
Maint Sq	14 Jan 55–12 Apr 55
5 Bomb Wg	14 Jan 55–12 Apr 55
5 Fld Maint Sq	14 Jan 55–12 Apr 55
5 Prdc Maint Sq	14 Jan 55–12 Apr 55
6 Bomb Wg	31 Oct 55–26 Jan 56
6 Prdc Maint Sq	31 Oct 55–26 Jan 56
23 Strat Recon Sq	14 Jan 55–12 Apr 55
24 Bomb Sq	31 Oct 55–26 Jan 56
28 Armnt & Elect	
Maint Sq	26 Apr 55–24 Jul 55
28 Fld Maint Sq	26 Apr 55–24 Jul 55
39 Bomb Sq	31 Oct 55–26 Jan 56
40 Bomb Sq	31 Oct 55–26 Jan 56
77 Strat Recon Sq	26 Apr 55–24 Jul 55

95 Armnt & Elect	
Maint Sq	1 Apr 55–3 Nov 55
95 Fld Maint Sq	1 Aug 55–3 Nov 55
95 Prdc Maint Sq	1 Aug 55–3 Nov 55
334 Bomb Sq	1 Aug 55–3 Nov 55
335 Bomb Sq	1 Aug 55–3 Nov 55
336 Bomb Sq	1 Aug 55–3 Nov 55
717 Bomb Sq	22 Apr 55–24 Jul 55
718 Bomb Sq	22 Apr 55–24 Jul 55
3960 AB Wg	
(3960 AB Gp;	
3960 Cmbt Spt Gp;	
3960 Strat Wg;	
3960 Cmbt Spt Gp;	
3960 Strat Wg)	1 Apr 55–1 Apr 70
3960 AP Sq	
(3960 Cmbt Def Sq;	
3960 Scty Pol Sq)	1 Apr 55–1 Apr 70
3960 Fld Maint Sq	
(3960 Consold Acft	
Maint Sq)	1 Apr 55–15 Sep 69
3960 Food Svc Sq	
(3960 Svcs Sq)	1 Apr 55–1 Apr 70
3960 Instls Sq	
(3960 CE Sq)	1 Apr 55–1 Apr 70
3960 Motor Trpt Sq	
(3960 Trnsp Sq)	1 Apr 55–1 Apr 70
3960 Ops Sq	1 Apr 55–1 Jul 56
3960 Sup Sq	1 Apr 55–1 Apr 70
3960 USAF Dispy	1 Apr 55–1 Oct 60
3961 Recon Tech Sq	1 Apr 55–1 Dec 59
Andersen Task	
Force, Prov	1 May 55–unk

1956

41 Ftr-Intcpr Sq	c. 5 Aug 56–8 Mar 60
92 Bomb Wg	26 Apr 56–5 Jul 56
92 Fld Maint Sq	26 Apr 56–5 Jul 56
92 Prdc Maint Sq	26 Apr 56–5 Jul 56
99 Armnt & Elect	
Maint Sq	29 Jan 56–25 Apr 56
99 Bomb Wg	29 Jan 56–25 Apr 56
99 Fld Maint Sq	29 Jan 56–25 Apr 56
99 Prdc Maint Sq	29 Jan 56–25 Apr 56
303 Armnt & Elect	
Maint Sq	12 Jul 56–4 Oct 56
303 Bomb Wg	12 Jul 56–4 Oct 56
303 Fld Maint Sq	12 Jul 56–4 Oct 56
303 Prdc Maint Sq	12 Jul 56–4 Oct 56
320 Armnt & Elect	
Maint Sq	5 Oct 56–11 Jan 57
320 Bomb Wg	5 Oct 56–11 Jan 57
320 Fld Maint Sq	5 Oct 56–11 Jan 57
320 Prdc Maint Sq	5 Oct 56–11 Jan 57
325 Bomb Sq	26 Apr 56–5 Jul 56
346 Bomb Sq	29 Jan 56–25 Apr 56
347 Bomb Sq	29 Jan 56–25 Apr 56
358 Bomb Sq	12 Jul 56–4 Oct 56

4

359 Bomb Sq	12 Jul 56–4 Oct 56
360 Bomb Sq	12 Jul 56–4 Oct 56
443 Bomb Sq	5 Oct 56–11 Jan 57
1957	
327 Air Div	1 Jul 57–8 Mar 60
1960	
863 Med Gp	
(USAF Dispy,	
Andersen; USAF	
Clinic, Andersen)	1 Oct 60–
1961	
79 Air Rscu Sq	
(79 Aerosp Rscu	
& Recovery Sq)	10 May 61–30 Jun 72
1962	
54 Wea Recon Sq	18 Apr 62–
1966	
605 Mil Alft Spt Sq	8 Jan 66–
Bomb Wg, Prov 4133	1 Feb 66–1 Jul 70
1969	
3960 Avncs Maint Sq	15 Sep 69–1 Apr 70
3960 Fld Maint Sq	15 Sep 69–1 Apr 70
3960 Orgnzl Maint Sq	15 Sep 69–1 Apr 70
1970	
43 Avncs Maint Sq	1 Apr 70–
43 CE Sq	1 Apr 70–

43 Cmbt Spt Gp	1 Jul 70–
43 Fld Maint Sq	1 Apr 70–
43 Scty Pol Sq	1 Apr 70–
43 Strat Wg	1 Apr 70–
43 Sup Sq	1 Apr 70–
43 Trnsp Sq	1 Apr 70–
Eighth AF	1 Apr 70–1 Jan 75
1971	
60 Bomb Sq	30 Jun 71–
1972	
43 Mun Maint Sq	1 Oct 72–
Air Div, Prov 57	1 Jun 72–15 Nov 73
Bomb Sq, Prov 63	15 Jun 72–30 Jun 75
Bomb Sq, Prov 64	15 Jun 72–15 Nov 73
Bomb Sq, Prov 65	15 Jun 72–15 Nov 73
Bomb Sq, Prov 329	1 Jun 72–15 Nov 73
Bomb Sq, Prov 486	1 Jun 72–15 Nov 73
Consold Acft Maint	
Wg, Prov 303	15 Jun 72–15 Nov 73
Strat Wg, Prov 72	1 Jun 72–15 Nov 73
1975	
3 Air Div	1 Jan 75–
1979	
43 Orgnzl Maint Sq	1 Apr 79–
1982	
44 Aerl Port Sq	1 Jan 82–

Ankara Air Station

Location: Located 2 mi SW of the city of Ankara, near the village of Balgat, Turkey.

Name: Named after a city in Turkey.

Date of Current Name: 28 Feb 1958.

Previous Names: Balgat Fld; Ankara Afld; Ankara AB.

Date of Establishment: 1 Aug 1955.

Date Construction Began: Jul 1962.

Date of Beneficial Occupancy: 15 May 1955.

Base Operating Units: 7217th Spt Gp, 15 May 1955–30 Jun 1958; 7250th Spt Gp, 1 Jul 1958–14 Oct 1971; 39th Tac Gp, 15 Oct 1971–14 Nov 1982; 7217th AB Gp, 15 Nov 1982–.

Base Commanders: Col William H. Smith, 15 May 1955; Col Richard D. Curtin, 31 Mar 1956; Col Gordon F. Thomas, 16 Jun 1956; Col Robert J. Goewey, 1 Jul 1956; Col James D. Jones, 29 May 1957; Col Frank O. Hinckley, c. Jul 1958; unk, 30 Jun 1959–Jun 1961; Col Julius J. Adleman, c. Jun 1961; Col Lawrence P. Mayland, c. Dec 1961; Lt Col Joseph A. Arduengo, 9 Jun 1963; Col George O. Commenator, 29 Jul 1963; Col William M. Wilson, c. Dec 1963; Lt Col Charles W. Fatzinger, c. Jun 1964; Col Delbert J. Salmon, 19 Aug 1964; Col Raymond J. Sealy, 11 Jul 1966; Col Henry C. Reed, 3 Aug 1966; Col Augustine C. Trapold, 20 Feb 1967; Col Chester H. Bohart, 9 Apr 1968; Col Harry D. Gilpin, 25 Mar 1970; Col Paul K. Smith, 8 Jul 1970; Col Roger W. Trueblood, 1 Oct 1971; Col Arnold E. Hector, Jan 1972; Col William A. Evans Jr, 28 May 1974; Col William H. Davidson, 20 Jun 1975; Col Robert W. Ruark, 15 Jul 1978; Col Robert J. Lines, 22 Jun 1979; Lt Col F. Dixon Jordan, 15 Nov 1982–.

Major Off-Base and Detached Installations:* Esenboga Intl Aprt (rdsgd Esenboga Flt Spt Anx), 1 Apr 1954 (asgnd)–; Sile Comms Stn #1, 10 Feb 1955 (asgnd)–1 Jun 1958 (dspd); Sile Comms Stn #2, 10 Feb 1955 (asgnd)–1 Jan 1958 (dspd); Ankara Reclamation Yard (rdsgd Ankara Stor Anx #3), 3 Mar 1956 (actvd)–30 Jun 1960 (inactvd); Samsun Comms Stn

---

*All installations are located in Turkey.

#1 (rdsgd Samsun Comms Fclty), 30 Mar 1956 (asgnd)–1 Jul 1958 (trsfd to Karamursel AS); Samsun Comms Stn #2 (rdsgd Samsun Rcvr Anx), 30 Mar 1956 (asgnd)–1 Jul 1958 (trsfd to Karamursel AS); Samsun Comms Stn #3 (rdsgd Samsun Trsmn Anx), 30 Mar 1956 (asgnd)–1 Jul 1958 (trsfd to Karamursel AS); Samsun DF Site, 30 Mar 1956 (asgnd)–1 Nov 1961 (dspd); Trabzon Comms Stn (rdsgd Trabzon Comms Anx), 30 Mar 1956 (asgnd)–1 Jul 1958 (trsfd to Karamursel AS); Trabzon Comms Stn #1 (rdsgd Trabzon Comms Fclty), 30 Mar 1956 (asgnd)–1 Jul 1958 (trsfd to Karamursel AS); Trabzon Comms Stn #3, 30 Mar 1956 (asgnd)–1 Jul 1958 (trsfd to Karamursel AS); Trabzon DF Site, 30 Mar 1956 (asgnd)–1 Jul 1958 (trsfd to Karamursel AS); Ankara Admn Anx (rdsgd Ankara Admn Anx #3; Ankara Admn Ofc #6), 31 Mar 1956 (actvd)–15 Dec 1969 (dspd); Ankara Admn Ofc #2, 31 Mar 1956 (asgnd)–; Ankara Svc Anx #2, 31 Mar 1956 (actvd)–5 Aug 1958 (dspd); Ankara Svc Anx #4, 1 May 1956 (actvd)–30 Jun 1967 (inactvd); Samsun Svc Fclty, 19 Sep 1956 (asgnd)–1 Jul 1958 (trsfd to Karamursel AS); Ankara Admn Ofc #1, 11 Oct 1956 (actvd)–; Ankara Stor Anx #1, 3 Nov 1956 (actvd)–30 Jun 1970 (inactvd); Ankara NCO Club (rdsgd Ankara Svc Anx #1), 8 Dec 1956 (actvd)–15 Apr 1971 (dspd); Trabzon Sch #1, 15 Feb 1957 (asgnd)–; Ankara Depnt Sch, 1 Apr 1957 (actvd)–; Ankara Sch #1 (rdsgd Ankara Spt Fclty Anx #2), 1 Apr 1957 (asgnd)–30 Jun 1972 (dspd); Ankara Stor Anx #2, 15 Jun 1957 (asgnd)–29 Nov 1977 (dspd); Ankara Recrn Anx (rdsgd Ankara Admn Anx #4; Ankara Admn Ofc), 1 Jul 1957 (asgnd)–30 Jun 1968 (dspd); Ankara Recrn Anx #2, 1 Jul 1957 (asgnd)–15 Mar 1970 (dspd); Ankara Recrn Anx #3 (rdsgd Ankara Pkg Anx), 1 Jul 1957 (asgnd)–10 Jan 1972 (dspd); Ankara Svc Anx #3, 1 Apr 1958 (asgnd)–1 Dec 1980 (dspd); Ankara Pkg Anx, Amn Hsg, 1 Jan 1959 (actvd)–30 Jun 1961 (dspd); Ankara Comms Stn (rdsgd Ankara Comms Anx; Ankara Admn Ofc #7), 1 Mar 1959 (actvd)–30 Jun 1976 (dspd); Ankara Pkg Anx #1, Hosp, 1 Mar 1959 (actvd)–30 Jun 1961 (dspd); Istanbul Stor Stn, 15 Apr 1959 (asgnd)–1 Sep 1962 (dspd); Yesilkoy Admn Ofc, 15 Apr 1959 (asgnd)–1 Sep 1962 (trsfd to Istanbul AS); Ankara Admn Ofc #3, (rdsgd Ankara Admn Anx), 1 Jul 1959 (actvd)–8 Jun 1974 (dspd); Ankara Recrn Anx #4, Gym, 25 Jul 1959 (actvd)–1 Feb 1968 (inactvd); Erzurum Off Hsg, 1 Jan 1960 (asgnd)–30 Nov 1967 (dspd); Sivas Off Hsg, 1 Jan 1960 (asgnd)–; Erzurum Off Hsg #2, 1 Mar 1960 (asgnd)–30 Jun 1963 (dspd); Ankara Recrn Anx #4 (rdsgd Ankara Stor Site), 10 Mar 1960 (asgnd)–30 Jun 1973 (dspd); Ankara Wea Stn Anx, 10 Mar 1960 (asgnd)–; Buyukdere Stor Anx, 14 Mar 1960 (asgnd)–1 Sep 1962 (trsfd to Istanbul AS); Ankara Stor Anx #4, 15 Mar 1960 (asgnd)–18 Jul 1963 (dspd); Konya Off Hsg #1, 1 Apr 1960 (asgnd)–30 Jun 1965 (dspd); Konya Off Hsg #3, 1 Apr 1960 (asgnd)–30 Jun 1965 (dspd); Konya Off Hsg #2, 1 May 1960 (asgnd)–30 Jun 1965 (dspd); Ankara Hsg Anx, Trnst Fam Qtrs, 14 May 1960 (asgnd)–; Ankara Maint

Anx (rdsgd Ankara Recrn Anx #4), 21 May 1960 (asgnd)–; Isparta Off Hsg, 1 Jul 1960 (asgnd)–30 Jun 1970 (dspd); Ankara Sch #3, Elementary (rdsgd Ankara Admn Anx #2; Ankara Admn Ofc #1), 16 Sep 1960 (asgnd)–; Afyon Off Hsg, 15 Nov 1960 (asgnd)–; Ankara Stor Anx #5, 31 Jan 1961 (asgnd)–14 Dec 1971 (dspd); Samsun Comms Fclty Anx, 1 Nov 1961 (asgnd)–; Ankara Stor Anx #6, 1 Jul 1962 (asgnd)–30 Jun 1964 (dspd); Samsun Comms Anx (rdsgd Samsun RRS), 9 Aug 1962 (asgnd)–; Alemdag RRS, 1 Jan 1963 (asgnd)–1 Jul 1974 (trsfd to Karamursel AS); Cakmakli RRS, 1 Jan 1963 (asgnd)–1 Jul 1974 (trsfd to Karamursel AS); Corlu RRS, 1 Jan 1963 (asgnd)–1 Jul 1974 (trsfd to Karamursel AS); Fenertepe RRS, 1 Jan 1963 (asgnd)–1 Jul 1974 (trsfd to Karamursel AS); Izmit RRS, 1 Jan 1963 (asgnd)–1 Jul 1974 (trsfd to Karamursel AS); Istanbul Admn Ofc #3, 1 Jan 1963 (asgnd)–1 Jul 1974 (trsfd to Karamursel AS); Ortakoy RRS, 1 Jan 1963 (asgnd)–1 Jul 1974 (trsfd to Karamursel AS); Salipazari Port, 1 Jan 1963 (asgnd)–1 Jul 1974 (trsfd to Karamursel AS); Yesilkoy Admn Ofc, 1 Jan 1963 (asgnd)–1 Jul 1974 (trsfd to Karamursel AS); Samsun Water Sys Anx, 18 Feb 1963 (asgnd)–; Trabzon Tacan Anx, 18 Feb 1963 (asgnd)–; Trabzon Water Sys Anx, 18 Feb 1963 (asgnd)–; Ankara Amn Hsg Anx #3, 25 Jun 1963 (asgnd)–30 Sep 1968 (dspd); Ankara Amn Hsg Anx #1, 1 Jul 1963 (asgnd)–30 May 1971 (dspd); Sahintepe Water Sys Anx, 6 Aug 1963 (asgnd)–; Ankara Spt Fclty Anx, 23 Aug 1963 (asgnd)–30 Jun 1972 (dpsd); Samsun Water Sys Anx #2, 28 Aug 1963 (asgnd)–25 Jun 1970 (dspd); Eskisehir RRS, 15 Sep 1963 (asgnd)–; Elmadag RRS, 1 Nov 1963 (asgnd)–; Ankara Spt Fclty Anx (rdsgd Ankara Fam Hsg Anx #1), 26 Dec 1963 (asgnd)–15 Dec 1969 (dspd); Ankara Fam Hsg Anx (rdsgd Ankara Fam Hsg Anx #1), 1 Jul 1964 (asgnd)–30 Sep 1979 (dspd); Ankara Amn Hsg Anx #4, 1 Jan 1965 (asgnd)–; Ankara Fam Hsg Anx #2, 1 May 1965 (asgnd)–30 Jun 1966 (dspd); Konya Off Hsg #4, 1 Jul 1965 (asgnd)–30 Jun 1968 (dspd); Ankara Maint Anx #2, 1 Nov 1967 (asgnd)–; Elmadag Water Sys Anx, 2 Feb 1968 (asgnd)–; Konya Off Hsg, 30 Jun 1968 (asgnd)–; Balikesir RRS, 15 Nov 1968 (asgnd)–; Istanbul Svc Anx, 1 Jan 1969 (asgnd)–1 Sep 1962 (trsfd to Istanbul AS); Samsun RRS, 31 Jan 1971 (asgnd)–; Ankara Rsch Site (rdsgd Ankara Wea Stn Site), 3 Jun 1971 (asgnd)–; Ankara Pkg Anx, 14 Dec 1971 (asgnd)–10 Jan 1972 (dspd); Ankara Fam Hsg Site, 1 Jul 1972 (asgnd)–; Ankara Hosp, 3 Dec 1973 (asgnd)–30 Jun 1982 (dspd); Iskenderun Stor Anx #2, 1 Jul 1974 (asgnd)–30 Jun 1978 (dspd); Istanbul Admn Ofc, 1 Jul 1974 (asgnd)–1 Oct 1978 (dspd); Istanbul Stor Site, 1 Jul 1974 (asgnd)–1 Jul 1976 (dspd); Ankara Fam Hsg Site #1, 1 Sep 1975 (asgnd)–30 Sep 1979 (dspd); Ankara Fam Hsg Site #3, 1 Sep 1975 (asgnd)–30 Sep 1978 (dspd); Ankara Fam Hsg Site #2, 1 Oct 1975 (asgnd)–30 Sep 1979 (dspd); Ankara Fam Hsg Site #4, 14 Sep 1977 (asgnd)–30 Sep 1981 (dspd); Alemdag RRS, 15 Oct 1978 (trsfd from Karamursel AS)–; Ankara Stor Anx, 15 Oct 1978 (asgnd); Cakmakli RRS, 15 Nov 1978 (trsfd from Karamursel AS)−; Corlu RRS, 15 Nov 1978 (trsfd from Karamursel AS)−; Izmit RRS, 15 Nov 1978 (trsfd from Karamursel AS)−; Ortakoy RRS, 15 Nov 1978 (trsfd from Karamursel AS)−; Sahin Tepesi RR Anx, 15 Nov 1978 (trsfd from Karamursel AS)−; Sahin Tepesi RRS, 15 Nov 1978 (trsfd from Karamursel AS)−; Sahin Tepesi Water Sys Anx, 15 Nov 1978 (trsfd from Karamursel AS)−; Salipazari Port, 15 Nov 1978 (trsfd from Karamursel AS)−; Yesilkoy Admn Ofc, 15 Nov 1978 (trsfd from Karamursel AS)−; Istanbul Fam Hsg Site, 1 Jul 1982 (asgnd)−.

Major Changes in Operational Capability: Established as an administrative headquarters without flying operations; Ankara AS's primary mission was to provide support for the U.S. military and diplomatic mission in Turkey, especially for the American military community situated in the greater Ankara area; base supported HQ The United States Logistics Group (TUSLOG) after May 1973, when that headquarters moved to Ankara AS from downtown Ankara.

Major Commands to Which Assigned: USAFE, 15 May 1955−.

Major Changes in Status: None.

Units Assigned:

1945		7217 Spt Gp	15 May 55−1 Jul 58
1271 AAF BU	1 May 45−11 Feb 46	**1956**	
1947		7250 Spt Sq	
37 AAF BU		(7250 Spt Gp;	
(37 AF BU; USAF		7250 AB Sq)	1 Apr 56−31 Mar 73
Gp, Air Mission		**1957**	
for Aid to Turkey)	3 Oct 47−c. 27 Nov 48	7250 USAF Hosp	8 Jun 57−30 Jun 71
1948		**1971**	
USAF Gp, American		HQ TUSLOG	15 Oct 71−
Mission for Aid		USAF Dispy, Ankara	
to Turkey	27 Nov 48−1 Jul 76	(USAF Hosp,	
1955		Ankara; USAF	
6933 Radio Sq,		Clinic, Ankara)	1 Jul 71−
Mobile		**1982**	
(6933 Radio		7217 AB Gp	15 Nov 82−
Gp, Mobile)	8 May 55−1 Jul 57	7217 AB Sq	15 Nov 82−
7217 AB Sq	1 Aug 55−5 Jan 57		

Aviano Air Base

Location: Located 2 mi N of downtown Aviano, 7 mi NNW of Pordenone, and about 50 mi NNE of Venice, Italy.

Name: Named after a town in Italy.

Date of Current Name: 1 Jan 1956.

Previous Names: Aeroporto Aviano; Aeroporto Pagliano e Gori, 1919;* Aviano Afld, 1955.

Date of Establishment: Originally established by the Italian government in 1911; Mediterranean Allied AFB, 1945; RAF installation, 1945–1947; Italian afld, 1947; established as a USAF air base 15 Feb 1955.

Date Construction Began: Originally built in 1911; improvements made in late 1930s and 1940–1944; further improvement undertaken preparatory to USAF occupancy of German-built World War II structures, 1952–1955.

Date of Beneficial Occupancy: 1 Oct 1955.

Base Operating Units: 7207th AB Sq, 15 Feb 1955; 7227th Spt Gp, 1 Dec 1957 (rdsgd 7227th Cmbt Spt Gp, 1 May 1962); 40th Cmbt Spt Sq, 1 Apr 1966–.

Base Commanders: Maj Ovid M. Rey (temp), 16 Feb 1955; Lt Col Eugene F. Miller, 8 May 1955 (temp), 24 May 1955 (perm); Lt Col Donald E. Ewing, early 1956; Col Kenneth D. Kienth, 1 Dec 1957; Col Clarence C. McPherson, 5 May 1958; Col Glenn A. Stell, 15 Apr 1961; Col Carl E. Lovell, 22 Jun 1964; Lt Col Gordon J. James, 1 Apr 1966; Col Robert R. Fowler, 16 Jul 1966; Col Joe Fry, 25 May 1967; Col Robert L. Herman, 1 Jul 1968; Col Charles M. Read, 16 Jul 1969; Lt Col Jack E. Ladds, 17 Aug 1971; Lt Col (later, Col) Joseph J. Hillner Jr, 2 Sep 1971; Lt Col Jack E. Ladds, 1 Jul 1972; Lt Col (later, Col) Leroy J. Salem, 23 Sep 1972; Col Wray C. Lasswell, 22 Jun 1974; Col Charles M. Fronzuto, 1 Nov 1974; Lt Col Wallace J. Gaber, 16 Jun 1975; Col Lowell D. Covington, 28 Jul 1975; Col Jimmy G. Martin, 30 Aug 1976; Col Dennis R. Fanning, 1 Dec 1977;

---

*This former Italian airdrome was named in memory of Italian Air Force aviators Capt Maurizio Pagliano and Lt Luigi Gori, killed in action during World War I.

Col Harold H. Gabby, 27 Jan 1978; Col Kenneth R. Thompson, 15 Jul 1980–.

Major Off-Base and Detached Installations:* Udine/Campoformido AC & W Stn, 1.1 mi NNE of Campoformido, 22 Nov 1954 (actvd)–18 Sep 1957 (inactvd); Longare RRS, Longare, 19 Jan 1955 (asgnd)–1 Jul 1976 (dspd); Aviano Amn Hsg Anx #1, Aviano, 15 Feb 1955 (asgnd)–; Aviano Amn Hsg Anx #2, Aviano, 15 Feb 1955 (asgnd)–; Aviano Ammo Stor Anx, 6 mi NNW of Pordenone, 15 Feb 1955 (asgnd)–; Aviano DF Anx, Roveredo in Piano, 15 Feb 1955 (asgnd)–25 Jan 1961 (dspd); Aviano Maint Anx, Aviano, 15 Feb 1955 (asgnd)–; Aviano Petrol Prods Stor Anx, 1 mi SSW of Aviano, 15 Feb 1955 (asgnd)–; Sacile RB Anx, Sacile, 15 Feb 1955 (asgnd)–21 Mar 1961 (dspd); Aviano RR Anx, 8 mi NNW of Pordenone, 6 Oct 1956 (asgnd)–; Aviano Railhead Anx, Aviano, 6 Oct 1956 (asgnd)–; San Vito Dei Normanni Comms Anx, San Vito Dei Normanni, 24 Jun 1959 (asgnd)–1 Mar 1961 (trsfd to San Vito Dei Normanni AS); Pordenone Svc Anx, Pordenone, 15 Oct 1959 (asgnd)–15 May 1962 (dspd); Monte Mancuso RRS, Gizzeria, 15 May 1962 (asgnd)–27 Jun 1967 (dspd); Monte Tolfa RRS, Tolfa, 15 May 1962 (asgnd)–1 Jul 1967 (dspd); Cima Gallina RRS, Colle Isarco, 30 Jan 1963 (asgnd)–; Monte Corna RRS, Grole, 30 Jan 1963 (asgnd)–; Monte Venda RRS, Teolo, 30 Jan 1963 (asgnd)–; Monte Pagnella RRS, Zambana, 30 Jun 1963 (asgnd)–; Monte Garibaldi RRS (rdsgd Monte Nardello RRS), Santo Stefano in Aspromonte, 6 Jul 1963 (asgnd)–; Martina Franca RRS, Martina Franca, 11 Jul 1963 (asgnd)–15 Apr 1981 (trsfd to San Vito Dei Normanni AS); Monte Limbara RRS, Tempio Pausiana, Sardinia, 16 Jul 1963 (asgnd)–; Monte Vergine RRS, Avellino, 8 Aug 1963 (asgnd)–Jul 1976 (dspd); Bressanone RRS, Elvas, 19 Jan 1965 (asgnd)–Jul 1976 (dspd); Ceggia RRS, Ceggia, 19 Jan 1965 (asgnd)–22 May 1979 (dspd); Codogne RRS, Codogne, 19 Jan 1965 (asgnd)–; Ghedi RRS, Ghedi, 19 Jan 1965 (asgnd)–22 May 1979 (dspd); Portogruaro RRS, Portogruaro, 19 Jan 1965 (asgnd)–Jul 1976 (dspd); San Damiano RRS, San Damiano, 19 Jan 1965 (asgnd)–13 Sep 1968 (dspd); Oderzo RRS, Oderzo, 19 Jan 1965 (asgnd)–1 Jul 1976 (dspd); Monte Telegrafo RRS, Eores, 2 Sep 1965 (asgnd)–; Martina Franca Water Sys Anx, Martina Franca, 6 Jan 1966 (asgnd)–15 Apr 1981 (trsfd to San Vito Dei Normanni AS); Conselve RRS, Conselve, 1 Mar 1966 (asgnd)–22 May 1979 (dspd); Monte Calvarina RRS, Ronca, 1 Mar 1966 (asgnd)–22 May 1979 (dspd); Rimini RRS, Mira Mare, 1 Mar 1966 (asgnd)–; La Comina Stor Anx (rdsgd La Comina Stor Site), Roveredo in Piano, Aug 1966 (asgnd)–; Monte Limbara Water Sys Anx, Tempio Pausiana, Sardinia, 1 Sep 1966 (asgnd)–; Monte Nardello Water Sys Anx, Santo Stefano

---

*All installations are located in Italy.

in Aspromonte, 1 Sep 1966 (asgnd)–; Aviano Hsg Anx (Trnst Fam Qtrs) (detchd), Aviano, 1 Sep 1967 (asgnd)–30 Jun 1975 (dspd); Aviano Fam Hsg Anx, Aviano, 1 Dec 1967 (asgnd)–30 Jun 1972 (dspd); Napoli Fam Hsg #1, Naples, 1 Jul 1968 (asgnd)–1 Jul 1969 (dspd); Napoli Fam Hsg #2, Naples, 1 Jul 1968 (asgnd)–1 Jul 1969 (dspd); Vicenza Fam Hsg (detchd), Vicenza, 1 Sep 1968 (asgnd)–1 Jul 1969 (dspd); Aviano Fam Hsg Anx #2, Aviano, 1 Sep 1970 (asgnd)–; Aviano Fam Hsg Anx #3, Aviano, 1 Mar 1971 (asgnd)–; Roveredo Fam Hsg Anx, Roveredo in Piano, 10 Apr 1972 (asgnd)–31 Mar 1974 (dspd); San Quirino Stor Anx, San Quirino, 1 Sep 1975 (asgnd)–30 Jun 1977 (dspd); Monte Serra RR Anx, Calei, 10 Feb 1978 (asgnd)–; Quartu Santa Elena Bach Hsg Anx, Quartu Santa Elena, 15 Mar 1979 (asgnd)–; Decimomannu AB (detchd), Decimomannu, 1 Jul 1979 (asgnd)–; Assemini Bach Hsg Anx, Assemini, 1 Aug 1979 (asgnd)–31 Jan 1982 (dspd); Uta Bach Hsg, Uta, 1 Oct 1979 (asgnd)–; Aviano Fam Hsg Anx #6, Aviano, 1 Jun 1981 (asgnd)–; Ciampino AB (rdsgd Ciampino Aprt; Ciampino Flt Svc Anx; Ciampino Admn Ofc), Ciampino, unk (asgnd)–.

Major Changes in Operational Capability: Airfield built as one of Italian Air Force's first flying training schools, 1911; airfield used during World War I for attacks against Austria; between 1919 and 1939 the base again used by the Italian Air Force for flying training; served Italian and German forces as airfield during World War II; captured by the U.S. Fifth Army and occupied by the Mediterranean Allied Air Forces (and later, Desert Air Forces), May 1945; RAF light bomber base 1945–47, then returned to Italian control; conclusion of a joint-use agreement between the U.S. and Italian governments made Aviano a NATO air base in 1954; began hosting TAC rotational units 13 Dec 1955; after USAFE assumed jurisdiction, major improvements included construction of weather observation site, replacement of revetments, installation of special lighting, resurfacing of runway, and paving of overruns 1957–1958; new control tower completed fall 1964; base population increased sharply when base mission changed from accommodating rotational F–100 squadrons to serving F–4 rotational weapons training for USAFE in spring 1970; throughout the 1970s the base also assumed alert commitments; 28 TAB VEE shelters completed spring 1977; airfield lighting upgraded in 1977.

Major Commands to Which Assigned: Mediterranean Allied Air Forces, 15 May–14 Jun 1945 (trsfd to Desert AF); USAFE, 15 Feb 1955–.

Major Changes in Status: Italian airfield 1911–1943; under German military control 1943–1945; under Allied control, 15 May 1945–1947 (returned to Italian jurisdiction); USAFE air base, 15 Feb 1955–.

Units Assigned:

	1955	7207 USAF Infmy
390 Ftr-Bmbr Sq	19 Dec 55–18 Jun 56	(7207 USAF Dispy;
7207 AB Sq	15 Feb 55–1 Dec 57	7227 USAF

Dispy)   15 Aug 55–1 Apr 66
                1956
391 Ftr-Bmbr Sq   6 Dec 56–11 Jun 57
614 Ftr-Bmbr Sq   18 Jun 56–10 Dec 56
1287 AACS Sq
  (2187 Comms Sq;
  2187 Comms Gp;
  2187 Information
  Sys Gp)   18 Feb 56–
                1957
389 Ftr-Bmbr Sq   10 Jun 57–19 Dec 57
7227 Spt Gp
  (7227 Cmbt Spt Gp)   1 Jul 57–1 Apr 66
                1958
308 Tac Ftr Sq   22 Aug 58–16 Jan 59
612 Tac Ftr Sq   27 Aug 58–17 Nov 58
614 Tac Ftr Sq   17 Nov 58–18 Apr 59
7227 Mat Sq   24 Oct 58–1 Jul 61
7227 Spt Sq   24 Oct 58–1 Jul 61
7230 USAF Dispy   25 Nov 58–20 Feb 59
                1959
353 Tac Ftr Sq   17 Sep 59–15 Jan 60
355 Tac Ftr Sq   18 Mar 59–17 Sep 59
356 Tac Ftr Sq   18 Mar 59–17 Sep 59
612 Tac Ftr Sq   14 Dec 59–19 Feb 60
613 Tac Ftr Sq   13 Aug 59–15 Dec 59

615 Tac Ftr Sq   18 Apr 59–10 Apr 60
                1960
306 Tac Ftr Sq   9 Apr 60–10 Jul 60
307 Tac Ftr Sq   13 Nov 60–11 Mar 61
309 Tac Ftr Sq   11 Jul 60–15 Nov 60
356 Tac Ftr Sq   13 May 60–12 Sep 60
                1961
308 Tac Ftr Sq   12 Mar 61–May 62
614 Tac Ftr Sq   13 Jan 61–unk 61
                1966
40 Cmbt Spt Sq   1 Apr 66–
40 Consold Acft
  Maint Sq   1 Apr 66–
40 Sup Sq   1 Aug 66–
40 Tac Gp   1 Apr 66–
                1971
USAF Dispy, Aviano
  (USAF Hosp,
  Aviano; USAF
  Clinic, Aviano)   1 Jul 71–
                1972
7004 Explosive Ord
  Dspl Flt   1 Jul 72–
                1980
40 Trnsp Sq   1 May 80–

14

Bitburg Air Base

Location: Located 2 mi SE of Bitburg, 20 mi N of Trier, and 135 mi W of Weisbaden, Federal Republic of Germany.

Name. Named after a city in the Federal Republic of Germany.

Date of Current Name: 1 Sep 1952.

Previous Names: None.

Date of Establishment: 1 Sep 1952.

Date Construction Began: French construction for USAF initiated spring 1951; USAF construction commenced Feb 1952.

Date of Beneficial Occupancy: Dec 1952.

Base Operating Units: Det 1, 31st Wea Sq, 20 May 1952; 53d Ftr-Bmbr Sq, 22 Jul 1952; 36th AB Gp, 13 Dec 1952 (rdsgd 36th Cmbt Spt Gp, 8 Mar 1962)–.

Base Commanders: Maj Herbert A. Curran, c. Feb–c. Jul 1952; Lt Col Darrell S. Cramer, Jul 1952; Col Robert L. Scott Jr, 17 Nov 1952; Col Thomas B. Whitehouse, 30 May 1953; Col Roy R. Brischetto, 17 Aug 1954; Col William H. Dick, 11 Jan 1955; Col John A. Brooks III, 7 Feb 1955; Col Leighton F. Downing, 8 Jun 1956; Lt Col Theodore D. Bradley, 1 Feb 1957; Lt Col Irving H. Gravin, 25 Jun 1957; Col John D. Wynne, 7 Aug 1957; Col Robert F. Whitlow, 18 Sep 1957; Lt Col Donald J. Quigley, 15 Jul 1959; Col James D. Berry, 27 Jul 1959; Col Alden G. Thompson, 9 Apr 1960; Col Walter J. Couser Jr, 4 Aug 1964; Col Eugene J. Budnik, 31 Jul 1967; Col Roberts L. Underwood, 23 Feb 1970; Col John P. Moore, 3 Jul 1970; Col Sterling E. Barrow, 15 Aug 1972; Lt Col Walter E. Bjorneby, 2 Oct 1974; Col George E. Wehling, 14 Nov 1974; Col Charles A. Dutton, 15 Aug 1977; Col James S. Brimm, 23 Aug 1978; Col Benedict E. Glyphis, 1 May 1980–.

Major Off-Base and Detached Installations:* Bitburg/Schoenfeld ACWS, Schoenfeld, 16 Oct 1953 (asgnd)–unk; Bitburg Hsg Anx (rdsgd Bitburg Fam Hsg Anx), Bitburg, 1 Jan 1958 (asgnd)–; Bitburg Hsg Water

---

*Unless otherwise indicated, all installations are located in the Federal Republic of Germany.

Pump Anx (rdsgd Bitburg Hsg Water Plant Anx; Ahlbach Water Sys Anx), Moetsch, 1 Jan 1958 (asgnd)–unk; Camp Hilvarenbeck (rdsgd Hilvarenbeck RB Site), Tilburg, Netherlands, 1 Jan 1958 (asgnd)–1 Feb 1960 (dspd); Camp New Amsterdam, Huis ter Heide, Netherlands, 1 Jan 1958 (asgnd)–7 Feb 1969 (trsfd to Hahn AB); Idenheim Msl Anx (rdsgd Idenheim Msl Site; Idenheim Anx; Idenheim Comms Stn), Idenheim, 1 Jan 1958 (asgnd)–unk; Oberweis Msl Anx (rdsgd Oberweis Msl Site; Oberweis Anx), Oberweis, 1 Jan 1958 (asgnd)–unk; Sulm Msl Anx (rdsgd Sulm Msl Site; Sulm Anx), Sulm, 1 Jan 1958 (asgnd)–unk; Trier AB/Eurem Kaserne, Trier, 1 Jan 1958 (asgnd)–unk; Trier Comms Anx (rdsgd Trier Comms Stn), Trier, 1 Jan 1958 (asgnd)–unk; Trier Hsg Anx (rdsgd Trier Fam Anx), Pfalzel, 1 Jan 1958 (asgnd)–1 Oct 1977 (trsfd to Spangdahlem AB); Echternacherbruck Comms Fclty Anx, Echternacherbruck, 1 Apr 1960 (asgnd)–31 Jul 1963 (dspd); Bitburg/Schoenfeld/ Pruem Hsg Anx (rdsgd Pruem Fam Hsg Anx), Pruem, 15 Feb 1961 (trsfd from Ramstein AB)–30 Jun 1965 (dspd); Pruem Fam Hsg Anx, Pruem, 15 Feb 1961 (trsfd from Ramstein AB)—unk; Schoenfeld Water Sys Anx (rdsgd Pruem Water Sys Anx), Ormont, 15 Feb 1961 (trsfd from Ramstein AB)–30 Jun 1965 (dspd); Erding AB, Erding, 1 Jul 1973 (trsfd from Ramstein AB)–12 May 1978 (trsfd to Zweibrucken AB); Bitburg Ammo Stor Stn (rdsgd Moetsch Ammo Stor Anx), Hullingen, 29 Jun 1974 (asgnd)–unk; Pruem AS, Pruem, 1 Jul 1975 (asgnd)–; Pruem Water Sys Anx, Ormont, 1 Jul 1975 (asgnd)–; Huis ter Heide Fam Hsg Anx, Huis ter Heide, Netherlands, unk–7 Jan 1978 (dspd); Lahr AB, Lahr, 12 May 1978 (trsfd from Ramstein AB)–; Rittersdorf Msl Site (rdsgd Rittersdorf Anx), Rittersdorf, unk–; Roehl Radio Rg Anx (rdsgd Roehl Anx), Roehl, unk–.

Major Changes in Operational Capability: Runway, hangars, and control tower to support the 53d Ftr-Bmbr Sq completed spring 1952; 985 dependent housing units completed mid-1953; runway upgraded for F–84s and F–86s that replaced F–80s, May 1961; base converted flight facilities to accommodate century series F–100 and F–102 operations late 1961; F–105 flight simulator, first in Europe, commissioned Feb 1962; camouflage/concealment project completed mid-1965; operational facilities upgraded to accommodate F–104D operations Mar 1966; hardened aircraft shelters completed 1969; operations merged with Spangdahlem AB as 36th Tac Ftr Wg assumed control, thus making it (with the tenant 40th Aerosp Rscu & Recovery Wg) USAFE's sole two-wing base, 15 Sep 1969; three underground fuel storage tanks completed Dec 1974; airmen dormitory rehabilitation project (two phases) completed 1971, 1974; additional construction and modification of facilities undertaken to support USAFE's first F–15 squadron, which arrived in Apr 1977; protective and maintenance shelters, with all support equipment and facilities, completed 15 Aug 1977; avionics shop completed mid-1978.

Major Commands to Which Assigned: USAFE, 23 Aug 1952–.
Major Changes in Status: None.
Units Assigned:

1952			
22 Ftr-Bmbr Sq		5 Tac Dep Sq	7 Aug 55–1 Jul 62
(22 Ftr-Day Sq;		1807 AACS Wg	
22 Tac Ftr Sq)	28 Oct 52–	(European-African-	
23 Ftr-Bmbr Sq		Middle-Eastern	
(23 Ftr-Day Sq;		AACS Area)	14 Nov 55–2 Feb 58
23 Tac Ftr Sq)	17 Nov 52–31 Dec 71	**1956**	
36 AB Gp		585 Msl Maint Sq	15 Sep 56–25 Sep 62
(36 Cmbt Spt Gp)	13 Dec 52–	585 Spt Sq	15 Sep 56–8 Jul 62
36 AP Sq		585 Tac Msl Gp	15 Sep 56–25 Sep 62
(36 Scty Pol Sq)	11 Dec 52–	**1957**	
36 Comms Sq	5 Nov 52–1 Jul 62	525 Ftr-Intcpr Sq	
36 Ftr-Bmbr Gp		(525 Tac Ftr Sq)	12 Feb 57–
(36 Ftr-Day Gp)	17 Nov 52–8 Dec 57	613 Ftr-Bmbr Sq	19 Dec 57–27 Jun 58
36 Ftr-Bmbr Wg		1892 AACS Engrg	
(36 Ftr-Day Wg;		& Instl Sq	18 Jan 57–12 Nov 57
36 Tac Ftr Wg)	13 Dec 52–	**1958**	
36 Food Svc Sq	6 Nov 52–8 Mar 62	71 Tac Msl Sq	18 Jun 58–30 Apr 69
36 Instls Sq		612 Tac Ftr Sq	24 Jun 58–27 Aug 58
(36 CE Sq)	8 Oct 52–	**1959**	
36 Maint & Sup Gp	8 Dec 52–8 Dec 57	36 Armnt & Elect	
36 MV Sq		Maint Sq	15 Nov 59–8 Mar 62
(36 Trnsp Sq)	12 Dec 52–	**1961**	
36 Sup Sq	8 Dec 52–	53 Tac Ftr Sq	3 Oct 61–
53 Ftr-Bmbr Sq		**1962**	
(53 Ftr-Day Sq)	22 Jul 52–17 Dec 56	2139 Comms Sq	1 Jul 62–
B1 AB Spt Sq, Prov	12 Mar 52–13 Dec 52	**1964**	
1953		36 Armnt & Elect	
36 Maint Sq		Maint Sq	
(36 Fld Maint Sq;		(36 Avncs	
36 Consold		Maint Sq;	
Acft Maint Sq;		36 Component	
36 Fld Maint Sq;		Rpr Sq)	1 Jul 64–
36 Equip Maint Sq)	3 Mar 53–	36 Orgnzl Maint Sq	1 Jul 64–1 Jan 66
36 Med Gp		336 Mun Maint Sq	1 Jul 64–7 Oct 72
(36 Tac Hosp)	26 Jul 53–	**1971**	
1954		USAF Hosp, Bitburg	1 Jul 71–
1 Pilotless Bmbr Sq	20 Mar 54–18 Jun 58	**1972**	
563 Ftr-Bmbr Sq	12 Dec 54–7 Jul 55	36 Orgnzl Maint Sq	
7424 USAF Hosp	1 May 54–25 Sep 57	(36 Acft Gnrtn Sq)	1 Feb 72–
1955		**1982**	
2 Wea Wg	6 Dec 55–23 Mar 58	36 Svcs Sq	1 Feb 82–

Camp New Amsterdam

Location: Located in Huis ter Heide, 7 mi ENE of Utrecht, on a part of Soesterberg AB (RNAFB), The Netherlands.*

Name: Named in honor of the first Dutch settlement in America, Nieuw Amsterdam, later renamed New York City.

Date of Current Name: 16 Nov 1954.

Previous Names: None.

Date of Establishment: 16 Nov 1954.

Date Construction Began: Soesterberg AB construction began after World War II; additional construction to accommodate USAF tenant units began in early 1950s.

Date of Beneficial Occupancy: 16 Nov 1954 (Camp New Amsterdam portion of Soesterberg AB).

Base Operating Units: 512th Ftr-Day Sq, 16 Nov 1954; 32d Ftr-Day Sq, 8 Sep 1955 (rdsgd 32d Tac Ftr Sq, 8 Jul 1958; 32d Ftr-Intcpr Sq, 8 Jul 1959; 32d Tac Ftr Sq, 1 Jul 1969)–.

Base Commanders: Lt Col Michael J. Quirk, c. 16 Nov 1954; Lt Col Alden E. West, 8 Sep 1955; Lt Col Donald H. Paap, 3 Dec 1957; Lt Col Frederick C. Blesse, 23 Oct 1958; Lt Col Alma R. Flake, 8 Jun 1961; Lt Col (later, Col) Gelvin S. Nicely, 24 Jun 1963; Lt Col Edward M. Walsh Jr, 7 Jul 1965; Lt Col (later, Col) Daniel C. Perry, 5 Jun 1967; Col Austin O. Davis, 16 Jul 1968; Lt Col Boyd E. Gibson, 17 Mar 1970; Lt Col Theodore Dowd, 18 Aug 1972; Col Robert E. Messerli, 2 Jul 1973; Col Kenny D. Cobb, 2 Jul 1974; Col Donald L. Poorman, 24 Sep 1975; Lt Col Charles J. Dutton, 1 Oct 1975;[†] Lt Col Donald G. Nutt, 22 Jul 1977; Lt Col James D. Ernst, 14 Jul 1980–.

Major Off-Base and Detached Installations: None. The dormitory area, called the W.S. Kamp, and the commissary, located at Kamp van

---

*The designation Camp New Amsterdam applies only to the U.S.-occupied segment of the Royal Netherlands Air Force Base—named after the nearby town which dates to 1911. Soesterberg RNAFB was named on 1 Jul 1913 and became the "cradle" of Dutch aviation.

[†]From this date on, the deputy commander for combat support became the designated base commander instead of the squadron commander.

19

Zeist in Soesterberg, house U.S. facilities; the housing area in Soesterberg, known as Apollo Housing, is leased and controlled by the squadron's housing office.

Major Changes in Operational Capability: Primary runway extended to 12,000 feet and new barriers installed to enable transition from F–86F to F–100C operations, Aug 1956; additional personnel arrived, facilities again upgraded, and 21 additional operational buildings (including alert hangar and dormitories) completed upon conversion to F–102A/B operations 1960–1961; extensive runway repairs (Mar–Jun 1963 and Sep–Nov 1966) necessitated temporary transfer of flying operations to nearby Deelen RNAF; phasing in of F–4Es resulted in more upgrading and construction of additional facilities 1969–1970; TAB VEE shelters completed fall 1972; new liquid oxygen plant completed mid-1973; 17 aircraft shelters and 4 ammunition igloos accepted Oct 1977; 190 family housing units occupied Jul 1977–May 1978; arrival of F–15A/Bs required further updating of operational facilities 1978–1980.

Major Commands to Which Assigned: USAFE, 15 Nov 1954–.

Major Changes in Status: Continuously active since 16 Nov 1954, when Dutch-U.S. agreement authorized stationing of a U.S. fighter squadron at Soesterberg RNAFB.

Units Assigned:

1954			1955
512 Ftr-Day Sq	1 Nov 54–8 Sep 55	32 Ftr-Intcpr Sq	
7475 USAF Infmy		(32 Tac Ftr Sq;	
(7475 USAF		32 Ftr-Intcpr Sq;	
Dispy)	8 Oct 54–25 Oct 58	32 Tac Ftr Sq)	8 Sep 55–

Clark Air Base

Location: Located 3 mi NNW of Angeles City, 60 mi N of Manila, Luzon, Republic of the Philippines.

Name: Named in honor of Maj Harold M. Clark (1890–1919). A native of St. Paul, Minnesota, Maj Clark grew up in the Philippines, was commissioned in the cavalry in 1913, and later transferred to the Aviation Section of the Air Service. He subsequently commanded an aero squadron in Hawaii, setting numerous records as the first military aviator in the islands. Major Clark became executive officer of the Aviation Section of the Signal Corps in Panama, and died when the Curtis HS2LS flying boat he was piloting crashed into the gates of the Miraflores Locks in the Panama Canal on 2 May 1919.

Date of Current Name: 3 Dec 1957.

Previous Names: Fort Stotsenburg (aka Camp Stotsenburg), 1 Sep 1903; Clark Fld, Sep 1919–20 Dec 1941; AAB Clark Fld, 10 Feb 1945; Clark AFB, 26 Mar 1948.*

Date of Establishment: 1 Sep 1903 (War Dept); Sep 1919 (Army Air Service).

Date Construction Began: 1902.

Date of Beneficial Occupancy: 1903 (War Dept); 2 Dec 1919 (Signal Corps).

Base Operating Units:[†] 3d Aero Sq (Obs), 2 Dec 1919 (rdsgd 3d Sq, 14 May 1921; 3d Pursuit Sq, 25 Jan 1923); 28th Bomb Sq, 16 Jun 1938; 24th Pursuit Gp, 1 Oct–c. 20 Dec 1941. Adv Echelon, Fifth Air Force, AAB Clark Fld, 10 Feb 1945; 29th Air Svc Gp, 16 Feb 1946; 358th Air Svc Gp, 1 Jan 1947; 24th Air Dep Wg, 1 Jul 1949; 6200th AB Wg, 1 Dec 1950; 6200th AB Gp, 1 Feb 1953; 405th AB Gp, 10 Apr 1959 (rdsgd 405th Cmbt Spt Gp,

---

*The original Clark Field was only a part of Fort Stotsenburg. After U.S. forces recaptured the area in 1945 the name Clark was applied to the entire Fort Stotsenburg area. This was recognized offically in 1948 when all of that reservation became Clark Air Force Base.

[†]The first five units were the main flying organizations on the field; presumably they also performed custodial functions.

8 Apr 1963); 6200th Cmbt Spt Gp, 8 Jan 1966; 636th Cmbt Spt Gp, 8 Jul 1966; 6200th AB Wg, 1 Aug 1968; 405th Cmbt Spt Gp, 1 Jan 1972; 3d Cmbt Spt Gp, 16 Sep 1974–.

Base Commanders: Unk, 1919–1938; Maj Guy L. McNeil, 1939; Maj Lester J. Maitland, 1940; Col Eugene L. Eubank, 1941–c. 30 Sep 1941; Col Orrin L. Grover, 1 Oct 1941; (under Japanese control Jan 1942–15 Feb 1945); Col Ernest K. Warburton, 16 Feb 1945; Col Charles H. MacDonald, 27 Mar 1945; Brig Gen Carl A. Brandt, 11 Feb 1946; Maj Edward J. Moriarty, 1 Jan 1947; Col Stoyte O. Ross, 23 Jun 1947; Maj Gen Eugene L. Eubank, Aug 1948; Col John A. Way, 14 Nov 1947; Brig Gen Robert C. Oliver, Oct 1948; Col Clinton W. Davis, 15 Nov 1949; Col Morley F. Slaght, 8 Nov 1951; Col Jack N. Donohew, 7 Jan 1952; Col Wilson H. Banks, 9 May 9 May 1953; Col William F. Stewart, 20 May 1955; Col Francis L. Rivard, 15 Aug 1955; Col Karl T. Barthelmes, 1 Feb 1956; Col James K. Dowling, 6 Jul 1957; Col Willard C. Woodbury, 10 Apr 1959; Col Cornelius S. Dresser, 23 Jul 1959; Col Vernon W. Froehlich, Jun 1962; Lt Col Jerome G. Schweickert, 1 Jul 1963; Col Gordon K. Stallings, 13 Aug 1963; Lt Col Richard D. Salter, 13 Jun 1965; Col William F. Kahley, 26 Aug 1965; Col Ernest F. Moore, 26 Jul 1967; Col Phillip C. Rawlins, Aug 1967; Col Ernest P. Pate, 1 Aug 1968; Col Robert M. Hansen, 2 Jan 1969; Col Averil F. Holman, 1 Aug 1969; Col Paul L. Maret, 21 Nov 1970; Col Aubrey M. Bobitt, 19 Apr 1971; Col John R. Geyer, 2 Sep 1971; Col William I. Truesdell, 1 Jan 1972; Col Donald A. Michela, 1 Aug 1973; Col George J. Schmidt, 15 Aug 1975; Col Boyd D. Hensley, 25 Aug 1975; Col Charles J. Corey, 12 Jul 1977; Col Paul C. Mathis, 24 Aug 1977; Col John A. Parrish Jr, 28 Aug 1978; Col Harrison M. Ward Jr, 8 Nov 1979; Col Arthur C. Weiner, 19 Feb 1982; Col Burton R. Moore, 27 Aug 1982–.*

Major Off-Base and Detached Installations:[†] John Hay AS, Baguio, Dec 1903 (asgnd), 15 Oct 1949 (officially asgnd)–; Wallace AS, San Fernando, 1903 (asgnd), 1949 (officially asgnd)–; Camp O'Donnell, 20 mi N of Angeles, Dec 1903 (asgnd), 1954 (officially asgnd)–16 Feb 1979 (trsfd to Philippine govt); Crow Valley Gunnery Rg, Capas, Dec 1903–16 Feb 1979; Manila Rsch Site, Manila, unk–Dec 1941 (abandoned); Del Monte AS, Mindanao, Oct 1941–15 Jan 1977; West Tinian Aux Afld, Tinian, Marianas, 2 Aug 1944 (actvd)–Apr 1949 (inactvd); McKinley Hosp and Hsg Anx (rdsgd William McKinley Anx), Manila, 1945 (asgnd)–1951 (inactvd), unk (actvd)–6 Dec 1956 (trsfd to Philippine govt); Angeles AP Anx,

---

*After 16 Feb 1979, the official Clark AB Commander has been the Chief of Staff, Armed Forces of the Philippines (AFP): Gen Romeo Espino, 16 Feb 1979; Gen Fabian C. Ver, Sep 1981-.

[†]Unless otherwise indicated, all installations are located in the Philippines.

Angeles, 1 Apr 1947 (asgnd)–Sep 1974 (lease term); Mariveles Mil Rsch Anx (rdsgd Mariveles Tng Anx), Mariveles, 1 May 1949 (actvd)–unk; Baja Pt Anx, 88 mi SW of Puerto Princesa, Apr 1954 (actvd)–28 Sep 1959 (deleted); Shu Lin Kou AS, Shu Lin Ku, Taiwan, ROC, 1 Jun 1955 (actvd)–31 Mar 1958 (trsfd to Tinian AS); Tainan AS (rdsgd Tainan AB), Tainan, ROC, 1 Jun 1955 (actvd)–31 May 1958 (chgd to prim instl); Taipei AS, Taipei, ROC, 1 Jun 1955 (asgnd)–31 Mar 1958 (trsfd to Tainan AS); North Tinian Aux Fld, Tinian, Marianas, unk–9 Jan 1978 (use rights term); West Tinian Aux Afld, Tinian, Marianas, 1 Jul 1957 (trsfd from Hickam AFB, HI)–9 Jan 1978 (use rights term); Bamban Anx (rdsgd Bamban RB Anx), Bamban, 3 Dec 1957 (asgnd)–; Bataan Fuel Stor Stn (rdsgd Bataan Ocean Petrol Dep; Bataan Petrol Prods Stor Anx; Bataan Ocean Petrol Dep), 10 mi SSE of Balanga, 3 Dec 1957 (trsfd from Manila AS)–30 Apr 1968 (trsfd to Philippine govt); Mariveles Tng Anx, Mariveles, 3 Dec 1957 (asgnd)–unk; Gozar AS, 1963 (actvd)–; Paranal AS, 1963 (actvd)–; Paredes AS, 1963 (actvd)–; Bamban RB Anx, 20 Oct 1964 (actvd)–; Bangkok Prcmt Ofc, Bangkok, Thailand, unk–1 Sep 1965 (dspd); Bangkok Hsg Anx, Bangkok, Thailand, unk–14 Oct 1965 (dspd); Saigon Hsg Anx, Saigon, Republic of Vietnam, unk–14 Oct 1965 (dspd); Silang Anx, Silang, unk–22 Dec 1965 (dspd); Manila Rsch Site, Manila, 1 Oct 1966 (asgnd)–15 Aug 1970 (lease term); Mactan AB, Mactan, unk–Apr 1967 (dspd); Can Tho Hsg Anx No. 1, unk–1 Jun 1967 (dspd); Clark Petrol Prods Stor Anx, Olongapo, 1 Jul 1967 (asgnd)–; Isley Aux Fld, Saipan, 30 Jun 1970 (asgnd)–9 Jan 1978 (use rights term); Quezon Bcn Anx, Quezon, 1 Oct 1970 (actvd)–; Taygaytay TB Anx, Taygaytay, 1 Oct 1970 (actvd)–; Angat Microwave Relay Stn, 15 Jun 1971 (asgnd)–; Mt Cabuyo Comms Site, Mt Cabuyo, 24 May 1972 (asgnd)–9 Jan 1978 (use rights term); Hong Kong Fam Hsg Anx, Hong Kong, unk–31 Jul 1972 (lease cancelled); Manila Prcmt Ofc, Manila, unk–14 Oct 1974 (dspd); Chia Yi Ammo Stor Anx, Chia Yi, ROC, 15 Jun 1979 (asgnd)–unk; Ching Chuan Kang AB, 10 mi N of Taichung, ROC, 15 Jun 1979 (asgnd)–18 Jun 1980 (dspd); Tainan AB, Tainan, ROC, Jun 1979 (asgnd)–unk; Manila Admn Ofc 02, Manila, Sep 1980 (actvd)–; Manila Beach Hsg Anx, Manila, 1 Oct 1980 (actvd)–; Manila Admn Ofc 01, 1 Feb 1981 (actvd)–; Manila Admn Ofc 03, Manila, 15 Apr 1981 (actvd)–; Sydney Air Trml, Sydney, Australia, Nov 1981 (actvd)–; Manila Admn Anx, 13 Jun 1982 (asgnd)–.

Major Changes in Operational Capability: Officers' quarters and water system constructed 1910–1911; construction of steel hangars and a dirt air strip 1917–1918; a portion of Ft Stotsenburg officially set aside for the Aviation Section of the Signal Corps and named Clark Fld, Sep 1919; Clark served as a landing field for medium bombers and accommodated half of the heavy bombers stationed in the Philippines during the 1930s; Clark and its subordinate airfield at Del Monte were the only fields capable of heavy bomber operations at the outbreak of World War II; Japanese bombers destroyed 36 aircraft and many facilities at Clark on 8 Dec 1941; last aircraft and personnel evacuated to Australia by 31 Dec 1941; during period of Japanese occupation, several auxiliary airfields constructed and used; first "kamikazi" flights operated from Clark and Mabalacat, 1944; elements of the Sixth U.S. Army cleared most Japanese from Ft Stotsenburg-Clark Fld area and flying activity commenced on least damaged runway while the field still drew Japanese fire, 25 Jan 1945; saboteurs and infiltrators sporadically damaged parked aircraft until 10 Feb 1945; general hospital rehabilitated and enlarged late 1945; various operational buildings, quonset huts, and 500 housing units for enlisted men and officers constructed 1948–1949; a new dive-bombing and skip-bombing range completed 1952; extensive repairs and maintenance work, including renovation of numerous older buildings to make them suitable for military housing, undertaken 1953–1959; SEA operations doubled base population to 60,000, making Clark the second most populous USAF installation 1963–1967; 350-bed hospital, which also served as medical center for SEA, completed 1964 (augmented by 180-bed nursing unit in 1970); 100-unit officer housing project completed mid-1967; aviation fuel hydrant system installed 1968; 300-unit duplex housing area completed early 1970; repair of NCO quarters and construction of family quarters completed May–Nov 1970; improvement of operational concrete areas, including 10,500-ft runway to permit C–5 operations, completed July 1970; storage facilities, sewage treatment and disposal plant, water treatment facilities, and a fire station constructed 1971–1973, thus making Clark the U.S. military logistics hub for SEA operations; 250-unit housing project completed late 1980.

Major Commands to Which Assigned: War Dept, 1903; Philippine Dept, 1917; The Adjutant General of the Army, Dept of the Philippines, 1919; Air Forces, United States Army Forces in the Far East, 4 Aug 1941; Philippines Dept Air Force, 20 Sep 1941 (rdsgd Far East Air Force, 20 Dec 1941); Sixth Army, 16 Feb 1945; Eighth Army, 15 May 1945; FEAF, Jun 1945 (rdsgd Pacific Air Command, USA, 6 Dec 1945; FEAF, 1 Jan 1947; PACAF, 1 Jul 1957)–.

Major Changes in Status: Clark AB was occupied by the Japanese 20 Dec 1941–10 Feb 1945.

Units Assigned:

			1940	
	1919	2 Obs Sq		c. 1 Nov 40–c. Nov 41
3 Pur Sq	2 Dec 19–16 Jun 38			1941
	1920	14 Bomb Sq		16 Sep 41–1 Jan 42
Sq A		17 Pur Sq		9 Dec 41–1 May 42
(3 Sq; 3 Pur Sq)	15 Oct 20–15 Jun 38	19 Bomb Gp		26 Oct 41–24 Dec 41
	1922	20 Pur Sq		Jul 41–25 Dec 41
28 Sq [Bomb]	1 Sep 22–4 Jun 23	24 Pur Gp		1 Oct 41–2 Apr 46
	1938	28 Mat Sq		1 Feb 41–2 Apr 46
28 Bomb Sq	16 Jun 38–24 Dec 41			

24

30 Bomb Sq	c. 23 Oct 41–c. 20 Dec 41
93 Bomb Sq	c. 23 Oct 41–c. 19 Dec 41
V Bomber Comd	14 Nov 41–c. 24 Dec 41
	1945
2 Bomb Sq	Mar 45–18 Aug 45
4 Adrm Sq	17 Sep 45–16 Aug 48
4 Recon Sq	Jun 45–Aug 45
5 Recon Sq	24 Dec 45–20 Oct 47
6 Recon Gp	1 May 45–31 Aug 45
7 Air Svc Gp	1 Apr 45–18 Jul 45
8 Photo Recon Sq	19 May 45–12 Aug 45
13 Emerg Rscu Gp	45–1 Oct 45
14 Comms Sq, Comd	4 Sep 45–15 May 46
14 Tow Target Sq	c. 17 Jul 45–1 Feb 46
17 Photo Recon Sq	Nov 45–1 May 46
19 Bomb Sq	c. 15 Mar 45–14 Aug 45
20 Recon Sq	17 May 45–4 Aug 45
21 Svc Gp	27 Apr 45–27 Aug 45
22 Bomb Gp	12 Mar 45–4 Aug 45
23 Bomb Sq	Dec 45–10 Mar 47
25 Photo Recon Sq	14 Jun 45–14 Jul 45
26 Photo Recon Sq	22 Jul 45–Sep 45
29 Air Svc Gp	26 Dec 45–11 May 46
31 Bomb Sq	Dec 45–10 Mar 47
35 Ftr Gp	19 Apr 45–28 Jun 45
36 Photo Recon Sq	c. 28 Apr 45–26 Jul 45
38 Photo Recon Sq	c. 5 Oct 45–15 Jan 46
39 Ftr Sq	18 Jan 45–2 Jul 45
39 Trp Carr Sq	28 Mar 45–19 Apr 45
40 Air Engrg Sq	23 Sep 45–1 Apr 46
40 Ftr Sq	19 Apr 45–30 Jun 45
40 Trp Carr Sq	5 Mar 45–c. 16 Aug 45
41 Ftr Sq	20 Apr 45–30 Jun 45
41 Trp Carr Sq	6 Apr 45–Aug 45
43 Bomb Gp	16 Mar 45–26 Jul 45
46 Trp Carr Sq	Mar 45–19 Aug 45
54 Trp Carr Wg	Jun 45–Sep 45
63 Bomb Sq	19 Mar 45–25 Jul 45
64 Bomb Sq	c. 22 Mar 45–26 Jul 45
65 Air Engrg Sq	26 Dec 45–20 May 46
65 Bomb Sq	c. 16 Mar 45–c. 24 Jul 45
67 Trp Carr Sq	c. 1 Jun 45–c. 27 Aug 45
68 Trp Carr Sq	c. 15 Jun 45–25 Aug 45
69 Trp Carr Sq	1 Jun 45–c. 25 Aug 45
70 Trp Carr Sq	28 Jun 45–26 Aug 45
71 Air Engrg Sq	1 Nov 45–1 Apr 46
72 Bomb Sq	Dec 45–10 Mar 47
91 Photo Recon Wg	23 Mar 45–30 Jul 45
301 Adrm Sq	c. 45–30 Jun 46
310 Bomb Wg	23 Aug 45–21 Oct 45
317 Trp Carr Gp	c. 17 Mar 45–24 Aug 45
370 Bomb Sq	10 Sep 45–27 Dec 45
371 Bomb Sq	1 Sep 45–27 Dec 45
372 Bomb Sq	c. 1 Sep 45–27 Dec 45
394 Bomb Sq	Dec 45–29 Apr 46
403 Bomb Sq	c. 15 Mar 45–22 Jul 45
408 Bomb Sq	13 Mar 45–c. 21 Aug 45

413 Bomb Sq	23 Dec 45–unk
421 Night Ftr Sq	26 Apr 45–16 Jul 45
424 Bomb Sq	5 Sep 45–7 Dec 45
431 Ftr Sq	28 Feb 45–19 Apr 45
432 Ftr Sq	27 Feb 45–19 Apr 45
433 Ftr Sq	28 Feb 45–19 Apr 45
433 Trp Carr Gp	31 May 45–11 Sep 45
437 Ftr Sq	23 Dec 45–unk
456 Ftr Sq	23 Dec 45–unk
475 Ftr Gp	28 Feb 45–c. 20 Apr 45
498 Bomb Sq	11 May 45–c. 20 Jul 45
499 Bomb Sq	12 May 45–28 Jul 45
500 Bomb Sq	12 May 45–27 Jul 45
501 Bomb Sq	12 May 45–28 Jul 45
771 AAF BU	
(141 AACS Sq)	6 Mar 45–15 May 45
1129 MP Co, Avn	
(427 AP Sq)	17 Sep 45–1 Apr 49
1715 Sig Svc Bn, Avn	c. Apr 45–13 Jun 45
1718 Sig Svc Co, Wg	6 Aug 45–15 Oct 45
V Bomber Comd	Mar 45–Aug 45
V Ftr Comd	Mar 45–Aug 45
XIII Bomber Comd	27 Aug 45–15 Mar 46
Fifth AF	Apr 45–Jul 45
Thirteenth AF	c. 45–19 May 46
	1946
1 Bomb Sq	14 Mar 46–8 Jun 47
2 Recon Sq	22 Jan 46–4 Feb 46
5 Bomb Sq	14 Mar 46–9 Jun 47
5 Recon Sq	15 Jun 46–20 Oct 47
6 Air Svc Gp	6 Jan 46–16 Aug 48
6 Bomb Gp	28 Jan 46–1 Jun 47
9 Bomb Gp	15 Apr 46–9 Jun 47
13 Motor Trpt Sq, Air Dep	c. 46–1 Dec 47
13 Trp Carr Sq	7 Jan 46–15 Jun 46
24 Bomb Sq	13 Mar 46–1 Jun 47
24 Cmbt Mapping Sq	29 Jan 46–15 Jun 46
25 Ln Sq	c. 10 Jan 46–22 Apr 47
39 Bomb Sq	13 Mar 46–1 Jun 47
40 Bomb Sq	13 Mar 46–1 Jun 47
63 Trp Carr Sq	23 Jan 46–15 May 46
64 Trp Carr Sq	c. Jan 46–15 May 46
65 Trp Carr Sq	27 Jan 46–9 Aug 47
72 Air Svc Gp	15 Mar 46–7 Jun 47
82 Air Engrg Sq	16 Jan 46–16 Aug 48
99 Bomb Sq	14 Mar 46–9 Aug 47
313 Bomb Wg	15 Mar 46–15 Jun 48
325 Sig Co, Wg (8 Comms Sq, Wg)	15 Mar 46–9 Jun 47
398 Bomb Sq	13 Mar 46–15 Jun 46
403 Trp Carr Gp	Jan 46–c. Jun 46
419 Night Ftr Sq	10 Jan 46–7 May 46
421 Bomb Sq	13 Mar 46–15 Jun 46
431 Bomb Sq	15 Jun 46–20 Oct 47
482 Bomb Sq	14 Mar 46–30 Jun 46
483 Bomb Sq	14 Mar 46–30 Jun 46

25

484 Bomb Sq	14 Mar 46–30 Jun 46
504 Bomb Gp	6 Mar 46–15 Jun 46
505 Bomb Gp	14 Mar 46–30 Jun 46
567 Air Mat Sq	13 Mar 46–16 Aug 48
568 Air Engrg Sq	13 Mar 46–16 Aug 48
570 Air Engrg Sq	c. Feb 46–30 Jun 46
579 Air Mat Sq	15 Mar 46–7 Jun 47
600 Army Band	
(600 AF Band)	1 Feb 46–1 Apr 49
675 Bomb Sq	13 Mar 46–15 Jun 46
680 Bomb Sq	13 Mar 46–15 Jun 46
801 Med Air Evac Sq	27 Jan 46–22 Aug 46
Clark Fld AAB	
Comd [Prov]	6 Jan 46–unk
Clark Fld AAB	
Food Svcs	
Sq [Prov]	2 Oct 46–15 Jan 48
Hq & Base Svcs Sq,	
358 Air Svc Gp	46–5 Feb 47
Thirteenth AF	c. 1 Jan 46–20 May 46
1947	
1 Recon Sq	11 Feb 47–10 Mar 47
8 Air Trpt Comps	
Sq [Prov]	30 Sep 47–3 Jun 48
12 Ftr Sq	16 Sep 47–28 Jul 50
14 Comms Sq, Comd	
(14 Comms Sq, AF)	c. 21 Jun 47–1 Jul 59
18 Ftr Gp	16 Sep 47–28 Jul 50
22 Trp Carr Sq	23 Apr 47–19 Sep 48
23 Recon Sq	20 Oct 47–15 May 48
25 Ln Sq	8 Sep 47–25 Mar 49
38 Recon Sq	15 Mar 47–6 May 49
44 Ftr Sq	16 Sep 47–15 Jul 55
67 Ftr Sq	16 Sep 47–28 Jul 50
622 AC & W Sq	15 Mar 47–10 Mar 48
771 AF BU	
(141 AACS Sq)	c. 47–3 Jun 48
Thirteenth AF	7 Aug 47–1 Dec 48
1948	
18 AB Gp	14 Aug 48–1 Dec 50
18 AP Sq	14 Aug 48–1 Dec 50
18 Base Svc Sq	14 Aug 48–23 Dec 49
18 Comms Sq	14 Aug 48–1 Dec 50
18 Ftr Wg	
(18 Ftr-Bmbr Wg)	14 Aug 48–1 Dec 50
18 Food Svc Sq	14 Aug 48–1 Dec 50
18 Instls Sq	14 Aug 48–1 Dec 50
18 Maint & Sup Gp	14 Aug 48–1 Dec 50
18 Maint Sq, Ftr, SE	
(18 Maint Sq, Ftr,	
Jet; 18 Maint Sq)	14 Aug 48–1 Dec 50
18 MV Sq, Ftr, SE	
(18 MV Sq, Ftr, Jet;	
18 MV Sq)	14 Aug 48–1 Dec 50
18 Sup Sq	14 Aug 48–1 Dec 50
141 AACS Sq	
(1961 AACS Sq;	

1961 AACS Gp;	
1961 Comms Gp)	1 Jun 48–
338 Recon Sq	9 Jan 48–6 May 49
6200 Trp Carr Sq	1 Dec 48–5 Aug 49
Thirteenth AF Food	
Svcs Sq [Prov]	16 Jan 48–15 Apr 48
1949	
24 AB Gp, Dep	1 Jul 49–17 Dec 49
24 Acft Rpr Sq, Dep	1 Jul 49–16 Feb 54
24 Air Dep Wg	1 Jul 49–12 Dec 49
24 Ammo Sup Sq, Dep	1 Jul 49–16 Feb 54
24 AP Sq, Dep	1 Jul 49–17 Dec 49
24 Comms Sq, Dep	1 Jul 49–17 Dec 49
24 Equip Rpr Sq, Dep	
(24 Acft Equip	
Rpr Sq)	1 Jul 49–16 Feb 54
24 Food Svc Sq, Dep	1 Jul 49–17 Dec 49
24 Gen Sup Sq, Dep	1 Jul 49–1 Sep 52
24 Instls Sq, Dep	1 Jul 49–17 Dec 49
24 Maint Gp, Dep	1 Jul 49–16 Feb 54
24 Med Gp, Dep	1 Jul 49–17 Dec 49
24 MV Sq, Dep	1 Jul 49–16 Feb 54
24 Sup Gp, Dep	1 Jul 49–16 Feb 54
24 Tech Sup Sq, Dep	1 Jul 49–1 Sep 52
24 VR Sq, Dep	1 Jul 49–16 Feb 54
600 AF Band	11 Jul 49–
6200 AP Sq	21 Nov 49–1 Jul 50
6201 Engr Const Sq	21 Nov 49–10 Mar 54
6201 Heavy Maint &	
Const Sq	16 May 49–5 Aug 49
6204 Photo	
Mapping Flt	
(6204 Photo	
Mapping Sq)	16 Sep 49–1 Jun 53
6205 AP Gp	21 Nov 49–1 Mar 53
6206 AP Sq	21 Nov 49–1 Mar 53
6207 AP Sq	21 Nov 49–1 Jul 50
6208 Dep Wg	17 Dec 49–1 Sep 52
Thirteenth AF	16 May 49–
1950	
2 Rscu Sq	
(2 Air Rscu Sq)	4 May 50–7 Nov 55
21 Trp Carr Sq	27 Jan 50–29 Jun 50
801 Med Air Evac Sq	1 Mar 50–14 Sep 50
6200 AB Gp	1 Dec 50–9 Apr 59
6200 AB Wg	1 Dec 50–1 Feb 53
6200 AP Sq	1 Dec 50–9 Apr 59
6200 Comms Sq	1 Dec 50–1 Oct 52
6200 Food Svc Sq	1 Dec 50–9 Apr 59
6200 Instls Sq	1 Dec 50–9 Apr 59
6200 Maint Sq	
(6200 Fld Maint Sq;	
6200 Consold	
Acft Maint Sq)	1 Dec 50–9 Apr 59
6200 Maint & Sup Gp	1 Dec 50–1 Jul 58
6200 MV Sq	
(6200 Trnsp Sq)	1 Dec 50–9 Apr 59

6200 Sup Sq	1 Dec 50–1 Oct 53	Sq, Prov	3 Feb 54–1 Sep 54	
	1951	**1955**		
1 Admntv Svcs		26 Ftr-Intcpr Sq	11 Jul 55–9 Apr 59	
Sq, Hosp	25 Jun 51–7 Jul 53	6200 AB Wg	5 Jan 55–9 Apr 59	
1 Hosp Gp	25 Jun 51–7 Jul 53	6200 Ops Sq	1 Nov 55–1 Jul 58	
1 Professional Svcs		**1957**		
Sq, Hosp	25 Jun 51–7 Jul 53	12 Ftr-Bmbr Sq	16 Aug 57–25 Mar 58	
854 AC & W Sq	25 Aug 51–20 Sep 52	**1958**		
	1952	72 Tac Ftr Sq	1 Jul 58–9 Apr 59	
24 Air Dep Wg	1 Sep 52–16 Feb 54	418 Ftr-Day Sq	25 Mar 58–1 Jul 58	
24 Receiving,		848 AC & W Sq	18 Oct 58–20 Dec 62	
Shipping &		6200 Sup Sq	18 Jun 58–9 Apr 59	
Svcs Sq, Dep	1 Sep 52–16 Feb 54	Air Tac Gp, Prov	1 Jul 58–9 Feb 59	
24 Stock Con Sq, Dep	1 Sep 52–16 Feb 54	**1959**		
24 Whse Sq, Dep	1 Sep 52–16 Feb 54	2 RR Sq	21 Oct 59–1 Oct 61	
29 Radio Sq, Mobile	1 Aug 52–8 May 55	5 Comms & Con Gp		
31 Air Rscu Sq	14 Nov 52–12 Aug 60	(5 Tac Con Gp)	21 Oct 59–31 Dec 71	
32 Air Rscu Sq	14 Nov 52–8 Sep 54	405 AB Gp		
581 Abn Mat		(405 Cmbt Spt Gp)	9 Apr 59–16 Oct 74	
Assembly Sq	18 Jul 52–20 Oct 54	405 AP Sq	9 Apr 59–8 Jan 66	
581 Air Resupply		405 Consold Acft		
& Comms Gp		Maint Sq	9 Apr 59–8 Jul 61	
(581 Air		405 Ftr Wg	9 Apr 59–16 Sep 74	
Resupply Gp)	18 Jul 52–20 Oct 54	405 Food Svc Sq	9 Apr 59–8 Apr 63	
581 Air Resupply		405 Instls Sq		
& Comms Wg	18 Jul 52–7 Sep 53	(405 CE Sq)	9 Apr 59–8 Jan 66	
581 Air Resupply Sq	18 Jul 52–20 Oct 54	405 Sup Sq	9 Apr 59–8 Jan 66	
581 Comms Sq	18 Jul 52–7 Sep 53	405 Trnsp Sq	9 Apr 59–8 Jan 66	
581 Maint Sq	18 Jul 52–7 Sep 53	509 Ftr-Intcpr Sq	9 Apr 59–24 Jul 50	
581 Reproduction Sq	18 Jul 52–7 Sep 53	510 Tac Ftr Sq	9 Apr 59–	
6207 AC & W Sq	20 Sep 52–18 Oct 58	605 Tac Con Sq	21 Oct 59–1 Oct 61	
	1953	608 Comms Sq	21 Oct 59–1 Oct 61	
6208 Dental Flt	8 Jul 53–1 Nov 54	656 Tac Hosp	16 Feb 59–	
6208 Hosp Gp		**1960**		
(6208 USAF Hosp;		Armnt & Elect		
USAF Hosp, Clark;		Maint Sq,		
USAF Regional		Prov, 6405	1 Apr 60–8 Jul 61	
Med Cen, Clark)	8 Jul 53–	Fld Maint Sq,		
	1954	Prov, 6405	1 Apr 60–8 Jul 61	
26 Ftr-Intcpr Sq	11 Nov 54–11 Dec 54	Flt Line Maint		
50 Trp Carr Sq	26 Jun 54–5 Sep 54	Sq, Prov, 6405	1 Apr 60–8 Jul 61	
816 Trp Carr Sq	16 Apr 54–25 Jun 54	**1961**		
6424 Acft Equip		1 Mobile Comms Sq		
Rpr Sq	16 Feb 54–1 Jan 55	(1 Mobile		
6424 Acft Rpr Sq	16 Feb 54–1 Sep 54	Comms Gp;		
6424 Air Dep Wg	16 Feb 54–25 Nov 54	1 Mobile		
6424 Med Mat Flt	16 Feb 54–1 Sep 54	Comms Sq)	1 Aug 61-15 Jan 75	
6424 MV Sq	16 Feb 54–1 Jan 55	405 Fld Maint Sq	8 Jul 61–16 Sep 74	
6424 Receiving,		405 Flt Line		
Shipping &		Maint Sq	8 Jul 61–8 Sep 62	
Svcs Sq	16 Feb 54–1 Sep 54	**1962**		
6424 Stock Con Sq	16 Feb 54–1 Jan 55	1 Med Svc Wg	30 Jun 62–31 Dec 77	
6424 VR Sq		405 Orgnzl Maint Sq	7 Aug 62–8 Jan 66	
(6424 MV Rpr Sq)	16 Feb 54–1 Jan 55	6203 Spt Sq	1 Jul 62–1 Jan 72	
6424 Whse Sq	16 Feb 54–1 Jan 55	**1963**		
Far East Air Logs		31 Air Rscu Sq		
Force Fld Maint		(31 Aerosp Rscu &		

Recovery Sq)	8 Jul 63–1 Jul 75
405 Mun Maint Sq	8 Apr 63–8 Jan 66
405 Svcs Sq	8 Apr 63–8 Jan 66
1867 Facility	
Checking Flt	
[Svc Evaluation]	
(1867 Facility	
Checking Sq)	1 Jun 63–8 Sep 75
1964	
5 Tac Con Maint Sq	8 Jul 64–1 Oct 68
8 Bomb Sq, Tac	24 Apr 64–15 Jan 68
13 Bomb Sq	24 Apr 64–15 Jan 68
657 Tac Hosp	1 Jun 64–
1965	
523 Tac Ftr Sq	20 Nov 65–31 Aug 73
608 Tac Con Sq	8 Jul 65–31 May 75
6200 Avncs & Elect(s)	
Maint Sq	1 Apr 65–1 Aug 68
6200 Fld Maint Sq	1 Apr 65–31 Dec 71
6200 Mat Wg	
(6200 AB Wg)	1 Apr 65–31 Dec 71
6200 Muns Maint Sq	1 Apr 65–31 Dec 71
6200 Orgnzl Maint Sq	1 Apr 65–1 Aug 68
6200 Spt Sq	24 Apr 65–23 Nov 65
1966	
19 Casualty	
Staging Flt	
(19 Aeromed	
Staging Flt)	15 Apr 66–
29 Trp Carr Sq	
(29 Tac Alft Sq)	27 Jan 66–31 Oct 70
57 Aeromed Evac Sq	13 Jan 66–1 Aug 72
64 Ftr-Intcpr Sq	10 Jun 66–15 Dec 69
69 Mil Alft Spt Gp	8 Jul 66–1 Jan 72
604 Mil Alft Spt Sq	8 Jan 66–1 Sep 75
636 AP Sq	
(636 Scty Sq)	8 Jul 66–1 Aug 68
636 CE Sq	8 Jul 66–1 Aug 68
636 Cmbt Spt Gp	8 Jul 66–1 Aug 68
636 Svcs Sq	8 Jul 66–1 Aug 68
902 Aeromed Evac Sq	8 Jul 66–30 Jun 72
6200 AP Sq	8 Jan 66–8 Jul 66
6200 CE Sq	8 Jan 66–8 Jul 66
6200 Cmbt Spt Gp	8 Jan 66–8 Jul 66
6200 Svcs Sq	8 Jan 66–8 Jul 66
6200 Trnsp Sq	8 Jan 66–31 Dec 71
1967	
13 Recon Tech Sq	15 Jun 67–15 Jun 71
6400 Test Sq	17 Apr 67–15 Oct 69
1968	
6 Air Div	1 Aug 68–15 Dec 69
463 Fld Maint Sq	15 Jul 68–31 Dec 71
463 Tac Alft Wg	15 Jul 68–31 Dec 71
774 Tac Alft Sq	15 Jul 68–15 Sep 72
6200 CE Sq	1 Aug 68–31 Dec 71
6200 Consold Avncs	
Maint Sq	1 Aug 68–1 Aug 69

6200 SP Sq	1 Aug 68–31 Dec 71
6200 Svcs Sq	1 Aug 68–31 Dec 71
1969	
1 Test Sq	15 Oct 69–
9 Aeromed Evac Gp	15 Mar 69–1 Jul 75
20 Ops Sq	
(20 Aeromed	
Alft Sq)	15 Oct 69–
463 Orgnzl Maint Sq	1 Jun 69–31 Dec 71
6200 Avncs Maint Sq	1 Aug 69–31 Dec 71
Orgnzl Maint Sq,	
Prov, 463	8 Mar 69–1 Jun 69
1970	
6922 Scty Gp	
(6922 Scty Sq;	
6922 Elect	
Scty Sq)	1 Apr 70–
1971	
405 CE Sq	31 Dec 71–16 Sep 74
405 Mun Maint Sq	31 Dec 71–16 Sep 74
405 Orgnzl Maint Sq	31 Dec 71–16 Sep 74
405 Scty Pol Sq	31 Dec 71–16 Sep 74
405 Svcs Sq	31 Dec 71–16 Sep 74
405 Sup Sq	31 Dec 71–16 Sep 74
405 Trnsp Sq	12 Nov 71–16 Sep 74
6204 Broadcasting	
Sq (6204 Aerosp	
Spt Sq; 6204	
Broadcasting Sq)	1 Jul 71–30 Sep 76
Air Rflg Sq,	
Prov, 4102	18 Dec 71–22 Jan 73
1972	
8 Sp Ops Sq	1 Oct 72–1 Mar 74
13 Bomb Sq, Tac	
(13 Ftr Sq)	24 Dec 72–30 Sep 73
90 Sp Ops Sq	
(90 Tac Ftr Sq)	15 Dec 72–
1973	
21 Tac Alft Sq	1 Nov 73–
26 Tac Ftr Sq	
(26 Tac Ftr Tng	
Sq; 26 Tac Ftr	
Tng Aggressor Sq)	30 Sep 73–
68 Tac Ftr Sq	30 Sep 73–30 Sep 75
374 Avncs Maint Sq	13 Nov 73–1 Apr 77
374 Orgnzl Maint Sq	15 Nov 73–
374 Trp Carr Wg	
(375 Tac Alft Wg)	15 Nov 73–
776 Tac Alft Sq	15 Nov 73–31 Oct 75
1974	
3 Avncs Maint Sq	
(3 Component	
Rpr Sq)	16 Sep 74–
3 CE Sq	16 Sep 74–
3 Cmbt Spt Gp	16 Sep 74–
3 Fld Maint Sq	
(3 Equip Maint Sq)	16 Sep 74–

3 Law Enforcement Sq	16 Sep 74–
3 Mun Maint Sq	16 Sep 74–1 Jun 77
3 Orgnzl Maint Sq	
(3 Acft Gnrtn Sq)	16 Sep 74–
3 Scty Pol Gp	16 Sep 74–
3 Scty Pol Sq	16 Sep 74–
3 Svcs Sq	16 Sep 74–30 Nov 76
3 Sup Sq	16 Sep 74–
3 Tac Ftr Wg	16 Sep 74–
3 Trnsp Sq	16 Sep 74–
7 Abn Comd &	
Con Sq	22 May 74–14 Aug 75
405 Law Enforce-	
ment Sq	15 Mar 74–16 Sep 74
405 Scty Pol Gp	15 Mar 74–16 Sep 74
	1975
3 Tac Ftr Sq	15 Dec 75–

9 Aeromed Evac Sq	1 Jul 75–
374 Aerl Port Sq	1 Sep 75–
421 Tac Ftr Sq	13 Dec 75–23 Dec 75
	1977
6200 Tac Ftr Tng Gp	1 Sep 77–
6201 Epidemiological	
Flt	31 Dec 77–1 Oct 78
	1980
6200 Tac Ftr Tng Sq	1 Jan 80–
Numbered AF	
Cmbt Ops Staff	
(Thirteenth AF)	15 Jul 80–
	1981
1 Sp Ops Sq	1 Jan 81–
31 Aerosp Rscu &	
Recovery Sq	8 Jan 81–

Hahn Air Base

Location: Located 1 mi N of Lautzenhausen, 60 mi W of Wiesbaden, and 1 mi S of Hahn, Federal Republic of Germany.

Name: Named after a village in the Federal Republic of Germany.

Date of Current Name: 8 Sep 1952.

Previous Names: None.

Date of Establishment: 8 Sep 1952.

Date Construction Began: French construction for USAF began Apr 1951; USAF construction commenced 2 Jun 1952.

Date of Beneficial Occupancy: 9 Sep 1952.

Base Operating Units: 7356th AB Gp, 9 Sep 1952; 50th AB Gp, 10 Aug 1953; 7425th AB Gp, 1 Aug 1956 (rdsgd 7425th Spt Gp, 1 Dec 1957); 50th AB Gp, 1 Sep 1959 (rdsgd 50th Cmbt Spt Gp, 1 Sep 1959); 50th Tac Ftr Wg, 1 Jul 1966–.*

Base Commanders: Lt Col Chester Brown, 9 Sep 1952; Col Wallace S. Ford, 12 Aug 1953; Col Melvin F. McNickle, 22 Jul 1954; Col Fred J. Ascani, 24 Jun 1955; Col Fred L. Rennels Jr, 1 Aug 1956; Col Thomas S. Torresson Jr, 10 Jul 1958; Col Bertil E. Hanson, 22 Jul 1960; Col John A. Andrews, 8 Jun 1962; Col Edward B. Burdett, 29 Mar 1964; Col Robert M. Hancock Jr, c. Jul 1965; Col Albert M. Ward, c. Jul 1967; Col Franklin C. Davies, 24 Jul 1969; Col Ralph W. Trousdale, c. 15 May 1970; Col Charles S. Allen, 16 Apr 1971; Col Clyde H. Garner, 15 Oct 1972; Col Reginald W. Shaleski, 1 Mar 1973; Col William G. Gibbons, 31 Aug 1973; Col James P. Albritton, 22 Apr 1974; Col Joseph K. Brown, 10 Sep 1974; Col Mary A. Marsh, 5 Jul 1977; Lt Col Robert F. Hermanson, 15 Jun 1978; Col Eugene F. Martin, 1 Aug 1978; Col Robert F. Hermanson, 16 Jul 1979; Col James L. McCleskey, 8 Jul 1980; Lt Col Thomas G. Hogg, 6 Apr 1981; Col Charles B. Neel, 23 Jul 1981–.

Major Off-Base and Detached Installations:[†] Birkenfeld Fam Hsg Site #1, Birkenfeld, 1 May 1952 (asgnd)–1 Sep 1959 (trsfd to Ramstein

---

*The wing histories identify the wing rather than the combat support group as the base operating unit as of this date.

[†]Unless otherwise indicated, all installations are located in the Federal Republic of Germany.

AB); Hinzerath RR Anx (rdsgd Hinzerath RRS), Hinzerath, 15 Sep 1952 (asgnd)–5 Aug 1965 (dspd); Buchenbeuren Waste Anx, Buchenbeuren, 15 Sep 1953–unk; Hahn Hsg Anx (rdsgd Hahn Fam Hsg Anx), Lautzen-hausen, 15 Sep 1953 (asgnd)–; Hahn/Leideneck LF Bcn Anx (rdsgd Leideneck Radio Bcn Anx), Leideneck, 15 Jan 1954 (asgnd)–13 Sep 1968 (dspd); Hahn Water Plt Anx (rdsgd Hahn Water Sys Anx #1), Heubult, 1 Apr 1954 (actvd)–; Hahn Water Sys Anx #2, Allenbach, 1 Apr 1954 (asgnd)–; Hahn Water Sys Anx #3, Sensweiler, 1 Apr 1954 (asgnd)–; Hahn Water Sys Anx #4, Schauren, 1 Apr 1954 (asgnd)–; Hahn Water Sys Anx #5, Stiphausen, 1 Apr 1954 (asgnd)–; Hahn Water Sys Anx #6, Krumme-nau, 1 Apr 1954 (asgnd)–; Ravensbeuren UHF/DF Anx (rdsgd Ravens-beuren DF Anx), 1 mi ESE of Ravensbeuren, 15 May 1954 (asgnd)–30 Jun 1960 (dspd); Hahn/Muehl-Zuesch Microwave Anx (rdsgd Muehl-Zuesch Microwave Anx), Muehl-Zuesch RRS, Hermeskeil, 31 Aug 1954 (asgnd)–1 Jul 1964 (trsfd to Ramstein AB); Birkenfeld Fam Hsg Anx #2 (rdsgd Birkenfeld Fam Hsg Site #2), Birkenfeld, 27 Sep 1954–1 Sep 1959 (trsfd to Ramstein AB); Koeterberg Msl Site, Fuerstenau, 27 Sep 1954 (asgnd)–1 Sep 1959 (trsfd to Sembach AB); Driedorf Water Sys Anx, 1 mi S of Driedorf, 26 Jan 1955 (asgnd)–; Hamm Comms Anx (rdsgd Hamm Msl Site; Hamm Relay Site), 4 mi NNW of Hamm, Jan 1955–1 Oct 1958 (trsfd to Ramstein AB); Hahn/Morbach Ammo Area (rdsgd Hahn/Morbach Ammo Stor Stn; Morbach Ammo Stor Area; Wenigerath Ammo Stor Area), Wenigerath, 20 Feb 1955 (asgnd)–; Marsburg RR Anx (rdsgd Marsburg RRS), Marsburg, 1 Aug 1955 (asgnd)–1958 (trsfd to Ramstein AB); Pferdsfeld Air Aux Fld (rdsgd Pferdsfeld AB), 1 mi N of Pferdsfeld, 15 Sep 1955 (trsfd from French Forces)–1 Sep 1959 (trsfd to Ramstein AB); Wueschheim Msl Site #1 (rdsgd Wueschheim Recrn Anx; Wueschheim Anx; Wueschheim Comms Stn), Hundheim, 1 Nov 1955 (asgnd)–1 Aug 1962 (dspd); Wueschheim Msl Site #2, Wueschheim, 1 Nov 1955 (asgnd)–13 Sep 1968 (dspd); Wueschheim Msl Site #4, Kappel, 1 Nov 1955 (asgnd)–16 Sep 1968 (dspd); Wueschheim Msl Site #5 (rdsgd Wueschheim Trng Anx; Wueschheim Msl Site #2; Wueschheim Comms Site 02), Kappel, 1 Nov 1955 (asgnd)–; Wueschheim Msl Site #6 (rdsgd Wueschheim Msl Site #1; Wueschheim Stor Anx [Med]; Wueschheim Comms Stn), Kappel, 1 Nov 1955 (asgnd))–; Marsburg Msl Site, Marsburg, 15 Jan 1956 (asgnd)–1958 (trsfd to Ramstein AB); Emstek Msl Site (rdsgd Emstek Comms Anx), Halen, 21 Apr 1956 (asgnd)–unk; Heubuelt Comms Stn, Heubuelt, 21 Apr 1956 (asgnd)–20 Sep 1960 (dspd); Oldenburg Msl Site, Loy, 31 May 1956 (asgnd)–20 Sep 1960 (dspd); Ilmspan Msl Site, Ilmspan, 7 Sep 1956 (asgnd)–1958 (trsfd to Ramstein AB); Hecken Msl Anx (rdsgd Hecken Msl Site; Hecken Anx), Hecken, 30 Oct 1956 (asgnd)–7 Sep 1971 (dspd); Tellig Msl Anx (rdsgd Tellig Msl Site), Moritzheim, 30

Oct 1956 (asgnd)−20 Jan 1965 (dspd); Zell Msl Site (rdsgd Idarkopf Msl Site), Stiphausen, c. 1956 (asgnd)−30 Oct 1961 (dspd); Langenbrand Msl Site, Langenbrand, 15 Jul 1957 (asgnd)−1958 (trsfd to Ramstein AB); Ludwigsturm Msl Site, Rhodt, 15 Jul 1957 (asgnd)−23 Aug 1960 (dspd); Birkenfeld AC & W Stn (rdsgd Birkenfeld Admn Ofc), Birkenfeld, 16 Dec 1957 (asgnd)−1 Sep 1959 (trsfd to Ramstein AB); Diepholz Hsg Anx, Steinfeld, 23 Jan 1958 (asgnd)−1 Sep 1959 (trsfd to Sembach AB); Diepholz Msl Site, Daume, 23 Jan 1958 (asgnd)−1 Sep 1959 (trsfd to Sembach AB); Wueschheim Msl Anx (rdsgd Wueschheim Msl Site #3; Wueschheim Ammo Stor Anx), Wueschheim, 28 Feb 1958 (asgnd)−; Driedorf AC & W Stn (rdsgd Driedorf Msl Site), Driedorf, 1 Oct 1958 (trsfd from Ramstein AB)−unk; Gelchsheim Msl Site, Gelchsheim, 6 Aug 1959 (asgnd)−Sep 1959 (trsfd to Sembach); Hundheim Msl Site, Hundheim, 1 Dec 1959 (asgnd)−16 Sep 1968 (dspd); Pferdsfeld Ammo Stor Anx, Pferdsfeld, 10 Dec 1959 (asgnd)−4 Oct 1960 (dspd); Volkel AB (detchd instl), Volkel, Netherlands, c. 1960 (asgnd)−1 Feb 1963 (trsfd to Ramstein AB); Birkenfeld Fam Hsg Site #1, Birkenfeld, 1 Feb 1963 (trsfd from Ramstein AFB)−1 Jul 1977 (trsfd to Ramstein AB); Erbeskopf Tech Anx (rdsgd Erbeskopf RS), Allenbach, 1 Feb 1963 (trsfd from Ramstein AB)−30 Jun 1965 (dspd); Pferdsfeld AB, Pferdsfeld, 1 Feb 1963 (trsfd from Ramstein AB)−unk (trsfd to the FRG); Birkenfeld Fam Hsg Site #2, Birkenfeld, 1 Sep 1963 (trsfd from Ramstein)−1 Jul 1977 (trsfd to Ramstein); Volkel AB, Volkel, 4 Dec 1970 (actvd)−; Wueschheim Recrn Anx (rdsgd Wueschheim Aux; Wueschheim Comms Stn), Hundheim, 1 Jan 1972 (reactvd)−; Den Dolder Fam Hsg Anx, Den Dolder, Netherlands, 1 Sep 1972 (asgnd)−31 Aug 1975 (dspd); Buechel Comms Stn, Buechel, 1 Jul 1976 (asgnd)−; Noervenich Comms Stn, Noervenich, 1 Jul 1976 (actvd)−; Jever AB (U.S. acty only), Jever, 1 Sep 1976 (actvd)−1 Jan 1981 (trsfd to RAF Bentwaters, UK); Gilze-Rijen AB (U.S. acty only), Gilze-Rijen, Netherlands, 1 May 1977 (asgnd)−; Soesterberg Fam Hsg Anx (detchd), Soesterberg, Nether-lands, 21 Sep 1977 (asgnd)−; Kastellaun Fam Hsg Anx, Kastellaun, 14 Aug 1978 (asgnd)−unk; Kirchberg Fam Hsg Anx, Kirchberg, 14 Aug 1978 (asgnd)−; Rhaunen Fam Hsg Anx, Rhaunen, 14 Aug 1978 (asgnd)−; Leck AB (U.S. acty only, detchd instl), Leck, 1 Jun 1979 (asgnd)−; Nordholz AB (U.S. acty only, detchd instl), Nordholz, 1 Jun 1979 (asgnd)−; Wueschheim AS, Hundheim, (detchd instl), 1 Jul 1982 (asgnd)−.

Major Changes in Operational Capability: Fifteen three-story dormi-tories, roads, guard posts, and fences completed early 1953; operational and support facilities completed for F−86F aircraft, Aug 1953; support facilities installed to accommodate a pilotless bomber squadron (later, redesignated a tactical missile squadron) Sep 1954; facilities for night flying constructed late 1954; underground operations room occupied Oct

1955; major runway repair and resurfacing projects completed in 1959 and 1963; runway barriers installed Aug 1961; earlier dependent housing shortage eliminated with completion of additional quarters late 1962; TAB VEE hardened maintenance shelters constructed 1968–1972; rescue alert facilities completed early 1969; aircraft hot fuel system completed in two phases 1973–1976; dormitory remodeling project (German-funded) completed mid-1976; contingency launch/recovery runway completed Dec 1977; 33 munitions storage igloos completed at Wueschheim Weapons Storage Area, mid-1978.

Major Commands to Which Assigned: USAFE, 8 Sep 1952–.

Major Changes in Status: None.

Units Assigned:

1952	
7356 AB Sq	1 Sep 52–25 Aug 53
1953	
2 AACS Sq	28 Jul 53–24 Jun 60
10 Ftr-Bmbr Sq	9 Aug 53–10 Jul 56
50 AB Gp	9 Aug 53–10 Jul 56
50 AP Sq	9 Aug 53–10 Jul 56
50 Comms Sq	9 Aug 53–10 Jul 56
50 Ftr-Bmbr Gp	9 Aug 53–15 Jul 56
50 Ftr-Bmbr Wg	9 Aug 53–17 Jul 56
50 Food Svc Sq	9 Aug 53–5 Jul 56
50 Instls Sq	9 Aug 53–15 Jul 56
50 Maint Sq	
(50 Fld Maint Sq)	9 Aug 53–2 Jul 56
50 Med Gp	
(50 Tac Hosp)	9 Aug 53–8 Jul 56
50 MV Sq	9 Aug 53–19 Jun 56
50 Sup Sq	9 Aug 53–27 Jun 56
81 Ftr-Bmbr Sq	10 Aug 53–10 Jul 56
417 Ftr-Bmbr Sq	9 Aug 53–15 Apr 56
1954	
69 Pilotless Bmbr Sq	
(69 Tac Msl Sq)	30 Sep 54–18 Jun 58
561 Tac Ftr Sq	12 Dec 54–1 Dec 55
1284 AACS Sq	
(2184 Comms Sq)	1 Nov 54–
7425 USAF Hosp	1 May 54–25 Sep 58
1956	
461 Ftr-Day Sq	
(461 Tac Ftr Sq)	2 May 56–1 Aug 59
496 Ftr-Intcpr Sq	
(496 Tac Ftr Sq)	8 Nov 56–
586 Comms &	
Guidance Sq	
(586 Msl Maint Sq)	15 Sep 56–25 Sep 62
586 Spt Sq	15 Sep 56–25 Sep 62
586 Tac Msl Gp	15 Sep 56–25 Sep 62
701 Tac Msl Wg	15 Sep 56–18 Jun 58
7245 AB Gp	
(7425 Spt Gp)	9 Apr 56–1 Sep 59

7382 Guided Msls	
Gp (Tac)	1 Feb 56–15 Sep 56
7425 AP Sq	9 Apr 56–1 Sep 59
7425 Fld Maint Sq	9 Apr 56–1 Sep 59
7425 Food Svc Sq	9 Apr 56–1 Sep 59
7425 Instlns Sq	9 Apr 56–1 Sep 59
7425 Mtr Veh Sq	
(7425 Trnsp Sq)	9 Apr 56–1 Sep 59
7425 Sup Sq	9 Apr 56–1 Sep 59
1958	
38 Tac Msl Wg	18 Jun 58–19 Aug 59
307 Tac Ftr Sq	27 Feb 58–13 Aug 58
308 Tac Ftr Sq	15 Aug 58–22 Aug 58
405 Tac Msl Sq	18 Jun 58–25 Sep 66
1959	
10 Tac Ftr Sq	10 Dec 59–
50 AB Gp	
(50 Cmbt Spt Gp)	1 Sep 59–
50 AP Sq	
(50 Scty Pol Sq)	1 Sep 59–
50 Armnt & Elects	
Maint Sq	10 Dec 59–8 Apr 62
50 Comms Sq	1 Sep 59–1 Jul 62
50 Consold Acft	
Maint Sq	
(50 Fld Maint Sq;	
50 Equip Maint Sq)	10 Dec 59–
50 Food Svcs Sq	1 Sep 59–8 Apr 62
50 Instls Sq	
(50 CE Sq)	1 Sep 59–
50 Sup Sq	1 Sep 59–
50 Tac Ftr Wg	10 Dec 59–
50 Tac Hosp	1 Sep 59–
50 Trnsp Sq	1 Sep 59–
1960	
81 Tac Ftr Sq	10 Jan 60–15 Jul 71
1962	
89 Tac Msl Sq	25 Sep 62–25 Sep 66

1964	
50 Armnt & Elects	
Maint Sq	
(50 Avncs	
Maint Sq;	
50 Component	
Rpr Sq)	1 Jul 64–
50 Orgnzl Maint Sq	1 Jul 64–1 Jan 66
350 Mun Maint Sq	1 Jul 64–7 Oct 72
586 Msl Maint Sq	1 Jul 64–25 Sep 66
1971	
USAF Hosp, Hahn	1 Jul 71–
1972	
50 Mun Maint Sq	8 Oct 72–8 Oct 78
50 Orgnzl Maint Sq	
(50 Acft Gnrtn Sq)	1 Jan 72–

1975	
6911 Scty Sq	
[Mobile]	
(6911 Elect	
Scty Gp;	
6911 Elect	
Scty Sq)	25 Jul 75–
1976	
313 Tac Ftr Sq	15 Nov 76–
1978	
7015 Explosive	
Ord Flt	1 Oct 78–
1982	
50 Svcs Sq	1 Feb 82–

Hellenikon Air Base

Location: Located 5 mi S of Athens, 1/2 mi W of Komnina, Greece.

Name: Named after the Greek city Elliniko (Elleniko).

Date of Current Name: 25 Feb 1976.

Previous Names: Hassani Aprt, Aug 1945–7 May 1946. Hassani Aprt, 1948; Ellinikon Afld, 1948; Athenai AB, 1948; Athenai Aprt, 28 Feb 1958.*

Date of Establishment: Established as AAF installation, 1 Oct 1945; established as USAF installation in 1947.

Date Construction Began: Reconstruction of existing Greek facilities commenced 1947.

Date of Beneficial Occupancy: 1 Oct 1945. 5 Apr 1948.

Base Operating Units: OL 4–Y, 1419th AAF BU, Aug 1945–1 May 1946; Det K,[†] 7907th AF BU, 2 Jun 1948; 1015th AB Sq, 1 Jul 1948; 1632d AB Sq, 1 Oct 1948; Det 3, 1602d Air Trpt Wg, 23 Nov 1949; 7206th AB Sq, 1 Apr 1954; 7206th Spt Gp, 15 May 1955 (rdsgd 7206th AB Gp, 1 Jan 1973)–.

Base Commanders: Unk, 1 Oct 1945–Oct 1946. Maj Daniel F. Riva, 6 Apr 1948–unk; Capt Lyle W. Melcher, 2 Jun 1948; Lt Col (later, Col) Harry E. Willard, 1 Jul 1948; Capt Raymond A. Finklea Jr, c. 7 Feb 1950; Maj (later, Lt Col) Adrien A. Talbot, 13 Sep 1950; Lt Col James F. Wiley, c. 30 Apr 1953; Lt Col Benjamin F. Chapman, 1 Apr 1954; Lt Col Benjamin M. Sheldon, 13 Apr 1956; Col William C. Allen, 12 Oct 1956; Col Henry B. Wilson, 1 Apr 1958; Lt Col Carl G. Nelson, 17 Sep 1959; Col David G. Alford, 11 Nov 1959; Col Henry S. Tyler Jr, 6 Jun 1962; Col Jean D. Tarbutton, 21 Jul 1964; Col William A. Trippet, 29 May 1966; Col Harvey C. Clymer, 12 Jun 1968; Col Teague G. Harris Jr, 11 Jul 1968; Col Joseph R. Cafarella, 16 Jul 1971; Col Glenn A. Carus, 3 Oct 1973; Col Paul G. Ziluca, 29 May 1976; Col Richard J. Toner, 13 Jul 1979; Col Philip E. Smith, 6 Jun 1980–.

---

*Also referred to unofficially as Hassani Airfield, Ellinikon Airport, and Athens/Kalamaki Airfield.

[†]Base unoccupied and inactive between May 1946 and May 1947, when a small supply unit was stationed at Hellenikon to handle air shipments of Marshall Plan aid for Greece.

Major Off-Base and Detached Installations:* Athenai Dispy (rdsgd Athens Dispy Anx) (detchd Instl), Athens, 27 Jun 1957 (asgnd)–1 Apr 1960 (dspd); Athenai Hosp, Athens, 27 Jun 1957 (asgnd)–30 Sep 1959 (dspd); Kifisia RRS (rdsgd Athenai RRS), Agia Trias, 18 Feb 1958 (asgnd)–12 Dec 1969 (dspd); Kifisia Rcvr Anx (rdsgd Athenai Rcvr Anx), Kato Souli, 18 Feb 1958 (asgnd)–1 May 1975 (dspd); Kifisia Tmtr Anx (rdsgd Athenai Tmtr Anx), Nea Makri, 18 Feb 1958 (asgnd)–1 May 1975 (dspd); Athenai Comms Stn (Geeia), Athens, 1 Feb 1961 (asgnd)–; Perivolaki RRS, Langadas, 23 Sep 1963 (asgnd)–; Argyroupolis RRS, Argyroupolis, 24 Sep 1963 (asgnd)–; Elevsis RRS, Elevsis, 2 Oct 1963 (asgnd)–; Pendelikon RRS, Kifisia, 2 Oct 1963 (asgnd)–23 May 1978 (dspd); Katsimidhi RRS, Dhekelia, 3 Oct 1963 (asgnd)–23 May 1978 (dspd); Parnia RRS, Agia Trias, 3 Oct 1963 (asgnd)–; Tanagra RRS, Assopia, 3 Oct 1963 (asgnd)–30 Sep 1977 (dspd); Sami RRS, Sami Kefallinia Isl, Greece, 5 Oct 1963 (asgnd)–23 May 1978 (dspd); Hortiatis RRS, Hortiatis, 20 Mar 1964 (asgnd)–; Araxos RRS, Kato Achaia, 7 May 1964 (asgnd)–; Soudha Bay RRS, Soudha, 16 Nov 1964 (asgnd)–23 May 1978 (dspd); Athenai Fam Hsg Anx, Voula, 1 Apr 1965 (asgnd)–unk; Leukas RRS, Megara, 1 Oct 1965 (asgnd)–; Paternas RRS, Megara, 1 Oct 1965 (asgnd)–; Yannitsa RRS, Yannitsa, 19 Jan 1966 (asgnd)–; Athenai Fam Hsg Site, Athens, 1 Apr 1970 (asgnd)–30 Jun 1974 (dspd); Athenai Bachelor Hsg Site, Glyfada, 1 Feb 1974 (asgnd)–; Malia Water Sys Anx #3, Hersonissos, unk–16 Jun 1975 (dspd); Athenai Fam Hsg Anx #3, Voula, 1 Nov 1978 (asgnd)–.

Major Changes in Operational Capability: Used as a staging field for Air Transport Command on flights between Rome and Middle East 1945–1946; reoccupied to process U.S. aid flow to Greece and Turkey under Truman Doctrine and Marshall Plan in May 1947; new control tower completed 15 Nov 1948; 10 C-47s based on the field 1 Jul 1948; new passenger and freight terminal opened 13 May 1951; USAF activities relocated to one side of the airport, while hitherto occupied part was acquired by Greek civil aviation authorities and designated Athenai International Airport, 1956–1958; an AACS network of four facilities beneficially occupied early 1961; seven major buildings constructed and three more leased 1962–1964; accommodated airlift evacuation operations from Middle East (1967), Cyprus (1975), Ethiopia (1977), and Iran (1979, 1981); base has continuously provided administrative and logistical support to U.S. units and organizations in Greece, the Middle East, Eastern Mediterranean, and parts of Africa.

Major Commands to Which Assigned: Air Trpt Comd, Aug 1945–7 May 1946; USAFE, 5 Apr 1948; MATS, 1 Jul 1948; USAFE, 1 Apr 1954–.

---

*Unless otherwise indicated, all installations are located in Greece.

Major Changes in Status: Active 1 Oct 1945–1 May 1946; inactive 2 May 1946; activated only to process Marshall Plan aid for Greece, May 1947; became active USAFE installation, 2 Jun 1948–.

Units Assigned:

1948	
1015 AB Sq	
(1632 AB Sq)	1 Jul 48–22 Nov 49
1954	
7206 AB Sq	1 Apr 54–1 Jan 58
1955	
1240 AACS Sq	
(2140 Comms Sq;	
2140 Comms Gp)	13 Jan 55–
7206 Air Trpt Sq,	
Med (7168 Air	
Trpt Sq, Med)	15 May 55–1 Nov 57
7206 Spt Gp	
(7206 AB GP)	15 May 55–
7206 USAF Dispy	1 Jun 55–30 Jun 71
1958	
8 Air Postal Sq	18 Apr 58–8 Jan 63
1966	
629 Mil Alft Spt Sq	8 Jan 66–17 Jan 71
1971	
USAF Dispy,	
Athens (USAF	
Hosp, Athens;	
USAF Hosp,	
Hellenikon)	1 Jul 71–
1973	
6916 Scty Sq	
(6916 Elect	
Scty Sq)	1 Jul 73–
1978	
922 Strat Sq	1 Jul 78–
1982	
7206 Scty Pol Sq	1 Mar 82–
7206 Tac Hosp	15 Feb 82–

Hessisch-Oldendorf Air Station

Location: Located 30 mi W of Hanover, 10 mi NW of Hameln, Federal Republic of Germany.

Name: Named after the town of Hessisch-Oldendorf in the Federal Republic of Germany.

Date of Current Name: 21 May 1976.

Previous Names: Royal Netherlands AF Caserne, Hessisch-Oldendorf.

Date of Establishment: 21 May 1976.

Date Construction Began: Reconstruction and modification of facility for tactical control operations commenced 5 Feb 1976.

Date of Beneficial Occupancy: 15 Jun 1976.

Base Operating Units: 609th Tac Con Sq, 15 Jun 1976; 600th Cmbt Spt Sq, 20 Sep 1976.

Base Commanders: Lt Col James S. Post, 15 Jun 1976; Maj John E. Allerheiligen, 20 Sep 1976; Lt Col Roy H. Inouye, 23 Mar 1978; Lt Col Gerald A. Warner, 19 Jul 1980; Maj William D. Reed Jr, 25 Jul 1980–.

Major Off-Base and Detached Installations:* Hessisch-Oldendorf Air Stn Off-Base Instl, Hessisch-Oldendorf, 5 Feb 1976–; Hessisch-Oldendorf Recrn Anx, Hessisch-Oldendorf, 1 Aug 1976; Hessisch-Oldendorf Fam Hsg Anx #1, Hessisch-Oldendorf, 1 Nov 1976–; Det 1, 600th Tac Con Gp, Kalkar, 1 Jan–1 May 1977. Hessisch-Oldendorf Stor Anx, Hessisch-Oldendorf, 1 Oct 1977–31 Mar 1982.

Major Changes in Operational Capability: An installation with no flying units. Under the 609th Tac Con Sq, station operated a Control and Reporting Post (CRP), and a computerized mobile radar that tied into the NATO Air Defense Ground Environment (NADGE) system for command and control of NATO aircraft on combat and training missions; as a northern extension of the 601st Tac Con Wg, the 609th Sq controlled installations of the 619th and 609th Tac Con Flts; the 600th Cmbt Spt Sq assumed responsibility for the base on 20 Sep 1976; it hosted the 600th Tac

---

*All installations are located in the Federal Republic of Germany.

Con Gp and all tenant organizations, and provided base support for off-base installations of the 600th Tac Con Gp in the North German area.

Major Commands to Which Assigned: USAFE, 21 May 1976–.

Major Changes in Status: None.

Units Assigned:

1976		600 Tac Con Gp	20 Sep 76–
600 Cmbt Spt Sq	20 Sep 76–	609 Tac Con Sq	15 Jun 76–

Howard Air Base

Location: Located 6 mi SW of Balboa, at the southern (Pacific) end of the Panama Canal.

Name: Named in honor of Maj Charles Harold Howard, 1892–1936, who was appointed a 2d lt in the U.S. Air Service in 1918. A pioneer in the Air Service/Air Corps operations in the Canal Zone during the 1920s, Howard was killed in an airplane crash near Bryans Mill, Texas, on 25 Oct 1936.

Date of Current Name: 1 Oct 1979.

Previous Names: Bruja Point Mil Reservation, 11 Aug 1928; Ft Bruja, 1929; Ft Kobbe (named after Maj Gen William A. Kobbe, USA, who died 1 Nov 1931) 1932; airfield section of Ft Kobbe named Howard Fld, 1 Dec 1939; Howard AB, 10 Jul 1941; Howard AFB, 1948.

Date of Establishment: Original establishment as Bruja Point Mil Reservation, 1 Aug 1938; Howard Fld part of base established as an independent post, 26 Jun 1941; reestablished 24 Oct 1954.

Date Construction Began: Although officially listed as 1 Oct 1939, War Dept approval for the field allowed grading to begin as early as 4 Sep 1939; further major construction commenced on 1 Jan 1943 and, later, in the 1960s.

Date of Beneficial Occupancy: 26 Jul 1940 (arrival of first troop unit).

Base Operating Units: 16th AB Gp (16th Svc Gp), 15 May 1941; 15th AB Sq, 10 Dec 1942; 2114th Svc Unit, Avn (Prov), 1 Oct 1945; HQ & Base Svc Sq, 582d Air Svc Gp, 20 Sep 1946; 5605th AB Gp, 26 Jul 1948; 23d AB Gp, 25 Apr 1949; 5601st AB Sq, 24 Sep–15 Dec 1949. 5700th AB Gp (5700th AB Wg), 24 Oct 1954; 24th AB Gp, 8 Nov 1967; 24th Sp Ops Gp (24th Comps Gp), 30 Jun 1972; 24th Cmbt Spt Gp, 1 Jan 1976–.

Base Commanders: Brig Gen Douglas B. Netherwood, 21 Apr 1941, CG of Ft Kobbe, also assumed command of Howard Fld on 15 May 1941; Lt Col Edmund P. Gaines, 15 May 1941, Comdr of Howard Fld; Col Charles L. Munroe, 2 Apr 1942; Lt Col Edward M. Fairfield, 7 Oct 1942; Lt Col Eugene Cunningham, 1 Jun 1943; Col Perry B. Griffith, 26 Dec 1943; Lt Col Arthur A. McGill, 22 Sep 1944; Col Donald H. Baxter, 9 Oct 1944; Lt Col George F. Keene Jr, 7 Sep 1945; Col Cornelius W. Cousland,

1 Oct 1945; Col Hanlon H. Van Auken, 15 Oct 1947; Col Murray C. Woodbury, 27 Jul 1948; Col Clair A. Peterson, 17 Sep 1948; Col Angier H. Foster, 22 Dec 1948; Col William R. Forbes, 25 Apr 1949; unk, 24 Sep–15 Dec 1949. Col John W. Oberdorf, 24 Oct 1954 (also Comdr of Albrook AFB); Lt Col Richard T. Lively, 13 Jun 1956 (also Comdr of Albrook AFB); Col Edwin M. Ramage, 1 Sep 1956 (also Comdr of Albrook AFB); Col Arthur P. Hurr, 21 Jul 1957 (also Comdr of Albrook AFB); Lt Col Clarence A. Dooley, 12 Jul 1960 (also Comdr of Albrook AFB); Col William R. Robertson, 30 Jul 1960 (also Comdr of Albrook AFB); Col Wilson Ralston, 18 Jul 1962 (also Comdr of Albrook AFB); Lt Col John E. McClure, 15 Aug 1963; Col Norman W. Campion, 5 May 1964; Lt Col John E. McClure, 3 May 1966; Col Jack R. Banks, 30 Jul 1966; unk, 9 Nov 1967–Jan 1968; Lt Col Paul T. Luttrell, Jan 1968; Col Robert A. Ports, c. Jan 1969; Col Rembert A. Ebert, c. Jul 1970; Col Kenneth B. Smith, c. 30 Jan 1971; unk, 31 Mar 1971–1 Apr 1973; Col Glendon T. Johnson, c. Apr 1973; Col William E. Roth, 3 May 1974; Col Kenneth V. Wilson, c. Jul 1975; Lt Col Robert L. Barrett, 1 Jan 1976;* Col James R. Arthur, 26 Jul 1977; Col David R. Hughes, 23 Sep 1980; Col Donald P. Adee, 18 Oct 1982–.

Major Off-Base and Detached Installations:† Galapagos Afld, 1 Jan 1943–31 Jan 1948 (trsfd to Albrook Fld, Republic of Panama); Las Margaritas Air Warning Stn, Feb 1944–2 Jan 1948 (trsfd to Republic of Panama); Aguadulce Adrm, 1 Dec 1944–Feb 1946; Chame Aux Afld, 1 Dec 1944–19 Sep 1947 (trsfd to Republic of Panama); Chorrera Afld, unk–unk; Poori Aux Adrm, 1 Dec 1944–Nov 1945 (trsfd to USN); Jaque Aux Fld, 15 Nov 1947–10 Jan 1948 (discd); Rey Isl Aux Fld, 15 Nov 1947–10 Jan 1948 (discd).

Major Changes in Operational Capability: The base served as integral part of overall defense of Western Hemisphere and Panama Canal during and after World War II and hosted primarily fighter units; runways put into use c. April 1941; two battalions of airborne infantry formed a part of the Canal Zone defenses based at Howard 1942–1945; operations at Howard drew down during the summer of 1949 and all training ceased on 11 Oct 1949; base transferred in inactive status to USA, Caribbean, in February 1950; in the 1950s, Albrook AFB used Howard to reduce aircraft activity at Albrook; a joint USA, Caribbean, and Caribbean Air Comd, USAF, agreement (18 Aug 1955) permitted the resumption of regular flying operations at Howard in Oct 1955; Albrook's flying operations ceased, its flying units transferred to Howard in Dec 1961; USAF assumed

---

*After 1 Jan 1976 all Howard commanders also commanded Albrook AS.
†All installations are located in the Republic of Panama.

full control and responsibility for Howard AFB on 1 Oct 1963; radar and communication equipment, airdrome facilities and newly acquired facilities from Ft Kobbe Army Post modernized 1964; project to widen aprons from operations building to NE-SE taxiway completed 31 Aug 1965; airmen's dormitories and education center rehabilitated 1965; air conditioning installed in 462 family housing units at Howard 1966; 32 acres of land acquired from USN and 250 family housing units constructed 1967–68; air passenger terminal, chapel annex, gymnasium, NCO Open Mess, repair shops, and recreation workshops refurbished late 1967; base streets and roads renovated and 50 units of enlisted men's housing completed 1968; taxiways, part of the main runway, and ramps repaired and reinforced in 1970s; central air conditioning provided for family housing units 1979; AN/GPN–24 Landing Control Radar installed to replace AN/MPN–13 GCA Radar 1981; since mid-1960s base hosted Navy air units operating from carriers in the area, supported military and tactical airlift operations, humanitarian and civic-action missions for the relief of victims of floods and earthquakes in Central and South America, and search and rescue operations; base also hosted C–130 rotational detachments from TAC and MAC, Nov 1967–Sep 1977, rotational A–7D detachment from TAC, Nov 1972–1982, and rotational UC–123 detachments from the Air Force Reserve and Air National Guard field training units, 1964–1982.

Major Commands to Which Assigned: Panama Canal AF, USA, 15 May–4 Aug 1941; Caribbean AF, 5 Aug 1941–4 Feb 1942; Sixth AF, 5 Feb 1942–30 Jul 1946; Caribbean Air Comd, 31 Jul 1946–15 Dec 1949. Caribbean Air Comd, 24 Oct 1954–7 Jul 1963; USAF Southern Comd, 8 Jul 1963–31 Dec 1975; TAC, 1 Jan 1976–.

Major Changes in Status: Became nonoperational 11 Oct 1949; inactivated 15 Dec 1949; transferred to USA, Caribbean, Feb 1950; USA, Caribbean, and Caribbean Air Comd, USAF, signed joint agreement for resumption of flying operations at Howard AFB 18 Aug 1955; HQ, USAF, assumed responsibility for the base, 1 Oct 1963; base became Panama property on 1 Oct 1979.

Units Assigned:

	1941		
		Co B, 550 Abn	
7 Recon Sq	26 Nov 41–11 Dec 41	Inf Bn	1 Jul 41–c. Dec 43
15 AB Sq	15 May 41–1 Oct 45	Co C, 550 Abn	
16 AB Gp		Inf Bn	1 Jul 41–c. Dec 43
(16 Svc Gp)	15 May 41–c. Jun 43	HQ & HQ Co,	
20 Mat Sq		550 Abn Inf Bn	1 Jul 41–c. Dec 43
(20 Svc Sq)	15 May 41–1 Nov 43	Det, 6 AACS Sq	5 Dec 41–15 May 44
44 Recon Sq	8 Jul 41–27 Oct 41	1942	
51 Pur Sq	10 Dec 41–23 Dec 41	1 Obs Sq	
59 Bomb Sq	28 Oct 41–11 Dec 41	(1 Recon Sq)	19 Jan 42–17 Apr 42
397 Bomb Sq	26 Nov 41–10 Dec 41	1 Obs Sq	
Co A, 550 Abn		(1 Recon Sq)	20 Jun 42–7 May 44
Inf Bn	1 Jul 41–c. Dec 43	10 Stat Con Unit	13 Mar 42–10 Jan 45

20 Trp Carr Sq	19 Feb 42–9 Jun 43
25 Bomb Sq	9 Jan 42–8 Dec 42
31 Ftr Sq	30 Sep 42–25 Mar 44
37 Ftr Gp	30 Sep 42–1 Nov 43
39 Obs Sq	20 Mar 42–6 Aug 42
40 Bomb Gp	16 Jun 42–16 Sep 42
44 Bomb Sq	16 Jun 42–6 Jul 42
53 Ftr Con Sq	3 Jun 42–3 Nov 42
59 Bomb Sq	19 Feb 42–10 Mar 42
72 Obs Gp	c. 18 Jan 42–1 Nov 43
108 Obs Sq (108 Recon Sq)	19 Jan 42–1 Nov 43
1161 Qm Svc Gp, Avn	5 Apr 42–1 Nov 43
1610 Ord Sup & Maint Co, Avn	10 May 42–1 Nov 43
2101 Qm Truck Co, Avn	27 May 42–8 Sep 43
VI AF Gnd Spt Comd	14 Oct 42–21 Aug 43
Co A, 551 Parachute Inf Bn	7 Dec 42–c. Dec 43
Co B, 551 Parachute Inf Bn	7 Dec 42–c. Dec 43
Co C, 551 Parachute Inf Bn	7 Dec 42–c. Dec 43
HQ & HQ Co, 551 Parachute Inf Bn	7 Dec 42–c. Dec 43
Det, 6 Wea Sq	30 Apr 42–unk
1943	
6 Bomb Gp	14 Jan 43–1 Nov 43
23 Tow Target Sq	31 Oct 43–20 Aug 46
24 Ftr Sq	9 Jun 43–8 Mar 44
25 Bomb Sq	22 May 43–16 Jun 43
40 Bomb Gp	2 Jun 43–16 Jun 43
44 Bomb Sq	c. 4 Jun 43–15 Jun 43
45 Bomb Sq	c. 22 May 43–15 Jun 43
1944	
3 Bomb Sq	6 Apr 44–c. 26 Aug 44
18 Svc Sq	12 Jan 44–c. 9 Mar 44
29 Bomb Sq	8 Dec 44–27 Jan 45
43 Ftr Sq	9 Feb 44–6 Apr 44
43 Ftr Sq	29 Aug 44–10 Jan 45
51 Ftr Sq	c. 10 Jun 44–15 Oct 46
1945	
10 Repl Con Dep	10 Jan 45–23 Sep 46
28 Ftr Sq	25 Sep 45–15 Oct 46
30 Ftr Sq	25 Jan 45–15 Oct 46
32 Ftr Sq	10 Jan 45–15 Oct 46
AAF Tropical Wea Sch	18 Mar 45–12 Oct 45
1946	
1 Emerg Rscu Sq (1 Rscu Sq)	1 Nov 46–1 Sep 49
22 Ftr Sq	15 Oct 46–13 Aug 48
23 Ftr Sq	15 Oct 46–13 Aug 48
36 Ftr Gp	15 Oct 46–13 Aug 48
39 Comms Sq, Wg	15 Oct 46–1 Dec 48
91 Recon Sq	26 Aug 46–1 Dec 47
530 AC & W Gp	15 Oct 46–16 Apr 48
631 AC & W Sq	15 Oct 46–16 Apr 48
HQ & Base Svcs Sq, 582 Air Svc Gp	15 Oct 46–6 Jul 48
1947	
53 Ftr Sq	1 Dec 47–13 Aug 48
629 AC & W Sq	15 Jul 47–16 Mar 48
1948	
4 Tac Recon Sq	20 Aug 48–14 Mar 49
5 Base Compl Sq	23 Jun 48–28 Jul 48
36 AB Gp	2 Jul 48–13 Aug 48
36 AP Sq	2 Jul 48–13 Aug 48
36 Base Svc Sq, Ftr, Jet	2 Jul 48–13 Aug 48
36 Comms Sq	2 Jul 48–13 Aug 48
36 Ftr Wg	2 Jul 48–13 Aug 48
36 Food Svc Sq, Ftr, Jet	2 Jul 48–13 Aug 48
36 Instls Sq, Ftr, Jet	2 Jul 48–13 Aug 48
36 Maint & Sup Gp	2 Jul 48–13 Aug 48
36 Maint Sq, Ftr, Jet	2 Jul 48–13 Aug 48
36 MV Sq, Ftr, Jet	2 Jul 48–13 Aug 48
36 Stn Med Gp	2 Jul 48–13 Aug 48
36 Sup Sq	2 Jul 48–13 Aug 48
1949	
23 AB Gp	25 Apr 49–24 Sep 49
23 AP Sq	25 Apr 49–24 Sep 49
23 Base Svc Sq	25 Apr 49–24 Sep 49
23 Comms Sq	25 Apr 49–24 Sep 49
23 Ftr Gp	25 Apr 49–24 Sep 49
23 Ftr Wg	25 Apr 49–24 Sep 49
23 Food Svc Sq	25 Apr 49–24 Sep 49
23 Instls Sq, Ftr, Jet	25 Apr 49–24 Sep 49
23 Maint & Sup Gp	25 Apr 49–24 Sep 49
23 Maint Sq	25 Apr 49–24 Sep 49
23 MV Sq, Ftr, Jet	25 Apr 49–24 Sep 49
23 Sup Sq	25 Apr 49–24 Sep 49
74 Ftr Sq	25 Apr 49–24 Sep 49
75 Ftr Sq	25 Apr 49–24 Sep 49
76 Ftr Sq	25 Apr 49–24 Sep 49
1963	
605 Air Commando Sq, Comps (605 Sp Ops Sq)	15 Nov 63–30 Sep 72
5700 Spt Sq	1 Oct 63–3 Aug 64
1964	
5700 AP Sq	15 May 64–15 Mar 68
5700 CE Sq	15 May 64–15 Mar 68
5700 Consold Acft Maint Sq	15 May 64–15 Mar 68
5700 Ops Sq	15 May 64–15 Mar 68

	1965	24 Fld Maint Sq	15 Mar 68–30 Jun 71
1977 Comms Sq	1 Jul 65–31 Mar 68	24 Orgnzl Maint Sq	15 Jul 68–30 Jun 71
	1967	24 Scty Pol Sq	15 Mar 68–
24 Trnsp Sq	13 Dec 67–	24 USAF Dispy	
Armnt & Elect		(USAF Clinic,	
Maint Sq, Prov	8 Nov 67–15 Mar 68	Howard)	15 Mar 68–
Fld Maint Sq, Prov	8 Nov 67–15 Mar 68		1970
Orgnzl Maint Sq,		24 Sp Ops Sq	
Prov	8 Nov 67–15 Mar 68	(24 Comps Sq)	1 Jul 70–1 Jul 75
	1968		1971
24 Air Trpt Sq	15 Mar 68–30 Jun 71	24 Consold Acft	
24 Armnt & Elect		Maint Sq	1 Jul 71–
Maint Sq			1973
(24 Avncs		24 Sup Sq	15 Dec 73–
Maint Sq)	15 Mar 68–30 Jun 71		1975
24 CE Sq	15 Mar 68–	1300 Mil Alft Sq	31 Mar 75–
24 Comps Wg			1976
(24 Air		24 Cmbt Spt Gp	1 Jan 76–
Commando Wg;		24 Comps Sq	1 Jan 76–
24 Sp Ops Wg;		24 Svcs Sq	1 Oct 76–
24 Sp Ops Gp;		1202 Air Postal Sq	1 Jul 76–1 Oct 79
24 Comps Gp;			1978
24 Comps Wg)	3 Jan 68–	1978 Comms Gp	15 Dec 78–

Incirlik Air Base

Location: Located 7 mi E of Adana, 2 mi NW of Incirlik, and about 250 mi SE of Ankara, Turkey.

Name: Named after the town of Incirlik, Turkey.

Date of Current Name: 28 Feb 1958.

Previous Names: Adana AB, 21 Feb 1955 (aka Incirlik Common Defense Installation).

Date of Establishment: 6 Dec 1954 (Turkish-U.S. joint-use agreement).

Date Construction Began: Spring 1951 (Turkish-U.S. Engrg Gp [TUSEG] began construction).

Date of Beneficial Occupancy: Nov 1954.*

Base Operating Units: Det, 7216th AB Sq, Nov 1954; 7216th AB Sq, 21 Feb 1955 (rdsgd 7216th AB Gp, 1 May 1958; 7216th Cmbt Spt Gp, 9 Jul 1962); 39th Cmbt Spt Sq, 1 Apr 1966–.

Base Commanders: Col James A. Smith, c. 15 Aug 1954; Lt Col James Giannatti, 10 Sep 1954; Maj Edward Stroupe, c. 1 Jul 1955; Maj Wilmer E. McDowell, Oct 1955; Col Gordon F. Thomas, 3 Jan 1956; Col Peter J. Markham, 20 Jul 1958; Col Charles F. Franklin, c. 1 Apr 1960; Col Travis Hoover, 4 Nov 1961; Col Albert B. Parsons, 23 Jul 1963; Col Rowan M. Perkins, 29 Jul 1966; Col Allen B. Cotton, 25 Jul 1968; Lt Col Joe D. Schneider, 25 May 1970; Col Robert L. Berg, Aug 1970; Col Alfred S. Allen, Aug 1972; Col Jack W. Hart, 3 May 1974; Col Richard J. Miles, 4 Sep 1975; Col Bobby J. Martin, 2 Dec 1976; Col Glenn W. Young, 19 Aug 1979; Col Thomas E. Dayton, 8 Aug 1980; Col Richard C. Craveiro, 26 Jun 1981; Lt Col William D. Doran, 26 Feb 1982; Lt Col Robert G. Guin, 24 Jun 1982; Col Howard L. King, 1 Oct 1982–.

Major Off-Base and Detached Installations:[†] Adana Sea Trml Anx (rdsgd Yumurtalik Pipe Line Trml Anx; Yumurtalik Ocean Petrol Sys; Yumurtalik Petrol Prods Stor Anx), Yumurtalik, 26 Aug 1955–; Iskenderun Whse Anx (rdsgd) Iskenderun Stor Anx Iskenderun Port), Isk-

---

*Arrival at Adana of a detachment of 3 officers and 17 airmen of the 7216th Air Base Squadron.

[†]All installations are located in Turkey.

enderun, 5 Sep 1956 (actvd)−; Adana Amn Hsg Anx, Adana, 15 Sep 1956 (asgnd)−unk; Iskenderun Amn Hsg Anx, Iskenderun, 1 Nov 1957 (asgnd)−30 Jun 1965 (dspd); Incirlik RB Anx, Adana, 10 Dec 1959 (asgnd)−unk; Karatas Trml Anx (rdsgd Karatas RRS), Karatas, 27 Jan 1961 (asgnd)−unk; Iskenderun Off Hsg Anx (rdsgd Iskenderun Bach Hsg Anx), Iskenderun, 1 Nov 1961 (asgnd)−; Malatya RRS, 16 mi NE of Akcadag, 1 Nov 1961 (asgnd)−; Adana Water Sys Anx, Koprukoyu, 16 Jan 1962 (asgnd)−; Tatvan RRS (detchd Instl), Tatvan, 18 Oct 1965 (asgnd)−; Karatas Rcvr Anx, Yemisli, unk−1 Jun 1966 (inactvd); Malatya Water Sys Anx, 16 mi N of Akcadag, 20 Aug 1970 (asgnd)−; Karatas Stor Anx, Kayarli, unk−27 Aug 1971 (dspd); Iskenderun Stor Anx #2, Iskenderun, 1 Jul 1974 (asgnd)−30 Jun 1978 (dspd); Adana Svc Anx, Adana, 1 Jan 1978 (asgnd)−unk.

Major Changes in Operational Capability: Immediately upon activation of the U.S. part of the field, winter 1954−1955, the base mission changed from support of a jet instrument and gunnery school to emergency support of long-range medium and heavy bomber operations, and support of all USAF activities in southern Turkey; 10,000-ft runway operational Nov 1954; base facilities became adequate to host first field exercise, with participation of seven B−47s and three KC−97s, May 1955; POL sea terminal at Yumurtalik and a connecting pipe line to the base became operational Oct−Nov 1955; living quarters considerably improved, primarily by completion of 200-man barracks, 1957; flying operations rose sharply during Lebanon crisis when 150 aircraft were on station Jun−Jul 1958; Jupiter missiles briefly stationed at the field 1962−1963; three BOQ and two airmen dormitory buildings completed early 1962; precision measurement equipment lab accepted spring 1965; F−100s replaced F−105s in May 1964; dining hall, dormitories, VOQ, and freight/passenger terminal completed early 1966; facilities updated to accommodate operations of one tactical fighter rotational squadron and three supporting C−131 aircraft, and standby war-readiness spares kits provided for 36 aircraft, 1970−1971; Cyprus crisis strained U.S.-Turkish relations and greatly curtailed base activities 1974−1978; 36 TAB VEE aircraft shelters completed during 1974−1976 and modified by Sep 1980; bachelor and family housing construction, major upgrading of utilities, and construction of munition igloos finished 1981.

Major Commands to Which Assigned: USAFE, 21 Feb 1955.

Major Changes in Status: Turkish AF owns installation and occupies part of base; USAFE has tenant status.

Units Assigned:

1955	2006 Comms Gp)	8 May 55−
2006 AACS Sq	7216 AB Sq	
(2006 Comms Sq;	(7216 AB Gp; 7216	

Cmbt Spt Gp)	21 Feb 55–1 Apr 66	1966	
7216 USAF Dispy	10 Apr 55–1 Apr 66	39 Cmbt Spt Sq	1 Apr 66–
Adana Task Force,		39 Consold Acft	
Prov	1 May 55–unk	Maint Sq	1 Apr 66–
1958		39 Sup Sq	1 Aug 66–
7216 Mat Sq	1 Sep 58–1 Apr 66	39 Tac Gp	1 Apr 66–
1959		39 USAF Dispy	1 Apr 66–30 Jun 71
428 Tac Ftr Sq	16 Feb 59–19 Jun 59	628 Mil Alft Spt Sq	8 Jan 66–
429 Tac Ftr Sq	19 Jun 59–15 Oct 59	1971	
522 Tac Ftr Sq	18 Oct 59–13 Feb 60	USAF Hosp, Incirlik	1 Jul 71–
1960		1972	
523 Tac Ftr Sq	21 Feb 60–	7005 Explosive	
1962		Ord Dspl Flt	1 Jul 72–
7216 AP Sq	9 Jul 62–1 Apr 66	1979	
		39 Tac Hosp	22 Aug 79–

Iraklion Air Station

Location: Located 10 mi E of Iraklion in the village of Gournes, in the north central section of Crete.

Name: Named after a city in Crete.

Date of Current Name: 1 Oct 1954.

Previous Names: Iraklion Radio Mobile Annex.

Date of Establishment: 1 Oct 1954.

Date Construction Began: 1 Jul 1954.

Date of Beneficial Occupancy: 1 Oct 1954.*

Base Operating Units: Det 1, 1603d Air Trnsp Wg, 1 Oct 1954; 7222d AB Sq, 1 Aug 1955; Det 1, 7206th Spt Gp, 1 Jan 1958; 6930th Radio Gp, Mobile (6931st Scty Gp), 1 Apr 1958; 7276th AB Gp, 1 Oct 1978–.

Base Commanders: Maj Robert L. Lee, 1 Oct 1954; Maj William A. Pelton, c. 1 Aug 1955; Capt Ronald M. Ryan, c. Nov 1955; Lt Col William Pugh, 24 Jan 1956; Lt Col Edward Corcoran, 5 Jul 1957; Col John P. Shean, 16 Jun 1958; Col Jonathan Leet, 18 Jul 1961; Col John P. Wells, 3 Jul 1963; Col Ross E. Spence, 22 Apr 1965; Col Willie R. Sturm, 13 Mar 1967; Col Louie Miller Jr, 7 Mar 1969; Col Robert F. Stark, Mar 1971; Col Robert L. Burt, 9 Feb 1973; Col James C. Embry, 28 Jan 1975; Col Edwin M. Binder, 25 Apr 1975; Lt Col Robert C. Hawkins, 21 Jun 1977; Col David J. Cade, 11 Jul 1977; Col Charles G. Luse, 1 Oct 1978; Col George D. Courington, 27 Jun 1980; Col William L. Spacy, 27 Jun 1982–.

Major Off-Base and Detached Installations:[†] Iraklion Comms Anx, 10 mi E of Iraklion, 15 Aug 1957 (actvd); Malia Water Sys Anx, 20 mi E of Iraklion, 15 Jan 1958 (actvd); Malia Water Sys Anx #2, 20 mi E of Iraklion, 15 Jan 1958 (actvd); Iraklion RRS, 14 mi W of Iraklion, 18 Jun 1965 (actvd).

Major Changes in Operational Capability: Base began operations in support of activities of the 1603d Air Trpt Wg and USAFE liaison operations in Crete; the base supported units of USAFE and NATO as

---

*Flag-raising ceremony took place on 15 Oct 1954.
[†]All installations are located on the island of Crete.

directed, and all units assigned and tenant at Iraklion from 1 Apr 1958 to 1 Oct 1978;* base provided administrative and logistical support to the 6931st Elect Scty Sq, as well as policy guidance in administrative, logistical and support matters for all regular and other tenant organizations at Iraklion AS, and dispersed DoD units located on the island of Crete from 1 Oct 1978 to the present; also provided liaison and base support services for the United States Embassy, Athens, Greece.

Major Commmands to Which Assigned: USAFE, 1 Oct 1954–.

Major Changes in Status: None.

Units Assigned:

	1955			1974	
7222 AB Sq		1 Aug 55–1 Jan 58	6931 AB Sq		1 Jul 74–1 Oct 78
	1957		6931 Scty Sq		
7222 USAF Dispy		8 Apr 57–30 Jun 71	(6931 Elect		
	1958		Scty Sq)		1 Jul 74–
6930 Radio Gp		1 Apr 58–1 Oct 78		1978	
	1971		7276 AB Gp		1 Oct 78–
USAF Dispy,				1979	
Iraklion (USAF					
Hosp, Iraklion)		1 Jul 71–	2115 Comms Sq		2 Mar 79–

---

*From 1 Apr 1958 to 1 Oct 1978 Iraklion AS continued to be an installation of USAFE, although the 6930th Radio Gp, Mobile (6931st Security Gp), an organization of the United States Air Force Security Service, operated the base and functioned as host unit.

Izmir Air Station

Location: Located 200 mi SSW of Istanbul, on the W coast of Turkey.
Name: Named after a city in Turkey.
Date of Current Name: 10 Sep 1970.
Previous Names: Cumaovasi AB; Izmir AB, 6 Dec 1956; Izmir Admntv Anx #6, 6 Jul 1962.
Date of Establishment: Established in rented facilities of Allied Land Forces Southeast Europe on 25 Aug 1953; activated as USAF installation on 1 Jan 1956.
Date Construction Began: Unk.
Date of Beneficial Occupancy: Sep 1952.
Base Operating Units: Det 2, 7206th AB Sq, 1 Apr 1954–1 Nov 1955; 7266th Spt Sq, 1 Nov 1955–6 Jul 1962; 7231st Cmbt Spt Gp, 6 Jul 1962–31 Mar 1966; 41st Tac Gp, 1 Apr 1966–30 Jun 1970; 7241st Spt Sq (7241st AB Sq; 7241st AB Gp), 1 Jul 1970–.
Base Commanders: Unk, 25 Aug 1953–31 Mar 1954; Capt John R. Gillis, 1 Apr 1954; Lt Col Richard E. Armstrong, 3 Oct 1955; Col Robert N. Wilkinson, 15 Jul 1957; Col Kelly W. Mitchim, 22 Oct 1959; Col Jack O. Brown, 12 Dec 1960; Col Charles D. Jantzen, 6 Jul 1962; Col Thomas L. Wiper, Sep 1963; Lt Col James R. Ames, 7 Jul 1964; Col Nathan J. Hirsh, 30 Jul 1966; Col Frank A. Zamboni, 3 Jul 1969; Col John E. Skaggs Jr, 15 May 1970; Lt Col Donald L. Stinson, 31 Dec 1971; Col John M. Taylor, 12 Jul 1972; Col Edward M. McDonald, 7 Aug 1973; Col Gordon E. Williams, 15 Jul 1975; Col Michael M. Miller, 6 Jul 1976; Col William F. Palmer, 29 Jun 1978; Col Lawrence E. Bustle Jr, 28 Jun 1979; Col Howard J. Hazlett, 17 Jul 1981–.
Major Off-Base and Detached Installations.* Izmir Svc Anx, 1 Jul 1954–6 Jul 1962 (trsfd to Cigli AB); Izmir Hosp, 20 Dec 1955–6 Jul 1962 (trsfd to Cigli AB); Izmir Cmsy (Izmir Svc Anx), 1 Jan 1956–6 Jul 1962 (trsfd to Cigli AB); Izmir Depnt Sch (Izmir Sch), 1 Jan 1956–6 Jul 1962 (trsfd to Cigli AB); Izmir Base Whse #3 (Izmir Stor Anx #3), 1 Apr

---

*All installations are located in Turkey.

1956–6 Jul 1962 (trsfd to Cigli AB); Izmir Recrn Anx #2, 9 Apr 1956–6 Jul 1962 (trsfd to Cigli AB); Izmir Stor Anx, 9 May 1956–30 Jun 1959 (dspd); Izmir Admn Ofc #2 (Izmir Admn Anx #2), 1 Aug 1956–10 Mar 1961 (dspd); Izmir Thtr (Izmir Recrn Anx #1, Thtr), 1 Dec 1956–6 Jul 1962 (trsfd to Cigli AB); Izmir Admn Ofc #1 (Izmir Admn Anx #1), 1 Jan 1957–31 Dec 1961 (dspd); Izmir Base Whse #1 (Izmir Stor Anx #1; Izmir Admn Anx #5), 1 Jan 1957–6 Jul 1962 (trsfd to Cigli AB); Izmir Base Whse #2 (Izmir Stor Anx #2), 1 Jan 1957–unk; Izmir Med Lab (Izmir Lab), 1 Jan 1957–6 Jul 1962 (trsfd to Cigli AB); Izmir Comms Fclty Anx, 11 Jan 1958–6 Jul 1962 (trsfd to Cigli AB); Izmir Recrn Anx #3, 15 Jul 1958–6 Jul 1962 (trsfd to Cigli AB); Izmir Recrn Anx #4, 15 Jul 1958–6 Jul 1962 (trsfd to Cigli AB); Izmir Stor Anx #4 (Izmir Bakery Anx), 15 Jul 1958–30 Jun 1962 (trsfd to Cigli AB); Izmir Fam Hsg Anx, 15 Dec 1958–6 Jul 1962 (trsfd to Cigli AB); Izmir Port Ofc, 1958–6 Jul 1962 (trsfd to Cigli AB); Izmir Stor Anx #6, 15 Mar 1959–6 Jul 1962 (trsfd to Cigli AB); Izmir Stor Anx #7, 15 Mar 1959–6 Jul 1962 (trsfd to Cigli AB); Izmir Recrn Anx #5, 1 Aug 1959–6 Jul 1962 (trsfd to Cigli AB); Izmir Recrn Anx #6, 1 Aug 1959–6 Jul 1962 (trsfd to Cigli AB); Izmir Stor Anx #5, 1 Aug 1959–6 Jul 1962 (trsfd to Cigli AB); Izmir Admn Ofc #3 (Izmir Admn Anx #3), 1 Sep 1959–6 Jul 1962 (trsfd to Cigli AB); Izmir Amn Hsg Anx, 1 Nov 1959–6 Jul 1962 (trsfd to Cigli AB); Cigli AB, 10 Nov 1959–1 Feb 1961; Izmir Stor Anx #8, 1 Sep 1960–6 Jul 1962 (trsfd to Cigli AB); Izmir Recrn Anx #8, 1 Jan 1961–6 Jul 1962 (trsfd to Cigli AB); Izmir Stor Anx #9, 1 Jan 1961–6 Jul 1962 (trsfd to Cigli AB); Izmir Maint Anx, 1 Jul 1961–6 Jul 1962 (trsfd to Cigli AB); Izmir Fam Hsg Anx #2, 1 Aug 1961–6 Jul 1962 (trsfd to Cigli AB); Izmir Recrn Anx #6, Thtr, 28 Jun 1963–; Izmir Stor Anx #4, 1 Jan 1964–; Izmir Stor Anx #1, 1 May 1964–; Izmir Stor Anx #14, 1 Sep 1966–unk; Balikesir RRS, 15 Nov 1968 (actvd)–; Izmir Fam Hsg Anx #3 (Izmir Fam Hsg Site), unk–1 Jul 1969 (asgnd to Cigli AB); Izmir Fam Hsg Anx #2, unk–3 Dec 1969 (dspd); Izmir Amn Hsg Anx, Sokak, unk–1 Feb 1970 (dspd); Izmir Stor Anx #14 (Izmir Stor Anx #2), Byarakli, 1 Jul 1971 (actvd)–; Izmir Admn Ofc, 1 Jul 1973 (actvd)–; Izmir Fam Hsg Anx, Bornova, unk–31 Jul 1973 (dspd); Izmir Recrn Anx #3, unk–31 Jan 1976 (dspd); Izmir Recrn Anx #5, 6 May 1976 (actvd)–; Izmir Fam Hsg Site #2, 1 Jun 1976 (actvd)–; Izmir Stor Anx #3, Bornova, 1 Oct 1978–.

Major Changes in Operational Capability: U.S. responsibilities in the Izmir area began on 8 Sep 1952 with the activation of Allied Land Forces Southeast Europe and the arrival on 14 Oct 1953 of the Sixth Allied Tac AF at Sirinyer Garrison south of Izmir; the USN supported these and other NATO organizations, while Det 2, 7206th AB Sq, supported USAF installations in the area after 1 Apr 1954; USAFE assumed support responsibility for U.S. and NATO entities in the Izmir area on 1 Jan 1956; assumed support responsibility for all U.S. and NATO units based at Cigli and off-base installations of Cigli situated throughout the Izmir area on 6 Jul 1962; concrete roofs of jet fuel tanks repaired and new water lines, fire hydrants and electric power lines installed, 1962; a reinforced concrete pad for wing-tank loading built at the north hangar and air conditioning installed in dependent quarters, 1963; Cigli gained control of all support activities in and around Izmir on 1 Apr 1966; Turkish AF assumed control of Cigli AB on 1 Jul 1970, and Izmir AS then assumed support responsibility for U.S. and USAF units in the Izmir area, with Cigli relegated to standby base status.

Major Commands to Which Assigned: USN, 25 Aug 1953; USAFE, 1 Jan 1956–.

Major Changes in Status: None.

Units Assigned:

1955
7266 Spt Sq   1 Nov 55–6 Jul 62
1956
7266 USAF Hosp   1 Jan 56–6 Jul 62
1960
7231 Spt Sq   1 Oct 60–1 Feb 61
7231 Tech Tng Gp   1 Oct 60–1 Feb 61
1961
7231 USAF Dispy
  (7231 USAF Hosp)   1 Feb 61–1 Apr 66

1970
7241 Spt Sq
  (7241 AB Sq;
   7241 AB Gp)   1 Jul 70–
7241 USAF Dispy   1 Jul 70–30 Jun 71
1971
USAF Dispy, Izmir
  (USAF Hosp,
   Izmir; USAF
   Clinic, Izmir)   1 Jul 71–

Kadena Air Base

Location: Located immediately adjacent to and SE of the town of Kadena, 1 mi S of Koza, and 12 mi NNE of Naha, Okinawa, Japan.

Name: Named after a town on the island of Okinawa.

Date of Current Name: 1 Nov 1949.

Previous Names: Kadena Afld (aka Afld #5, AAB, APO 953), c. Apr 1945; Kadena AAB, 20 Nov 1945; Kadena AFB, 8 Mar 1948.

Date of Establishment: Japanese afld, unk; 1 Apr 1945 (troops of the 7th U.S. Inf Div captured the Japanese field).

Date Construction Began: U.S. construction began on 6 Apr 1945.

Date of Beneficial Occupancy: 5 Sep 1945.

Base Operating Units: 13th Cmbt Bn, 7th U.S. Inf Div, 2 Apr 1945; 807th Engr Avn Bn, 23 May 1945; 316th Bomb Wg, 5 Sep 1945; 71st AB Gp, 18 Aug 1948; 32d AB Gp, 21 Sep 1948; 6332d Stn Wg, 1 Apr 1949 (rdsgd 6332d AB Wg, 25 Jan 1950); 18th Ftr-Bmbr Wg, 1 May 1955; 18th AB Gp, 1 Feb 1957; 6313th AB Wg, 1 Oct 1957; 824th Cmbt Spt Gp, 8 Dec 1964; 18th Cmbt Spt Gp, 1 Oct 1974–.

Base Commanders: Unk, 1 Apr–Jun 1945; Lt Col William J. Niemi, Jun 1945–unk; Lt Col Robert J. Colleran, unk–4 Sep 1945; Col Lee B. Coats, c. 15 Sep 1945; Col Thomas J. DuBose, unk–30 Nov 1945; Col Joseph J. Nazzaro, 1 Dec 1945; Brig Gen Richard C. Lindsay, 21 Jan 1946; Col Clarence A. Neely, 3 Mar 1947; Col Francis L. Rivard, 13 Sep 1947; Brig Gen Charles T. Myers, 1 Oct 1947; Col John F. Wadman, 11 Dec 1947; Col Walter E. Arnold, 1 May 1948; Col Edwin M. Day, 16 Aug 1948; Col Charles P. Prime, 1 Feb 1949; Col Walter E. Arnold, 21 Mar 1949; Col John W. Egan, 1 Apr 1949; Lt Col Guy W. Saunders, 26 Aug 1949; Col George A. McHenry, 1 Dec 1949; Col Henry B. Fisher, 23 Jul 1951; Col Franklin S. Henley, 3 Dec 1952; Col James C. Cochran, 5 Aug 1954; Col Glendon P. Overing, 5 Apr 1955; Col Robert C. Orth, 3 May 1956; Col William C. Adams, 1 Feb 1957; Col Glenn T. Eagleston, 26 Jul 1958; Col Joe C. Briley, 25 Apr 1960; Col Charles H. Pierce, 22 Jun 1961; Col George B. Simler, 24 Jul 1961; Col John R. Roche, 1 Jun 1963; Col Cornelius G. Brosnan, 4 Jun 1964; Col James D. Robinson, 10 Jul 1964; Col Frank E. Marek, 1 Aug 1965; Col Thomas L. Murphy, 9 Jul 1969; Col

Allen W. Carver Sr, 20 Oct 1970; Col Thomas M. Beneagh, 12 Mar 1973; Col Earl S. Barnett III, 17 Feb 1976; Col David L. Elliott, 26 May 1978; Col Richard S. Beyea Jr, 29 May 1979; Col Francis R. Fanning, 14 May 1980; Col Ronnie C. Covert, 11 Jun 1982-.

Major Off-Base and Detached Installations:* Bolo Afld (rdsgd Bolo Aux AB; Bolo Aux Afld), Sobe, 28 Jul 1945 (actvd)-1 Jul 1961 (trsfd to the USA); Ie Shima Alternate Adrm (rdsgd Ie Shima Aux AB; Ie Shima Aux Afld; Ie Shima Air Rg), Agarii, 15 Nov 1945 (asgnd)-; Bishagawa Dock Anx, 5 mi NW of Koza, 1945 (actvd)-30 Jun 1958 (dspd); Kadena/Bishagawa Hsg Anx (rdsgd Bishagawa Billeting Anx; Kadena Ammo Stor Anx), 1 mi N of Kadena, 1945 (asgnd)-11 Mar 1958 (dspd); Awase Aux AB (rdsgd Awase Comms Site; Awase Globecom Tmtr Anx; Awase Tmtr Anx; Awase Comms Anx), 2 mi ESE of Koza, 1946 (asgnd)-31 May 1977 (trsfd to the Japanese govt); Kadena/Higashionna Ammo Dep (rdsgd Higashi Onna Ammo Dep; Higashionna Anx; Higashionna Ammo Stor Site; Higashionna Ammo Stor Anx), 2 mi S of Ishikawa, 1946 (asgnd)-unk; Koza Contractor Hsg Anx (rdsgd Koza Billeting Anx; Koza Anx #2; Koza Hsg Anx), Koza, 1946 (asgnd)-1 Jul 1958 (trsfd to the U.S. Marine Corps); Deragawa Tmtr Site (rdsgd Kadena/Deragawa Tmtr Anx; Deragawa Comms Anx; Deragawa Tmtr Anx; Deragawa Comms Anx), 1 mi E of Tairagawa, 1947 (asgnd)-1 Jul 1962 (trsfd to the Dept of the Army); Kadena/Sobe Globecom Tmtr Anx (rdsgd Sobe Comms Anx #1; Sobe Tmtr Anx; Sobe Anx), 7 mi NW of Koza, 1947 (asgnd)-Dec 1954 (trsfd to the USN); Kadena Village Area "C" Hsg Anx (rdsgd Kadena Anx #1; Kadena Hsg Anx; Kadena Fam Hsg Anx; Kadena Hsg Anx), Kadena, 1947 (actvd)-24 May 1965 (dspd); Yontan Aux AB (rdsgd Yontan AS; Yontan Tacan Anx; Yontan Aux Afld; Yomitan Aux Afld; Yomitan Anx), 1 mi S of Kurutake, 1950 (trsfd from the U.S. Marine Corps)-27 Jul 1977 (trsfd to the USN); Microwave Relay Stn (rdsgd Kadena/Koza Globecom Relay Anx; Koza Anx #3; Koza Relay Anx; Koza RR Anx), 1 mi SW of Koza, Apr 1952 (asgnd)-31 May 1973 (trsfd to the Japanese govt); Bishagawa POL Anx (rdsgd Bishagawa Anx #2), unk; Onna Point AFSS Radio Rcvr Anx (rdsgd Onna Point Rcvr Anx; Onna Admin Anx; Onna Comms Site), 5 mi NNE of Ishikawa, 13 Apr 1953 (asgnd)-1 Feb 1973 (trsfd to the U.S. Marine Corps); Bishagawa Fuel Stor Anx (rdsgd Bishagawa Power Line Anx), 4 mi WNW of Koza, 15 Jul 1953 (asgnd)-30 Jun 1958 (trsfd to the Japanese govt); Kadena SBRAZ AACS Radio Rg Anx (rdsgd Yonagusuku

---

*Unless otherwise indicated, all installations are on Okinawa, Ryukyu Islands, which was administered by the U.S. military government from 1945 until returned to Japan in 1972. Installations for which no initial assignment date could be established are listed separately at the end.

Anx; Yonagusuku RR Anx), 5 mi E of Koza, 1 Dec 1953 (asgnd)–25 Sep 1961 (trsfd to owner); Bolo Aux Afld, Kadena Site #1, Sobe, 8 Mar 1954 (actvd)–30 Jun 1973 (trsfd to the Japanese govt); Okuma Homer Bcn Stn, 18 mi NE of Nago, 1 Apr 1956–25 Sep 1961 (trsfd to the Dept of the Army); Sobe Anx, 7 mi NW of Koza, unk (asgnd)–12 Apr 1958 (trsfd to the USN); Kadena Site #2, Yonagusuku, 1 Apr 1960–31 Dec 1976 (trsfd to the Japanese govt); Kadena Site #3, Ginbaru, 1 Apr 1960 (asgnd)–31 May 1971 (trsfd to the Japanese govt); Kadena Site #4, Onna, 1 Apr 1960 (asgnd)–18 Apr 1972 (returned to owner); Kadena Tacan Anx, Chibana, 1 Jul 1960 (trsfd from the Dept of the Army)–unk; Irisuna Shima Air Range (rdsgd Idesuna Air Rg), 38 mi SE of Naha, 28 Apr 1961 (trsfd from Naha AB)–unk; Motobu Aux AB (rdsgd Motobu Aux Afld), 8 mi NW of Nago, 1 Mar 1962 (trsfd from Naha AB)–30 Jun 1965 (trsfd to the U.S. Marine Corps); Yogi Gasoline Stor Site, Yogi, unk–13 Jun 1971 (returned to the Japanese govt); Kadena VORTAC Site, adjacent to base, 1 Jul 1968 (asgnd)–8 Feb 1974 (merged w/base); Kume Shima AS (rdsgd Kume Jima AS; Kume Jima Air Rg), Kanegusuku, 30 Jun 1971 (trsfd from Naha AB)–14 May 1973 (trsfd to the Japanese govt); Miwa RB Anx, Kiyan, 30 Jun 1971 (trsfd from Naha AB)–15 May 1972 (trsfd to the Japanese govt); Miyako Jima AS, Hirara, 30 Jun 1971 (trsfd from Naha AB)–15 Feb 1973 (trsfd to the Japanese govt); Naha AB (rdsgd Naha Fam Hsg Anx), Naha, 30 Jun 1971 (asgnd and chgd from prim to off-base instl)–; Okino AS (rdsgd Okino VORTAC Site), Kagoshima-Ken, Japan, 30 Jun 1971 (trsfd from Naha AB)–22 Jan 1973 (trsfd to the Japanese govt); Okino Erabu Shima AS, Serikaku, Japan, 30 Jun 1971 (trsfd from Naha AB)–22 Jan 1973 (trsfd to the Japanese govt); Yaedake Comms Anx (rdsgd Yaedake Comms Anx), Motobu, 30 Jun 1971 (trsfd from Naha AB)–; Yoza Dake AS (rdsgd Yozadake AS), Yoza, 30 Jun 1971 (trsfd from Naha AB)–30 Jun 1976 (trsfd to the Japanese govt); Sunabe Stor Anx (rdsgd Sunabe Spt Anx), Kadena, 15 May 1972 (asgnd)–; Hanza Ord Demolition Anx (rdsgd Hanza Ammo Stor Anx), Zakimi, unk–2 Feb 1976 (merged w/Kadena Ammo Stor Anx); Camp Kuwae Fam Hsg Anx, 1 mi NNE of Jagaru, 28 Feb 1977 (asgnd)–; Makiminato Fam Hsg Anx, Urasoe, 28 Feb 1977 (asgnd)–; Tengan Comms Stn, Tengan, 28 Feb 1977 (asgnd)–; Zukeran Fam Hsg Anx, 1 mi NNE of Okinawa City, 28 Feb 1977 (asgnd)–; Kadena Hsg Anx, Kadena, unk (asgnd)–30 Nov 1977 (trsfd to the Japanese govt); Yomitan Anx, 1 mi S of Kurutake, unk (actvd)–30 Apr 1978 (trsfd to the Japanese govt); Chibana Comms Anx, Chibana, 15 Mar 1978 (asgnd)–; Kadena Village Ammo Dep, unk; Joint Explosive Ord Dep Anx, unk; Kina RR Anx, Kina, unk–15 Apr 1971 (lease cancelled); Torishima Bombing Rg (rdsgd Torishima Target Rg; Itazuke Bombing and Gunnery Rg; Torii Air Rg; Torishima Bombing and Gunnery Rg; Torishima Ryukyus Air Rg; Ryukyus Air Rg), Naha, unk.

AIR FORCE BASES OVERSEAS

Major Changes in Operational Capability: U.S. 7th Inf Div captured Kadena Afld on 1 Apr 1945, and artillery spotting aircraft began to use the field when the runway became serviceable on 6 Apr 1945; Army Air Forces engineers constructed new fuel tank farms, a new 6,500-ft bituminous runway, and a 7,500-ft runway for bomber aircraft by Aug 1945; Japanese forces in the Kadena area surrendered at the field to Lt Gen James H. Doolittle on 7 Sep 1945; field closed for resurfacing of runways, Sep–Oct 1945; in Oct 1945 the base suffered severe hurricane damage with some amphibious aircraft lying offshore destroyed; 100 hardstands completed for B–29 operations, late 1945; base improvements allowed for the support of tactical air units between 1945 and 1949 and instrument flying programs in 1950; base roads, quarters, runways, and base operations facilities renovated and enlarged, and the main runway lengthened to 12,000 ft, 1951–1953; Kadena became a fighter base in Nov 1954 with assignment of the 18th Ftr-Bmbr Wg; four hardened eight-bay Mace missile launch sites installed, 1961–1968; engineers completed first increment of a 500-unit family housing project in Aug 1964; base dedicated its largest housing project to date, Sebille Manor, in Sep 1965; 14 major construction projects, including hangar installations, dining halls, ammunition maintenance facilities, and an extensive arresting barrier system completed by mid-1967; base hosted a SAC refueling wing and several large tenant units from other MAJCOMs during late 1960s; U.S.-Japanese Reversion Agreement of 15 May 1972 returned the Ryukyus Islands to Japan and transferred several Kadena off-base installations to Japanese jurisdiction; responsibility for air defense of the Okinawa Air Defense Sector transferred to the Japanese Air Self-Defense Force on 1 Jul 1973; the USAF undertook a vast construction program of operational facilities under the Japanese Facilities Adjustment Program, including a taxiway, ground equipment building, and two hangars for the USN between 1973–1975; the Japanese Facilities Adjustment program also reduced U.S. presence on Okinawa, beginning 27 Jul 1973; other U.S.-Japanese agreements permitted Okinawans to farm unused portions of Kadena AB and some parts of its off-base installations beginning in Jul 1973; several operational facilities were shared with or transferred to the USN and USMC in 1975; the POL pipe line project from Chimuwan Bay completed in the fall of 1976; a 200-unit family housing facility for U.S. Navy families, several BOQs, EM quarters, and the expanded medical facility also accepted in 1976; functions performed by the U.S. Army, including the milk plant, laundry plant, all family housing on the island, the telephone exchanges, and consolidated servicing for civilian personnel transferred to the base during 1977; Okuma Recreation Center transferred from the Army in 1978; a number of older structures, including school buildings and warehouses returned to Japanese control 1979–1980; F–15 engine test stand and maintenance facilities for supporting F–15 operations completed 1980; the base converted from F–4D to F–15 aircraft and added an Airborne Warning and Control System (AWACS) squadron of E–3As during 1980; new facilities, including a commissary and primary school, 50 aircraft weather shelters, a large number of family housing units, and the first of many programmed hardened aircraft shelters completed 1981–1982.

Major Commands to Which Assigned: U.S. Tenth Army, 1 Apr 1945; Eighth AF, 16 Jul 1945; Pacific Air Comd, USA, 6 Dec 1945 (rdsgd FEAF, 1 Jan 1947; PACAF, 1 Jul 1957)–.

Major Changes in Status: None.

Units Assigned:

	1945		
1 Ftr Sq	c. 17 Nov 45–29 Jan 46	40 Bomb Sq	1 Jun 47–18 Oct 48
21 Ftr Sq	21 Nov 45–29 Jan 46	72 Air Svc Gp	7 Jun 47–20 Sep 48
34 Ftr Sq	c. 17 Nov 45–29 Jan 46	535 Air Svc Sq	7 Jun 47–20 Sep 48
46 Trp Carr Sq	18 Aug 45–21 Sep 45	579 Air Mat Sq	7 Jun 47–20 Sep 48
317 Trp Carr Gp	22 Aug 45–21 Sep 45	722 AF BU [HQ]	16 Dec 47–3 Jun 48
346 Stn Compl Sq	24 Sep 45–30 Nov 45		1948
347 Stn Compl Sq	c. 1 Aug 45–Dec 45	9 Comms Sq, AF	c. 8 Mar 48–20 Jan 49
413 Sig Co,		23 Recon Sq	15 May 48–16 Mar 49
Avn (13 Comms		29 Air VR Sq	19 May 48–24 May 48
Sq, Comd;		32 AB Gp	24 Aug 48–1 Apr 49
13 Comms		32 AP Sq	24 Aug 48–1 Apr 49
Sq, AF;		32 Base Svc Sq	24 Aug 48–1 Apr 49
13 Comms		32 Comms Sq	24 Aug 48–1 Apr 49
Sq, Div)	16 Aug 45–1 Oct 57	32 Comps Wg	24 Aug 48–1 Apr 49
430 AP Sq	1 Sep 45–1 Jun 53	32 Food Svc Sq	24 Aug 48–1 Apr 49
435 Bomb Sq	5 Aug 45–28 May 46	32 Instls Sq	24 Aug 48–1 Apr 49
437 Bomb Sq	2 Jul 45–21 Jul 45	32 Maint & Sup Gp	24 Aug 48–1 Apr 49
438 Bomb Sq	3 Jul 45–21 Jul 45	32 Maint Sq	24 Aug 48–1 Apr 49
439 Bomb Sq	2 Jul 45–21 Jul 45	32 MV Sq	24 Aug 48–1 Apr 49
440 Bomb Sq	2 Jul 45–21 Jul 45	32 Stn Med Gp	24 Aug 48–1 Apr 49
460 Avn Sq	24 Dec 45–15 May 46	32 Sup Sq	24 Aug 48–1 Apr 49
460 Bomb Sq	5 Aug 45–28 May 46	71 AB Gp	18 Aug 48–25 Oct 48
461 Bomb Sq	13 Aug 45–30 Jun 46	71 AP Sq	18 Aug 48–25 Oct 48
462 Bomb Sq	13 Aug 45–30 Jun 46	71 Base Svc Sq,	
463 Bomb Sq	13 Aug 45–30 Jun 46	Tac Recon	18 Aug 48–25 Oct 48
507 Bomb Sq	5 Aug 45–28 May 46	71 Comms Sq	18 Aug 48–25 Oct 48
989 Air Engrg Sq	24 Jul 45–18 Aug 48	71 Food Svc Sq	18 Aug 48–25 Oct 48
994 Air Mat Sq	23 Jul 45–18 Aug 48	71 Instls Sq	18 Aug 48–25 Oct 48
HQ & Base Svcs Sq,		71 Maint & Sup Gp	18 Aug 48–25 Oct 48
559 Air Svc Gp	20 Jul 45–18 Aug 48	71 Maint Sq,	
	1946	Tac Recon	18 Aug 48–25 Oct 48
349 Stn Compl Sq	15 Aug 46–30 Jun 48	71 Sup Sq	18 Aug 48–25 Oct 48
	1947	Adrm Gp [Prov],	
2 Emerg Rscu Sq		316 Bomb Wg	1 Jan 48–unk
(2 Rscu Sq)	31 Mar 47–4 May 50	Air Ammo Gp	
7 Adrm Sq	1 Jun 47–25 Mar 48	[Prov],	
11 Comms Sq, Comd	30 Mar 47–25 Mar 48	316 Bomb Wg	1 Jan 48–unk
15 Wea Sq	1 Jul 47–8 Aug 59	Sixth Area,	
24 Bomb Sq	1 Jun 47–18 Oct 48	6001 Counter	
25 Ln Sq	22 Apr 47–8 Sep 47	Intelligence Sq	
39 Bomb Sq	1 Jun 47–18 Oct 48	(Sixth Area,	
		6001 Sp	

Investigation Unit; Sixth Area, 6001 Sp Investigation Sq)	1 Sep 48–1 Mar 58
Thirteenth AF	1 Dec 48–16 May 49

1949

9 Air VR Sq (9 MV Rpr Sq)	15 Jun 49–8 Feb 55
31 Recon Sq (31 Strat Recon Sq)	16 Mar 49–c. 12 Jul 50
6332 AB Gp	1 Apr 49–1 Jun 53
6332 Comps Gp	1 Apr 49–20 Jul 49
6332 Finance Disbursing Unit	1 Apr 49–27 Dec 49
6332 Food Svc Sq	1 Apr 49–1 Jun 53
6332 Instls Sq	1 Apr 49–1 Jun 53
6332 Maint Sq	1 Apr 49–1 Jun 53
6332 Maint & Sup Gp	1 Apr 49–1 May 55
6332 MV Sq	1 Apr 49–1 Jun 53
6332 Stn Med Gp (6332 Med Gp)	16 Nov 49–1 Jun 53
6332 Sup Sq	1 Apr 49–1 Jun 53
Stn Med Gp (Prov) 6332	1 Apr 49–16 Nov 49
Twentieth AF	16 May 49–1 Mar 55

1950

2 Bomb Sq	c. 9 Jul 50–c. 30 Oct 50
13 Ammo Sup Sq, Dep	c. 1 Oct 50–12 Jan 51
19 Bomb Gp	5 Jul 50–1 Jun 53
28 Bomb Sq	5 Jul 50–14 May 54
30 Bomb Sq	1 Jul 50–16 May 54
93 Bomb Sq	1 Jul 50–18 May 54
6301 Rock Plant Co	5 May 50–25 Jun 51

1951

6307 Spt Sq	25 Feb 51–25 Oct 51
6332 Comms Sq	25 Jan 51–1 Feb 52

1952

33 Air Rscu Sq	14 Nov 52–14 Apr 55
34 Air Rscu Sq	14 Nov 52–8 Sep 54
307 Armnt & Elect Maint Sq	22 Jul 52–13 Nov 54
307 Bomb Wg	22 Jul 52–13 Nov 54
307 Fld Maint Sq	22 Jul 52–13 Nov 54
307 Prdc Maint Sq	22 Jul 52–13 Nov 54
370 Bomb Sq	22 Jul 52–13 Nov 54
371 Bomb Sq	22 Jul 52–13 Nov 54
372 Bomb Sq	22 Jul 52–13 Nov 54

1953

3 Mat Recovery Sq	13 Apr 53–31 Jan 54
4 Ftr-Intcpr Sq	18 Feb 53–25 Feb 54
11 Air Postal Sq	8 May 53–1 Jan 67
12 Avn Fld Dep Sq (12 Avn Dep Sq)	21 Sep 53–1 Oct 59
17 Comms Const Sq	10 Sep 53–1 Jan 59
19 AB Gp (9 Cmbt Spt Gp)	1 Jun 53–8 May 54
19 AP Sq	1 Jun 53–8 May 54
19 Armnt & Elect Maint Sq	1 Jun 53–5 Jun 54
19 Bomb Wg	1 Jun 53–14 May 54
19 Fld Maint Sq	1 Jun 53–5 Jun 54
19 Food Svc Sq	1 Jun 53–8 May 54
19 Instls Sq	1 Jun 53–8 May 54
19 MV Sq	1 Jun 53–8 May 54
19 Ops Sq	1 Jun 53–8 May 54
19 Prdc Maint Sq	1 Jun 53–5 Jun 54
19 Sup Sq	1 Jun 53–8 May 54
370 Bomb Sq	15 Aug 53–19 Nov 54
371 Bomb Sq	15 Aug 53–19 Nov 54
372 Bomb Sq	15 Aug 53–19 Nov 54
6332 AB Wg	1 Nov 53–1 May 55
6332 Fld Maint Sq	1 Sep 53–1 May 55
Armnt & Elect Maint Sq, 19, Prov	1 Mar 53–1 Jun 53

1954

3 Tac Spt Sq (3 Tac Dep Sq; 7 Tac Dep Sq; 400 Mun Maint Sq [Thtr])	1 Apr 54–
12 Ftr-Bmbr Sq	30 Oct 54–10 Nov 54
12 Ftr-Bmbr Sq	12 Dec 54–29 Jan 55
18 AB Gp	30 Oct 54–10 Nov 54
18 AB Gp	12 Dec 54–1 Oct 57
18 AP Sq	30 Oct 54–10 Nov 54
18 AP Sq	12 Dec 54–1 Oct 57
18 Comms Sq	30 Oct 54–1 Oct 57
18 Fld Maint Sq (18 Equip Maint Sq)	12 Dec 54–
18 Ftr-Bmbr Gp	30 Oct 54–1 Oct 57
18 Ftr-Bmbr Wg	30 Oct 54–10 Nov 54
18 Ftr-Bmbr Wg (18 Tac Ftr Wg)	12 Dec 54–
18 Food Svc Sq	30 Oct 54–1 Oct 57
18 Instls Sq (18 CE Sq)	30 Oct 54–1 Oct 57
18 Maint & Sup Gp	30 Oct 54–1 Oct 57
18 Maint Sq (18 Fld Maint Sq)	30 Oct 54–10 Nov 54
18 MV Sq	30 Oct 54–10 Nov 54
18 MV Sq (18 Trnsp Sq)	12 Dec 54–1 Oct 57
18 Sup Sq	30 Oct 54–10 Nov 54
18 Sup Sq	12 Dec 54–1 Oct 57
67 Ftr-Bmbr Sq	30 Oct 54–12 Dec 54
80 Ftr-Bmbr Sq	21 Oct 54–6 Aug 56
546 Ammo Sup Sq [Dep]	1 May 54–18 Dec 59

64

581 Abn Mat	
Assembly Sq	20 Oct 54–18 Sep 56
581 Air Resupply Gp	20 Oct 54–18 Sep 56
581 Air Resupply Sq	20 Oct 54–18 Sep 56
6332 AB Gp	8 May 54–1 May 55
6332 AP Sq	8 May 54–1 May 55
6332 Comms Sq	25 Nov 54–1 May 55
6332 Food Svc Sq	8 May 54–1 May 55
6332 Instls Sq	8 May 54–1 May 55
6332 MV Sq	8 May 54–1 May 55
6332 Ops Sq	8 May 54–25 Nov 54
6332 Sup Sq	8 May 54–1 May 55
6332 USAF Dispy	8 May 54–8 Dec 64
1955	
12 Ftr-Bmbr Sq	19 Feb 55–1 Sep 55
44 Ftr-Bmbr Sq	
(44 Tac Ftr Sq)	15 Jul 55–25 Apr 67
67 Ftr-Bmbr Sq	
(67 Tac Ftr Sq)	16 Feb 55–1 Jul 55
67 Ftr-Bmbr Sq	
(67 Tac Ftr Sq)	1 Oct 55–15 Dec 67
313 Air Div	1 Mar 55–1962
AACS Sq	
(1962 AACS Gp;	
1962 Comms Sq;	
1962 Comms Gp)	18 Feb 55–
6332 Tech Tng Sq	
[Survival]	1 Oct 55–1 Sep 57
6927 Scty Flt	
(6927 Scty Sq,	
Mobile)	8 May 55–7 Aug 58
Kadena Task Force,	
Prov	1 May 55–unk
1956	
15 Tac Recon Sq	18 Aug 56–
25 Ftr-Intcpr Sq	17 Jul 56–1 Aug 57
322 Trp Carr Sq	18 Sep 56–8 Dec 57
336 Ftr-Day Sq	7 Aug 56–8 Dec 57
1957	
2 RR Sq	1 Sep 57–20 Oct 59
5 Comms Gp	
(5 Comms &	
Con Gp)	1 Sep 57–20 Oct 59
24 Comms Const Sq	1 Sep 57–15 Apr 59
608 Comms Sq	1 Sep 57–20 Oct 59
6313 AB Wg	1 Oct 57–8 Dec 64
6313 AP Sq	1 Oct 57–8 Dec 64
6313 Comms Sq	1 Oct 57–1 Jul 59
6313 Food Svc Sq	1 Oct 57–5 Jan 61
6313 Instls Sq	
(6313 CE Sq)	1 Oct 57–8 Dec 64
6313 Ops Sq	
(6313 Spt Sq;	
6313 Svcs Sq)	1 Oct 57–8 Dec 64
6313 Sup Sq	
(6313 Mat Sq)	1 Oct 57–8 Jan 64
6313 Trnsp Sq	1 Oct 57–8 Dec 64

6318 Armnt &	
Elect Maint Sq	15 Mar 57–15 May 59
Fly Tng Sq, Prov	15 Oct 57–25 Mar 58
1958	
12 Ftr-Bmbr Sq	
(12 Tac Ftr Sq)	25 Mar 58–
1959	
18 Armnt & Elect	
Maint Sq	
(18 Avncs	
Maint Sq;	
18 Component	
Rpr Sq)	15 May 59–
605 Tac Con Sq	8 Apr 59–20 Oct 59
6902 Sp Comms Gp	27 Oct 59–1 Dec 59
6922 Radio Gp,	
Mobile	
(6922 Scty Wg)	15 Jan 59–1 Jul 65
1961	
498 Msl Maint Sq	8 Feb 61–8 Jul 65
873 Tac Msl Sq	8 Feb 61–8 Jul 65
874 Tac Msl Sq	8 Sep 61–8 Jul 65
1962	
18 Orgnzl Maint Sq	8 Sep 62–8 Jun 66
Orgnzl Maint Sq,	
Prov, 6018	1 Mar 62–8 Sep 62
1963	
418 Mun Maint Sq	8 Apr 63–1 Dec 73
6002 Standardization/	
Evaluation Gp	1 Feb 63–15 Nov 67
1964	
18 Sup Sq	8 Jan 64–1 Apr 68
824 AP Sq	8 Dec 64–30 Sep 74
824 CE Sq	8 Dec 64–30 Sep 74
824 Cmbt Spt Gp	8 Dec 64–30 Sep 74
824 Svcs Sq	8 Dec 64–30 Sep 74
824 Trnsp Sq	8 Dec 64–30 Sep 74
1966	
603 Mil Alft Spt Sq	8 Jan 66–
1967	
6990 Scty Sq	
(6990 Scty Gp;	
6990 Scty Sq;	
6990 Elect	
Scty Sq;	
6990 Elect	
Scty Gp)	15 Jul 67–
1968	
824 Sup Sq	1 Apr 68–30 Sep 74
1969	
19 Tac Elect	
Warfare Sq	15 May 69–31 Oct 70
1970	
376 Avncs Maint Sq	1 Apr 70–
376 Fld Maint Sq	1 Apr 70–
376 Mun Maint Sq	1 Apr 70–31 Dec 70
376 Orgnzl Maint Sq	1 Apr 70–

AIR FORCE BASES OVERSEAS

376 Strat Wg	1 Apr 70–
1971	
18 Orgnzl Maint Sq	
(18 Acft Gnrtn Sq)	24 Jan 71–
33 Aerosp Rscu &	
Recovery Sq	1 Jul 71–
44 Tac Ftr Sq	15 Mar 71–
67 Tac Ftr Sq	15 Mar 71–
909 Air Rflg Sq	1 Jul 71–
6011 RR Sq	1 Mar 71–30 Jun 74
USAF Dispy,	
Kadena	
(USAF Clinic,	
Kadena)	17 May 71–
1972	
1 Sp Ops Sq	15 Dec 72–1 Jan 81
90 Sp Ops Sq	15 Apr 72–15 Dec 72
1973	
18 Mun Maint Sq	1 Dec 73–1 Jun 77
345 Tac Alft Sq	1 Dec 73–1 Sep 75
1974	
18 CE Sq	30 Sep 74–31 Oct 76
18 Cmbt Spt Gp	30 Sep 74–
18 Scty Pol Sq	30 Sep 74–
18 Svcs Sq	30 Sep 74–

18 Sup Sq	30 Sep 74–
18 Trnsp Sq	30 Sep 74–
6928 Scty Sq	1 Jul 74–1 Feb 76
1975	
25 Tac Ftr Sq	19 Dec 75–1 Feb 81
1976	
18 CE Ops Sq	31 Oct 76–
18 CE Spt Sq	31 Oct 76–
6100 Logs Spt Sq	
(Tac AF Logs	
Spt Sq)	15 Jan 76–
1977	
418 Acft Gnrtn Sq	1 Jun 77–
6007 Sch Sq	1 Sep 77–15 Jul 79
Acft Gnrtn Sq,	
Prov, 6101	1 Jan 77–30 Jun 77
1978	
18 Tac Ftr Gp	1 May 78–11 Feb 81
1979	
961 Abn Warning	
& Con Spt Sq	
(961 Abn Warning	
& Con Sq)	1 Oct 79–
1981	
81 Tac Con Flt	1 Apr 81–

Keflavik Airport

Location: Located 5 mi SW of Keflavik, about 35 mi SW of Reykjavik, Iceland.

Name: Named after a town in Iceland.

Date of Current Name: 25 Oct 1946.

Previous Names: Reykjavik Adrm, 6 Aug 1941 (U.S. occupation); Meeks Fld, c. Jul 1942.

Date of Establishment: 1 Mar 1943.

Date Construction Began: 2 Jul 1942.

Date of Beneficial Occupancy: 24 Mar 1943.

Base Operating Units: 824th Engrg Bn, Avn, Feb 1942; 14th Det, North Atlantic Wg, Air Trpt Comd, 28 Aug 1943 (rdsgd Stn 14, North Atlantic Wg, Air Trpt Comd, 18 Oct 1943); 1386th AAF BU, 1 Aug 1944; OL 53, 1100th AAF BU, 25 Mar–7 Apr 1947. 1400th AB Gp, 23 May 1951; Iceland AD Force, 15 Jan 1954 (rdsgd Air Forces Iceland,* 1 Jan 1960)–.

Base Commanders: Col Charles W. Yuill (USA)[†] (also, Comdr, Keflavik Sector), 21 Jun 1942; Col Edward G. Sherburne (USA), 20 Jun 1943; Col James G. Pratt, 12 Aug 1943; Col Eugene F. Gillespie, 3 Jan 1944; Lt Col Hugh R. Gilchrist, 27 Sep 1944; Lt Col (later, Col) Ronald C. McLaughlin, 25 May 1945; Brig Gen Clinton B. Vincent, 19 Jan 1946; Col Ira D. Snyder, 29 Dec 1946–c. 7 Apr 1947. Col Andrew D. Moore, 23 May 1951; Lt Col Leonard A. Peterson, c. 1 Oct 1951; Col Marshall A. Elkins, c. 10 Jan 1952; Col J. C. Bailey, 3 Feb 1953; Col Salvatore E. Manzo, 23 Jul 1955; Col Richard W. Philbrick, 15 Mar 1957; Col Paul P. Douglas Jr, 7 Jun 1959; Col Benjamin J. Willis, 24 Jul 1959; Col Oscar B. Steely, 1 Jul 1961; Col August E. Weil, 14 Aug 1962; Col Alan G. Long, 25 Jul 1964; Col Richard H. Broach, 21 Jul 1966; Col Maurice D. Surratt, c. Jul 1968; Col Robert L. Sowers, 16 Jul 1969; Col Budd H. Butcher, 19 Jan 1971; Col Ewell D. Wainwright, c. May 1973; Col William E. Lindeman, 8 Jul 1975;

---

*Air Forces Iceland changed from host to tenant status on 1 Jul 1961, when the U.S. Navy gained jurisdiction; the installation was renamed U.S. Naval Station Keflavik, and Keflavik Airport became one of its tenants.

[†]The first two commanders of Keflavik were officers of the Army Ground Forces.

Col Leon W. Babcock Jr, 27 Jun 1977; Col Paul D. Wagoner, 7 Jul 1978; Col Gary K. Carroll, 29 Jun 1980; Col Jerry E. Smith, 24 Jul 1981–.

Major Off-Base and Detached Installations:* Keflavik/Broadstreet Tmtr Anx (rdsgd Broadstreet Tmtr Anx; Keflavik Tmtr Site; Broadstreet Globecom Anx), 4 mi SE of Keflavik, 1 Apr 1952; Keflavik FM Anx (rdsgd Keflavik/ Grindavik FM Anx; Grindavik FM Anx), Grindavik, 1 Apr 1952 (asgnd); Keflavik ILS OM Anx (rdsgd Keflavik OM Anx), 4 mi NNW of Keflavik, 1 Apr 1952 (asgnd); Keflavik/Sandgerdi RR Anx (rdsgd Keflavik RR Anx; Sandgerdi RR Anx; Sandgerdi RR Stn), 4 mi S of Sandgerdi, 1 Apr 1952 (asgnd); Reykjavik Billet Anx, Reykjavik, 1 Sep 1952 (asgnd); Hvalfjordur Scty Anx, 10 mi E of Akranes, 8 Jun 1953 (asgnd); H–1 AC & W Stn (rdsgd Keflavik AC & W Stn #1; Keflavik/H–1 AC & W Stn; Rockville AC & W Stn), 5 mi N of Keflavik, 1 Oct 1953 (asgnd); H–3 AC & W Stn (rdsgd Hofn ACW Stn; Hofn AC & W Stn), 7 mi E of Hofn, 8 Jun 1955 (asgnd); Ytri Njardvik Billet Bldg, 1 mi S of Keflavik, 9 Jun 1955 (asgnd)–7 Feb 1957 (dspd); Grindavik Globecom Anx, 1 mi NW of Grindavik, 14 Jun 1955 (asgnd); H–2 AC & W Site (rdsgd Keflavik AC & W Stn #2; Keflavik/H–2 AC & W Stn; Langanes ACW Stn), 11 mi NE of Thorshofn, 25 Oct 1955 (asgnd); H–4 AC & W Stn (rdsgd Keflavik/H–4 AC & W Stn; Latrar AC & W Stn), 25 mi N of Isafjord, 25 Oct 1955 (asgnd); Grindavik Forward Scatter Anx, 1 mi NW of Grindavik, 1 Nov 1955 (asgnd); Reykjavik Off Hsg Anx, Reykjavik, 1 Dec 1957 (asgnd)–30 Apr 1960 (dspd); Sandur Loran Bcn Anx, 3 mi W of Sandur, 18 Feb 1960.

Major Changes in Operational Capability: First runway completed Sep 1942; runway, control tower, and first hangar became operational Mar–May 1943; all major construction, including four 6,500-ft runways, completed Jul 1943; field served as refueling stopover for two-and four-engine aircraft on flights between U.S. and U.K. during 1943; base also became transit point for aircraft returning from the European Theater of Operations to the United States; runways lengthened slightly following World War II; U.S. flying operations phased down in preparation for transfer of the base to the Icelandic government at the end of 1946; the Office of Foreign Liquidation Commissioner, established on 16 Feb 1947, assisted in disposing of noncritical surplus equipment and supplies; all U.S. air activity ended on 11 Mar 1947; American Overseas Airlines, followed by Airport Overseas Corporation personnel, operated the military portion of Keflavik Fld after its reversion to Icelandic control at the end of Mar 1947; operation of Keflavik Aprt assumed by Military Air Transport

---

*All installations are located in Iceland and transferred to the U.S. Navy on 1 Jul 1961.

Service (MATS) following signing of a defense agreement between the United States and Iceland in May 1951; general rehabilitation project, chiefly construction of barracks, completed mid-1952; despite 50-plus knot winds, field served as refueling station along the Great Arctic Circle route starting 1953; main runway extended to 10,000 ft, taxiways completed, and aprons extended 1954; concrete surfaces upgraded, additional hangars constructed to accommodate an F–89 squadron, and two air rescue squadrons and TAC and SAC transient aircraft accommodated, 1955–1956; hangar, dormitories, operations building, and underground POL tanks accepted by USAF 1956–1957; retrenchment of USAF operations, including the reduction of F–89 and elimination of F–102 and SAC (tenant) activities occurred in 1959–1960; USAF assigned field to USN, which named it U.S. Naval Station Keflavik, although Keflavik Aprt remained a tenant USAF activity with one fighter-interceptor and two aircraft warning squadrons, on 1 Jul 1961; Keflavik Aprt supported the air defense interception and identification of non-NATO aircraft, mostly Soviet long-range bombers, that penetrated Iceland's military air defense identification zone after 1 Jul 1961; operation of the air terminal and hotel turned over to Icelandic Civil Aeronautics Administration and the Loftleidir Icelandic Airlines, 15 May 1962; major plumbing and electrical lines repaired, flight-line maintenance facilities and all roadways rebuilt, runway arresting barriers and night visibility markers installed, 1962–1965; airmen's dormitories and operations building renovated, and new dining hall constructed, 1966–1967; runways and major surfaced areas repaired, seven Butler-type aircraft ready shelters and an addition to base power plant built, runway approach lights for runway 21 and a BAK–12 aircraft arrester system installed, 1974–1975; extensive maintenance and repair of surfaced areas, 1976–1978; maintenance and repair of igloos at Patterson ramp completed, hangar 884 renovated, and flammable and munitions storage facilities constructed, 1979–1981.

Major Commands to Which Assigned: Iceland Base Comd, Feb 1942; European Thtr of Ops, USA (ETOUSA), 10 Jun 1942; Eastern Def Comd, USA, 30 Jul 1944; Air Trpt Comd, 1 Jan 1946–7 Apr 1947. Joint Task Force #109, 7 May 1951; Iceland Def Force, 6 Jul 1951; Mil Air Trpt Service, 1 Sep 1951;* ADC, 1 Jul 1962 (rdsgd Aerosp Def Comd, 15 Jan 1968); TAC, 1 Oct 1979–.

Major Changes in Status: Returned to Iceland on 7 Apr 1947; returned to joint Icelandic-USAF control, 23 May 1951.

---

*After 1 Jul 1961, the USAF MAJCOMs operated in a tenant status only.

Units Assigned:

1944	
1386 AAF BU	
(1386 AAF BU	
[FTS]; 1386 AAF	
BU [BC])	1 Aug 44–1 Mar 46
1946	
Iceland Base Comd	18 Feb 46–24 Mar 47
1951	
1400 AB Gp	23 May 51–1 Jul 60
1400 AB Sq	2 Jun 51–1 Oct 61
1400 AP Sq	2 Jun 51–1 Jul 60
1400 Instls Sq	
(1400 CE Sq)	2 Jun 51–1 Oct 61
1400 Maint &	
Sup Sq	
(1400 Mat Sq)	2 Jun 51–1 Mar 55
1400 Med Sq	
(1400 USAF	
Hosp)	2 Jun 51–1 Oct 61
1952	
20 WAF Sq	14 Sep 52–18 Sep 53
53 Air Rscu Sq	14 Nov 52–24 Mar 60
192 Ftr-Bmbr Sq	1 Sep 52–1 Dec 52
435 Ftr-Bmbr Sq	1 Dec 52–27 Mar 53
436 Ftr-Bmbr Sq	1 Dec 52–2 Dec 53
932 AC & W Sq	1 Oct 52–1 Aug 57
1953	
82 Ftr-Intcpr Sq	1 Apr 53–22 Oct 54
1400 Food Svc Sq	1 Feb 53–1 Jul 60
1400 Maint Sq	1 Feb 53–15 Jan 54
1400 MV Sq	

(1400 Trnsp Sq)	1 Feb 53–1 Oct 61
1400 Ops Sq	1 Feb 53–1 Jul 60
1400 Sup Sq	1 Feb 53–1 Oct 61
1954	
57 Ftr-Intcpr Sq	12 Nov 54–
HQ, Iceland Air	
Def Force	
(HQ, Air	
Forces Iceland)	1 Apr 52–
1955	
1400 Fld Maint Sq	
(1400 Consold	
Acft Maint Sq)	1 Mar 55–1 Jul 61
1400 Ops Gp	18 Dec 55–1 Jul 60
1956	
667 AC & W Sq	8 Aug 56–16 Apr 57
934 AC & W Sq	8 Sep 56–30 May 57
Keflavik Task	
Force, Prov	1 Jul 56–unk
1959	
1400 Maint &	
Sup Gp	1 May 59–1 Jul 60
1961	
1400 Spt Sq	1 Oct 61–1 Jul 62
1979	
960 Abn Warning	
& Con Spt Sq	
(960 Abn	
Warning &	
Con Sq)	1 Sep 79–

Kunsan Air Base

Location: Located 9 mi SW of Kunsan, about 120 mi S of Seoul, on the W coast of the Republic of Korea.

Name: Named after a town in the Republic of Korea.

Date of Current Name: Nov 1950.

Previous Names: Kunsan AB, K-8, 1946.

Date of Establishment: 1946.

Date Construction Began: Japanese commenced construction in 1938.

Date of Beneficial Occupancy: May 1951.

Base Operating Units:* 27th AB Gp, 1 Apr 1951; 931st Engr Avn Gp, May 1951; 3d AB Gp, 25 Aug 1951; 6170th AB Gp, 1 Sep 1954; 6170th AB Sq, 8 Apr 1956; 6175th AB Gp, 25 Mar 1959; 354th Cmbt Spt Gp, 1 Aug 1968; 6175th AB Gp, 15 Jun 1970; 3d Cmbt Spt Gp, 15 Mar 1971; 8th Cmbt Spt Gp, 16 Sep 1974-.

Base Commanders: Lt Col Lawrence W. Hall, 28 Apr 1951; Col Nils O. Ohman, c. 22 Aug 1951; Col Marshall R. Gray, 4 Mar 1952; Col Eugene B. LeBailly, 14 Aug 1952; Col Roger E. Phelan, 12 Aug 1953; Col William H. Matthews, 2 Feb 1954; Col Edwin A. Doss, 22 Feb 1954; Col William B. Reed, 2 Apr 1954; Col Homer C. Munson, 1 Aug 1954; Col Howard F. Bronson, 6 Aug 1954; Col Cecil P. Lessig, 10 Sep 1954; Col Homer C. Munson, 25 Oct 1954; Col Ormand J. Mosman, 1 May 1955; Col Roger W. Page, 11 Aug 1955; Maj Ervin J. Ludwig, 16 Jul 1956; Maj Clarence A. Jungman, 19 Aug 1956; Lt Col J. Mac Beall, 25 Nov 1956; Lt Col Joseph M. Matthews, 18 Mar 1957; Lt Col (later, Col) Harold C. Collins, 25 Aug 1957; Lt Col John W. Bohn Jr, 20 Jun 1958; Col Edward A. Jurgens, 8 Aug 1958; Lt Col Vincent A. Evers, 5 Jul 1959; Col John O. Moench, 14 Jul 1959; Col William J. Feallock II, 1 Sep 1959; Lt Col George R. Kauffman, 1960; Col Robert A. Sauer, 17 Oct 1960; Lt Col Roger D. Barton, 1 Jun 1961; Col Donnell Massey, 1 Aug 1961; Col Glen W. Thompson, 29 Jul

---

*The only USAF organizations at the field between V-J Day and the outbreak of the Korean conflict were those intermittently stationed detachments servicing USAF liaison aircraft for the U.S. Army Forces in Korea (1945-1948), the Provisional Military Advisory Group (1948), and the U.S. Military Advisory Group to the Republic of Korea (Jul 1949-1951).

1962; Col Charles E. Sullivan Jr, 1 Aug 1963; Col Carl M. Hillstrom, 2 Jul 1964; Col John J. LaRoche, 25 Jul 1965; Col Clower F. Ashley, 21 Sep 1966; Col Marvin R. Boothe, 29 Sep 1967; Col Henry W. Ritter, 17 Jul 1968; Col Allen W. Carver Sr, 29 Aug 1969; Col Ross M. Fountain, 5 Aug 1970; Lt Col Matthew E. Loar, 1 Apr 1971; Col Ross M. Fountain, 1 May 1971; Col Kenneth I. Gunnarson, 3 Sep 1971; Col Dwight W. Blanton, 24 Aug 1972; Lt Col Frederick C. Franklin, 15 Mar 1973; Col Lawrence E. Bortness, 3 May 1973; Col Robert H. Lee, 13 Oct 1973; Col Boyd W. Hensley, 7 Sep 1974; Col Eugene D. Levy, 9 Aug 1975; Col Paul C. Mathis, 31 Jul 1976; Col Eugene L. Vosika, 26 Jul 1977; Col Melvin P. Clarke, 21 Jul 1978; Lt Col Tom W. Brumfield Jr, 17 Mar 1979; Col Lester R. Terrell, 25 Jun 1979; Col Weston T. Smith, 1 Jul 1980; Col Wayne E. Clark, 23 Jun 1981; Lt Col Tatom A. Fisher, 24 Jun 1982; Col Wade S. Gatling, 9 Jul 1982–.

Major Off-Base and Detached Installations:* Taegu Radio Tmtr Anx (rdsgd Taegu Tmtr Anx), Taegu, 1 Sep 1950 (asgnd); Taegu Relay Anx (rdsgd Taegu RR Anx), 4 mi SE of Taegu, 5 May 1951 (asgnd); Naktong Bombing & Gunnery Rg, 3 mi SE of Sangu, 30 Sep 1951 (asgnd); Pochon Radar Anx (rdsgd Pochon Homer Bcn Anx), 1 mi NW of Pochon, 1 Oct 1952 (asgnd from Pohang AB)–unk; So-Hyongie Air Rg (rdsgd So-Hyongie Island Bombing & Gunnery Rg), 18 mi W of Chulpo-Ri, 23 Dec 1952 (actvd), 10 Mar 1958 (asgnd)–unk; Pohang Bore Site Anx (rdsgd Pohang Small Arms Rg Anx), 20 mi SE of Pohang, 1 Sep 1953 (asgnd); Cheju-Do Afld (rdsgd Cheju-Do Tacan Anx), 2 mi SE of Mosulpo, 26 Mar 1955 (asgnd); Cheju-Do Wea Stor (rdsgd Cheju-Do Wea Anx), 2 mi SE of Mosulpo, 26 Mar 1955 (asgnd); Kunsan Crash Boat Anx, Kunsan, 15 Apr 1955 (asgnd); Chain Homer Bcn Anx, Chain, 9 May 1956 (asgnd)–10 Jul 1957 (inactvd); Chinhae Homer Bcn Anx, 1 mi SE of Chinhae, 9 May 1956 (asgnd); Taegu AB, Taegu, 1 Oct 1978–1 Apr 1982 (trsfd to Osan AB); Kwang Ju AB, 15 Apr 1975 (asgnd)–.

Major Changes in Operational Capability:† North Korean troops occupied base 13 Jul–Oct 1950; 5,000-ft runway (later lengthened to 9,000 ft), taxiways, parking apron constructed Jul 1951; completion of basic facilities to accommodate an entire B–26 bomb wing and a USMC aviation squadron completed Apr 1952; F–84 operations began Jul–Aug 1952; flying operations sharply curtailed after wind down of Korean conflict in the spring of 1954; base accommodated periodic rotation of fighter and light bomber squadrons during mid-1950s; upgrading of taxiways and

---

*All installations are located in the Republic of Korea and transferred to Osan AB on 10 Mar 1958.
†For period up to Korean conflict see explanatory note on page 154.

construction of dormitories undertaken in 1957–1958; base hosted a U.S. Army Hawk missile battalion and a Korean AF F–86 squadron, and served as recurrent "safe haven" for typhoon-evacuated C–130s from Okinawa and Guam, 1965–1968; dispensary completed 7 May 1966; base population rose sharply and a command post established in wake of *USS Pueblo* crisis, spring 1968; POL pipe line connecting base with sea completed Apr 1968; additional revetments, bunkers, arresting barriers constructed and flight facilities updated, mid-1968; C–130s flying ECM missions along Korean demilitarized zone (DMZ) accommodated 1968–1969; plans for wind down of operational activities reversed when F–4s arrived from Japan, temporarily bolstering base's F–100 force, after a North Korean aircraft downed an EC–121 on 15 Apr 1969; host organization changed from F–100s to F–4s, 1969–1970; extensive runway rehabilitation began after reduction of flying activities in spring 1971; base population rose sharply preparatory to the arrival of an entire TAC fighter wing in Mar 1971; arrival of 3d Tac Ftr Wg provided Kunsan with greater USAF strike force in Apr 1971; extensive dormitory upgrading program completed and new accounting and finance building occupied Mar 1978; barrier ramp and concrete surfaces upgraded, passenger terminal enlarged mid-1979; elaborate bomb loading facility completed fall 1980; improved fuel storage facility in progress mid-1981; field readied to accommodate F–16s Sep 1981.

Major Commands to Which Assigned: Pacific Air Comd, 1946 (rdsgd FEAF, 1 Jan 1947; PACAF, 1 Jul 1957)–.

Major Changes in Status: U.S./Korean "acquisition agreement" of 1953 established USAF's right to operate the base.

Units Assigned:

1951		
3 AB Gp	25 Aug 51–1 Oct 54	
3 AP Sq	24 Aug 51–1 Oct 54	
3 Bomb Gp	22 Aug 51–1 Oct 54	
3 Bomb Wg	22 Aug 51–1 Oct 54	
3 Comms Sq	16 Aug 51–1 Oct 54	
3 Food Svc Sq	25 Aug 51–1 Oct 54	
3 Instls Sq	22 Aug 51–1 Oct 54	
3 Maint & Sup Gp	13 Aug 51–1 Oct 54	
3 Maint Sq	11 Aug 51–1 Oct 54	
3 MV Sq	14 Aug 51–1 Oct 54	
3 Sup Sq	13 Aug 51–1 Oct 54	
8 Bomb Sq	18 Aug 51–5 Oct 54	
13 Bomb Sq	c. 15 Aug 51–5 Oct 54	
27 AB Gp	1 May 51–24 Jun 51	
27 AP Sq	1 May 51–24 Jun 51	
27 Food Svc Sq	1 May 51–24 Jun 51	
27 Instls Sq	1 May 51–24 Jun 51	
90 Bomb Sq	21 Aug 51–5 Oct 54	
1952		
428 Ftr-Bmbr Sq	10 Jul 52–1 Apr 53	
430 Ftr-Bmbr Sq	10 Jul 52–16 Apr 53	

474 Ftr-Bmbr Gp	10 Jul 52–1 Apr 53
1953	
7 Ftr-Bmbr Sq	1 Apr 53–2 Nov 53
8 Ftr-Bmbr Sq	1 Apr 53–4 Nov 53
49 Ftr-Bmbr Gp	1 Apr 53–2 Nov 53
49 Ftr-Bmbr Wg	1 Apr 53–6 Nov 53
1954	
6170 AB Gp	1 Sep 54–8 Apr 56
6170 Mat Sq	20 Sep 54–8 Apr 56
6170 Spt Sq	20 Sep 54–8 Apr 56
6181 Tac Hosp	2 Dec 54–1 Jan 56
1955	
334 Ftr-Bmbr Sq	27 May 55–17 Jun 55
1956	
6043 USAF Dispy	1 Jan 56–1 Aug 68
6170 AB Sq	8 Apr 56–25 Mar 59
1959	
6175 AB Gp	25 Mar 59–1 Aug 68
6175 Fld Maint Sq	8 Aug 59–31 Oct 70
6175 Mat Sq	25 Mar 59–1 Aug 68
6175 Spt Sq	25 Mar 59–22 Sep 65

	1962	
6175 AP Sq		1 Apr 62–1 Aug 68
	1964	
6175 RR Sq		8 Jun 64–17 May 71
	1965	
6175 CE Sq		22 Sep 65–15 Mar 71
	1968	
354 CE Sq		1 Aug 68–15 Jun 70
354 Cmbt Spt Gp		1 Aug 68–15 Jun 70
354 Consold Acft Maint Sq		1 Dec 68–1 Dec 69
354 Fld Maint Sq		1 Aug 68–1 Dec 68
354 Scty Pol Sq		1 Aug 68–15 Jun 70
354 Svcs Sq		1 Aug 68–15 Aug 70
354 Sup Sq		1 Aug 68–1 Dec 68
354 Tac Ftr Wg		5 Jul 68–15 Jun 70
354 Tac Hosp (354 USAF Dispy)		1 Aug 68–15 Jun 70
354 Trnsp Sq		1 Aug 68–15 Jun 70
6354 Consold Acft Maint Sq		5 Jul 68–1 Aug 68
	1969	
6175 Avncs Maint Sq		8 Aug 69–31 Oct 70
6175 Muns Maint Sq		1 May 69–15 Mar 71
	1970	
54 Tac Ftr Sq		15 Jun 70–31 Oct 70
6043 USAF Dispy		15 Jun 70–15 Mar 71
6175 AB Gp		15 Jun 70–15 Mar 71
6175 SP Sq		15 Jun 70–15 Mar 71
	1971	
3 Avncs Maint Sq		15 Mar 71–16 Sep 74
3 CE Sq		15 Mar 71–16 Sep 74
3 Cmbt Spt Gp		15 Mar 71–16 Sep 74
3 Fld Maint Sq		15 Mar 71–16 Sep 74
3 Orgnzl Maint Sq		15 Mar 71–16 Sep 74
3 RR Sq		17 May 71–16 Sep 74
3 Scty Pol Sq		15 Mar 71–16 Sep 74
3 Svcs Sq		15 Mar 71–16 Sep 74
3 Sup Sq		15 Mar 71–16 Sep 74
3 Tac Ftr Wg		15 Mar 71–16 Sep 74
3 Trnsp Sq		15 Mar 71–16 Sep 74
7 Aerl Port Sq		30 Jun 71–1 Nov 73
35 Tac Ftr Sq		15 Mar 71–
36 Tac Ftr Sq		15 May 71–1 Sep 71
80 Tac Ftr Sq		1 Sep 71–
303 Mun Maint Sq		15 Mar 71–1 Dec 73
USAF Dispy, Kunsan (USAF Hosp, Kunsan)		17 May 71–
	1973	
3 Mun Maint Sq		1 Dec 73–16 Sep 74
	1974	
8 Avncs Maint Sq (8 Component Rpr Sq)		16 Sep 74–
8 CE Sq		16 Sep 74–
8 Cmbt Spt Gp		16 Sep 74–
8 Fld Maint Sq (8 Equip Maint Sq)		16 Sep 74–
8 Orgnzl Maint Sq (8 Acft Gnrtn Sq)		16 Sep 74–
8 Scty Pol Sq		16 Sep 74–
8 Svcs Sq		16 Sep 74–28 Feb 75
8 Sup Sq		16 Sep 74–
8 Tac Ftr Wg		16 Sep 74–
8 Trnsp Sq		16 Sep 74–
1982 Comms Sq		16 Sep 74–
6012 RR Sq		16 Sep 74–

Kwang Ju Air Base

Location: Located 8 mi SW of Kwang Ju, about 130 mi W of Pusan, Republic of Korea.

Name: Named after a city in the Republic of Korea. (Alternate designation Kwang Ju Afld K-57.)

Date of Current Name: 26 Dec 1968.

Previous Names: Kwang Ju Aux Afld, 30 Jun 1957; Kwang Ju Liaison Anx, 12 Jun 1963.

Date of Establishment: 3 Feb 1968.

Date Construction Began: Feb 1968.

Date of Beneficial Occupancy: Jun 1968.

Base Operating Units: Det, 6146th AF Advisory Gp, c. 1950–3 Feb 1968 (intermittently stationed, atchd to Korean AF); 6171st AB Sq, 3 Feb 1968; 107th Cmbt Spt Sq, 1 Aug 1968; 6171st Cmbt Spt Sq, 1 May 1969 (rdsgd 6171st AB Sq, 1 Jul 1975)–.

Base Commanders: Lt Col Hubert A. Kutsch, 3 Feb 1968; Lt Col Clarence R. Williams, 8 Oct 1968; Col Cecil N. Liles, c. Jun 1969; Col Ernest R. Wilson, 4 Jul 1969; Col Dale E. Borgen, 2 Jul 1970; Col William J. White, 7 Jul 1971; Lt Col Charles H. Davis IV, 13 Jul 1972; Col Francis J. Kramer Jr, 5 Aug 1973; Col Cary L. Broadway, 8 Aug 1974; Lt Col Edmund H. Crandall, c. Jun 1975; Lt Col Thomas E. Dayton, 15 Jun 1976; Lt Col Robert N. Harrington, 7 Jun 1977; Lt Col James M. Monsees, 31 Jul 1978; Lt Col Robert H. Custer, 10 Jul 1979; Lt Col Clifton T. Windham, 5 Jul 1980; Lt Col Eldon D. Henderson, 25 Jun 1981; Lt Col James H. Sledge, 14 Jun 1982–.

Major Off-Base and Detached Installations: None.

Major Changes in Operational Capability: The *USS Pueblo* crisis of Mar 1968 impelled the USAF to prepare facilities at Kwang Ju AB for a tactical fighter squadron; from 1970–1973 base accommodated rotating fighter squadrons deploying to the Far East and supported the COLLEGE EYE Task Force; no aircraft were assigned permanently at the base after 1972; base converted to a forward operating location in Apr 1973; concurrently, base experienced a drastic personnel reduction resulting in conversion to caretaker status on 1 Sep 1975; supported C-130 exercises and served as deployment site of USMC Harrier AV–8s and F–4s, and as a "safe haven" for hurricane-evacuated aircraft from various PACAF bases 1973–1974; base designated a deployment installation for "various forces" to support tactical missions of USAF and Allied units operating from or through Kwang Ju in the event of hostilities after 1976; Kwang Ju converted from caretaker status to a "readiness base," 1976–1977; facilities improved with completion of AGM–45 missile shop and storage area Jan 1977; facility and airfield improvement projects undertaken to support forces deploying to this "bare base," 1977–.

Major Commands to Which Assigned: PACAF, Feb 1968–.

Major Changes in Status: Republic of Korea AF owned and administered Kwang Ju, where it operated the 1st Ftr Wg (ROKAF); PACAF operated a portion as co-host and housekeeper; activated on 3 Feb 1968; assigned as off-base installation of Osan AB 26 Dec 1968; converted to a forward OL, Apr 1973; reduced to caretaker status on 1 Sep 1975; converted to a "readiness base" in 1977.

Units Assigned:

	1968		6171 Cmbt Spt Sq	
6171 AB Sq		3 Feb 68–1 Aug 68	(6171 AB Sq)	1 May 69–
	1969		6171 USAF Dispy	1 May 69–17 May 71

Lajes Field

Location: Located 10 mi NE of Angra do Heroismo, Terceira Isl, Azores Archipelago, about 2,300 mi E of New York, and about 1,000 mi W of Lisbon, Portugal.

Name: Named after a village in the Azores.

Date of Current Name: 15 Sep 1980.

Previous Names: Azores Air Trpt Stn, c. Jan 1943; Lagens Fld, 23 Jul 1949;* Lages Fld, 17 Nov 1950; Lajes Fld, 3 May 1953 (DAF GO), 24 Jun 1952 (MATS communication); Lajes AB, 11 Aug 1980.

Date of Establishment: 17 Jan 1944.

Date Construction Began: RAF personnel began readying facilities for U.S. occupancy, 8 Oct 1943; USAF construction personnel arrived 25 Aug 1944.

Date of Beneficial Occupancy: Jan 1944.

Base Operating Units:[†] Stn #15, North Atlantic Wg, 17 Jan 1944 (rdsgd Stn #15, North Atlantic Div, 28 Jul 1944); 1390th AAF BU, 1 Aug 1944; 1391st 1Y OL, 1 Nov 1945; 1391st AAF BU, 1 Sep 1946 (rdsgd 1391st AF BU, 26 Sep 1947); 523d AB Gp, 1 Jun 1948 (rdsgd 1605th AB Gp, 1 Oct 1948); 1605th AB Wg, 1 Feb 1953; 1605th AB Gp, 1 Nov 1967; 1605th AB Wg, 1 Jan 1975; 1605th AB Gp, 1 Jan 1982–.

Base Commanders: Lt Col Arthur F. Callahan, 11 Dec 1943; Col David A. Morris, 28 Dec 1943; Col (later, Brig Gen) Albert D. Smith, 24 Jan 1944; Lt Col (later, Col) Harry L. Putnam, 13 Oct 1944; Col Sigmund F. Landers, 17 Dec 1944; Col George O. Bond, 19 Jun 1945; Col Sam W. Agee, 16 Dec 1945; Col John W. Warren, 16 Mar 1947; Maj Robert C. Morris Jr, 1 Jun 1948; Col Joseph A. Wilson, 16 Jul 1948; Col George S. Cassady, 12 Jan 1950; Col (later, Brig Gen) Harold L. Smith, 1 Jul 1952;

---

*Azores Air Transport Station changed from an installation designation to an organization on this date.

[†]The field is within part of Air Base #4, owned and operated by the Portuguese Air Force. After 1942 PAF allotted part of it to the RAF and after 1945 also to USAAF. The RAF left in 1946 and the AAF (later, USAF) operated the base in tenancy status, sharing the runway and other facilities with the Portuguese hosts.

Brig Gen (later, Maj Gen) George B. Dany, 16 Aug 1958; Brig Gen Eugene B. LeBailly, 9 Aug 1961; Brig Gen George S. Boylan Jr, 6 Jan 1964; Brig Gen (later, Maj Gen) William H. Brandon, 19 Oct 1965; Brig Gen John H. Buckner, 17 Jul 1967; Col Thomas M. Glassburner, 1 Nov 1967; Col David M. Sweeney, 7 Aug 1969; Col Reynaldo A. Rodriguez, Aug 1971; Col George C. Pinyerd, 19 Jun 1973; Brig Gen Erskine Wigley, 1 Jan 1975; Brig Gen Richard T. Drury, 24 Oct 1977; Brig Gen Duane H. Erickson, 11 Jun 1980–.

Major Off-Base and Detached Installations:* Calderia Nav Aid Anx #1 (rdsgd Calderia Naval Maint & Stor Anx; Calderia Ammo Stor Anx), 1 mi NW of Lajes, 2 Feb 1948–; Fontinhas Water Well Anx #1 (rdsgd Fontinhas Water Sys Anx), 1 mi N of Fontinhas, 2 Feb 1948–; Fontinhas Water Well Anx #2, 1 mi N of Fontinhas, 2 Feb 1948–7 Mar 1967 (merged w/Fontinhas Water Sys Anx); Fontinhas Water Well Anx #3, 1 mi N of Fontinhas, 2 Feb 1948–7 Mar 1967 (merged w/Fontinhas Water Sys Anx); Juncal Nav Aid Anx, 1 mi NW of Praia da Victoria, 2 Feb 1948–21 Apr 1966 (dspd); Praia da Victoria Dock Anx, Praia da Victoria, 2 Feb 1948–; Praia da Victoria Fuel Stor Anx, Praia da Victoria, 2 Feb 1948–; Santa Maria Aprt (rdsgd Santa Maria Tacan Anx), 1 mi NW of Villa do Porto, Santa Maria Isl, 2 Feb 1948–unk; Villa Nova GLOBECOM Anx, 1 mi S of Villa Nova, 2 Feb 1948–; Agualva Nav Aid Anx (rdsgd Agualva Comms Anx), 1 mi E of Agualva, 16 Mar 1953–; Santa Maria Tacan Anx, 1 mi NW of Villa do Porto, Santa Maria Isl, 1954 (actvd)–28 Apr 1970 (dspd); Praia Ridge Nav Aid Anx #2 (rdsgd Praia Ridge Nav Anx #2; Cume da Praia RR Anx), 9 Feb 1954–; Cova das Cinzas Fuel Stor Anx #1 (rdsgd Cova das Cinzas Petrol Stor Anx), 2 mi SSW of Praia da Victoria, 1 Jun 1954–; Cova das Cinzas Fuel Stor Anx #2, 2 mi W of Praia da Victoria, 1 Jun 1954–7 Mar 1967 (merged w/Cova das Cinzas Petrol Prods Stor Anx); Cova das Cinzas Fuel Stor Anx #3, 1 mi WSW of Praia da Victoria, 1 Jun 1954–7 Mar 1967 (merged w/Cova das Cinzas Petrol Prods Stor Anx); Lajes Ammo Anx (rdsgd Agualva Mun Stor Anx), 4 mi NNE of Angra do Heroismo, 1 Jun 1954–; Praia Ridge Comms Anx (rdsgd Cume da Praia Comms Anx #1), 2 mi NNW of Praia da Victoria, 1 Jun 1954–7 Mar 1967 (merged w/Cume da Praia Tacan Anx #3); San Miguel RR Anx, 6 mi NW of Ponte Delgada, San Miguel Isl, 1 Jun 1954–unk; Santa Maria Fuel Stor Anx, 2 mi N of Villa do Porto, Santa Maria Isl, 14 Jul 1954–2 Jan 1964 (dspd); Caldeira Nav Aid Anx #3 (rdsgd Caldeira VOR Anx), 1 mi N of Lajes, 18 Aug 1954–; Santa Barbara Nav Aid Anx, 1 mi W of Santa Barbara, 19 Aug 1954 (asgnd)–30 Jun 1960 (dspd); Caldeira Nav Aid Anx

---

*All installations are located in the Azores Archipelago and unless otherwise noted are on Terceira Island. Initial dates are those of assignment.

#2 (rdsgd Caldeira Comms Fclty Anx #2), 1 mi N of Lajes, 10 Feb 1955–unk; Santa Maria Water Sup Anx, 3 mi NE of Villa do Porto, Santa Maria Isl, 15 Feb 1955–2 Jan 1964 (dspd); Caldeira Anx #4 (rdsgd Caldeira RB Anx), 1 mi N of Lajes, 2 Mar 1955–; Portella Nova Nav Aid Anx (rdsgd Portella Nova Nav Aid Anx #1; Portella Nova DF Anx), 2 mi NNW of Praia da Victoria, 25 Oct 1955–; Praia Ridge Nav Aid Anx #1 (rdsgd Cume da Praia Nav Aid Anx #1; Cume da Praia Tacan Anx), 5 mi WNW of Cume da Praia, 8 Apr 1957–; Portella Nova Nav Aid Anx #2 (rdsgd Portella Nova Radar Anx), 2 mi NNW of Praia da Victoria, 24 May 1957–; Graciosa RB Anx, Santa Cruz, Graciosa Isl, 19 Mar 1958–unk; Lajes Water Well #6, Lajes, 15 May 1958–unk; Lajes Water Well #4 (rdsgd Lajes Water Sys Anx), 1 mi SW of Lajes, 20 Sep 1958–; Lajes Water Well #5, 1 mi SW of Lajes, 20 Sep 1958–7 Mar 1967 (merged w/Lajes Water Sys Anx); Cabrito Fuel Stor Anx, Angra do Heroismo, 1 Aug 1960 (actvd)–.

Major Changes in Operational Capability: RAF engineers readied two 6,000-ft runways for U.S. occupancy, late 1943, both lengthened by U.S. units in 1944; base served as staging and refueling point for aircraft en route between Continental U.S., and the European-African-Middle East and China-Burma-India Theaters 1944–1945; main intercontinental flight operations shifted to Santa Maria Aprt (Santa Maria Isl) after it became operational, 15 May 1945, and these operations returned to Lajes in 1946; first dependents began arriving spring 1948; stopover operations, which declined following World War II, increased during Berlin Airlift 1948–1949; considerable construction activity including new barracks, family housing project, docks, power plant, transmitter site, and facilities to support SAC training missions and accommodate an Army transport terminal unit completed 1952–1953; new headquarters building occupied 1953; 300-bed hospital, maintenance hangars completed fall 1956; 15-hydrant fuel system, additional hangar, and upgrading of concrete surfaces completed spring 1956; Naval Air Facility established 18 Jan 1957; liquid fuel bulk storage facility completed spring 1958; major port and pier facilities, capable of direct ship-to-base POL delivery, completed early 1963; runway extension project completed Jul 1965; increased intercontinental nonstop flights caused traffic decline, and field became maintenance and overhaul center for C–118s and C–135s based at Rhein-Main, 1966–1967; with the reduction of USAF intercontinental flight staging operations, Lajes primarily supported flying activities of USN during late 1960s and early 1970s; Lajes' strategic importance reconfirmed in 1973 Arab-Israeli war, when base became key to resupply of Israel; a plan to assign base to USN cancelled 18 Jan 1974; runway upgraded Apr 1974–1976; extensive rehabilitation of parking ramp and other concrete areas finished 1980; 150-unit housing project completed 1981–1982.

Major Commands to Which Assigned: Air Trpt Comd, Jan 1944–1 Jun 1948; MATS, 1 Jun 1948 (rdsgd MAC, 1 Jan 1966)–.

Major Changes in Status: U.S.-Portuguese agreement provided for U.S. forces in Azores to act as technical advisers to British forces, 8 Oct 1943; U.S. and British forces returned operational control of military facilities to Portugal, with both governments retaining rights of transit for military aircraft and personnel, May 1946; U.S. granted military rights on Lajes Fld, Sep 1946; thereafter, rights periodically renewed and extended through international agreements.

Units Assigned:

1944		**1949**	
1390 AAF BU	1 Aug 44–1 Nov 45	1605 Instls Sq	
1946		(1605 CE Sq)	11 Jul 49–
1391 AAF BU		**1955**	
[HQ, Azores		Lajes Task	
Base Comd]		Force, Prov	1 May 55–unk
(1391 AAF BU		**1967**	
[HQ, Azores		1605 Sup Sq	8 Jan 67–
Air Trpt Stn];		1605 Trnsp Sq	8 Jan 67–
1391 AF BU)	1 Sep 46–3 Jun 48	**1970**	
1947		USAF Hosp, Lajes	13 Oct 70–
770 AAF BU		**1977**	
[140 AACS Sq]		1605 Scty Pol Sq	1 Jul 77–
(770 AF BU		**1982**	
[140 AACS Sq])	5 Jul 47–3 Jun 48	1605 AB Gp	1 Jan 82–
1948		1605 Mil Alft	
140 AACS Sq		Spt Sq	1 Jan 82–
(1936 AACS Sq;		1605 Mil Alft	
1936 Comms Sq)	1 Jun 48–	Spt Wg	1 Jan 82–

Lindsey Air Station

Location: Located in the NW part of the city of Wiesbaden, Federal Republic of Germany.

Name: Named in honor of Capt Darrel R. Lindsey, who received the Medal of Honor posthumously for heroism in aerial combat as a member of the 394th Bomb Gp, 9 Aug 1944. Capt Lindsey led a formation of 30 B–26 bombers in an attack on the strategically important L'Isle Adam railroad bridge over the Seine River.

Date of Current Name: 28 Nov 1958.

Previous Names: Installation formed from three contiguous base caserns: name unk, 1875–31 Mar 1897; Gersdorff *Kaserne*, 1 Apr 1897; Oranien *Kaserne*, 25 Sep 1909; Infanterie *Kaserne*, Nov 1909; complex called Schiersteiner *Kaserne* Displaced Persons' Camp No. 563 in Apr 1945; Camp Lindsey, 13 Nov 1946; Lindsey AB, 15 May 1954.

Date of Establishment: Established in 1875 as a German Army infantry barracks; occupied by the USA on 28 Mar 1945; established as an AAF installation on 13 Nov 1946 (confirmed 28 Feb 1947); established as a USAF installation on 18 Sep 1947.

Date Construction Began: Original construction by German Army, 1875–1876, with several buildings added 1907–1915; modern renovation, and construction work initiated under German Armed Forces contract in 1935; following World War II, U.S. restoration, renovation, and rehabilitation work undertaken in 1946.

Date of Beneficial Occupancy: Apr 1945.

Base Operating Units: Unk, 1875–Apr 1945; United Nations Relief and Rehabilitation Agency (UNRRA), Apr 1945; 501st Air Svc Gp, 1 Jun 1946; 7120th AB Gp, 1 Jul 1948 (rdsgd 7100th AB Gp, 1 Nov 1953; 7100th Spt Gp, 1 Jan 1958; 7101st AB Wg, 15 Nov 1959; 7101st AB Wg [USAFE Base Comd], 24 Nov 1964); 601st Cmbt Spt Gp, 1 Jun 1973; Det 5, 601st Cmbt Spt Wg, 1 Jan 1976; 7100th AB Gp, 1 Jul 1977–.

Base Commanders: Lt Col James T. Patterson, 1 Jun 1946; Lt Col Render D. Denson, 11 Jul 1948; Lt Col Frank D. B. G. Hutchins, 3 Jun 1949; Col Curtis I. Pullig, 5 Oct 1949; Lt Col Frank D. B. G. Hutchins, 12 May 1950; Lt Col John G. Taylor, 10 Sep 1951; Col James H. Starbuck, 9

Nov 1951; Col Robert H. Workman, 14 May 1952; Col John R. Ulricson, 9 Sep 1955; Col William B. David, 30 Jul 1957; Col Joseph F. Mooney, 15 May 1961; Col Harold P. Sparks, 29 Jul 1963; Col Gail L. Stubbs, 1965; Col Kendall S. Young, 16 Aug 1966; Col Norbert C. Treacy, 9 Jun 1967; Col Richard G. McKittrick, 2 Sep 1969; Col Warren T. Whitmire, 19 Jul 1971; Col David H. Finley, 14 Sep 1972; Col James R. Hyde, 1 Jun 1973; Col Louis D. Braun Jr, 17 Sep 1974; Col Robert E. Edge, 1 Jul 1977; Col George J. Vehrs, 9 Jun 1978; Col Lewis G. Vale, 6 Jun 1980–.

Major Off-Base and Detached Installations: * Schiersteiner Adm Ofc, Biebricherstrasse, Wiesbaden-Schierstein, 1 Apr 1978 (trsfd from Sembach AB)–; Wiesbaden Hosp, Wielandstrasse, Wiesbaden, 1 Apr 1978 (trsfd from Sembach AB)–.

Major Changes in Operational Capability: Prior to and during World War I the base served as a training camp for the German Army; hosted the German 80th and 87th Inf Regts after 1920; at the close of World War II provided barracks for various USA ground force units; Lindsey, without an airfield, was a barracks and administrative center for displaced persons under the direction of the United Nations Relief and Rehabilitation Administration (UNRRA), providing logistical support for this agency as well as for the American Red Cross in Germany, United States Air Forces in Europe, United States Forces European Theater, Office of Military Government, United States, and the War Crimes Commission from Apr 1945 to 13 Nov 1946; off-base installation of Wiesbaden AB from Nov 1946 to 1 Jul 1976, when Sembach AB assumed control of Lindsey; Lindsey achieved its greatest prominence between Dec 1953 and 14 Mar 1973 when it was host base for HQ Comd, USAFE; Lindsey assumed primary installation status under USAFE on 1 Oct 1977; provided support for various assigned and attached Air Force units in the Wiesbaden area since 1 Oct 1977.

Major Commands to Which Assigned: USAFE, 13 Nov 1946–.

Major Changes in Status: German Army barracks, 1875–1945; USA barracks, 28 Mar 1945; United Nations Relief and Rehabilitation Administration Displaced Persons Camp, Apr 1945; off-base installation of Wiesbaden AB, 13 Nov 1946; off-base installation of Sembach AB, 1 Jul 1976; primary installation under USAFE, 1 Oct 1977–.

Units Assigned:

	1946			1954
501 Air Svc Gp		1 Jun 46–8 Oct 48	7260 HQ Spt Sq	
	1948		(7260 Spt Sq	
7120 AB Gp		1 Jul 48–9 Oct 54	[Stat Svcs])	1 Mar 54–1 Jul 63

---

*All installations are located in the Federal Republic of Germany.

	1956	2063 Comms Sq	
7135 Sch Sq		(2063 Comms Gp;	
(7135 Sch		2063 Comms Sq)	1 Jul 62–
Gp [Gen		1966	
Education])	7 May 56–1 Jan 67	7225 Spt Sq	1 Jul 66–31 Mar 72
7170 Spt Gp	9 Nov 56–6 Aug 59	1972	
	1958	7102 Computer	
1892 AACS		Svcs Sq	1 Jan 72–15 Sep 73
Instls Sq	30 Jun 58–29 Oct 59	7113 Sp Activities	
7370 Flt Svcs Sq	15 Aug 58–1 Jan 70	Gp (7113 Sp	
	1959	Activities Sq)	1 Nov 72–
7230 Spt Sq	20 Feb 59–1 Dec 59	1973	
7230 USAF Disp	20 Feb 59–1 Dec 59	7012 Computer	
	1960	Svcs Flt	15 Sep 73–
1157 Tech Ops Sq		1975	
[Central Fld Ofc]	1 Jul 60–27 May 63	1836 Elect Instls Sq	1 Oct 75–
7231 Spt Sq	1 Jul 60–28 Sep 60	1977	
7260 Spt Gp		7100 AB Gp	1 Jul 77–
(7260 Spt Sq)	1 Jul 60–15 Feb 73	1981	
	1962	6910 Elect Scty Wg	1 Jul 81–

Misawa Air Base

Location: Located adjacent to the city of Misawa, 3 mi W of the Pacific Ocean on northern Honshu Island, 10 mi SW of Towada, 18 mi NW of Hachinohe City, and 425 mi N of Tokyo, Japan.

Name: Named after the city of Misawa, Aomori-ken Prefecture, Honshu, Japan.

Date of Current Name: 12 Nov 1949.

Previous Names: Unk, 1870–1939; Misawa Imperial Japanese Naval AB, 10 Feb 1942; Misawa AAB, Sep 1945.

Date of Establishment: Established as Imperial Japanese Cavalry Stud Farm in 1870; at outbreak of war in Manchuria in 1931, established as Imperial Japanese Cavalry Tng Cen; established as Imperial Japanese Naval AB, 10 Feb 1942; established as USAAF base, Sep 1945; established as USAF base, 4 Nov 1947.

Date Construction Began: Minor construction, 1870–1930; construction as Cavalry Tng Cen for Japanese Army 1931–1933; construction for Japanese Naval AB began 1939; U.S. reconstruction began in 1945.

Date of Beneficial Occupancy: Japanese Army, 1870–1939; Japanese Naval AF, 17 Mar 1942; USAAF occupancy began Sep 1945.

Base Operating Units: Unk, 1870–1945; 32d Army Engrg Const Gp, Sep 1945; 49th AB Wg, 18 Aug 1948; 6163d AB Wg, 1 Dec 1950; 116th Ftr-Bmbr Wg, 2 Nov 1951; 6016th AB Wg, 10 Jul 1952; 49th Ftr-Bmbr Wg, 18 Nov 1953; 49th AB Gp, 15 Apr 1957; 6139th AB Gp, 15 Oct 1957; 439th Cmbt Spt Gp, 8 Jan 1964; 475th AB (475th Cmbt Spt) Gp, 15 Jan 1968; 6122d AB Gp, 15 Mar 1971; 6920th AB Sq (6920th AB Gp), 1 Jul 1972; 6112th AB Wg, 1 Oct 1978–.

Base Commanders: Capt Davis K. Stark, Sep 1945; Col Louis R. Hughes Jr, Dec 1946; Col Brooks A. Lawhon, Apr 1948; Col Jack S. Jenkins, 22 Apr 1950; Brig Gen George E. Price, 27 Feb 1951; Col George R. Stanley, 1 Nov 1951; Col George W. Pardy, 14 Aug 1952; Col John P. Randolph, 24 May 1954; Col Thomas C. Conroy, May 1956 (temp); Col Elbert Helton, 14 Aug 1956; Col Charles L. Stafford, 15 Apr 1957; Col Donald A. Baccus, 1 Jun 1959; Col Vic L. Byers Jr, Jul 1961; Col Jesse L. Harris, 1 May 1962; Col Eric Linhof, 6 Jul 1964; Col Clifford G. Long,

May 1966 (temp); Col Oliver B. Bucher Jr, 3 Aug 1966; Col James B. Argersinger, 1 Jul 1967 (temp); Col Anthony W. Monaco Jr, 10 Aug 1967; Col John W. Bogan, 29 Aug 1969; Col Edward H. Aune, 6 Aug 1970; Lt Col David T. Kuntz, 1 Jul 1972 (actg); Col Nathan J. Hirsh, 26 Jul 1972; Lt Col David T. Kuntz, 26 Jun 1973 (actg); Lt Col Clarence G. Knight, 10 Jul 1973 (actg); Col Robert D. Edgren, 9 Aug 1973; Lt Col John Forrester, 7 May 1976; Col Howard J. Bear, 29 Sep 1978; Col Stephen L. Sutton, 18 Dec 1979; Col Harry K. Rogers Jr, 14 Jun 1982–.

Major Off-Base and Detached Installations:* Ominato Aux Afld, 3 mi SW of Ominato, Nov 1945–Oct 1950 (inactvd); Wakkanai RR Anx, Sep 1946–19 Jun 1953 (inactvd); Matsumae Loran Bcn Anx, 2 mi W of Matsumae-Machi, 1 Oct 1950–14 Jun 1954 (inactvd); Nemuro AS, Nemuro, 16 Oct 1952–13 May 1960 (inactvd); Bihora Aux Afld (rdsgd Bihora #2 Afld; Bihora Air Strip), 2 mi SSW of Memanbetsu, Nov 1952–24 Jul 1958 (trsfd to Japanese govt); Ominato Aux Afld (rdsgd Ominato Liaison Anx), 17 Nov 1953–; Kamo AS, 20 mi NW of Funagawa-shi, Aug 1954–22 May 1959 (dspd); Misawa/Tomari AC & W Stn (rdsgd Tomari AS; Tomari Liaison Anx), Jun 1955–; Kawai Relay Anx (rdsgd Kawai RR Anx), 4 mi NNE of Matrushima, 15 Nov 1956–31 Mar 1958 (dspd); Kurosaki AC & W Site (rdsgd Misawa/Yamada AC & W Stn; Yunijin-Yama AS), 6 mi N of Yamada, 1 Aug 1957–22 Sep 1959 (trsfd to Japanese govt); Asoiwayama AS (used jointly with Japanese Air Self-Defense Force [JASDF], 6 mi NNE of Tobetu-Machi, 27 Mar 1958–18 Jan 1960 (trsfd to Japanese govt); Bikuni RR Anx, 5 mi S of Bikuni-cho, 27 Mar 1958 (trsfd from Chitose AB)–; Crawford Svc Anx, Sapporo, 27 Mar–19 Jun 1958 (trsfd to Dept of the Army); Abashiri AS (rdsgd Abashiri Shoran Bcn Anx), 4 mi NNW of Abashiri-shi, 1 Apr 1958 (trsfd from Chitose AB)–; Chitose AB (rdsgd Chitose Aux Afld; Chitose AS), 1 mi S of Chitose, 1 Apr 1958–15 May 1974 (trsfd to Japanese govt); Erimosaki AS, 1 Apr 1958 (trsfd from Chitose AB)–17 Oct 1958 (trsfd to Japanese govt); Mashuko RR Anx, 1 Apr 1958 (trsfd from Chitose AB)–; Matsumae Loran Bcn Anx, 1 Apr 1958 (trsfd from Chitose AB)–; Nemuro AS, 1 Apr 1958 (trsfd from Chitose AB)–; Numanohata Homing Bcn Anx, 25 mi WSW of Tomakomai-shi, 1 Apr 1958 (trsfd from Chitose AB)–5 Aug 1958 (trsfd to Japanese govt); Obiri RR Anx, 8 mi S of Rumov-shi, 1 Apr 1958 (trsfd from Chitose AB)–; Otaru Adm Anx, Otaru, 1 Apr 1958 (trsfd from Chitose AB)–21 Apr 1958 (trsfd to Japanese govt); Rumoi AS, 1 Apr 1958 (trsfd from Chitose AB)–7 Apr 1958 (trsfd to Japanese govt); Shakubetsu RR Anx, 1 Apr 1958 (trsfd from Chitose AB)–; Shimamatsu Air Rg, 7 mi SSE of Sapparo-shi, 1 Apr 1958 (trsfd from Chitose AB)–1 Apr 1959 (trsfd to

---

*All installations are located in Japan.

Japanese govt); Teshio RR Anx, 1 Apr 1958 (trsfd from Chitose AB)−; Tomanae RR Anx, 1 Apr 1958 (trsfd from Chitose AB)−; Toyoni-Dake RR Anx, 6 mi NE of Horoizumi-Machi, 1 Apr 1958 (trsfd from Chitose AB)−; Wakkanai AS, 2 mi NNW of Wakkanai-shi, 1 Apr 1958 (trsfd from Chitose AB)−; Wakkanai Air Strip, 2 mi ESE of Koitoi, 1 Apr 1958 (trsfd from Chitose AB)−28 Dec 1959 (trsfd to Japanese govt); Fukagawa RR Anx, 1 Jul 1958 (trsfd from Chitose AB)−22 Sep 1959 (trsfd to Japanese govt); Misawa Tacan Anx, 12 Jun 1963−; Shiraoi Comms Site, Shiraoi, 19 Jun 1967 (actvd)−28 Jan 1971 (trsfd to Japanese govt); Memoisli Comms Site, 15 Mar 1970 (actvd)−15 May 1974 (trsfd to Japanese govt); Amagamori Air Rg, unk−1 Jun 1972 (trsfd to USN).

Major Changes in Operational Capability: In 1870 the Japanese Emperor established a stud farm for the household cavalry in the area that later became Misawa AB, and kept his own (Tenno Heika) cavalry there until 1931, when the Sino-Japanese conflict required their use in China; Misawa remained a training center for Japanese Cavalry until the Japanese Army constructed the first runway at Misawa for military aircraft in 1938; the Imperial Japanese Navy began construction of a base for long-range bombers in 1939; by early 1941 the Gensan Flying Corps trained at Misawa, and the 22d Imperial Naval Air Wg assumed control of the base on 10 Feb 1942; the Misawa area was heavily damaged (base 90 percent destroyed) in the latter part of World War II, and Misawa had to be almost completely reconstructed by occupying U.S. forces; the USA commenced work in Feb 1945; E-W concrete runway added 1948; operational use of the base began on 31 Mar 1948; a number of fighter, fighter-interceptor, fighter-bomber, reconnaissance and support units operated from Misawa AB between 1950 and 1971; parallel taxiways finished, 1954; the first Japanese Air Self-Defense Force (JASDF) unit arrived at Misawa in Oct 1954, and the Japanese Northern Air Defense Force began operations from Misawa in 1957; as early as 1953 units of the USAF Security Service (USAFSS) were stationed at Misawa; 1,500-ft extension added to E-W runway in 1958; the USN controlled all U.S. flight line facilities, and the JASDF controlled its own flight lines and the airspace over Misawa after 1 Oct 1978; base hosted various Allied exercises in the region and provided support for 13 AF Associate units, 14 Department of Defense agencies, and the JASDF units stationed in the Misawa area between 1 Oct 1978 and Sep 1982.

Major Commands to Which Assigned: FEAF, Sep 1945; Pacific Air Comd, USA, 6 Dec 1945; FEAF, 1 Jan 1947; PACAF, 1 Jul 1957; USAFSS, 1 Jul 1972; PACAF, 1 Oct 1978−.

Major Changes in Status: None.

AIR FORCE BASES OVERSEAS

Units Assigned:

1946	
613 AC & W Sq	15 Jul 46–6 Jan 57
1948	
7 Ftr Sq	
(7 Ftr-Bmbr Sq;	
7 Ftr-Bmbr Sq,	
Jet Propelled;	
7 Ftr-Bmbr	
Sq, Jet)	2 Apr 48–14 Aug 50
8 Ftr Sq	
(8 Ftr-Bmbr Sq;	
8 Ftr-Bmbr Sq,	
Jet Propelled;	
8 Ftr-Bmbr	
Sq, Jet)	2 Apr 48–30 Jun 50
9 Ftr Sq	
(9 Ftr-Bmbr Sq;	
9 Ftr-Bmbr Sq,	
Jet Propelled;	
9 Ftr-Bmbr	
Sq, Jet)	2 Apr 48–27 Jun 50
49 AB Gp	18 Aug 48–1 Dec 50
49 Base Svc Sq,	
Ftr, Jet	18 Aug 48–10 Feb 50
49 Comms Sq	18 Aug 48–1 Dec 50
49 Ftr-Bmbr Gp	31 Mar 48–c. 23 Jan 50
49 Ftr Wg	
(49 Ftr-Bmbr Wg)	18 Aug 48–1 Dec 50
49 Food Svc Sq	18 Aug 48–1 Dec 50
49 Instls Sq	18 Aug 48–1 Dec 50
49 Maint & Sup Gp	18 Aug 48–1 Dec 50
49 Maint Sq, Ftr, Jet	
(49 Maint Sq)	18 Aug 48–1 Dec 50
49 MV Sq	18 Aug 48–1 Dec 50
49 Stn Med Gp	
(49 Med Gp)	18 Aug 48–1 Dec 50
49 Sup Sq	18 Aug 48–1 Dec 50
601 Air Engrg Sq	2 Apr 48–20 Aug 48
609 Air Mat Sq	2 Apr 48–20 Aug 48
794 AF BU	
[164 AACS Sq]	48–3 Jun 48
6113 All Wea Flt	18 Aug 48–10 Apr 49
HQ & Base Svcs Sq,	
385 Svc Gp	31 Mar 48–20 Aug 48
1950	
41 Ftr-Intcpr Sq	6 Sep 50–20 Feb 51
6163 AB Gp	1 Dec 50–1 Jan 52
6163 AB Wg	1 Dec 50–2 Nov 51
6163 AP Sq	1 Dec 50–2 Nov 51
6163 Comms Sq	1 Dec 50–2 Nov 51
6163 Food Svc Sq	1 Dec 50–2 Nov 51
6163 Instls Sq	1 Dec 50–2 Nov 51
6163 Maint Sq	1 Dec 50–2 Nov 51
6163 Maint & Sup	
Gp (6163 Maint	
& Sup Sq)	1 Dec 50–1 Jan 52

6163 Med Gp	
(6163 Med Sq)	1 Dec 50–1 Apr 52
6163 MV Sq	1 Dec 50–2 Nov 51
6163 Sup Sq	1 Dec 50–2 Nov 51
1951	
40 Ftr-Intcpr Sq	25 May 51–1 Jul 51
56 Strat Recon Sq	21 Feb 51–15 Sep 51
511 AC & W Gp	25 Aug 51–15 Mar 55
847 AC & W Sq	25 Aug 51–15 Mar 55
6013 Ops Wg	
[Northern Area]	2 Nov 51–1 Mar 52
6163 Base Svc Sq	2 Nov 51–1 Jan 52
1952	
27 Armnt & Elect	
Maint Sq	9 Oct 52–20 Jan 53
27 Fld Maint Sq	9 Oct 52–20 Jan 53
27 Ftr-Esct Wg	
(27 Strat Ftr Wg)	9 Oct 52–20 Jan 53
27 Prdc Maint Sq	9 Oct 52–20 Jan 53
31 Armnt & Elect	
Maint Sq	20 Jul 52–11 Oct 52
31 Fld Maint Sq	20 Jul 52–11 Oct 52
31 Ftr-Esct Wg	20 Jul 52–11 Oct 52
31 Prdc Maint Sq	20 Jul 52–11 Oct 52
38 Air Rscu Sq	14 Nov 52–18 Sep 57
39 Air Div	1 Mar 52–15 Jan 68
307 Ftr-Esct Sq	20 Jul 52–11 Oct 52
308 Ftr-Esct Sq	20 Jul 52–11 Oct 52
309 Ftr-Esct Sq	20 Jul 52–11 Oct 52
474 AB Gp	10 Jul 52–1 Apr 53
474 AP Sq	10 Jul 52–1 Apr 53
474 Comms Sq	10 Jul 52–1 Apr 53
474 Food Svc Sq	10 Jul 52–1 Apr 53
474 Instls Sq	10 Jul 52–1 Apr 53
474 Maint &	
Sup Gp	10 Jul 52–1 Apr 53
474 Maint Sq	10 Jul 52–1 Apr 53
474 MV Sq	10 Jul 52–1 Apr 53
474 Sup Sq	10 Jul 52–1 Apr 53
524 Ftr-Esct Sq	9 Oct 52–20 Jan 53
6016 AB Sq	
(6016 AB Wg)	1 Jan 52–18 Nov 53
6016 Maint Sq	1 Aug 52–1 Apr 53
1953	
8 Ftr-Bmbr Sq	4 Nov 53–10 Dec 57
12 Armnt & Elect	
Maint Sq	15 May 53–10 Aug 53
12 Fld Maint Sq	15 May 53–20 Jun 53
12 Prdc Maint St	15 May 53–10 Aug 53
12 Strat Ftr Wg	15 May 53–10 Aug 53
31 Armnt & Elect	
Maint Sq	11 Nov 53–12 Feb 54
31 Fld Maint Sq	11 Nov 53–12 Feb 54
31 Prdc Maint Sq	11 Nov 53–12 Feb 54
31 Strat Ftr Wg	11 Nov 53–12 Feb 54
49 AB Gp	1 Apr 53–10 Dec 57

49 AP Sq	1 Apr 53–10 Dec 57
49 Comms Sq	1 Apr 53–10 Dec 57
49 Ftr-Bmbr Wg	7 Nov 53–10 Dec 57
49 Food Svc Sq	1 Apr 53–24 Oct 57
49 Instls Sq	1 Apr 53–10 Dec 57
49 Maint & Sup Gp	1 Apr 53–10 Dec 57
49 Maint Sq (49 Fld Maint Sq)	1 Apr 53–10 Dec 57
49 Med Gp (49 Tac Hosp)	1 Apr 53–10 Dec 57
49 MV Sq (49 Trnsp Sq)	1 Apr 53–10 Dec 57
49 Sup Sq	1 Apr 53–10 Dec 57
83 Bomb Sq	15 Aug 53–10 Sep 53
307 Strat Ftr Sq	11 Nov 53–12 Feb 54
309 Strat Ftr Sq	11 Nov 53–12 Feb 54
457 Strat Ftr Sq	15 Aug 53–5 Nov 53
462 Ftr Sq	15 Aug 53–5 Nov 53
466 Strat Ftr Sq	8 Feb 53–5 May 53
506 Fld Maint Sq	15 Aug 53–5 Nov 53
506 Ftr-Esct Wg	15 Aug 53–15 Nov 53
506 Prdc Maint Sq	15 Aug 53–8 Nov 53
508 Armnt & Elect Maint Sq	7 Feb 53–5 May 53
508 Fld Maint Sq	17 Feb 53–5 May 53
508 Prdc Maint Sq	17 Feb 53–5 May 53
560 Strat Ftr Sq	15 May 53–10 Aug 53
586 Strat Ftr Sq	8 Feb 53–5 May 53

1954

4 Ftr-Intcpr Sq	1 Aug 54–20 Jun 65
12 Armnt & Elect Maint Sq	12 May 54–11 Aug 54
12 Fld Maint Sq	12 May 54–11 Aug 54
12 Prdc Maint Sq	12 May 54–12 Aug 54
12 Strat Ftr Wg	12 May 54–11 Aug 54
16 Ftr-Intcpr Sq	Jul 54–1 Aug 54
336 Ftr-Intcpr Sq (336 Ftr-Bmbr Sq; 336 Ftr-Day Sq)	19 Nov 54–7 Aug 56
407 Armnt & Elect Maint Sq	8 Aug 54–8 Nov 54
407 Fld Maint Sq	13 Aug 54–10 Nov 54
407 Prdc Maint Sq	11 Aug 54–26 Oct 54
466 Strat Ftr Sq	16 Feb 54–16 May 54
468 Strat Ftr Sq	16 Feb 54–16 May 54
508 Armnt & Elect Maint Sq	16 Feb 54–16 May 54
508 Fld Maint Sq	16 Feb 54–16 May 54
508 Prdc Maint Sq	16 Feb 54–16 May 54
515 Strat Ftr Sq	10 Aug 54–10 Nov 54
517 Ftr-Bmbr Sq	15 Aug 54–8 Nov 54
559 Strat Ftr Sq	12 May 54–11 Aug 54
560 Strat Ftr Sq	12 May 54–12 Aug 54
6038 USAF Hosp	2 Dec 54–8 Jan 64

1955

45 Tac Recon Sq	3 Mar 55–
6921 Radio Sq, Mobile (6921 Radio Gp, Mobile; 6921 Scty Wg)	8 May 55–31 Mar 70

1956

7 Ftr-Bmbr Sq	7 Aug 56–c. 30 Jun 57

1957

49 Ftr-Bmbr Gp	1 Jun 57–10 Dec 57
334 Ftr-Day Sq	1 Jul 57–8 Dec 57
418 Ftr-Day Sq	10 Dec 57–25 Mar 58
6139 AB Gp	15 Oct 57–8 Jan 64
6139 AP Sq	15 Oct 57–8 Jan 64
6139 Comms Sq	15 Oct 57–1 Jul 58
6139 Fld Maint Sq	15 Oct 57–1 Jul 58
6139 Food Svc Sq	15 Oct 57–18 Sep 60
6139 Instls Sq (6139 CE Sq)	15 Oct 57–8 Jan 64
6139 Ops Sq (6139 Spt Sq)	15 Oct 57–8 Jan 64
6139 Sup Sq (6139 Mat Sq)	15 Oct 57–8 Jan 64
6139 Trnsp Sq	15 Oct 57–18 Sep 60

1958

21 Armnt & Elect Maint Sq	1 Jul 58–8 Jan 64
21 Fld Maint Sq	1 Jul 58–8 Jan 64
416 Ftr-Bmbr Sq (416 Tac Ftr Sq)	25 Mar 58–15 Jun 64
531 Tac Ftr Sq	1 Jul 58–8 Jan 64
613 AC & W Sq	6 Jan 58–8 Sep 60
Fl Tng Wg [Prov]	18 May 58–1 Jul 58
6989 Radio Sq, Mobile (6989 Scty Sq)	1 Jul 58–1 Oct 64

1962

21 Orgnzl Maint Sq	8 Sep 62–8 Jan 64
Orgnzl Maint Sq, Prov, 6021	1 Mar 62–8 Sep 62

1963

421 Mun Maint Sq	8 Apr 63–8 Jan 64

1964

439 Armnt & Elect Maint Sq	8 Jan 64–8 Sep 66
439 CE Sq	8 Jan 64–15 Jan 68
439 Cmbt Spt Gp	8 Jan 64–15 Jan 68
439 Fld Maint Sq	8 Jan 64–8 Sep 66
439 Mun Maint Sq	8 Jan 64–8 Apr 65
439 Orgnzl Maint Sq	8 Jan 64–8 Jan 66
439 Scty Pol Sq	8 Jan 64–15 Jan 68
439 Svcs Sq	8 Jan 64–15 Jan 68
439 Sup Sq	8 Jan 64–15 Jan 68
439 Trnsp Sq	8 Jan 64–15 Jan 68
439 USAF Hosp	8 Jan 64–15 Jan 68
6139 Mat Sq	12 Jun 64–8 Sep 66
6989 Spt Sq	

(6921 Spt Sq)	1 Oct 64–31 Mar 70	Maint Sq	24 Jan 71–15 Mar 71
1965		6112 AB Gp	15 Mar 71–1 Jul 72
356 Tac Ftr Sq	29 Nov 65–15 May 71	6122 CE Sq	15 Mar 71–15 Oct 71
612 Tac Ftr Sq	3 Nov 65–15 Mar 71	6122 Svcs Sq	15 Mar 71–1 Aug 71
1966		6122 Sup Sq	15 Mar 71–1 Aug 71
439 Consold Acft		6122 USAF Hosp	15 Mar 71–17 May 71
Maint Sq	8 Sep 66–15 Jan 68	Consold Acft	
1967		Maint Sq,	
67 Tac Ftr Sq	15 Dec 67–15 Mar 71	Prov, 6122	15 Mar 71–1 Aug 71
1968		USAF Hosp,	
391 Tac Ftr Sq	22 Jul 68–28 Feb 71	Misawa	15 May 71–
475 AB Wg	15 Jan 68–15 Mar 71	**1972**	
475 Avncs Maint Sq	1 Dec 68–15 Mar 71	6920 AB Sq	
475 CE Sq	15 Jan 68–15 Mar 71	(6920 AB Gp)	1 Jul 72–1 Oct 78
475 Cmbt Spt Gp	15 Jan 68–15 Mar 71	**1974**	
475 Consold Acft		6920 Scty Gp	1 Jul 74–1 Oct 78
Maint Sq	15 Jan 68–1 Dec 68	**1976**	
475 Fld Maint Sq	1 Dec 68–15 Mar 71	6920 Scty Wg	1 Feb 76–1 Oct 78
475 Mun Maint Sq	1 Dec 68–15 Mar 71	**1977**	
475 Scty Pol Sq	15 Jan 68–15 Mar 71	6920 CE Sq	1 Nov 77–1 Oct 78
475 Svcs Sq	1 Dec 68–15 Mar 71	**1978**	
475 Sup Sq	15 Jan 68–15 Mar 71	6112 AB Wg	1 Oct 78–
475 Trnsp Sq	15 Jan 68–15 Mar 71	6112 CE Sq	1 Oct 78–
1970		6920 Scty Sq	
16 Tac Recon Sq	16 Mar 70–15 Feb 71	(6920 Elect	
6921 Scty Gp		Scty Gp)	1 Oct 78–
(6921 Scty Wg)	1 Apr 70–1 Feb 76	**1979**	
1971		2114 Comms Sq	1 Feb 79–
475 Orgnzl			

Osan Air Base

Location: Located 4.7 mi SW of Osan-Ni, 40 mi S of Seoul, Republic of Korea. (Part of base covers "Hill 180," site of a bloody USA bayonet charge during the Korean conflict.)

Name: Named after a town in the Republic of Korea.

Date of Current Name: 18 Sep 1956.

Previous Names: Osan-Ni (K−55) AB, Nov 1951.

Date of Establishment: Nov 1951.

Date Construction Began: Aug 1952.

Date of Beneficial Occupancy: Dec 1952.

Base Operating Units: 841st Engr Avn Bn, 24 Jun 1952; 18th AB Gp, 27 Dec 1952; 6171st AB Wg, 1 Nov 1954; 58th AB Gp, 18 Mar 1955; 6314th AB Gp, 8 Nov 1957 (rdsgd 6314th AB Wg, 25 Mar 1959); 6316th AB Gp, 20 Jul 1961; 6314th Spt Wg, 1 Jul 1964; 51st AB Wg, 1 Nov 1971; 51st Cmbt Spt Gp, 30 Sep 1974−.

Base Commanders: Unk, Aug−26 Dec 1952; Col John C. Edwards, 27 Dec 1952; Col Amos F. Riha, 9 May 1953; Col Andrew F. Gordon, 23 Jun 1953; Col Kermit D. Messerschmitt, 27 May 1954; Col Neil A. Newman, 1 Nov 1954; Col Richard T. Carlisle, 2 Dec 1955; Col Clifford D. Nash, 13 Jun 1956; Col Wayne E. Rhynard, 1 Aug 1956; Col Frederick W. Searles, 1 Aug 1957; Col Walter J. Wilson, 29 May 1958; Col Robert W. Springfield, 11 Jun 1958; Col Owen F. Clarke, 23 Jul 1958; Col James H. Starbuck, 24 Jul 1959; Lt Col Robert H. Farrell, 15 May 1961; Col John D. Bridges, 27 Jul 1961; Col Francis B. Howes Jr, 7 Dec 1961; Col Milton C. Barnard II, c. Jan 1962; Col Benjamin T. Chapman, Jul 1963; Col John R. Wilbraham, Jul 1964; Col Raymond M. Gehrig, 22 Jun 1965; Col Thomas B. Summers, 30 Jun 1966; Col Bestow R. Rudolph, Nov 1966; Col Lewis S. Beall, 21 Aug 1967; Col William J. Cook, 15 Aug 1968; Col Cecil N. Liles, 23 Jul 1969; Col Robert L. Collie, 25 Sep 1969; Col Frank J. Behan, 26 Jun 1970; Col Hewitt E. Lovelace Jr, 7 Jul 1971; Col John H. Allison, 1 Aug 1972; Col Billie J. Norwood, 7 Jun 1973; Col Alonzo L. Ferguson, 1 May 1974; Col Charles M. Summers, 15 Feb 1975; Col Gordon D. Alldredge, 7 Feb 1976; Col Robert C. Hess, 1 Feb 1978; Col Charles J. Corey, 15 Jul 1978; Col Dennis J. O'Brien, 7 Jul 1980; Col Charles D. Link, 2 Jul 1982−.

Major Off-Base and Detached Installations:* Suwon Ammo Stor Stn (rdsgd Suwon Ammo Stor Anx), 2 mi S of Suwon, Nov 1952 (asgnd)–20 Dec 1957 (trsfd to ROK); Hoeng-Song RB Anx (K–46), 4 mi SSW of Hoeng-Song, 18 May 1954 (actvd)–23 Sep 1957 (trsfd to ROK); Anyang Sig Maint Anx (rdsgd Anyang-Ni Comms Maint Anx; Anyang-Ni Comms Anx), 1 mi NNE of Anyang, 9 May 1956 (trsfd from Kimpo AB)–30 Jun 1958 (inactvd); Cheju-Do Tacan Anx, 2 mi SE of Mosulpo, 10 Mar 1958 (trsfd from Kunsan AB)–19 Jun 1958 (trsfd to Itazuke AB, Japan); Cheju-Do Weather Stn Anx, 2 mi SE of Mosulpo, 10 Mar 1958 (trsfd from Kunsan AB)–19 Jun 1958 (trsfd to Itazuke AB); Chinch On-Ni AC & W Stn, 1 mi N of Chinch On-Ni, unk; Chinhae RB Anx, 1 mi SE of Chinhae, 10 Mar 1958 (trsfd from Kunsan AB)–5 Jan 1969 (trsfd to ROK); Kangnung AS (rdsgd Kangnung Ln Anx), 4 mi SE of Kangnung, 10 Mar 1958 (trsfd from Kimpo AB)–unk; Kangnung Aux AB, 1 mi S of Kamdong-Ni, 10 Mar 1958 (trsfd from Kimpo AB)–4 Mar 1959 (inactvd); Kangnung RR Anx, 1 mi S of Hanjibu-Ri, 10 Mar 1958 (trsfd from Kimpo AB)–31 Dec 1959 (trsfd to ROK); Kimpo AB (rdsgd Kimpo AC & W Stn), 2 mi WNW of Kimpo, 10 Mar 1958 (trsfd from Kimpo AB)–unk; Kimpo/Seoul AS, 10 mi WNW of Seoul, 10 Mar 1958 (trsfd from Kimpo AB)–unk; Kimpo-Songjong-Ni AC & W Stn, 1 mi E of Songjong-Ni, 10 Mar 1958 (trsfd from Kimpo AB–unk; Kongsa-Ri Air Rg, 1 mi SE of Kongsa-Ri, unk–30 Jan 1958 (trsfd to ROK); Koon-Ni Air Rg, 1 mi NNW of Koon-Ni, 10 Mar 1958 (trsfd from Kimpo AB)–unk; Kwangchow-Ni RR Anx, 2 mi NNE of Kwangchow-Ni, 10 Mar 1958 (trsfd from Kimpo AB)–unk; Ligsungchon-Ni RR Anx, 1 mi SE of Ligsungchon-Ni, 10 Mar 1958 (trsfd from Kimpo AB)–1 Jul 1960 (trsfd to Dept of the Army); Naktong Bomb & Gnry Rg, 3 mi SE of Sanju, 10 Mar 1958 (trsfd from Kunsan AB)–30 Jun 1960 (trsfd to ROK); Ok-ku Myun Bomb & Gnry Rg, 4 mi SW of Ok-ku Myun, 10 Mar 1958 (trsfd from Kunsan AB)–17 May 1958 (trsfd to ROK); Osan-Ni Antiaircraft Anx (rdsgd Osan-Ni Antiaircraft Artillery Anx #3), 5 mi S of Osan-Ni, 10 Mar 1958 (trsfd from Kimpo AB)–unk; Osan-Ni Bomb & Gnry Rg, 10 Mar 1958 (asgnd)–unk; Osan-Ni Comms Anx #1, 5 mi SSW of Osan-Ni, 10 Mar 1958 (asgnd)–unk; Osan-Ni Comms Anx #2, 5 mi SSW of Osan-Ni, 10 Mar 1958 (asgnd)–2 Apr 1962 (trsfd to Dept of the Army); Osan-Ni Comms Anx #3, 5 mi SSW of Osan-Ni, 10 Mar 1958 (asgnd)–1 Jan 1962 (trsfd to ROK); Osan-Ni RR Anx #1, 6 mi SSE of Osan-Ni, 10 Mar 1958 (asgnd)–unk; Osan-Ni RR Anx #2, 5 mi SSE of Osan-Ni, 10 Mar 1958 (asgnd)–unk; Pochon RB Anx, 1 mi W of Pochon, 10 Mar 1958 (trsfd from Pohang AB)–unk; Pochon Water Sys Anx, 1 mi SE of Pochon, 10 Mar 1958 (trsfd from Phang AB)–15 Sep 1960 (trsfd to ROK); Pohang Small

---

*All installations are located in the Republic of Korea.

Arms Rg, 6 mi SE of Pohang, 10 Mar 1958 (trsfd from Pohang AB)–unk; Seoul Aux AB, 2 mi SW of Seoul, 10 Mar 1958 (asgnd)–unk; Seoul Hsg Anx, Seoul, 10 Mar 1958 (asgnd)–1 Aug 1958 (trsfd to ROK); So-Hyongie Air Rg, 18 mi W of Chulpo-Ri, 10 Mar 1958 (trsfd from Kunsan AB)–unk; Sokpong-Ni RR Anx, 3 mi SE of Sokpong, 10 Mar 1958 (asgnd)–unk; Sonjong-Ni AS, Songjong-Ni, 10 Mar 1958 (asgnd)–31 Mar 1960 (trsfd to Dept of the Army); Songjong-Ni Wea Stn Anx, 1 mi E of Songjong-Ni, 10 Mar 1958 (asgnd)–31 Oct 1958 (trsfd to Dept of the Army); Sosa Tng Anx, 3 mi NNE of Sosa, 10 Mar 1958 (asgnd)–8 Feb 1960 (trsfd to ROK); Suwon Aux Afld, 4 mi S of Suwon, 10 Mar 1958 (asgnd in inactive status)–3 Feb 1968; Tachwanggyo-Ri Petrol Prods Stor Anx, 1 mi SSW of Tachwanggyo-Ri, 10 Mar 1958 (asgnd)–unk; Taegu AB (K–2), 3 mi NNE of Taegu, 10 Mar 1958 (trsfd from Kunsan AB)–unk; Taegu Comms Anx, Taegu, 10 Mar 1958 (trsfd from Kunsan AB)–unk; Taegu RR Anx, 4 mi SE of Taegu, 10 Mar 1958 (asgnd)–21 May 1960 (trsfd to ROK); Tae-So Air Rg, Tae-So, 10 Mar 1958 (asgnd)–unk; Tokchok-To RR Anx, 27 mi WSW of Inchon, 10 Mar 1959 (asgnd)–unk; Tunpo-Ri Air Stn, 1 mi NE of Tunpo-Ri, 10 Mar 1958 (asgnd)–unk; Yongdong-Po Trnsp Anx, Yongdong-Po, 10 Mar 1958 (asgnd)–1 Apr 1961 (trsfd to Dept of the Army); Pohang RR Anx, 9 mi SE of Pohang, unk–20 Apr 1958 (trsfd to ROK); Pyong Taek Aux AB, 8 mi NE of Pyong Taek, unk–15 May 1958 (trsfd to Dept of the Army); Taeyonpyong RR Anx, Taeyonpyong, 1 Jul 1959 (asgnd)–unk; Changam-Ni RR Anx, 5 mi SSE of Changam-Ni, 5 Feb 1960 (trsfd to ROK); Kwang Ju Liaison Anx, 28 Aug 1963 (asgnd)–unk; Kwang Ju AB, 26 Dec 1968 (asgnd)–unk; Suwon AB, 26 Dec 1968 (asgnd)–30 Sep 1972 (inactvd); Taegu AB, 26 Dec 1968 (asgnd)–1 Oct 1978 (trsfd to Kunsan AB); Chakpyang Comms Site, 9 mi SE of Hasangok-Ni, 1 Oct 1971 (asgnd)–13 Jul 1973 (trsfd to Dept of the Army); Chowan Comms Anx, 15 mi SW of Ipchong-Ni, 25 Nov 1971 (asgnd)–26 Jun 1973 (trsfd to ROK); Inchon Stor Anx, Inchon, 25 Mar 1977 (asgnd)–30 Nov 1977 (trsfd to Dept of the Army); Changsan RRS, Changsan, 20 Nov 1978 (asgnd)–; Taegu AB, 1 Apr 1982 (trsfd from Kunsan AB)–.

Major Changes in Operational Capability: Osan AB is the only USAF facility within the Republic of Korea built by the United States during the Korean conflict; 9,000-ft runway completed Nov 1952; Republic of Korea relocated four villages, allowing the USAF to acquire 1,250.5 acres for expansion of the Osan base 1952; hosted 18th Ftr-Bmbr Wg and several units flying F–51s and F–86s during Korean conflict; a fifth Korean village relocated to enlarge the Osan (K–55) compound area for the arrival of Fifth AF Headquarters in 1953; Fifth AF maintained an advanced headquarters at Osan AB until activation of the 314th Air Div in 1954; Osan AB retained on standby status and hosted only temporary duty or transient units involved in tactical operations for PACAF, 1954–1957, during which time some of the facilities and structures at Osan fell into disrepair; concrete base surfaces restored in 1957 and base renovated as regular peacetime permanent installation in 1958; F-100s hosted at Osan late 1950s; replaced by F-105s in 1962-1963; new control tower for base completed 5 Jan 1966, and elaborate fence, alarm and security system completed to thwart thievery in Feb 1966; spectrometric oil analysis lab completed 1967; *USS Pueblo* seizure by North Korea prompted an increase in forces at Osan, including arrival of 6,500,000 lbs of cargo and 1,000 additional personnel, Jan-Mar 1968; F-106s joined F-105s to reinforce USAF and ROKAF F-5 complements, 1968-1969; new base operations building completed 15 Jan 1970 and main runway rehabilitated Oct 1971; new and modernized base headquarters complex and additional dormitories completed early 1974; base-wide housing and dormitory construction projects, new and renovated, accomplished 1974-1975; 26 aircraft shelters and revetments for arrival of F-111, F-15, and A-10 aircraft completed 1977-1979; taxiway/runway overhaul project finished 1978; tactical air control center opened 1981.

Major Commands to Which Assigned: FEAF, Nov 1951 (rdsgd PACAF, 1 Jul 1957)-.

Major Changes In Status: Active, 27 Dec 1952; standby status, 1954-1956; activated as primary installation, 9 May 1956.

Units Assigned:

	1951	503 Tac Con Gp	25 Jan 54-1 Oct 57
6147 AB Sq	25 Apr 51-1 Nov 54	601 Comms Sq	11 Jan 54-13 Oct 55
	1952	605 Tac Con Sq	25 Jan 54-8 Apr 59
18 AB Gp	27 Dec 52-30 Oct 54	611 Comms Sq	11 Jan 54-13 Oct 55
18 AP Sq	27 Dec 52-30 Oct 54	1246 AACS Sq	
18 Comms Sq	27 Dec 52-30 Oct 54	(2146 Comms Sq;	
18 Food Svc Sq	27 Dec 52-30 Oct 54	2146 Comms Gp)	15 Jul 54-
18 Ftr-Bmbr Wg	26 Dec 52-30 Oct 54	6147 Mat Sq	30 Oct 54-3 Mar 55
18 Instls Sq	27 Dec 52-30 Oct 54	6148 Tac Con	
18 MV Sq	27 Dec 52-30 Oct 54	Sq [Air]	20 Oct 54-3 Mar 55
18 Sup Sq	27 Dec 52-30 Oct 54	6149 Tac Con	
	1953	Sq [Air]	20 Oct 54-1 Mar 55
12 Ftr-Bmbr Sq	11 Jan 53-30 Oct 54	6154 AB Gp	28 Feb 54-20 Aug 54
18 Ftr-Bmbr Gp	11 Jan 53-30 Oct 54	6157 Ops Sq	1 Jan 54-3 Oct 55
18 Maint Sq	12 Feb 53-30 Oct 54	6171 AB Gp	1 Nov 54-18 Mar 55
67 Ftr-Bmbr Sq	11 Jan 53-30 Oct 54	6171 AB Wg	1 Nov 54-15 Mar 55
6154 Base Svc Sq	1 Oct 53-16 Mar 54	6171 AP Sq	1 Nov 54-18 Mar 55
6154 Maint &		6171 Food Svc Sq	1 Nov 54-18 Mar 55
Sup Sq	1 Oct 53-16 Mar 54	6171 Instls Sq	1 Nov 54-18 Mar 55
	1954	6171 Maint &	
2 Comms Sq,		Sup Gp	1 Nov 54-18 Mar 55
Ops (2 Comms		6171 MV Sq	1 Nov 54-18 Mar 55
Sq, Div)	11 Jan 54-1 Oct 57	6171 Sup Sq	1 Nov 54-18 Mar 55
2 RR Sq	11 Jan 54-13 Oct 55	6171 Tac Hosp	1 Nov 54-18 Mar 55
5 Comms Gp	10 Jan 54-13 Oct 55	6174 Mat Sq	
10 Air Postal Sq	25 Feb 54-8 Feb 55	(6171 Fld	
10 Ln Sq	28 Jan 54-15 Mar 55		
30 Wea Sq	25 Jan 54-9 May 57		

Maint Sq)	20 Oct 54–18 Mar 55
Fifth AF	25 Jan 54–1 Sep 54
1955	
36 Ftr-Bmbr Sq	3 Feb 55–10 Feb 55
58 AB Gp	15 Mar 55–8 Nov 57
58 AP Sq	15 Mar 55–8 Nov 57
58 Comms Sq	15 Mar 55–8 Nov 57
58 Fld Maint Sq	15 Mar 55–1 Jul 58
58 Food Svc Sq	15 Mar 55–8 Nov 57
58 Ftr-Bmbr Gp	15 Mar 55–8 Nov 57
58 Ftr-Bmbr Wg	
(58 Tac Ftr	
Tng Wg)	15 Mar 55–15 Oct 69
58 Instls Sq	15 Mar 55–8 Nov 57
58 Maint & Sup Gp	15 Mar 55–8 Nov 57
58 MV Sq	
(58 Trnsp Sq)	15 Mar 55–8 Nov 57
58 Sup Sq	15 Mar 55–8 Nov 57
69 Ftr-Bmbr Sq	9 Mar 55–1 Jul 58
310 Ftr-Bmbr Sq	
(310 Tac Msl Sq)	19 Mar 55–25 Mar 62
311 Ftr-Bmbr Sq	7 Apr 55–1 Jul 58
314 Air Div	15 Mar 55–7 Nov 78
334 Ftr-Bmbr Sq	1 Mar 55–10 Mar 55
335 Ftr-Bmbr Sq	2 Feb 55–27 Feb 55
607 Comms Sq, Ops	21 Feb 55–13 Oct 55
HQ, Korean Air	
Div, Prov [314]	1 Mar 55–15 Mar 55
1956	
6045 USAF Hosp	1 Jan 56–17 May 71
1957	
6122 AC & W Gp	1 Oct 57–18 Oct 58
6314 AB Gp	
(6314 Spt Wg;	
6314 AB Wg)	8 Nov 57–1 Nov 71
6314 AP Sq	
(6314 Scty Pol Sq)	8 Nov 57–1 Nov 71
6314 Comms Sq	8 Nov 57–1 Jul 59
6314 Food Svcs Sq	8 Nov 57–25 Mar 59
6314 Instls Sq	
(6314 CE Sq)	8 Nov 57–1 Nov 71
6314 Ops Sq	
(6314 Fld Maint	
Sq; 6314 Consold	
Acft Maint Sq)	8 Nov 57–1 Nov 71
6314 Sup Sq	8 Nov 57–1 Nov 71
6314 Trnsp Sq	8 Nov 57–1 Nov 71
1958	
58 Comms &	
Guidance Sq	15 Jul 58–25 Mar 62
58 Spt Sq	15 Jul 58–8 Jul 60
58 Tac Msl Gp	15 Jul 58–25 Mar 62
6053 Radio Flt,	
Mobile	6 Mar 58–25 Jun 64
6929 Radio Sq,	
Mobile	
(6929 Scty Sq)	1 Oct 58–1 Apr 64

1959	
6314 Spt Sq	
(6314 Svcs Sq)	25 Mar 59–1 Nov 71
1961	
6316 AB Gp	20 Jun 61–8 Sep 64
1967	
6314 Mun Maint Sq	1 Jun 67–1 Nov 71
1968	
557 CE Sq	30 Aug 68–10 Dec 69
603 Direct Air	
Spt Sq	15 May 68–15 Jan 72
6060 Direct Air	
Spt Sq	15 Apr 68–1 Sep 68
Aerosp Rscu &	
Recovery Sq,	
Prov, 1646	9 Feb 68–8 Aug 68
Comms Sq,	
Prov, 2072	24 May 68–1 Oct 68
Far East	
Comms Region	
ADVON, Prov	19 Feb 68–1 Aug 68
1970	
6903 Scty Sq	
(6903 Elect	
Scty Sq; 6903	
Elect Scty Gp)	1 May 70–
1971	
36 Tac Ftr Sq	1 Sep 71–
51 AB Wg	
(51 Comps	
Wg [Tac])	1 Nov 71–
51 CE Sq	1 Nov 71–
51 Consold Acft	
Maint Sq (51	
Fld Maint Sq)	1 Nov 71–
51 Scty Pol Sq	1 Nov 71–
51 Svcs Sq	1 Nov 71–28 Feb 75
51 Sup Sq	1 Nov 71–
51 Trnsp Sq	1 Nov 71–
80 Tac Ftr Sq	15 Feb 71–1 Sep 71
451 Mun Maint Sq	1 Nov 71–1 Dec 73
611 Mil Alft Spt Sq	29 Aug 71–
USAF Hosp, Osan	17 May 71–
1972	
19 Tac Air Spt Sq	15 Jan 72–
51 Avncs Maint Sq	
(51 Component	
Rpr Sq)	29 Feb 72–
51 Orgnzl Maint	
Sq (51 Acft	
Gnrtn Sq)	29 Feb 72–
1973	
51 Mun Maint Sq	1 Dec 73–1 Jan 78
1974	
51 Cmbt Spt Gp	30 Sep 74–

95

AIR FORCE BASES OVERSEAS

1976

554 CE Sq,
  Heavy Rpr   5 Jan 76–
603 Tac Air Con
  Cen Sq   15 Apr 76–
621 Tac Con Sq   8 Jan 76–

1978

6008 Tac Air
  Con Flt   26 May 78–

1979

314 Air Div   1 Apr 79–

6130 Tac Con Flt   15 Jan 79–

1980

5 Tac Air Con Sq   8 Jan 80–
6140 Tac Con Flt   15 Mar 80–1 Jan 82

1981

6 Tac Intelligence
  Gp   1 Oct 81–
38 Aerosp Rscu
  & Recovery Sq   8 Jan 81–
51 Svcs Sq   1 May 81–

RAF Alconbury

Location: Located 3 mi E of Alconbury, about 60 mi N of London, England.

Name: Named after a village in England.

Date of Current Name: 18 Dec 1955.

Previous Names: RAF Stn #102 (aka RAF Stn Abbotts Ripton), 1938–9 Sep 1942; Alconbury Adrm, AAF Stn #102, 9 Sep 1942; USAAF Stn #102, c. Jul–26 Nov 1945. Alconbury RAF Stn, 24 Aug 1951.

Date of Establishment: 9 Sep 1942; 24 Aug 1951.

Date Construction Began: RAF construction began in 1938; USAF construction commenced in 1951.

Date of Beneficial Occupancy: c. 1 Jun 1952.

Base Operating Units: 93d Bomb Gp, 7 Sep 1942; 92d Bomb Gp, Jan 1943; 482d Bomb Gp, 20 Aug 1943; 435th Air Svc Gp, 15 Apr 1945–c. 20 Oct 1945. OL, Third AF, 1 Jun 1952; Det 1, 7523d Spt Sq, 1 Jun 1953; 7560th AB Sq, 7 Nov 1954; 7560th AB Gp, 25 Mar 1955; 10th AB Gp, 25 Aug 1959 (rdsgd 10th Cmbt Spt Gp, 15 Feb 1962)–.

Base Commanders:* Col Edward J. Timberlake Jr, 6 Dec 1942; Col James S. Sutton, Jan 1943; Lt Col Baskin R. Lawrence Jr, 2 May 1943; Col Howard Moore, 1 Dec 1943; Lt Col Clement W. Bird, 15 Dec 1944–c. 29 May 1945; Lt Col (later, Col) Robert F. Hambaugh, 30 May 1945–c. 26 Nov 1945. Lt Col Winfield H. Brown, 5 May 1953; Lt Col Harley N. Cox, 25 Mar 1955; Maj Roger C. Graham, 22 Apr 1955; Lt Col Neal H. Impaglazzio, 22 May 1955; Col James B. Baker, 3 Jun 1955; Col Thomas A. Holdiman, c. 1 Oct 1957; Lt Col James A. Caselli, 20 Mar 1958; Col George H. Kneen Jr, 11 Jul 1958; Col Henry S. Taylor, 25 Aug 1959; Lt Col Harold T. Snyder, 1 Jan 1962; Lt Col Chester B. Hackett, 28 Jun 1962; Lt Col George D. Rawlings, 6 Aug 1962; Lt Col Donald J. Martell, 1 Aug 1963; Lt Col (later, Col) Sidney O. Ingram, 4 Sep 1963; Col Bertram L. Hambleton Jr, 22 Aug 1966; Col James D. Naler, 10 Jul 1967; Col Dwight

---

*The RAF owns this USAFE-administered installation and maintains a permanent RAF station commander there.

W. Blanton, 17 Jul 1969; Col Dexter E. Martin, 18 Jun 1971; Lt Col (later, Col) Ray R. Kropp, 6 Mar 1973; Col Robert E. Edge, 22 Jul 1974; Col Charles L. Ferguson, 19 Jan 1977; Col Richard A. Virant, 17 Jul 1978; Col Stephen H. Cowles, 9 Jul 1980; Lt Col (later, Col) David T. Fee, 11 Feb 1981; Col Charles A. Lehman, 17 Jul 1982–.

Major Off-Base and Detached Installations: * RAF Bruntingthorpe Fam Hsg Anx, 1 mi SW of Bruntingthorpe, 15 Feb 1957–unk; RAF Mepal Stor Stn, 1 mi S of Mepal, 22 May 1958–8 Jul 1960 (dspd); Sandy POL Retail Distr Stn, Sandy, 1 Nov 1958 (asgnd)–29 Apr 1969 (dspd); RAF Alconbury-Wyton TVOR Anx (rdsgd RAF Wyton TVOR Anx), Wyton, 1 Jan 1959 (asgnd)–7 Sep 1961 (dspd); Crowland RRS, Crowland, 1 Mar 1962 (asgnd)–9 Nov 1973 (dspd); Daventry RR Stn, 1 mi E of Staverton, 1 May 1962 (trsfd from RAF Bruntingthorpe)–; Chelveston Stor Anx, Rushden, 1 Oct 1962 (asgnd)–; RAF Stn Chelveston, Rushden, 1 Oct 1962 (asgnd)–; RAF Barkway Comms Site, Barkway, 1 Nov 1963 (trsfd from RAF Wethersfield)–; RAF St. Mawgan RB Anx, 4 mi NE of Newquay, 1 Jan 1965 (trsfd from RAF Brize Norton)–30 Jun 1965 (trsfd to RAF South Ruislip); RAF Brize Norton Stor Anx, Witney, 1 Apr 1965 (asgnd)–unk; Fylingdales Comms Stn, Fylingdales, 1 Jul 1965 (trsfd from RAF Mildenhall)–1 Jul 1972 (trsfd to RAF Bentwaters); Garrowby Hill RRS, Garrowby Hill, 1 Jul 1965 (trsfd from RAF Mildenhall)–7 Dec 1973 (dspd); Kirton-in-Lindsey RRS, Kirton-in-Lindsey, 1 Jul 1965 (trsfd from RAF Mildenhall)–6 Nov 1973 (dspd); Spitalgate RRS, Grantham, 1 Jul 1965 (trsfd from RAF Mildenhall)–9 Nov 1973 (dspd); RAF Molesworth Stor Site, Thrapston, Jul 1966 (asgnd)–unk; Mormond Hill Comms Stn, Mormond Hill, 1 Jul 1967 (trsfd from RAF Upper Heyford)–1 Jul 1972 (trsfd to RAF Stanwick Fam Hsg Anx, Wellingborough, 3 Jun 1968 (asgnd)–24 Jun 1971 (dspd); Brampton Fam Hsg Anx, Brampton, 3 Jul 1968 (asgnd)–unk; March Fam Hsg Anx, March, 26 Aug 1968 (asgnd)–26 Mar 1971 (dspd); Stilton Fam Hsg Anx, Stilton, 26 Aug 1968 (asgnd)–26 Mar 1971 (dspd); Godmanchester Fam Hsg Anx, Godmanchester, 3 Feb 1969 (asgnd)–14 Aug 1977 (dspd); RAF Upwood Stor Anx, 1 mi N of Upwood, 2 Oct 1975 (asgnd)–; RAF Ridgewell Stor Anx, Ridgewell, 1 Jan 1977 (trsfd from RAF Wethersfield)–; RAF Wethersfield, 1 mi SSW of Wethersfield, 1 Jan 1977 (asgnd)–; RAF Wethersfield Hosp, Wethersfield, 1 Jan 1977 (asgnd)–; RAF Brampton Fam Hsg Anx, Rectory Close, 31 Aug 1979–; RAF Coltishall, Coltishall, 25 Jun 1980 (asgnd)–; Haverhill Fam Hsg Anx, Haverhill, 1 Oct 1980 (trsfd from RAF Lakenheath)–.

Major Changes in Operational Capability: Runways extended to

---

*All installations are located in England.

4,200 and 6,000 ft, additional hardstands and hangars constructed and taxiways altered preceding transfer to USAAF, fall 1942; first USAAF combat mission flown from field 9 Oct 1942; base accommodated B–17 and B–24 units flying missions to the European continent 1942–1945; accidental explosion while loading a B–17 killed 18 men and destroyed four B–17s on 27 May 1943; base reverted to RAF's Maintenance Command and became a bomb disposal site on 26 Nov 1945; facilities rehabilitated upon USAFE reoccupancy, with much new construction, 1951–1952; field also served as a storage and supply point 25 Aug 1951–1953; main runway extended, taxiway and apron completed 1955–1956; flying operations commenced May 1957; French insistence upon control of all nuclear weapons at French bases prompted the USAF to transfer 10th Tac Recon Wg to Alconbury in Aug 1959, at which time Alconbury temporarily headed up a four-base complex including RAF Bruntingthorpe, RAF Chelveston, and RAF Molesworth; electronic reconnaissance missions began after B–66s arrived 1959–1960; base also supported routine day and night visual photographic reconnaissance, electronic reconnaissance, and electronic counter measures commencing in the 1960s; because of noise complaints from nearby communities RF–4s replaced RB–66s 1965–1966; additional base buildings and facilities added in 1968 and major runway rehabilitation completed 1969–1970; facilities provided for a newly arrived, dual-based tactical reconnaissance squadron Jul 1970; facilities added for newly activated tactical squadron 15 Jun 1971; aircraft maintenance shop and bulk jet fuel storage facility completed 1973–1974; F–5 operations began 1976; 36 F–5 aircraft shelters constructed 1976–1978; two operations buildings, wing operations center, communications facility, and liquid oxygen and POL shelters completed 1977–1980; major housing renovation project finished 1978–1979; photo interpretation facility completed mid-1981; inactivation of two of Alconbury's three reconnaissance squadrons enabled beddown of additional F–5s in 1981; field training facility and maintenance complex projected for 1982–1983.

Major Commands to Which Assigned: Eighth AF, 9 Sep 1942 (rdsgd U.S. Strategic Air Forces in Europe, 22 Feb 1944; USAFE, 7 Aug 1945)–26 Nov 1945. USAFE, 24 Aug 1951–.

Major Changes in Status: AAF assumed beneficial occupancy Sep 1942, using field as a bomber base until 26 Nov 1945; under jurisdiction of RAF Maint Comd (later, merged with Bmbr Comd) used as a bomb disposal site from 26 Nov 1945–Aug 1951; Third AF authorized construction and rehabilitation program for Alconbury and designated it a primary USAFE installation 24 Aug 1951; designated a USAF construction site 1 Sep 1953; a satellite base of RAF Sculthorpe 20 Sep 1955–Apr 1957; reassigned primary base status on 1 May 1957.

Units Assigned:

1942	
36 Svc Sq	8 Dec 42–unk
93 Bomb Gp	7 Sep 42–5 Dec 42
328 Bomb Sq	7 Sep 42–c. 6 Dec 42
329 Bomb Sq	7 Sep 42–c. 6 Dec 42
330 Bomb Sq	7 Sep 42–c. 6 Dec 42
357 Svc Sq	
(357 Air Svc Sq)	18 Aug 42–unk 45
409 Bomb Sq	7 Sep 42–c. 6 Dec 42

1943	
36 Bomb Sq	c. 6 Nov 43–c. 7 Feb 44
41 Stn Compl Sq	21 Aug 43–15 Apr 45
92 Bomb Gp	6 Jan 43–15 Sep 43
325 Bomb Sq	6 Jan 43–15 Sep 43
326 Bomb Sq	6 Jul 43–15 Sep 43
327 Bomb Sq	6 Jan 43–15 Sep 43
328 Svc Gp	c. 14 Sep 43–11 Feb 44
406 Bomb Sq	11 Nov 43–c. 7 Feb 44
407 Bomb Sq	6 Jan 43–15 Sep 43
482 Bomb Gp	20 Aug 43–c. 21 May 45
812 Bomb Sq	20 Aug 43–Jun 45
813 Bomb Sq	20 Aug 43–Jun 45
814 Bomb Sq	20 Aug 43–Jun 45

1945	
1 Air Div	20 Sep 45–31 Oct 45
1 Bomb Wg	26 Jun 45–26 Aug 45
2 Bomb Wg	12 Jun 45–25 Aug 45
36 Bomb Sq	28 Feb 45–15 Oct 49
94 Bomb Wg	12 Jun 45–18 Jun 45
435 Air Svc Gp	15 Apr 45–c. 20 Oct 45
652 Bomb Sq	13 Jul 45–25 Oct 45
857 Bomb Sq	11 Jun 45–6 Aug 45

1953	
1 Motor Trpt Maint Sq (1 Motor Trpt Sq, Maint)	1 Sep 53–1 Mar 55

1954	
7560 AB Sq (7560 AB Gp)	7 Nov 54–25 Aug 59
7560 USAF Infmy (7560 USAF Dispy)	1 Oct 54–25 Sep 58

1955	
86 Bomb Sq (86 Bomb Sq, Tac)	15 Sep 55–5 Aug 59
7560 AB Gp	25 Mar 55–25 Aug 59
7560 AP Sq	25 Mar 55–25 Aug 59
7560 Mat Sq	25 Mar 55–25 Aug 59

1956	
4 Tac Dep Sq (304 Mun Maint Sq)	1 Feb 56–1 Oct 64

1957	
42 Trp Carr Sq	31 May 57–8 Dec 57

1266 AACS Sq (2166 Comms Sq)	1 Nov 57–
7560 Trnsp Sq	23 May 57–25 Aug 59

1958	
30 Sup Sq	15 Feb 58–10 Sep 59
37 Bomb Sq	11 May 58–12 May 58

1959	
1 Tac Recon Sq	25 Aug 59–
10 AB Gp (10 Cmbt Spt Gp)	25 Aug 59–
10 AP Sq (10 Scty Pol Sq)	25 Aug 59–
10 Armnt & Elect Maint Sq	25 Aug 59–15 Feb 62
10 Comms Sq	25 Aug 59–1 Sep 59
10 Consold Acft Maint Sq (10 Fld Maint Sq; 10 Equip Maint Sq)	25 Aug 59–
10 Food Svc Sq	25 Aug 59–15 Feb 62
10 Instls Sq (10 CE Sq)	25 Aug 59–
10 Sup Sq	25 Aug 59–
10 Tac Recon Wg	25 Aug 59–
10 Trnsp Sq	25 Aug 59–
30 Tac Recon Sq	25 Aug 59–6 Apr 76
53 Wea Recon Sq	25 Apr 59–9 Aug 59
7518 Comms Sq	1 Sep 59–1 Jul 62

1964	
10 Armnt & Elect Maint Sq (10 Avncs Maint Sq; 10 Component Rpr Sq)	1 Jul 64–
10 Orgnzl Maint Sq	1 Jul 64–1 Jan 66

1966	
32 Tac Recon Sq	24 Aug 66–1 Jan 76

1968	
7510 Mun Maint Sq	1 Jan 68–7 Oct 72

1969	
10 Recon Tech Sq	1 Jul 69–1 Oct 82

1971	
USAF Dispy, Alconbury (USAF Clinic, Alconbury)	1 Jul 71–

1972	
10 Mun Maint Sq	8 Oct 72–31 Jul 79
10 Orgnzl Maint Sq (10 Acft	

Gnrtn Sq)	1 Feb 72–	17 Fld Maint Sq	1 Oct 82–
1976		17 Orgnzl Maint Sq	1 Oct 82–
527 Tac Ftr Tng		95 Recon Sq	1 Oct 82–
Aggressor Sq	1 Apr 76–	496 Recon Tech Sq	1 Oct 82–
1982		6952 Elect Scty Sq	1 Jan 82–
17 Avncs Maint Sq	1 Oct 82–		

RAF Bentwaters

Location: Located 85 mi NE of London, 10 mi ENE of Ipswich, England.

Name: Named after a house, "Bentwaters," originally located on the site of the base's main runway.

Date of Current Name: 18 Dec 1955.

Previous Names: RAF Butley, AAF Stn 151, c. 1942; Bentwaters RAF Stn, 28 Jan 1943; Bentwaters RAF, 16 Mar 1955.

Date of Establishment: Established by the RAF in 1942; established as a USAFE base on 16 Mar 1951.

Date Construction Began: British commenced construction work in 1942; further construction undertaken by USAFE 1951–1952.

Date of Beneficial Occupancy: 16 Mar 1951.

Base Operating Units: 7506th Air Spt Gp, 16 Mar 1951; 81st AB (rdsgd 81st Spt; 81st Cmbt Spt) Gp, 5 Sep 1951–.

Base Commanders:[*] Lt Col Kermit A. Tyler, 7 Sep 1951; Col Miles A. Connor, c. 30 Sep 1953; Col David W. Hassemer, 31 Dec 1954; Col Wesley A. Anderson, 30 Jun 1955; Lt Col William H. Parkins, 1 Aug 1956; Col John W. Robie, 7 Mar 1957; Lt Col William H. Parkins, 28 Feb 1958; Col Elmer C. Blaha, 21 Apr 1958; Col Jack R. Best, 11 Jul 1959; Col Harry F. Alexander, 10 Jul 1962; Col William W. Parramore Jr, 19 Jul 1965; Col Bernie S. Bass, 5 Jul 1968; Col Philip R. Safford, 1 Dec 1969; Col Ernest R. Wilson, 17 Aug 1970; Col Morton D. Orzen, 13 Oct 1972; Lt Col Walter J. Schenning, 10 Jun 1974; Col Walter A. Williams, 26 Jul 1974; Col Jarrell S. Mitchell, 6 Sep 1977; Col Jackie K. Snow, 20 Jun 1979; Col Theodore J. Conrad, 3 Jul 1980; Col Sam P. Morgan Jr, 14 Mar 1981; Col Henry J. Cochran, 15 Jul 1982–.

Major Off-Base and Detached Installations:[†] RAF Bentwaters Waste Anx, 3 mi NW of Wickham Market, 16 Mar 1951–; RAF Bentwaters/Framlingham Stor Anx, 1 mi E of Parham, 2 Mar 1955–; RAF Martlesham

---

[*]The RAF owns this USAFE-administered installation and maintains a permanent RAF station commander there.

[†]All installations are located in England.

Heath RRS, 4 mi W of Ipswich, 10 Jan 1956–; RAF Bentwaters Tacan Anx, 1 mi SW of Woodbridge, 18 Sep 1957 (asgnd in UC status)–30 Nov 1979 (dspd); RAF Bentwaters RB Anx, Hazlewood, 17 Jun 1958–16 Apr 1962 (dspd); RAF Bentwaters Off Hsg Anx (rdsgd RAF Bentwaters Bachelor Hsg Anx), 3 mi NW of Wickham Market, 1 Oct 1959–; RAF Woodbridge, 12 mi ENE of Ipswich, 1 Oct 1959–; Great Bromley RRS, Great Bromley, 1 Sep 1960–; Hopton RB Anx, Hopton-on-Sea, 1 Sep 1962–c. Jan 1974 (dspd); RAF Woodbridge Waste Anx, 3 mi W of Woodbridge, 19 Feb 1965–; Sproughton Court Fam Hsg Anx, Ipswich, 15 Jan 1968–14 Jul 1978 (dspd); Grundisburgh Fam Hsg Anx, 11 mi NE of Ipswich, 2 Feb 1968–; Melton Farm Fam Hsg Anx, 9 mi NE of Ipswich, 5 Feb 1968–; Kesgrave Fam Hsg Anx, 3 mi NE of Ipswich, 15 May 1968–; Martlesham Fam Hsg Anx, 5 mi NE of Ipswich, 15 May 1968–; Rushmere Fam Hsg Anx, 1 mi NE of Rushmere, 4 Aug 1968–30 Nov 1979 (dspd); Ipswich Fam Hsg Anx, Ipswich, 14 Oct 1968–; RAF Bentwaters/Framlingham Fam Hsg Anx, Framlingham, 15 Nov 1968–c. 1980 (dspd); Orford Rsch Site (rdsgd RAF Orfordness), Orford, 3 Jan 1969–31 Dec 1973 (dspd); Trimley St. Martin Fam Hsg Anx, Trimley St. Martin, 10 Mar 1969–; Alderton Fam Hsg Anx, Alderton, 1 Sep 1969–31 Aug 1974 (dspd); Mormond Hill Comms Stn, Mormond Hill, 1 Jul 1972 (trsfd from RAF Alconbury)–; RAF Wattisham Radar Site, Fylingdales, 1 Jul 1972–; Rosehearty Fam Hsg Anx (rdsgd Rosehearty Fam Hsg Site), Rosehearty, 1 Jun 1976–; RAF Felixstowe Fam Hsg Anx, Felixstowe, 10 Apr 1980–; Shotley Fam Hsg Anx, Shotley, 13 Jan 1981–; Rendelsham Fam Hsg Anx, 1982–.

Major Changes in Operational Capability: Base became operational under RAF Bomber Command and transferred to No. 11 Group RAF Fighter Command on 22 Nov 1944; USAAF fighters flew escort missions for RAF Bomber Command beginning 4 May 1945; RAF training base from end of World War II to 26 Aug 1949; inactive from 1 Sep 1949 to 30 Jun 1950, when Bentwaters was placed in caretaker status prior to transfer from RAF to USAF; assigned to USAF control on 16 Mar 1951; designated a primary installation of HQ USAFE on 7 Sep 1951; supported fighter-bomber and later tactical fighter operations of the 81st Wg 5 Sep 1951 to the present; HQ USAFE operated RAF Bentwaters and Woodbridge as "twin bases" after 8 Jul 1958; RAF Bentwaters supported aircraft from RAF Woodbridge when Woodbridge closed its runways for major repairs, 5 Nov–5 Dec 1958; eight Victor Alert aircraft shelters and eight periodic maintenance docks constructed, 1958–1960; taxiways resealed, a new wing added to base dependent school, and 12 family housing units built, 1960–1962; medical warehouse, EES (EUCOM Exchange Service) facility, and ammunition storage facility constructed and security fencing erected around all aircraft parking areas, 1966–1967; base theater completed in 1969; Ready Crew facility and a 50,000-barrel jet fuel storage facility constructed 1970–1972; Victor Alert bypass taxiway, base supply management facility, and base rescue service hangar built, 1972–1974; base commissary addition constructed, base clinic renovated, taxiway lighting renovated, BAK–13 aircraft arrester barriers installed, and base fire fighting facilities modernized, 1974–1975; 14 TAB VEE aircraft shelters, a parachute building, and clinic constructed, 1977–1978; 22 TAB VEE aircraft shelters erected and entire airfield paved, 1979; a parallel taxiway, 8,200-ft long, a 300-unit housing project "Rendelsham Park," and a fuel system maintenance dock constructed 1980–1981; airmen's dining hall, a new dormitory, and additional POL storage facilities built in 1982.

Major Commands to Which Assigned: USAFE, 16 Mar 1951–.

Major Changes in Status: Caretaker status on 17 Apr 1944; operational, 22 Nov 1944; inactivated on 1 Sep 1949; caretaker status 1 Jul 1950; activated, and transferred to HQ USAFE on 16 Mar 1951; opened as primary installation of USAFE on 7 Sep 1951–.

Units Assigned:

1951

81 AB Gp	
(81 Spt Gp; 81 Cmbt Spt Gp)	5 Sep 51–
81 AP Sq	
(81 Scty Pol Sq)	5 Sep 51–
81 Comms Sq	
(81 Ops Sq)	5 Sep 51–1 Apr 58
81 Ftr-Intcpr Gp	
(81 Ftr-Bmbr Gp)	5 Sep 51–8 Feb 55
81 Ftr-Intcpr Wg	
(81 Ftr-Bmbr Wg; 81 Tac Ftr Wg)	5 Sep 51–
81 Food Svc Sq	5 Sep 51–26 Jan 56
81 Instls Sq	5 Sep 51–26 Jan 56
81 Maint & Sup Gp	5 Sep 51–26 Jan 56
81 Maint Sq	
(81 Fld Maint Sq)	5 Sep 51–14 May 62
81 MV Sq	
(81 Trnsp Sq)	5 Sep 51–
81 Sup Sq	5 Sep 51–
91 Ftr-Bmbr Sq	
(91 Tac Ftr Sq)	5 Sep 51–1 Feb 80
7506 Air Spt Gp	16 Mar 51–16 Oct 51
7506 Air Spt Sq	16 Mar 51–16 Oct 51

1952

7554 Tow Target Flt	22 Feb 52–16 Dec 52

1954

87 Ftr-Intcpr Sq	13 Dec 54–8 Sep 55
7564 USAF Infmy (7564 USAF Dispy)	1 May 54–26 Jan 56

1955

512 Ftr-Intcpr Sq	8 Sep 55–24 Mar 58
1264 AACS Sq (2164 Comms Sq)	15 Jul 55–

7581 AB Sq	8 Feb 55–26 Jan 56

1956

81 AB Sq	26 Jan 56–14 May 62

1958

81 Armnt & Elect Maint Sq	8 Jul 58–14 May 62
81 Prdc Maint Sq	8 Jul 58–14 May 62
92 Ftr-Bmbr Sq (92 Tac Ftr Sq)	30 Apr 58–

1959

7519 Comms Sq	1 Sep 59–1 Jul 62

1962

81 Consold Acft Maint Sq	12 May 62–1 Jul 64

1964

81 Armnt & Elect Maint Sq (81 Avncs Maint Sq; 81 Component Rpr Sq)	1 Jul 64–
81 Fld Maint Sq (81 Equip Maint Sq)	1 Jul 64–
81 Orgnzl Maint Sq	1 Jul 64–1 Jan 66
381 Mun Maint Sq	1 Jul 64–7 Oct 72

1971

USAF Dispy, Bentwaters (USAF Clinic, Bentwaters)	1 Jul 71–

1972

81 Mun Maint Sq	8 Oct 72–15 Feb 79
81 Orgnzl Maint Sq (81 Acft	

Gnrtn Sq)	1 Feb 72–		1980
	1978	509 Tac Ftr Sq	1 Feb 80–
510 Tac Ftr Sq	1 Oct 78–	511 Tac Ftr Sq	1 Jan 80–
	1979		1981
581 Acft Gnrtn Sq	16 Feb 79–	81 Svcs Sq	1 Nov 81–

RAF Chicksands

Location: Located 40 mi N of London, 9 mi S of Bedford, 11 mi N of Luton, and 3 mi W of Shefford, England.

Name: Named after an ancient priory in Bedfordshire, England, on which RAF Chicksands is situated.

Date of Current Name: 1 Jul 1959.

Previous Names: Chicksands Priory (ancient); Chicksands Priory RAF Stn, 20 Sep 1951; Chicksands RAF Stn, 30 Jan 1954; RAF Chicksands Priory, 18 Dec 1955; RAF Chicksands Comms Anx, 28 Feb 1958.

Date of Establishment: RAF establishment 1939; USAF establishment 8 Nov 1950.

Date Construction Began: RAF construction for a communications center commenced in 1939; USAF construction initiated in 1951.

Date of Beneficial Occupancy: RAF occupancy, 1939; USAF occupancy, 8 Nov 1950.

Base Operating Units: 10th Radio Sq, Mobile, 8 Nov 1950; 7534th AB Sq, 25 May 1951; 6950th Radio Gp, Mobile (rdsgd 6950th Scty Wg), 1 Jul 1958; 6950th Scty Gp, 20 Jan 1967; 7274th AB Gp, 1 Oct 1978–.

Base Commanders:* Lt Col Donald A. Robinson Jr, 8 Nov 1950; Capt Philip Rekoon, 1 Jan 1952; Capt David Gutshall, 2 Apr 1952; Maj Albert G. Arnold, 7 May 1952; Maj John F. Fritzer, 17 Jul 1952; Maj Kenneth D. Blackshaw, c. Mar 1954; Maj Edward F. Veiluva, 4 Oct 1954; Maj Edmund C. Straus, 1955; Maj George E. Cross Jr, 31 Dec 1956; Maj Daniel E. Redington, 27 Nov 1957; Col Walter W. Lavell, 1 Jul 1958; Col Joseph Bush, 25 Jul 1959–unk; unk, 1 Jul 1961–8 Jul 1963; Col Robert W. Relfe, 9 Jul 1963; Lt Col William H. Croft, c. 15 Jan 1964; Maj Samuel P. Schmehl, c. Jun 1964 (temp); Maj Charles V. Chapman, 1964 (temp); Lt Col George J. Hoerter, Jan 1965; Col Clifford G. Summers, 22 Aug 1966; Col Harrison R. Christy Jr, c. Sep 1966; Col Richard A. Wilson, 31 Jul 1967; Col Ross D. Norton, 5 Jun 1970; Col James L. George, 21 Jan 1972; Lt Col Walter M. Langford, c. 15 Aug 1974 (temp); Col James W. Johnson Jr, 29 Sep 1974;

---

*The RAF owns this USAFE-administered installation and maintains a permanent RAF station commander there.

Col William H. Ernest, Aug 1976; Col Francis E. Brandon Jr, 1 Oct 1978; Lt Col Robert C. Hyde, 10 Feb 1979; Col Donald J. Maxwell, 4 Nov 1980; Col Leland M. Martin, 7 Aug 1981–.

Major Off-Base and Detached Installations:* Chicksands DF Anx, 10 mi S of Bedford, 1 mi W of Shefford, Nov 1950–unk; Chicksands DF Site, 2 mi NNE of Shefford, 5 mi NNW of Hitchin, 1 May 1952 (actvd)–22 May 1964 (dspd); Chicksands DF Stn (Chicksands DF Anx), RAF Chicksands, 1 Jun 1952–.

Major Changes in Operational Capability: Base originally occupied by communications units of RAF 1939–late 1946; first cadre of 10th Radio Sq, Mobile, arrived at Chicksands to assume U.S. control of base on 10 Nov 1950; USAF units took possession of 39 buildings held by RAF 1950–1951; 7534th AB Sq hosted units of Third AF and Field Unit #2 of the National Security Agency 1951–Jul 1958; general base reconstruction and rehabilitation, partly with RAF funding, 1951–1955; central heating plant, bowling alley, housing units, and a 143-pupil school constructed 1956–1957; base library and base exchange added in 1957; USAFSS (later, Electronic Security Command) assumed control of RAF Chicksands 1 Jul 1958; RAF contingent on base gradually phased out 1958–1960; over the next decade extensive construction took place, including a theatre in 1960, the 700 and 800 housing areas in 1967, a commissary in 1969, and an officer housing area 900 in 1970; Chicksands, known as "Electronic Stonehenge," provided continuous support for assigned and attached units of the USAFSS and had no flying facilities; USAFE has supported tenant organizations and off-base installations of Chicksands since 1 Oct 1978.

Major Commands to Which Assigned: USAFSS, 8 Nov 1950; USAFE, 25 May 1951; USAFSS, 1 Jul 1958; USAFE, 1 Oct 1978–.

Major Changes in Status: RAF Comms Stn, 1939; activated as primary installation of the Third AF, 8 Nov 1950; off-base installation of RAF Alconbury, 1 Jul 1956; became primary installation, 1 Jul 1958–.

Units Assigned:

1950			1958	
10 Radio Sq, Mobile	8 Nov 50–8 May 55		6950 Radio Gp, Mobile	
	1951		(6950 Sec Wg)	1 Jul 58–20 Jan 67
7534 AB Sq	25 May 51–1 Jul 58		1959	
	1952		7518 Comms Sq	1 Sep 59–1 Jul 62
6906 Scty Flt	1 Jun 52–1 Aug 55		1963	
	1953		6950 Spt Sq	
6950 Sec Gp	2 Dec 53–1 Sep 56		(6950 Spt Gp)	1 Aug 63–20 Jan 67
	1954		1967	
7534 USAF Dispy	1 May 54–30 Jun 71		6950 Sec Gp	20 Jun 67–1 Oct 78

---

*All installations are located in England.

	1971	6950 AB Sq	1 Jul 74–1 Oct 78
USAF Dispy, Chicksands (USAF Clinic, Chicksands)		6950 Scty Sq (6950 Elect Scty Gp)	1 Jul 74–
	1 Jul 71– 1973		1978
6900 Scty Sq	13 Jul 73–30 Jun 75	7274 AB Gp	1 Oct 78– 1979
	1974	2112 Comms Sq	1 Feb 79–

RAF Fairford

Location: Located about 75 mi WNW of London, 13 mi N of Swindon, and 1 1/4 mi S of Fairford, England.

Name: Named after a village in England.

Date of Current Name: 18 Dec 1955.

Previous Names: RAF Stn Fairford, 1944; Fairford RAF Stn, 27 Jun 1950.

Date of Establishment: Established as RAF base 1944; established as USAFE (later, SAC) base 7 Jul 1950; returned to United Kingdom, 26 Jun 1964; established again as USAFE installation, 1 Jun 1979.

Date Construction Began: RAF construction began 1943; USAF began reconstruction of base and expansion of base facilities, including runways, Aug 1950.

Date of Beneficial Occupancy: 7 Jul 1950; 31 Jan 1979.

Base Operating Units: 7507th AB Sq, 7 Jul 1950 (rdsgd 7507th AB Gp, 25 May 1951; 3919th AB Gp, 16 Oct 1952; 3919th AB Sq, 15 Oct 1955; 3919th Spt Sq, 1 Jul 1962); 3919th Cmbt Spt Gp, 1 Jan 1959–30 Jun 1964. 7020th AB Gp, 1 Feb 1979–.

Base Commanders:* Maj William S. Flood, 7 Jul 1950; Lt Col George R. Geer, 10 Oct 1950; Col Jerome Tarter, c. Sep 1952; Col Kenneth D. Thompson, c. Apr 1955; Col Edwin A. Loberg, 15 Jul 1955; Lt Col Bruce H. Rogers, 18 Jun 1956; Col William M. Crampton, 27 Aug 1956; Col George P. Birdsong Jr, 13 Aug 1960; Col Carlton R. Lee, 18 Jul 1962–30 Jun 1964. Col Hiram R. Sullivan, 31 Jan 1979; Col William M. Brown, 17 Jul 1980; Col Thomas R. Johnson, 1 Jul 1982–.

Major Off-Base and Detached Installations:† RAF Fairford RB Anx, Kelmscot, 27 Nov 1950 (actvd)–26 Jun 1964 (dspd); South Cerney RAF/Radio Anx, 5 mi E of South Cerney, 8 Jun 1953 (actvd)–19 Sep 1955 (inactvd); Marston Hill Hsg Depnt Sch Anx, 1 mi E of Marston, 1 Jul 1954 (actvd)–30 Jun 1959 (inactvd); RAF Brize–Norton Fam Hsg Anx, Carter-

---

*The RAF owns this USAFE-administered installation and maintains a permanent RAF station commander there.

†All installations are located in England.

ton, 1 Jun 1979 (asgnd)–; Kempsford Fam Hsg Anx, Kempsford, 10 Aug 1979 (actvd)–; Bampton Fam Hsg Anx, Bampton, 26 Sep 1979–; Kingston Bagpuize Fam Hsg Anx, Kingston Bagpuize, 25 Oct 1979 (asgnd)–; Swindon Fam Hsg Anx, Swindon, 29 Oct 1979 (asgnd)–; Grove Fam Hsg Anx, Grove, 28 Mar 1980 (actvd)–1 Jan 1981 (dspd); South Cerney Fam Hsg Anx, South Cerney, 10 Oct 1980 (actvd)–; Faringdon Fam Hsg Anx, Faringdon, 19 Nov 1980 (actvd)–; RAF Little Rissington, Little Rissington, 15 Jan 1981 (actvd)–.

Major Changes in Operational Capability: Used by two RAF squadrons and the USAAF Ninth AF as a staging base for D-Day and Arnhem operations in World War II; reduced to caretaker status 1946; runways lengthened to 10,000 feet in preparation for hosting SAC B–47 bomber rotations 1950; supported SAC reflex operations Jan 1958 to Jun 1964; base returned to United Kingdom 26 Jun 1964; between 1969 and 1977 base served as field for testing "Concorde" supersonic airliner; returned to USAF when USAFE activated 7020th AB Gp at Fairford 1 Feb 1979 to prepare for KC–135 tanker operations; USAFE officially designated Fairford a primary installation 1 Jun 1979, with first KC–135s arriving 13 Sep 1979; base also hosted SAC B–52 deployments beginning Apr 1980.

Major Commands to Which Assigned: USAFE, 7 Jul 1950; SAC, 16 Oct 1952–26 Jun 1964. USAFE, 1 Jun 1979–.

Major Changes in Status: Active as RAF base Jan 1944; reduced to caretaker status 1946; under construction by USAFE Aug 1950–1951; operational as USAFE installation 1 Jul 1951; inactivated and returned to United Kingdom 26 Jun 1964; testing field for "Concorde" 1969–1977; activated by USAFE 1 Jun 1979.

Units Assigned:

1950			
7507 AB Sq			
(7507 AB Gp;			
3919 AB Gp;			
3919 AB Sq;			
3919 Spt Sq)	7 Jul 50–30 Jun 64		
1951			
2 Avn Fld Dep Sq			
(2 Avn Dep Sq)	19 May 51–15 Jun 56		
7507 AP Sq			
(3919 AP Sq)	25 May 51–15 Oct 55		
7507 Food Svc Sq			
(3919 Food			
Svc Sq)	25 May 51–15 Oct 55		
7507 Instls Sq			
(3919 Instls Sq;			
3919 CE Sq)	25 May 51–30 Jun 64		
7507 Med Sq			
(3919 Med Sq;			
3919 USAF Infmy)	25 May 51–15 Oct 55		
7507 MV S			
(3919 MV Sq)	25 May 51–15 Oct 55		
7507 Ops Sq			
(3919 Ops Sq)	25 May 51–30 Jun 64		
7507 Sup Sq			
(3919 Sup Sq)	25 May 51–30 Jun 64		
1952			
7522 AB Sq	10 Mar 52–10 Nov 52		
7582 AB Sq	1 Jul 52–1 Aug 52		
1953			
306 Bomb Wg	11 Jun 53–7 Sep 53		
1954			
43 Air Rflg Sq	18 Sep 54–9 Dec 54		
43 Armnt & Elect			
Maint Sq	18 Sep 54–9 Dec 54		
43 Bomb Wg	18 Sep 54–9 Dec 54		
43 Fld Maint Sq	18 Sep 54–9 Dec 54		
43 Prdc Maint Sq	18 Sep 54–9 Dec 54		
43 Tac Hosp	18 Sep 54–9 Dec 54		
63 Bomb Sq	18 Sep 54–9 Dec 54		

64 Bomb Sq	18 Sep 54–9 Dec 54	99 Bomb Sq	22 May 55–9 Jul 55
65 Bomb Sq	18 Sep 54–9 Dec 54	Fairford Task	
68 Fld Maint Sq	19 Jun 54–4 Aug 54	Force, Prov	1 May 55–unk
303 Air Rflg Sq	28 Apr 54–5 Jun 54	**1959**	
303 Armnt & Elect		3919 Cmbt Spt Gp	1 Jan 59–30 Jun 64
Maint Sq	28 Apr 54–5 Jun 54	3919 Consold Acft	
303 Bomb Wg	28 Apr 54–5 Jun 54	Maint Sq	1 Jan 59–30 Jun 64
303 Fld Maint Sq	28 Apr 54–5 Jun 54	**1962**	
303 Prdc Maint Sq	28 Apr 54–5 Jun 54	3919 Cmbt Def Sq	1 Jul 62–30 Jun 64
303 Tac Hosp	28 Apr 54–5 Jun 54	3919 Trnsp Sq	1 Jul 62–30 Jun 64
358 Bomb Sq	28 Apr 54–5 Jun 54	**1978**	
359 Bomb Sq	28 Apr 54–5 Jun 54	11 Strat Gp	15 Nov 78–
360 Bomb Sq	28 Apr 54–5 Jun 54	**1979**	
1955		2160 Comms Sq	1 Apr 79–
1 Bomb Sq	22 May 55–8 Jul 55	7020 AB Gp	1 Feb 79–
9 Armnt & Elect		**1981**	
Maint Sq	24 May 55–9 Jul 55	7020 CE Sq	5 Nov 81–
9 Fld Maint Sq	22 May 55–9 Jul 55	USAF Clinic,	
9 Prdc Maint Sq	24 May 55–9 Jul 55	Fairford	1 Aug 81–

RAF Greenham Common

Location: Located 45 mi W of London, 2 mi SE of Newbury, England.

Name: Named after a thousand-acre tract of land of the same name situated south of Newbury, Berkshire, England.

Date of Current Name: 20 Oct 1969.

Previous Names: Greenham Common, unk; RAF Stn Greenham Common, AAF Stn 486, May 1941; Greenham Common RAF, 16 Dec 1955; RAF Greenham Common Stor Anx, 1 Nov 1968.

Date of Establishment: Originally established as RAF Stn, a satellite of Aldermaston RAF Stn, May 1941; established as USAAF base, 4 Nov 1943; established as USAF base, 18 Jun 1951; after base returned to RAF, 30 Jun 1964, again established as USAF installation on 1 Nov 1968.

Date Construction Began: RAF began construction in 1940, with additional construction 1942–1944; USAF began improvements in 1951.

Date of Beneficial Occupancy: 14 Sep 1942; 23 Apr 1951; 1 Nov 1968.

Base Operating Units: 81st Adrm Sq, 4 Nov 1943; 96th Stn Compl Sq, 8 Dec 1943; 306th Stn Compl Sq, 21 Feb 1944–16 Apr 1945. 7501st AB Sq, 21 May 1951; 3909th AB Gp (rdsgd 3909th Cmbt Spt Gp), 15 Sep 1953–30 Jun 1964. 7551st Cmbt Spt Sq (rdsgd 7551st Cmbt Spt Gp), 1 Nov 1968; OL A, 20th Tac Ftr Wg, 1 Jun 1976; Det 3, 20th Tac Ftr Wg, 25 Jun 1976; 7273d AB Gp, 1 Jan 1979; 501st Cmbt Spt Gp, 1 Oct 1982–.

Base Commanders:* Maj Paul W. Albrecht, 4 Nov 1943; Maj Raymond P. Palmer, 8 Dec 1943; Maj Clinton W. Uhr, 16 Mar 1944–16 Apr 1945. Maj Benjamin H. Ashmore, 21 May 1951; Lt Col George R. Geer, 23 Jul 1951; Lt Col Walter A. Smith, 8 Sep 1952; Col Gerald G. Robinson, 1 Sep 1953; Col Harry R. Burrell, Sep 1954; Col Arthur S. Cresswell, 27 Jun 1957; Col Everett T. Chrisman, 5 Jul 1960; Col Eugene Q. Steffes, 5 Jul 1961; Col Harry C. Bayne, 23 Jul 1963–30 Jun 1964. Lt Col Paul E. Meuser, 1 Nov 1968; Col Ronald E. Dunlap, 2 Feb 1969; Col Dwight W. Blanton, 22 Jun 1971; Col Ernest R. Wilson, 6 Aug 1972; Col Leland M.

---

*The RAF owns this USAFE-administered installation and maintains a permanent RAF station commander there.

Martin, 8 Aug 1974; Lt Col Lester R. Gibson, 25 Jun 1976; Maj George P. Pehlvanian, 2 May 1977; Lt Col James E. Salminen, 21 Mar 1979; Lt Col Daryl D. Cook, 1 Jul 1982–.

Major Off-Base and Detached Installations:* Greenham Common RAF RB Anx (rdsgd RAF Greenham Common RB Anx), Pamber Heath, 21 May 1951 (actvd)–26 Jun 1964 (dspd); Bishops Green Fam Hsg Anx, Newbury, 20 Oct 1969–1 Jan 1977 (trsfd to RAF Upper Heyford); Blackbushe Fam Hsg Anx, Yately, 20 Oct 1969 (trsfd from South Ruislip AS)–1 Jan 1977 (trsfd to RAF Upper Heyford); Bulbarrow RRS, Hilton, 20 Oct 1969 (trsfd from South Ruislip AS)–3 Apr 1973 (dspd); Dean Hill RRS, West Dean, 20 Oct 1969 (trsfd from South Ruislip AS)–2 Apr 1973 (dspd); Golden Pot RRS, Alton, 20 Oct 1969 (trsfd from South Ruislip AS)–30 Mar 1973 (dspd); Portland RRS, Portland, 20 Oct 1969 (trsfd from South Ruislip AS)–3 Apr 1973 (dspd); RAF Christmas Common Comms Anx (rdsgd RAF Christmas Common RRS), Watlington, 20 Oct 1969 (trsfd from South Ruislip AS)–1 Jan 1977 (trsfd to RAF Upper Heyford); RAF Greenham Common Fam Hsg Anx, Newbury, 20 Oct 1969 (trsfd from South Ruislip AS)–1 Jan 1977 (trsfd to RAF Upper Heyford); RAF Greenham Common Waste Anx, Newbury, 20 Oct 1969 (trsfd from South Ruislip AS)–1 Jan 1977 (trsfd to RAF Upper Heyford); RAF Ringstead Comms Stn, Ringstead, 20 Oct 1969 (trsfd from South Ruislip AS)–3 Apr 1973 (dspd); RAF St. Mawgan RB Anx (rdsgd RAF St. Mawgan Comms Stn), 20 Oct 1969 (trsfd from South Ruislip AS)–1 Jan 1977 (trsfd to RAF Upper Heyford); RAF Welford (rdsgd RAF Welford Ammo Stor Area), Newbury, 20 Oct 1969 (trsfd from South Ruislip AS)–1 Jan 1977 (trsfd to RAF Upper Heyford); RAF Welford Waste Anx, Newbury, 20 Oct 1969 (trsfd from South Ruislip AS)–1 Jan 1977 (trsfd to RAF Upper Heyford); Felixstowe Port, Felixstowe, 16 Oct 1972 (actvd)–unk; St. Columb Fam Hsg Anx, St. Columb, 23 Jan 1974 (asgnd)–1 Jan 1977 (trsfd to RAF Upper Heyford); Bishops Green Fam Hsg Anx, Newbury, 1 Oct 1982 (trsfd from RAF Upper Heyford)–; Blackbushe Fam Hsg Anx, Yately, 1 Oct 1982 (trsfd from RAF Upper Heyford)–; RAF Clayhill Fam Hsg Anx, Burghfield, 1 Oct 1982 (trsfd from RAF Upper Heyford)–; RAF Greenham Common Fam Hsg Anx, Newbury, 1 Oct 1982 (trsfd from RAF Upper Heyford)–; RAF Greenham Common Waste Anx, Newbury, 1 Oct 1982 (trsfd from RAF Upper Heyford)–; RAF Welford Ammo Stor Area, Newbury, 1 Oct 1982 (trsfd from RAF Upper Heyford)–; RAF Welford Waste Anx, Newbury, 1 Oct 1982 (trsfd from RAF Upper Heyford)–; Swindon Fam Hsg Anx, Swindon, 1 Oct 1982 (trsfd from RAF Upper Heyford)–; Wantage Fam Hsg Anx, Wantage, 1 Oct 1982 (trsfd from RAF

---

*All installations are located in England.

116

Upper Heyford)–.

Major Changes in Operational Capability: Tract known as Greenham Common acquired by British Air Ministry May 1941 and opened as satellite of Aldermaston RAF Station; operational control of base transferred to Andover RAF Station Dec 1942; USAAF assumed control 4 Nov 1943, hosting fighter and troop carrier aircraft, 1944–1945; served as glider staging area for Normandy invasion, 6 Jun 1944; most Greenham Common units transferred to France by Feb 1945, leaving only USAAF detachment; base reverted to RAF control Jun 1945, and served as RAF basic training center until closed in Jun 1946; as tensions of Cold War increased, RAF Greenham Common named a Reflex Action deployment base for SAC bombers and tankers; USAF occupied base 23 Apr 1951 and began major construction work on runways and taxiways, 21 May 1951; most of base facilities constructed 1951–1953; RAF assigned complete control of base to USAF Jun 1953; first SAC B–47 unit deployed from Davis-Monthan AFB to Greenham Common early 1954, but soon transferred to RAF Fairford because Greenham Common's runways could not support the weight of B–47s; runways reinforced 1954–1956, and base selected as deployment base for KC–97G tankers, Apr 1956; SAC bombers deployed to RAF Greenham Common 1956–1964; base inactivated and transferred to RAF control on 30 Jun 1964; activated as off-base U.S. installation of South Ruislip AS on 1 Jun 1968; established as NATO standby base and reopened to support relocation of USAF units transferring from French airfields, 1 Nov 1968; base responsible for RAF Welford area 20 Oct 1969–Jan 1977; RAF Upper Heyford assumed control over RAF Greenham Common, 1 Jun 1976; 7273d AB Gp assumed control of Greenham Common on 1 Jan 1979, reinforcing runways, aprons and hardstands, renovating existing buildings and equipment required for the 501st Tac Msl Wg, which arrived in Jul 1982.

Major Commands to Which Assigned: Ninth AF, 4 Nov 1943–25 Apr 1945. USAFE, 18 Jun 1951–30 Jun 1964. USAFE, 1 Nov 1968–.

Major Changes in Status: RAF detached installation of Aldermaston RAF Stn, May 1941; USAAF primary installation (AAF Stn #486), 4 Nov 1943–25 Apr 1945. Activated as off-base installation of South Ruislip AS, 1 Jun 1968; primary installation and standby deployment base, 20 Oct 1969–.

Units Assigned:

1942		1943	
51 Trp Carr Wg	14 Sep 42–Nov 42	12 Tac Recon Sq	16 Dec 43–9 Jan 44
201 Prov Stn Gas		70 Ftr Wg	29 Nov 43–6 Dec 43
Def Det	42–unk	81 Adrm Sq	31 Nov 43–5 Apr 44
901 Engr Bn	18 Aug 42–1 Sep 42	96 Stn Compl Sq	31 Dec 43–5 Apr 44
AF Filler Trp Gp	42–unk	100 Ftr Wg	6 Dec 43–13 Jan 44
TCC Eighth AF		334 Sig Co, Wg	31 Dec 43–5 Apr 44
(Prov)	42–16 Oct 43	353 Ftr Sq	4 Nov 43–13 Nov 43

354 Ftr Gp	4 Nov 43–13 Nov 43	Weapons Bn	1 May 44–unk
355 Ftr Sq	4 Nov 43–13 Nov 43	**1951**	
356 Ftr Sq	4 Nov 43–13 Nov 43	7501 AB Sq	21 May 51–1 Sep 53
1052 Qm Svc		**1953**	
Co, Avn	11 May 43–15 Dec 45	8 Avn Fld Dep Sq	16 Oct 53–14 Jun 54
1183 MP Co	26 Nov 43–27 May 45	3909 AB Gp	
1814 Ord Sup &		(3909 Cmbt	
Maint Co, Avn	25 Mar 43–6 Apr 44	Spt Gp)	15 Sep 53–30 Jun 64
1944		3909 AP Sq	1 Sep 53–1 Jan 59
2 Qm Bn [Mobile],		3909 Instls Sq	
HQ & HQ Det		(3909 CE Sq)	1 Sep 53–30 Jun 64
[Prov]	20 Oct 44–8 Dec 44	3909 Med Sq	
2 Qm Dep Sup Co		(3909 USAF	
[Prov]	20 Oct 44–8 Dec 44	Infmy; 3909	
26 Mobile		USAF Dispy)	1 Sep 53–1 Jan 59
Reclamation		3909 MV Sq	
& Rpr Sq	c. Jan 44–Apr 44	(3909 Trnsp Sq)	1 Sep 53–30 Jun 64
29 Mobile		3909 Ops Sq	1 Sep 53–30 Jun 64
Reclamation		3909 Sup Sq	1 Sep 53–1 Jan 59
& Rpr Sq	c. Jan 44–Apr 44	**1954**	
53 Trp Carr Wg	11 Mar 44–20 Feb 45	303 Air Rflg Sq	17 Mar 54–28 Apr 54
71 Ftr Wg	14 Jan 44–1 Mar 44	303 Armnt &	
87 Trp Carr Sq	11 Mar 44–20 Feb 45	Elect Maint Sq	17 Mar 54–28 Apr 54
88 Trp Carr Sq	11 mar 44–20 Feb 45	303 Bomb Wg	17 Mar 54–28 Apr 54
89 Trp Carr Sq	11 Mar 44–20 Feb 45	303 Fld Maint Sq	17 Mar 54–28 Apr 54
90 Trp Carr Sq	11 Mar 44–20 Feb 45	303 Prdc Maint Sq	17 Mar 54–28 Apr 54
97 Svc Sq	6 Apr 44–25 Apr 45	303 Tac Hosp	17 Mar 54–28 Apr 54
205 Med Dispy Avn	6 Apr 44–14 Oct 44	358 Bomb Sq	17 Mar 54–28 Apr 54
306 Stn Compl Sq	21 Feb 44–25 Apr 45	359 Bomb Sq	17 Mar 54–28 Apr 54
312 Ftr Con Sq	c. 18 Feb 44–6 Apr 44	360 Bomb Sq	17 Mar 54–28 Apr 54
321 Sig Co, Wg	c. 18 Feb 44–6 Apr 44	804 Engr Avn Bn	27 Apr 54–1 Mar 56
337 Sig Co, Trp		**1955**	
Carr Wg	c. 22 Feb 44–25 Apr 45	4 Avn Dep Sq	
368 Ftr Gp	13 Jan 44–15 Mar 44	(4 Mun Maint Sq)	1 Oct 55–30 Jun 64
395 Ftr Sq	13 Jan 44–15 Mar 44	39 AAA Bn	c. 55–c. Jul 57
396 Ftr Sq	13 Jan 44–15 Mar 44	3909 Fld Maint Sq	
397 Ftr Sq	13 Jan 44–15 Mar 44	(3909 Consold	
438 Trp Carr Gp	11 Mar 44–20 Feb 45	Acft Maint Sq)	15 Oct 55–30 Jun 64
490 Qm Dep Spt Co	c. 21 Aug 44–unk	Greenham Common	
811 Med Aerovac		Task Force, Prov	1 Nov 55–unk
Trnsp Sq	4 Aug 44–31 May 45	**1956**	
816 Med Aerovac		97 Air Rflg Sq	5 May 56–13 Jul 56
Trnsp Sq	c. 6 Apr 44–c. Aug 44	307 Air Rflg Sq	11 Jul 56–5 Oct 56
1074 Sig Co, Svc Gp	c. 6 Jun 44–4 Aug 44	310 Armnt & Elect	
1183 MP Co, Avn	6 Apr 44–27 May 45	Maint Sq	3 Oct 56–9 Jan 57
1228 MP Co, Avn	1 Jan 44–10 Jul 44	310 Bomb Wg	3 Oct 56–9 Jan 57
1478 Ord Mun		310 Fld Maint Sq	3 Oct 56–9 Jan 57
Maint Co, Avn	c. 6 Apr 44–1 Feb 45	310 Prdc Maint Sq	3 Oct 56–9 Jan 57
2049 Engr Fire		379 Bomb Sq	3 Oct 56–9 Jan 57
Fighting Platoon	c. 6 Jun 44–25 Apr 45	380 Bomb Sq	3 Oct 56–9 Jan 57
2059 Engr Fire		**1957**	
Fighting Platoon	7 Jan 44–6 Apr 44	25 Bomb Sq	1 Jul 57–1 Oct 57
Battery A, 473		40 Air Rflg Sq	1 Jul 57–1 Oct 57
AAA Automatic		40 Bomb Wg	1 Jul 57–1 Oct 57
Weapons Bn	1 May 44–unk	40 Fld Maint Sq	1 Jul 57–1 Oct 57
HQ Battery 473		40 Med Gp	1 Jul 57–1 Oct 57
AAA Automatic		40 Prdc Maint Sq	1 Jul 57–1 Oct 57

118

44 Bomb Sq	1 Jul 57–1 Oct 57		1976
45 Bomb Sq	1 Jul 57–1 Oct 57	OL A, 20 Tac	
	1959	Ftr Wg	1 Jun 76–25 Jun 76
3909 AB Sq			1979
(3909 Spt Sq)	1 Jan 59–30 Jun 64	7273 AB Gp	1 Jan 79–30 Sep 82
	1962		1982
3909 Sup Sq	1 Jul 62–30 Jun 64	11 Tac Msl Sq	1 Oct 82–
3909 Cmbt Def Sq	1 Jul 62–30 Jun 64	501 CE Sq	1 Oct 82–
	1968	501 Cmbt Spt Gp	1 Oct 82–
7551 Cmbt Spt Sq		501 Scty Pol Sq	1 Oct 82–
(7551 Cmbt Spt Gp)	1 Nov 68–31 May 76	501 Sup Sq	1 Oct 82–
	1972	501 Tac Msl	
USAF Dispy,		Maint Sq	1 Oct 82–
Greenham		501 Tac Msl Wg	1 Jul 82–
Common		501 Trnsp Sq	1 Oct 82–
(USAF Clinic,		2161 Comms Sq	1 Jul 82–
Greenham		USAF Clinic,	
Common)	1 Jul 72–1 Jan 76	Greenham	
		Common	1 Oct 82–

RAF Lakenheath

Location: Located 12 mi NW of Bury St. Edmunds, 12 mi NNE of Newmarket, 20 mi NE of Cambridge, and 2 mi SSW of Lakenheath, England.

Name: Named after a village in England.

Date of Current Name: 18 Dec 1955.

Previous Names: Lakenheath RAF Stn, c. 24 Nov 1941; Lakenheath RAF, 1 Jun 1950.

Date of Establishment: RAF establishment, 24 Nov 1941; USAF establishment, 1 Jun 1950.

Date Construction Began: RAF construction commenced early 1941; USAF construction began Jul 1948.

Date of Beneficial Occupancy: RAF occupancy, 24 Nov 1941; USAF occupancy, 27 Nov 1948.

Base Operating Units: 7460th Base Compl Sq, 27 Nov 1948; 7504th Base Compl Sq (7504th AB Gp; 3909th AB Gp), 17 Jan 1949; 3913th AB Sq, 1 Sep 1953; 3910th AB Gp, 15 Apr 1955; 99th Avn Dep Sq, 1 Oct 1959; 48th Cmbt Spt Gp, 15 Jan 1960 (trsfd from Chaumont AB, France)–.

Base Commanders:* Unk, 27 Nov 1948–1 Aug 1949; Lt Col Anthony J. Perna, 2 Aug 1949; Col Harold A. Gunn, Oct 1950; Col Gerald G. Robinson, 13 Oct 1951; Lt Col Archie C. Thomas, 1 Sep 1953; Col Ellery D. Preston Jr, 15 Apr 1955; Col Maynard E. White, 11 Jul 1956; Col David A. Tate, 29 Jul 1957; Col William A. Delahay, 1 Sep 1959; Lt Col Thomas C. McGuire, 15 Jan 1960; Col Evans G. Stephens, 11 Jul 1960; Lt Col Harold D. Collins, 5 Jul 1963 (temp); Col Robert E. Carlson, 22 Jul 1963; Col Robert A. O'Donnell, 22 Jun 1966; Lt Col David T. Mold, Jul 1968 (temp); Col Stephen A. Farris Jr, 16 Aug 1968; Col Edward R. Johnston, 10 Jul 1970; Col Louie A. Babbitt, 1 Jun 1974; Col Robert I. Platenberg, 21 Nov 1975; Col James E. Kelm, 8 May 1978; Col Merle E. Bollenbach, 9 May 1980–.

---

*The RAF owns this USAFE-administered installation and maintains a permanent RAF station commander there.

Major Off-Base and Detached Installations:* Gravel Hill Bcn Anx, Gravel Hill, 1 Jun 1950 (actvd)−; RAF Shepherd's Grove, Stanton, 16 Mar 1951 (actvd)−unk; Cambridge Svc Club Anx, 16 mi NW of Cambridge, 25 Mar 1951 (actvd)−; RAF Lakenheath RB Anx, Stanton, 1 Jul 1958 (asgnd)−24 May 1973 (dspd); RAF Shepherd's Grove Fam Hsg Anx, Stanton, unk−1 Sep 1959 (trsfd to RAF Mildenhall); RAF Sturgate Fam Hsg Anx, Upton, unk−1 Oct 1959 (trsfd to RAF Mildenhall); RAF Lakenheath Tacan Anx, 9 mi SSW of Newmarket, 18 Mar 1960 (actvd)−1 Jun 1960 (trsfd to RAF) Mildenhall); Hopton RB Anx, Hopton-on-Sea, 14 Dec 1960 (asgnd)−1 Sep 1962 (trsfd to RAF Bentwaters); RAF Barnham Amn Hsg Anx, Thetford, 14 Dec 1960 (asgnd)−31 Aug 1962 (trsfd to RAF Bentwaters); Fakenham Stor Anx, Fakenham, 27 Aug 1962 (actvd)−17 Dec 1968 (dspd); RAF Mildenhall Ammo Stor Anx, 30 Jan 1963 (actvd)−unk (trsfd to RAF Mildenhall); RAF Feltwell Fam Hsg Anx, Feltwell, 14 Sep 1966 (actvd)−unk; RAF Sculthorpe Stor Anx (rdsgd RAF Sculthorpe), 5 mi WNW of Fakenham, 10 Jan 1967 (asgnd) (dsgd detchd instl, 1 Oct 1970)−; Thetford Fam Hsg Anx, Thetford, 1 Jul 1968 (asgnd)−31 Dec 1974 (dspd); Feltwell Stor Anx, 10 mi WNW of Thetford, 8 Jul 1968 (actvd)−; Caxton Stor Anx, Caxton, 9 Oct 1968 (asgnd)−17 Jun 1970 (dspd); Lakenheath Fam Hsg Anx, Lakenheath, 4 Nov 1968 (actvd)−30 Jun 1978 (dspd); Weeting Fam Hsg Anx, Weeting, 5 Aug 1969 (asgnd)−31 May 1978 (dspd); RAF Mildenhall Ammo Stor Anx, 1 Jan 1972 (trsfd from RAF Mildenhall)−; Thetford Fam Hsg Anx #3, Thetford, 5 Jan 1972 (asgnd)−20 Dec 1974 (dspd); Red Lodge Fam Hsg Anx, Freckenham, 1 Jun 1974 (asgnd)−; Isleham Fam Hsg Anx, Isleham, 1 Nov 1974 (asgnd)−; RAF Feltwell Fam Hsg Anx (rdsgd Feltwell Stor Anx; RAF Feltwell Stor Site), Feltwell, 30 Nov 1974 (actvd)−; RAF Bircham Newton Fam Hsg Anx, Docking, 16 Dec 1974 (actvd)−; RAF Watton Stor Anx, Watton, 29 Sep 1976 (actvd)−; Bury St. Edmunds Fam Hsg Anx, Bury St. Edmunds, 1 Dec 1976 (actvd)−; Haverhill Fam Hsg Anx, Haverhill, 1 Dec 1976−1 Oct 1980 (trsfd to RAF Alconbury); Peterborough Fam Hsg Anx, Peterborough, unk−31 Dec 1976 (dspd); RAF West Raynham Fam Hsg Anx, Fakenham, 6 Jan 1977 (actvd)−; Bury St. Edmunds Fam Hsg Anx #2, Bury St. Edmunds, 26 Apr 1977−1 May 1979 (dspd); RAF Waddington, Waddington, 16 Aug 1978 (asgnd)−; Newmarket Fam Hsg Anx #3, Newmarket, 7 Sep 1979 (actvd)−; Soham Fam Hsg Anx, Soham, 7 Sep 1979 (asgnd)−; RAF Wittering, Wittering, 11 Jun 1980 (asgnd as detchd instl)−.

Major Changes in Operational Capability: Established by RAF as satellite base of Mildenhall RAF Station, 24 Nov 1941; three concrete runways, hangars, and huts for personnel housing completed Nov 1941;

---

*All installations are located in England.

operated by RAF as decoy base 1941, as heavy bomber operations and training base 1942–1943, and as radar countermeasures base 1944; flying operations ceased for repair, resurfacing, and extension of one runway May 1944 to Apr 1947; reopened as independent station of RAF Bomber Command Apr 1947; two remaining runways repaired, resurfaced, and readied for operations by May 1948; allocated to USAFE along with Scampton and Waddington in Lancashire, and Marham in Norfolk, for use by SAC as short-term deployment bases Jul 1948; B–29s of 2d Bomb Gp arrived 11 Aug 1948, the first of a continuous flow of B–29, KB–29, C–97, B–50, B–36, and B–47 rotational units; U.S. presence in the U.K. strengthened after Berlin Airlift 1948–1949 and outbreak of the Korean conflict in Jun 1950; Lakenheath transferred from USAFE to SAC, 1 May 1951; base fenced for security 1952; returned to USAFE control as part of RED RICHARD operation, 1 Oct 1959; withdrawal of American units from French bases brought 48th Tac Ftr Wg to Lakenheath on 15 Jan 1960; expansion of base facilities became necessary to accommodate increased permanent base population, and numerous construction projects commenced in 1960: new theater opened in Mar, junior high school on 9 May, high school on 6 Sep 1960, and auditorium in May 1961; 45 Phase III brick housing units constructed in 1961; 48th Tac Ftr Wg operated from RAF Mildenhall while Lakenheath runways were resurfaced May–Sep 1961; large base hospital constructed, which became major medical referral facility for U.S. Armed Forces in Britain, 1962–1965; the final increment of 408 Phase III housing units accepted 14 Jan 1966; airmen's dining hall completed 3 Jan 1967; 53 base elementary school classrooms finished, Aug 1969; three-story, brick dormitories for military personnel completed 1970; runways resurfaced and flight simulator building constructed in preparation for F–4 aircraft, 1971; additional family housing built adjacent to Phase III area in 1973; conversion of 48th Tac Ftr Wg to F–111 aircraft prompted hardening programs to protect base from attack and included 60 hardened aircraft shelters, avionics facility, squadron operations buildings, and a command post in late 1970s.

Major Commands to Which Assigned: USAFE, 27 Nov 1948; SAC, 28 Apr 1951; USAFE, 1 Oct 1959–.

Major Changes in Status: Activated as detached installation of RAF Mildenhall 24 Nov 1941; closed for repairs and construction May 1944; reopened Apr 1947 as primary installation of RAF Bomber Command; established as USAF primary installation on 1 Jun 1950–.

Units Assigned:

	1948		65 Bomb Sq	15 Aug 49–15 Nov 49
			830 Bomb Sq	Jun 49–21 Aug 49
7460 Base			7504 Base	
Compl Sq	27 Nov 48–17 Jan 49		Compl Sq	
	1949		(7504 AB Gp;	
33 Bomb Sq	20 Nov 49–18 Feb 50			

3909 AB Gp)	17 Jan 49–1 Sep 53	3912 AB Sq	1 Sep 53–6 Dec 54
	1950	3913 AB Sq	1 Sep 53–15 Apr 55
32 Bomb Sq	17 May 50–28 Nov 50	3932 AB Sq	16 Jun 53–15 Apr 55
96 Bomb Sq	22 Feb 50–12 May 50	3934 AB Sq	16 Jun 53–15 Apr 55
301 Air Rflg Sq	17 May 50–28 Nov 50		1954
301 Bomb Gp	17 May 50–28 Jun 50	8 Avn Dep Sq	15 Jun 54–1 Oct 59
301 Bomb Wg	28 Jun 50–28 Nov 50	320 Air Rflg Sq	5 Jun 54–3 Sep 54
7504 AP Sq		321 Bomb Wg	9 Dec 54–9 Mar 55
(3909 AP Sq)	16 Oct 50–1 Sep 53	321 Fld Maint Sq	9 Dec 54–9 Mar 55
7504 Air Spt Wg	26 Sep 50–16 May 51	321 Prdc Maint Sq	9 Dec 54–9 Mar 55
7504 Comms Sq		445 Bomb Sq	9 Dec 54–9 Mar 55
(3909 Ops Sq)	26 Sep 50–1 Sep 53	446 Bomb Sq	9 Dec 54–9 Mar 55
7504 Food Svc Sq		447 Bomb Sq	9 Dec 54–9 Mar 55
(3909 Food			1955
Svc Sq)	26 Sep 50–1 Sep 53	25 Bomb Sq	9 Jun 55–9 Sep 55
7504 Instls Sq		40 Armnt & Elect	
(3909 Instls Sq)	26 Sep 50–1 Sep 53	Maint Sq	9 Jun 55–9 Sep 55
7504 Maint &		40 Bomb Wg	9 Jun 55–9 Sep 55
Sup Gp	26 Sep 50–16 May 51	40 Fld Maint Sq	9 Jun 55–7 Sep 55
7504 Maint Sq		40 Prdc Maint Sq	9 Jun 55–9 Sep 55
(7504 Fld		44 Bomb Sq	9 Jun 55–9 Sep 55
Maint Sq)	26 Sep 50–16 May 51	45 Bomb Sq	9 Jun 55–9 Sep 55
7504 Med Sq		98 Armnt & Elect	
(3909 USAF		Maint Sq	12 Nov 55–28 Jan 56
Infmy; 3909		98 Bomb Wg	12 Nov 55–28 Jan 56
USAF Dispy)	26 Sep 50–1 Sep 53	98 Fld Maint Sq	18 Nov 55–28 Jan 56
7504 MV Sq		98 Prdc Maint Sq	12 Nov 55–28 Jan 56
(3909 MV Sq)	26 Sep 50–1 Sep 53	340 Air Rflg Sq	15 Sep 55–3 Nov 55
7504 Sup Sq)		340 Armnt & Elect	
(3909 Sup Sq)	26 Sep 50–1 Sep 53	Maint Sq	13 Sep 55–3 Nov 55
	1951	340 Bomb Wg	14 Sep 55–3 Nov 55
2 Air Rflg Sq	4 May 51–3 Dec 52	340 Fld Maint Sq	13 Sep 55–3 Nov 55
8 Avn Fld Dep Sq	26 Nov 51–16 Oct 53	340 Prdc Maint Sq	12 Sep 55–3 Nov 55
19 Bomb Sq	6 Sep 51–13 Dec 51	343 Bomb Sq	12 Nov 55–28 Jan 56
53 Ord Svc Co	May 51–unk 55	344 Bomb Sq	12 Nov 55–28 Jan 56
60 AAA AW Bn	May 51–c. Jul 57	345 Bomb Sq	12 Nov 55–28 Jan 56
81 Chemical Smoke		486 Bomb Sq	13 Sep 55–3 Nov 55
Generator Co	c. May 51–c. Jul 57	487 Bomb Sq	13 Sep 55–3 Nov 55
329 Bomb Sq	9 Dec 51–27 Feb 52	488 Bomb Sq	13 Sep 55–3 Nov 55
330 Bomb Sq	10 Dec 51–4 Mar 52	3910 AB Gp	
352 Bomb Sq	25 Sep 51–4 Dec 51	(3910 Cmbt	
353 Bomb Sq	25 Sep 51–4 Dec 51	Spt Gp)	15 Apr 55–1 Oct 59
509 Avn Sq	23 Jan 51–20 Jul 51	3910 AP Sq	15 Apr 55–1 Jan 59
1979 AACS Sq		3910 Comms Sq	15 Apr 55–1 Oct 59
(1979 Comms Sq)	20 Oct 51–	3910 Fld Maint Sq	
	1952	(3910 Consold	
97 Bomb Gp	15 Mar 52–4 Jun 52	Acft Maint Sq)	15 Oct 55–1 Oct 59
97 Bomb Wg	15 Mar 52–1 Apr 52	3910 Food Svc Sq	15 Apr 55–1 Jan 59
97 Maint Sq	4 Mar 52–1 Apr 52	3910 Instls Sq	15 Apr 55–1 Oct 59
340 Bomb Sq	5 Mar 52–4 Jun 52	3910 MV Sq	
341 Bomb Sq	2 Mar 52–3 Jun 52	(3910 Trnsp Sq)	15 Apr 55–1 Jan 59
342 Bomb Sq	2 Mar 52–3 Apr 52	3910 Sup Sq	15 Apr 55–1 Jan 59
715 Bomb Sq	4 Jun 52–3 Sep 52	3910 USAF Infmy	
830 Bomb Sq	4 Jun 52–4 Sep 52	(3910 USAF	
3910 AB Sq	1 Apr 52–15 Jan 53	Dispy)	15 Apr 55–1 Oct 59
	1953	Lakenheath Task	
43 Air Rflg Sq	21 Mar 53–5 Jun 53	Force, Prov	1 May 55–unk

1956

307 Armnt & Elect Maint Sq	11 Jul 56–5 Oct 56
307 Bomb Wg	11 Jul 56–5 Oct 56
307 Fld Maint Sq	11 Jul 56–5 Oct 56
307 Prdc Maint Sq	11 Jul 56–5 Oct 56
370 Bomb Sq	11 Jul 56–5 Oct 56
371 Bomb Sq	11 Jul 56–5 Oct 56
372 Bomb Sq	11 Jul 56–5 Oct 56
509 Air Rflg Sq	26 Jan 56–30 Apr 56
Wea Recon Sq, Prov, No 1	15 May 56–14 Jul 56

1958

99 Avn Dep Sq (99 Mun Maint Sq)	23 May 58–20 Dec 63
705 Strat Msl Wg	20 Feb 58–15 Mar 58

1959

672 Tech Tng Sq	17 Aug 59–1 Oct 59
3910 AB Sq	1 Jan 59–1 Oct 59
7510 USAF Hosp	1 Oct 59–15 Jan 60

1960

48 AB Gp (48 Cmbt Spt Gp)	15 Jan 60–
48 AP Sq (48 Scty Pol Sq)	15 Jan 60–
48 Armnt & Elect Maint Sq	15 Jan 60–15 Jan 62
48 Consold Acft Maint Sq (48 Fld Maint Sq; 48 Equip Maint Sq)	15 Jan 60–
48 Food Svc Sq	15 Jan 60–15 Jan 62

48 Instls Sq (48 CE Sq)	15 Jan 60–
48 Sup Sq	15 Jan 60–
48 Tac Ftr Wg	15 Jan 60–
48 Tac Hosp	15 Jan 60–
48 Trnsp Sq	15 Jan 60–
492 Tac Ftr Sq	11 Jan 60–
493 Tac Ftr Sq	6 Jan 60–
494 Tac Ftr Sq	15 Jan 60–

1964

48 Armnt & Elect Maint Sq (48 Avncs Maint Sq; 48 Component Rpr Sq)	1 Jul 64–
48 Orgnzl Maint Sq	1 Jul 64–1 Jan 66
348 Mun Maint Sq	1 Jul 64–7 Oct 72

1971

USAF Hosp, Lakenheath	1 Jul 71–

1972

48 Mun Maint Sq	8 Oct 72–31 Aug 81
48 Orgnzl Maint Sq (48 Acft Gnrtn Sq)	1 Feb 72–
7008 Explosive Ord Dspl Flt	1 Jan 72–

1977

495 Tac Ftr Sq	1 Apr 77–

1981

48 Svcs Sq	1 Oct 81–
548 Acft Gnrtn Sq	31 Aug 81–
7448 Comptroller Sq	1 Apr 81–

RAF Mildenhall

Location: Located adjacent to and SE of Mildenhall, 16 mi NE of Cambridge, 10 mi NW of Bury St. Edmunds, and 7 mi NNE of Newmarket, England.

Name: Named after a village in England.

Date of Current Name: 18 Dec 1955.

Previous Names: RAF Stn Mildenhall, 16 Oct 1934; Mildenhall RAF, 11 Jul 1950.

Date of Establishment: RAF establishment, 16 Oct 1934; USAF establishment, 11 Aug 1950.

Date Construction Began: Original RAF construction commenced late 1930; USAF construction work undertaken 1950.

Date of Beneficial Occupancy: RAF occupancy, 16 Oct 1934; USAF occupancy, 11 Jul 1950.

Base Operating Units: 7511th AB Sq (7511th AB Gp; 3910th AB Gp), 11 Jul 1950; 3913th AB Sq (3913th Cmbt Spt Gp), 15 Apr 1955; 7513th AB Gp (7513th Tac Gp), 1 Sep 1959; 513th Cmbt Spt Gp, 1 Jul 1966–.

Base Commanders:* Col Anthony J. Perna, 11 Jul 1950; Lt Col Preston P. Pender, 15 Jun 1951; Col Lawrence M. Thomas, 21 Aug 1951; Col Ellery D. Preston Jr, 20 May 1954; Lt Col Archie C. Thomas, 15 Apr 1955; Col Clifford V. Warden, Sep 1955; Col Clark A. Tate, 28 Apr 1958; Col Thomas C. Kelly, 4 Jul 1961; Col Vaughan Miller Jr, 27 Aug 1964; Col Sheldon S. Brinson, 24 Jun 1965; Col John W. Bogan, 1 Jul 1966; Col Elsey Harris Jr, 15 Jul 1967; Col Johnie R. Godwin, 27 Jul 1968; Col John D. McClung, 8 Jul 1972; Col Paul D. Davis, 21 Jan 1974; Lt Col Willard F. Langford, 28 Feb 1975; Col Merrill A. McPeak, 23 Jul 1976; Col Lyle E. Darrow, 8 Jul 1977; Col Charles J. Wingert, 4 Jun 1979; Col Peter W. Bent, 22 Jul 1981–.

Major Off-Base and Detached Installations:† Mildenhall RAF ILS Middle Marker Anx, 8 mi ENE of Newmarket, 11 Jul 1950 (actvd)–23 Apr

---

*The RAF owns this USAFE-administered installation and maintains a permanent RAF station commander there.

†All installations are located in England.

1979 (dspd); Mildenhall RAF ILS Outer Marker Anx, Icklingham, 11 Jul 1950 (actvd)–23 Apr 1979 (dspd); Mildenhall RAF Waste Anx, 13 mi SSW of Newmarket, 11 Jul 1950 (actvd)–unk; Mildenhall/Chalk Hill Bcn Anx, Mildenhall, 1 Aug 1950 (actvd)–31 Oct 1956 (inactvd); Shepherd's Grove RAF Fam Hsg Anx, 10 mi SW of Bury St. Edmunds, 16 Mar 1951 (actvd)–unk; Mildenhall RB Anx, Icklingham, 23 Aug 1957 (actvd)–27 Sep 1961 (dspd); Upper Heyford ILS Middle Marker Anx, 14 mi NW of Banbury, 14 Aug 1959 (actvd)–unk; Shepherd's Grove RAF Fam Hsg Anx, 10 mi SW of Bury St. Edmunds, 1 Sep 1959 (actvd)–unk; RAF Sturgate Fam Hsg Anx, Upton, 1 Oct 1959 (trsfd from RAF Lakenheath)–13 Nov 1963 (dspd); Cowden Air Rg, Great Cowden, 1 Jun 1960 (actvd)–unk; RAF Mildenhall Tacan Anx, Mildenhall, 1 Jun 1960 (trsfd from RAF Lakenheath)–30 Jul 1982 (dspd); Kirton-in-Lindsey RRS, Kirton-in-Lindsey, 16 Nov 1961 (asgnd)–1 Jul 1965 (trsfd to RAF Alconbury); Spitalgate RRS, Grantham, 16 Nov 1961 (actvd)–1 Jul 1965 (trsfd to RAF Alconbury); Garrowby Hill RRS, Garrowby Hill, 17 Nov 1961 (actvd)–1 Jul 1965 (trsfd to RAF Alconbury); Fylingdales Comms Stn, Fylingdales, 29 Nov 1961 (asgnd)–1 Jul 1965 (trsfd to RAF Alconbury); RAF Mildenhall Ammo Stor Anx, 11 mi SSW of Newmarket, 30 Jan 1963 (asgnd)–unk; Mildenhall Fam Hsg Anx, Mildenhall, 25 Mar 1968 (actvd)–unk; Thetford Fam Hsg Anx #2, Thetford, 1 Jul 1968 (actvd)–22 Jul 1982 (dspd); Brandon Fam Hsg Anx, Brandon, 8 Jul 1968 (actvd)–22 Jul 1982 (dspd); Feltwell Fam Hsg Anx #2, 8 Jul 1968 (actvd)–30 Nov 1974 (trsfd to RAF Lakenheath); Tuddenham Fam Hsg Anx, Tuddenham, 9 Jul 1968 (asgnd)–unk; RAF Mildenhall Ammo Stor Anx, Mildenhall, 7 Apr 1969 (actvd)–1 Jan 1972 (trsfd to RAF Lakenheath); RAF Mildenhall Waste Anx, Mildenhall, 7 Apr 1969 (actvd)–unk; Tuddenham Fam Hsg Anx, Tuddenham, 5 Jan 1971 (actvd)–; Newmarket Fam Hsg Anx #1, Newmarket, 10 Feb 1971 (actvd)–; Newmarket Fam Hsg Anx #2, Newmarket, 10 Feb 1971 (actvd)–; Mildenhall ILS Middle Marker Anx, Mildenhall, 11 Feb 1971 (actvd)–; Mildenhall ILS Outer Marker Anx, Icklingham, 11 Feb 1971 (actvd)–; Thetford Fam Hsg Anx #4, Thetford, 5 Jan 1972 (actvd)–31 Dec 1974 (dspd); Newmarket Fam Hsg Anx #3, Newmarket, 1 Jun 1972 (actvd)–3 Nov 1972 (dspd); Freckenham Fam Hsg Anx, 5 mi NE of Freckenham, 1 Jul 1973 (actvd)–; Monkton Fam Hsg Site, Monkton, 22 Nov 1974 (actvd)–.

Major Changes in Operational Capability: RAF bomber base 1934–1945; on standby status 1946; USAF B–29 SAC base 11 Jul 1950; B–50 base 1952–1953; B–47 and KC–97 base 1953–1958; runway closed for repairs 1958–1959; upon drawdown at Burtonwood Depot, Military Air Transport Service transferred its main U.K. terminal to Mildenhall on 1 Mar 1959; called "The Gateway to the United Kingdom," most U.S. military personnel and dependents arrived or departed through RAF Mildenhall; base transferred from SAC to USAFE, 1 Sep 1959; RAF ceased regular flying operations and U.S. Armed Forces became sole operators of base 1 Sep 1959; thereafter supported various aircraft and units to meet national security needs of the U.S. and U.K.; United States European Command (USEUCOM) moved its Airborne Command Post from France to Mildenhall, 1 Jul 1966; hosted 513th Trp Carr Wg (rdsgd 513th Tac Alft Wg) and other transient and deployed U.S. and Allied units as directed by HQ USAFE since 1 Jul 1966; NCO Club renovated, runways repaired, and general base utilities and maintenance facilities improved, 1966–1968; airmen's dormitory and service club completed in 1969; base runways closed for resurfacing, 1 Jul–30 Sep 1970, during which time flying units operated out of RAF Lakenheath; combat operations center completed and central runway lights installed, 1970; 48-unit bachelor officers' quarters, and aircraft parking and loading apron constructed, 1971–1972; base hosted HQ Third AF, which transferred from South Ruislip 12 Jun 1972; major construction, including an airmen's dormitory, base gymnasium, POL storage plant, and four large aircraft hangars completed 1973–1976; NATO maintenance dock and water softening plant constructed, extensive base roof repairs completed and east taxiways concreted 1976–1978; improved airfield lighting system installed, revetments erected for protection of aircraft, south taxiways resurfaced and major base structures, including housing, modernized and insulated, 1979–1982.

Major Commands to Which Assigned: RAF Bmbr Comd, 1934–1950; USAFE, 11 Jul 1950; SAC, 16 May 1951; USAFE, 1 Sep 1959.

Major Changes in Status: Active RAF base, 1934–1946; standby status, 1946; reduced to caretaker status, 1 Apr 1950; active base (cooperative USAF-RAF operation), 11 Jul 1950; sole USAF operation, 1 Sep 1959–.

Units Assigned:

1950			
7511 AB Sq			
(7511 AB Gp;			
3910 AB Gp)	11 Jul 50–15 Apr 55		
7511 AP Sq			
(3910 AP Sq)	16 Oct 50–15 Apr 55		
7511 Air Spt Wg	26 Sep 50–16 May 51		
7511 Comms Sq			
(3910 Ops Sq)	26 Sep 50–15 Apr 55		
7511 Food Svc Sq			
(3910 Food			
Svc Sq)	16 Oct 50–15 Apr 55		
7511 Instls Sq			
(3910 Instls Sq)	26 Sep 50–15 Apr 55		
7511 Maint &			
Sup Gp	26 Sep 50–16 May 51		
7511 Maint Sq			
(7511 Fld			
Maint Sq)	22 Aug 50–16 May 51		
7511 Med Sq			
(3910 Med Sq;			
3910 USAF			
Infmy)	26 Sep 50–15 Apr 55		
7511 MV Sq			
(3910 MV Sq)	26 Sep 50–15 Apr 55		
7511 Sup Sq			
(3910 Sup Sq)	22 Aug 50–15 Apr 55		
1951			
2 Bomb Gp	4 May 51–30 Aug 51		
2 Bomb Sq	12 Oct 51–6 Dec 51		
2 Bomb Wg	4 May 51–30 Aug 51		
2 Maint Sq	16 May 51–30 Aug 51		
22 Bomb Wg	7 Sep 51–12 Dec 51		
22 Maint Sq	11 Sep 51–11 Dec 51		
49 Bomb Sq	4 May 51–4 Sep 51		
93 Bomb Gp	11 Dec 51–16 Mar 52		
93 Bomb Wg	16 Dec 51–8 Mar 52		
93 Maint Sq	10 Dec 51–2 Mar 52		
328 Bomb Sq	11 Dec 51–26 Feb 52		

	1952		1965
97 Air Rflg Sq	52–2 Jun 52	7036 Tac Sq	1 Jun 65–1 Jul 65
97 Bomb Wg	1 Apr 52–11 Jun 52	7120 Abn Comd	
97 Maint Sq	1 Apr 52–6 Jun 52	& Con Sq	15 Nov 65–1 Jan 70
342 Bomb Sq	3 Apr 52–3 Jun 52	7120 Spt Sq	15 Nov 65–1 Jan 77
393 Bomb Sq	4 Jun 52–3 Sep 52	7513 Cmbt Spt Sq	1 Jun 65–21 Jun 66
509 Bomb Gp	4 Jun 52–16 Jun 52	7513 Consold Acft	
509 Bomb Wg	4 Jun 52–2 Sep 52	Maint Sq	1 Jun 65–21 Jun 66
509 Fld Maint Sq	4 Jun 52–3 Sep 52	7513 Mat Sq	1 Jun 65–21 Jun 66
509 Maint &			1966
Sup Gp	4 Jun 52–16 Jun 52	5 Aerl Port Sq	
	1953	(5 Mobile Aerl	
22 Air Rflg Sq	7 Dec 53–5 Mar 54	Port Sq)	25 Jul 66–15 Sep 78
305 Air Rflg Sq	6 Sep 53–4 Dec 53	513 AP Sq	
306 Air Rflg Sq	11 Jun 53–7 Sep 53	(513 Scty Pol Sq)	1 Jul 66–
3912 AB Sq	1 Feb 53–1 Sep 53	513 CE Sq	1 Jul 66–
3913 AB Sq	15 Apr 53–1 Sep 59	513 Cmbt Spt Gp	1 Jul 66–
	1954	513 Fld Maint Sq	1 Jul 66–
303 Air Rflg Sq	17 Mar 54–5 Jun 54	513 Sup Sq	1 Jul 66–
3912 AB Sq	6 Dec 54–1 Mar 57	513 Trnsp Sq	1 Jul 66–
	1955	513 Trp Carr Wg	
98 Air Rflg Sq	7 Nov 55–31 Jan 56	(513 Tac Alft Wg)	1 Jul 66–
3932 AB Sq	15 Apr 55–15 Oct 55	627 Mil Alft Spt Sq	8 Jan 66–15 Sep 78
3934 AB Sq	15 Apr 55–15 Oct 55	Trp Carr Sq,	
	1956	Prov, 7441	20 Jul 66–1 Apr 67
Mildenhall Task		Trp Carr Sq,	
Force, Prov	1 Jul 56–unk	Prov, 7442	20 Jul 66–1 Apr 67
	1957		1968
380 Air Rflg Sq	3 Apr 57–3 Jul 57	Mil Alft Sq,	
	1959	Prov, 1648	8 Jul 68–25 May 69
19 Avn Dep Sq	1 Feb 59–1 Sep 59		1970
53 Wea Recon Sq	10 Aug 59–18 Mar 60	10 Abn Comd &	
1625 Spt Sq	1 Mar 59–8 Jan 66	Con Sq	1 Jan 70–
3913 Cmbt Spt Gp	1 Jan 59–1 Sep 59		1972
3913 Consold Acft		513 Orgnzl	
Maint Sq	1 Jan 59–1 Sep 59	Maint Sq	1 Jul 72–
3913 Instls Sq	1 Jan 59–1 Sep 59		1974
3913 Ops Sq	1 Jan 59–1 Sep 59	6954 Scty Sq	
6931 Comms Scty		(6954 Elect	
Flt		Scty Sq;	
(6931 Comms		6988 Elect	
Scty Dep Sq)	23 Feb 59–1 Oct 61	Scty Sq)	1 Apr 74–
7513 AB Gp			1975
(7513 Tac Gp)	1 Sep 59–1 Jul 66	435 Tac Alft Gp	1 Jul 75–15 Sep 78
7513 Cmbt Spt Sq	1 Jun 59–21 Jul 66		1977
7513 Consold Acft		513 Avncs	
Maint Sq	1 Jun 59–21 Jul 66	Maint Sq	1 Apr 77–
7513 Mat Sq	1 Jun 59–21 Jul 66		1978
7543 AB Sq	1 Sep 59–1 Mar 62	306 Strat Wg	30 Jun 78–
	1962	313 Tac Alft Gp	15 Sep 78–
3 Aeromed			1980
Evac Sq	6 Sep 62–25 Jan 63	28 Wea Sq	1 Jul 80–
1858 Fclts			1982
Checking Flt	23 Aug 62–1 Jun 63	513 Svcs Sq	1 Feb 82–
2147 Comms		2176 Comms Sq	1 Aug 82–
Sq		Numbered AF	
(2147		Cmbt Ops Staff	
Comms Gp)	1 Aug 62–	[Third AF]	1 Jan 82–

RAF Upper Heyford

Location: Located adjacent to and N of Upper Heyford, 15 mi N of Oxford, 60 mi NW of London, and 4 mi NW of Bicester, England.

Name: Named after a village in England.

Date of Current Name: 18 Dec 1955.

Previous Names: Unk, 1916–1919; RAF Stn Upper Heyford, 1928; Upper Heyford RAF, 15 May 1951.

Date Established: Originally established as a Royal Flying Corps base in 1916; inactive 1919–1928; reestablished as a RAF station in 1928; joint USAF-RAF establishment, 27 Jun 1950; USAF establishment, 15 May 1951.

Date Construction Began: Original construction initiated by Royal Flying Corps in 1916, with further construction work 1926–1928; USAF construction commenced 7 Jul 1950.

Date of Beneficial Occupancy: 7 Jul 1950.

Base Operating Units: 7509th AB Sq (7509th AB Gp; 3918th AB Gp; 3918th Cmbt Spt Gp; 3918th Strat Wg), 7 Jul 1950; 7514th Cmbt Spt Gp (7514th Tac Gp), 1 Apr 1965; 66th Cmbt Spt Gp, 10 Aug 1966; 20th Cmbt Spt Gp, 1 Apr 1970–.

Base Commanders:* Lt Col Frank A. Roper, 7 Jul 1950; Capt James Volosen, 16 Mar 1951 (temp); Col William L. Snowden, 1951 (temp); Lt Col Frank A. Roper, 2 Jan 1952; Col Floyd E. Wikstrom, 3 Jun 1953; Col Timothy J. Dacey Jr, 13 Aug 1954; Lt Col John T. Allen, 20 Jun 1957 (temp); Col Kenneth W. Schultz, 1 Aug 1957; Col John W. Carroll, 30 Jun 1960; Col Arthur W. Holderness Jr, 17 Jul 1961; Col Reuben A. Baxter, 10 Jan 1963; Col Peter M. Childress, 1 Apr 1965; Col John J. Davis, 6 Jul 1966; Col Ronald E. Dunlap, 18 Jul 1968; Col Robert A. Bennett, 30 Jan 1969; Col Don D. Pittman, 1 Aug 1970; Col Glen T. Noyes, 1 Apr 1971; Col Kenneth D. Burns, 18 Sep 1972; Col Jude R. McNamara, 25 Apr 1973; Col James M. Dunn Jr, 14 Jan 1974; Lt Col Rodney H. Fauser, 27 May

---

*The RAF owns this USAFE-administered installation and maintains a permanent RAF station commander there.

1975; Col James A. Heathcote, 18 Jun 1976; Col Donald G. Waltman, 9 Jun 1978; Col Fred R. Nelson, 24 Sep 1979; Col Frederick A. Zehrer III, 1 Jun 1981; Col William H. Lace, 15 Aug 1982–.

Major Off-Base and Detached Installations:* Upper Heyford Waste Anx, 14 mi N of Oxford, 27 Nov 1950 (actvd)–unk; Upper Heyford Water Sys Anx, 14 mi N of Oxford, 27 Nov 1950 (actvd)–unk; RAF Croughton, c. Jan 1951 (asgnd)–10 Jan 1952; RAF Middleton Stoney, c. Jan 1951 (asgnd)–10 Jan 1952 (trsfd to RAF Croughton); RAF Stn Barford St. John, c. Jan 1951 (asgnd)–10 Jan 1952 (trsfd to RAF Croughton); Upper Heyford ILS Outer Marker Anx, 14 mi N of Oxford, 14 Aug 1959 (asgnd)–unk; Upper Heyford RB Anx, 14 Aug 1959 (actvd)–unk; RAF Upper Heyford ILS Outer Marker Anx, Bicester, 1 Jul 1966 (asgnd)–7 Jun 1976 (inactvd); RAF Upper Heyford RB Anx (RAF Upper Heyford ILS Middle Marker Anx), Fringford, 1 Jul 1966 (actvd)–22 Nov 1978 (inactvd); RAF Upper Heyford Waste Anx, Bicester, 1 Jul 1966 (asgnd)–; RAF Upper Heyford Water Sys Anx, Bicester, 1 Jul 1966 (asgnd)–25 Apr 1977 (inactvd); Mormond Hill Comms Stn, Mormond Hill, Scotland, 1 Oct 1966 (trsfd from RAF Croughton)–1 Jul 1967 (trsfd to RAF Alconbury); RAF Barford St. John Trsmn Anx, 1 Oct 1966 (trsfd from RAF Croughton)–; RAF Croughton, Croughton, 1 Oct 1966 (trsfd from RAF Croughton)–unk; Chipping Norton Fam Hsg Anx, Chipping Norton, 24 Oct 1966–28 May 1970 (dspd); Coombe Fam Hsg Anx, Woodstock, 3 Nov 1966–; Steeple Aston Fam Hsg Anx, 14 mi N of Oxford, 1 Dec 1966 (actvd)–1 Aug 1977 (dspd); Banbury Fam Hsg Anx, Banbury, 12 Dec 1966 (actvd)–; Ardley Fam Hsg Anx, 9 mi S of Banbury, 17 Jan 1968 (asgnd)–; Hastoe Park Fam Hsg Anx, Aylesbury, 1 Jul 1969 (trsfd from South Ruislip AS)–13 Dec 1973 (dspd); Bicester Fam Hsg Anx, Bicester, 15 Dec 1969–; Bicester Sch, Bicester, 1 Feb 1971 (actvd)–; St. Columb Fam Hsg Anx, 8 mi NE of Newquay, 23 Jan 1974 (actvd)–unk (trsfd to RAF Greenham Common); RAF Gaydon Fam Hsg Anx, 9 mi SE of Warwick, 12 Jan 1976 (asgnd)–2 Sep 1981 (dspd); Bishop's Green Fam Hsg Anx, Newbury, 1 Jan 1977 (trsfd from RAF Greenham Common)–1 Oct 1982 (trsfd to RAF Greenham Common; Blackbushe Fam Hsg Anx, Yately, 1 Jan 1977 (trsfd from RAF Greenham Common)–1 Oct 1982 (trsfd to RAF Greenham Common); RAF Christmas Common RRS, Waddington, 1 Jan 1977 (trsfd from RAF Greenham Common)–1 Oct 1981 (trsfd to RAF High Wycombe); RAF Greenham Common Fam Hsg Anx, Newbury, 1 Jan 1977 (trsfd from RAF Greenham Common)–1 Oct 1982 (trsfd to RAF Greenham Common); RAF Greenham Common Waste Anx, Newbury, 1 Jan 1977 (trsfd from RAF Greenham Common)–1 Oct 1982 (trsfd to RAF Greenham Com-

---

*Unless otherwise indicated, all installations are located in England.

mon); RAF St. Mawgan Comms Stn, Newquay, 1 Jan 1977 (trsfd from RAF Greenham Common)–; RAF Welford Ammo Stor Anx, Newbury, 1 Jan 1977 (trsfd from RAF Greenham Common)–1 Oct 1982 (trsfd to RAF Greenham Common); St. Columb Fam Hsg Anx, St. Columb, 1 Jan 1977 (trsfd from RAF Greenham Common)–; Wantage Fam Hsg Anx, 1 Jan 1977 (trsfd from RAF Greenham Common)–1 Oct 1982 (trsfd to RAF Greenham Common); RAF Welford Waste Anx, Newbury, 1 Jul 1977 (trsfd from RAF Greenham Common)–1 Oct 1982 (trsfd to RAF Greenham Common); RAF Bicester, Bicester, 22 Nov 1978 (asgnd)–; Wincombe RB Site (RAF Wincombe RB Site), 3 May 1979 (asgnd)–; Long Hanborough Fam Hsg Anx, Long Hanborough, 11 Jan 1980 (actvd)–; Blackbushe Fam Hsg Anx, Yately, 8 Oct 1980 (asgnd)–; Swindon Fam Hsg Anx, Swindon, 1 Jan 1981 (trsfd from RAF Fairford)–1 Oct 1982 (trsfd to RAF Greenham Common); RAF Boscombe Down, Boscombe, 23 Mar 1981 (actvd & asgnd)–; RAF Clayhill Fam Hsg Anx, Burghfield, 16 Sep 1981 (asgnd in UC status)–1 Oct 1982 (trsfd to RAF Greenham Common).

Major Changes in Operational Capability: Established as Royal Flying Corps field in 1916 and closed 1919; reopened as RAF bomber training base 1928; RAF training base in World War II; following the Berlin Crisis of 1948 and onset of the Cold War, USAF and RAF planned to base U.S. strategic bombers at RAF Marham, Scampton and Waddington, with four other bases, including Upper Heyford, designated as standby or strategic dispersal bases; 7509th AB Sq arrived to take command of and coordinate airfield construction work at Upper Heyford 7 Jul 1950; after extensive runway renovation and construction of base and support facilities, the Third AF (USAFE) relinquished operational and administrative control of base to the 7th Air Div (SAC) on 10 Apr 1952; SAC commenced KC–50 tanker rotations in 1951 and B/RB–36 bomber rotations in 1952, followed by B–47 rotations 1953–1965; SAC reflex operations drew down late in 1964 and ended in Jan 1965; USAFE again assumed operational and administrative control of RAF Upper Heyford on 1 Apr 1965, initially using it as a dispersal base; with arrival of the 66th Tac Recon Wg from Laon AB, France, Heyford became main operating base on 1 Sep 1966; provided support for 20th Tac Ftr Wg after its arrival from RAF Wethersfield 1 Apr 1970; construction of two airmen's dormitories (140-man capacity each), two maintenance hangars, two aircraft maintenance docks on the north Taxiway, a 72-unit officer housing facility, and a helicopter pad completed by the end of 1972; construction of additional equipment storage sheds completed in 1973; base engineers renovated two airmen's dormitories, with construction completed on a base bowling alley, NCO Club, Base Exchange shopping center, taxitrack, aircraft weather shelter, two fuel storage tanks, and an ammunition storage facility, 1974–1975; contract workmen reinforced the main runway, built a base gymnasium, and erected dual BAR–12 arrester devices in 1976; 19 ammunition storage igloo structures and eight multi-barrel ammunition storage igloo structures constructed, base water system modernized, and up-to-date fire fighter equipment installed, including a 350,000 gallon ground-level tank with pumphouse, 1977–1978; POL facility completed in 1979; more recent improvements included fencing, lighting, and general improvement of perimeter security for base ammunition storage, a new parallel taxiway, widening of the NATO taxitrack, construction of 31 weatherproof aircraft shelters, a hardened alert area, and a composite medical facility, 1979–1982.

Major Commands to Which Assigned: USAFE, 7 Jul 1950; SAC, 10 Jan 1952; USAFE, 1 Apr 1965–.

Major Changes in Status: Royal Flying Corps field, 1916; base closed, 1919; reopened as active RAF training and bomber base, 1928; RAF training base, 1939–1950; operated by USAF in cooperation with RAF, 27 Jun 1950; under sole operational control of USAF, 15 May 1951; reduced to dispersal base status, 1 Apr 1965; assigned main operating base status, 1 Sep 1966.

Units Assigned:

1950			
801 Engr Avn Bn	20 Jun 50–30 Aug 52	7509 Ops Sq	
7509 AB Sq		(3918 Ops Sq)	25 May 51–31 Mar 65
(7509 AB Gp;		7509 Sup Sq	
3918 AB Gp;		(3918 Sup Sq)	25 May 51–31 Mar 65
3918 Cmbt		1952	
Spt Gp;		2 Armnt Elect	
3918 Strat Wg)	7 Jul 50–31 Mar 65	Maint Sq	9 Sep 52–7 Dec 52
Co A, 801 Engr		2 Bomb Wg	17 Dec 52–6 Mar 53
Avn Bn	20 Jun 50–30 Aug 52	2 Fld Maint Sq	7 Sep 52–3 Dec 52
Co B, 801 Engr		2 Prdc Maint Sq	4 Sep 52–3 Dec 52
Avn Bn	20 Jun 50–30 Aug 52	20 Bomb Sq	6 Sep 52–3 Dec 52
1951		44 Chemical Smoke	
1 Avn Fld Dep Sq		Generator Co	14 May 52–unk 54
(1 Avn Dep Sq)	19 May 51–1 May 58	49 Bomb Sq	4 Sep 52–3 Dec 52
93 Air Rflg Sq	9 Dec 51–3 Mar 52	96 Bomb Sq	4 Sep 52–3 Dec 52
7509 AP Sq		97 Air Rflg Sq	5 Mar 52–unk 52
(3918 AP Sq)	25 May 51–1 Jan 59	98 Chemical Smoke	
7509 Food Svc Sq		Generator Co	14 May 52–Jul 57
(3918 Food		301 Armnt & Elect	
Svc Sq)	25 May 51–1 Jan 59	Maint Sq	17 Dec 52–6 Mar 53
7509 Instls Sq		301 Bomb Wg	17 Dec 52–6 Mar 53
(3918 Instls Sq;		301 Fld Maint Sq	17 Dec 52–6 Mar 53
3918 CE Sq)	25 May 51–31 Mar 65	301 Prdc Maint Sq	17 Dec 52–6 Mar 53
7509 Med Sq		352 Bomb Sq	17 Dec 52–6 Mar 53
(3918 Med Sq;		509 Air Rflg Sq	4 Jun 52–3 Sep 52
3918 USAF		1953	
Infmy;		2 Bomb Sq	9 Dec 53–5 Mar 54
3918 Dispy)	25 May 51–31 Mar 65	4 AAA AW Bn	14 Feb 53–Jul 57
7509 MV Sq		19 Bomb Sq	12 Dec 53–5 Mar 54
(3918 MV Sq;		22 Armnt & Elect	
3918 Trnsp Sq)	25 May 51–31 Mar 65	Maint Sq	7 Dec 53–5 Mar 54
		22 Bomb Wg	7 Dec 53–5 Mar 54
		22 Fld Maint Sq	4 Dec 53–5 Mar 54

22 Prdc Maint Sq	8 Dec 53–5 Mar 54	Maint Sq)	1 Dec 58–30 Apr 65
33 Bomb Sq	9 Dec 53–5 Mar 54	**1959**	
1954		3918 AB Sq	
3 Strat Recon Sq	16 Sep 54–27 Oct 54	(3918 Spt Sq)	1 Jan 59–31 Mar 65
4 Strat Recon Sq	16 Sep 54–27 Oct 54	**1962**	
10 Strat Recon Sq	16 Sep 54–27 Oct 54	3918 Cmbt Def Sq	1 Jul 62–31 Mar 65
26 Armnt & Elect		**1965**	
Maint Sq	16 Sep 54–27 Oct 54	7514 Cmbt Spt Gp	
26 Fld Maint Sq	16 Sep 54–27 Oct 54	(7514 Tac Gp)	8 Feb 65–1 Sep 66
26 Prdc Maint Sq	16 Sep 54–27 Oct 54	7514 Cmbt Spt Sq	1 Jan 65–1 Sep 66
32 Army Band	20 Oct 54–20 Jun 55	7514 Consold Acft	
1268 AACS Sq		Maint Sq	1 Jan 65–10 Jan 66
(2168 Comms Sq)	1 Nov 54–25 Mar 65	7514 USAF Dispy	8 Feb 65–1 Sep 66
1955		**1966**	
83 Chemical Smoke		17 Tac Recon Sq	10 Aug 66–1 Nov 69
Generator Co	55–c. Jul 57	18 Tac Recon Sq	10 Aug 66–15 Jan 70
310 Armnt & Elect		66 AP Sq	
Maint Sq	12 Mar 55–8 Jun 55	(66 Scty Pol Sq)	10 Aug 66–1 Apr 70
310 Bomb Wg	10 Mar 55–8 Jun 55	66 Armnt & Elect	
310 Fld Maint Sq	11 Mar 55–8 Jun 55	Maint Sq	
376 Armnt & Elect		(66 Avncs	
Maint Sq	16 Jul 55–16 Oct 55	Maint Sq)	10 Aug 66–1 Apr 70
376 Bomb Wg	16 Jul 55–16 Oct 55	66 CE Sq	10 Aug 66–1 Apr 70
376 Fld Maint Sq	16 Jul 55–16 Oct 55	66 Cmbt Spt Gp	10 Aug 66–1 Oct 70
376 Prdc Maint Sq	16 Jul 55–16 Oct 55	66 Consold Acft	
379 Bomb Sq	10 Mar 55–8 Jun 55	Maint Sq	10 Aug 66–1 Apr 70
380 Bomb Sq	12 Mar 55–8 Jun 55	66 Fld Maint Sq	10 Aug 66–1 Apr 70
381 Bomb Sq	12 Mar 55–8 Jun 55	66 Sup Sq	10 Aug 66–1 Apr 70
512 Bomb Sq	8 Jul 55–16 Oct 55	66 Tac Recon Wg	10 Aug 66–1 Apr 70
513 Bomb Sq	8 Jul 55–16 Oct 55	66 Trnsp Sq	10 Aug 66–1 Apr 70
514 Bomb Sq	8 Jul 55–16 Oct 55	2168 Comms Sq	1 Apr 66–
3918 Fld Maint Sq		**1969**	
(3918 Consold		20 Avncs Maint Sq	
Acft Maint Sq)	15 Oct 55–31 Mar 65	(20 Component	
Upper Heyford		Rpr Sq)	1 Dec 69–
Task Force,		20 CE Sq	1 Dec 69–
Prov	1 May 55–unk	20 Cmbt Spt Gp	1 Dec 69–
1956		20 Fld Maint Sq	
97 Armnt & Elect		(20 Equip	
Maint Sq	5 May 56–4 Jul 56	Maint Sq)	1 Dec 69–
97 Bomb Wg	5 May 56–4 Jul 56	20 Scty Pol Sq	1 Dec 69–
97 Fld Maint Sq	5 May 56–4 Jul 56	20 Sup Sq	1 Dec 69–
97 Prdc Maint Sq	5 May 56–4 Jul 56	20 Tac Ftr Wg	1 Dec 69–
340 Bomb Sq	5 May 56–4 Jul 56	20 Tac Hosp	1 Dec 69–
341 Bomb Sq	5 May 56–4 Jul 56	20 Trnsp Sq	1 Dec 69–
342 Bomb Sq	5 May 56–4 Jul 56	55 Tac Ftr Sq	1 Dec 69–
393 Bomb Sq	26 Jan 56–30 Apr 56	77 Tac Ftr Sq	1 Dec 69–
509 Armnt & Elect		79 Tac Ftr Sq	1 Dec 69–
Maint Sq	26 Jan 56–30 Apr 56	320 Mun Maint Sq	1 Dec 69–1 Oct 72
509 Bomb Wg	26 Jan 56–30 Apr 56	**1971**	
509 Fld Maint Sq	26 Jan 56–30 Apr 56	USAF Dispy,	
509 Prdc Maint Sq	26 Jan 56–30 Apr 56	Upper Heyford	
715 Bomb Sq	26 Jan 56–30 Apr 56	(USAF Hosp,	
830 Bomb Sq	26 Jan 56–30 Apr 56	Upper Heyford)	1 Jul 71–
1958		**1972**	
11 Avn Dep Sq		20 Mun Maint Sq	1 Oct 72–31 Oct 81
(11 Mun		20 Orgnzl Maint Sq	

AIR FORCE BASES OVERSEAS

(20 Acft Gnrtn Sq)	1 Feb 72–		1981
	1978	520 Acft Gnrtn Sq	31 Oct 81–
7016 Explosive			1982
Ord Flt	1 Oct 78–	20 Svcs Sq	1 Feb 82–

RAF Woodbridge

Location: Located 5 mi E of town of Woodbridge, 85 mi NE of London, 12 mi ENE of Ipswich, and 2 mi ENE of Melton, England.

Name: Named after a town in England.

Date of Current Name: 18 Dec 1955.

Previous Names: RAF Stn Woodbridge (also known as RAF Stn Sutton Heath), 15 Nov 1943; Woodbridge RAF, 5 Jun 1952.

Date of Establishment: Opened as RAF emergency airfield 15 Nov 1943; established as USAF base 5 Jun 1952.

Date Construction Began: Original construction initiated by RAF in Jul 1942; USAF construction commenced 16 Apr 1952.

Date of Beneficial Occupancy: 16 Apr 1952.

Base Operating Units: 3928th AB Sq, 16 Apr 1952; 3938th AB Sq, 1 Apr 1954; 3928th AB Gp, 1 Nov 1954; 7546th Spt Sq, 26 Jan 1956; 81st Cmbt Spt Gp, 8 Jul 1960–.

Base Commanders:* Maj Olen L. Waters, 16 Apr 1952; Capt John V. Popp, 1 May 1952; 1st Lt Frank Maxey Jr, 6 Oct 1952; Maj William H. Noel, 10 Jan 1953; Maj Henry W. Mitzner, 1 Apr 1954; Col Rollin M. Winningham, 1 Nov 1954; Maj William A. Brady, 26 Jun 1956; Lt Col Benjamin F.Uhrich, 31 Jul 1956; Maj Sherwood F. Lapping, 8 Aug 1957; Col Elmer C. Blahn,† 1 Feb 1959; Col Jack R. Best, 11 Jul 1959; Col Harry F. Alexander, 10 Jul 1962; Col William W. Parramore Jr, 19 Jul 1965; Col Bernie S. Bass, 5 Jul 1968; Col Philip R. Safford, 1 Dec 1969; Col Ernest R. Wilson, 17 Aug 1970; Col Morton D. Orzen, 13 Oct 1972; Lt Col Walter J. Schenning, 10 Jun 1974; Col Walter A. Williams, 26 Jul 1974; Col Jarrell S. Mitchell, 6 Sep 1977; Col Jackie K. Snow, 20 Jun 1979; Col Theodore J. Conrad, 3 Jul 1980; Col Sam P. Morgan Jr, 14 Mar 1981; Col Henry J. Cochran, 15 Jul 1982–.

---

*The RAF owns this USAFE-administered installation and maintains a permanent RAF station commander there.

†All commanders after 1 Feb 1959 are identical to those of RAF Bentwaters since the two bases were administered as a single entity.

Major Off-Base and Detached Installations: RAF Woodbridge Waste Anx, 3 mi E of Woodbridge, 5 Jun 1952 (actvd)–19 Feb 1965 (trsfd to RAF Bentwaters); RAF Woodbridge Fam Hsg Anx, 19 Feb 1968 (actvd)–.

Major Changes in Operational Capability: RAF opened original station as a RAF emergency landing field 15 Nov 1943 and closed it on 14 Mar 1948; first USAF units arrived 1 Apr 1952; base provided support as satellite of Bentwaters RAF and operated as a SAC fighter-bomber (later, fighter) base; received logistical and administrative support from RAF Sturgate 30 Sep 1952; base evacuated on 1 Oct 1954 and throughout much of 1955 for major construction work, including repair and reinforcement of runway, preparation of hardstands, erection of hangars, etc; Woodbridge became solely a USAFE installation, logistically supported by RAF Bentwaters on 5 Jun 1952; operated as "twin base" with Bentwaters from 8 Jul 1958 and as a single unit with Bentwaters under the 81st Tac Ftr Wg after 1 Feb 1959; nonoperational 3 Nov–4 Dec 1958 during major runway repairs; 67th Air Rscu and Recovery Sq moved to Woodbridge from Moron AB, Spain, on 15 Jan 1970; as part of the expansion of the 81st Tac Ftr Wg to six A–10 squadrons, USAFE activated the 509th Tac Ftr Sq at Woodbridge in 1979 and moved the 91st Tac Ftr Sq there on 1 Feb 1980.

Major Commands to Which Assigned: USAFE, 5 Jun 1952–.

Major Changes in Status: Activated as secondary installation supported by RAF Wethersfield, 5 Jun 1952; placed on standby status, 1 Oct 1954; became active twin-base with RAF Bentwaters, 1 Oct 1958–.

Units Assigned:

1952		1964	
79 Ftr-Bmbr Sq		20 Flt Line	
(79 Tac Ftr Sq)	1 Jun 52–1 Dec 69	Maint Sq	1 Jul 64–15 Dec 65
3928 AB Sq	1 Apr 52–15 Jan 53	1970	
1954		67 Aerosp Rscu	
3938 AB Sq	1 Apr 54–1 Nov 54	& Recovery Sq	15 Jan 70–
1956		1979	
7546 Spt Sq	26 Jun 56–8 Jul 60	509 Tac Ftr Sq	1 Oct 79–1 Feb 80 1980
1958		91 Tac Ftr Sq	1 Feb 80–
78 Tac Ftr Sq	22 Dec 58–		

Ramstein Air Base

Location: Located 7 mi W of Kaiserslautern, 3 mi NE of Landstuhl, and 2 1/2 mi ESE of Ramstein, Rheinland-Pfalz, Federal Republic of Germany.

Name: Named after a town in the Federal Republic of Germany.

Date of Current Name: 15 Aug 1958.

Previous Names: Landstuhl AB, 5 Aug 1952; Ramstein AB, 1 Jun 1953 (Landstuhl and Ramstein separate bases until 1957) Ramstein-Landstuhl AB, 1 Dec 1957.

Date of Establishment: 5 Aug 1952.

Date Construction Began: French construction work initiated Apr 1951; USAF construction commenced Apr 1952.

Date of Beneficial Occupancy: 2 Feb 1952.

Base Operating Units: 86th AB Gp, 5 Apr 1952; 7030th HQ Spt Gp (7030th Spt Gp; 7030th AB Wg; 7030th Cmbt Spt Wg), 6 Apr 1953; 26th Cmbt Spt Gp, 5 Oct 1966; 86th Cmbt Spt Gp, 31 Jan 1973–.

Base Commanders: Lt Col William F. Barnard Jr, 5 Apr 1952; Col Franklin S. Allen, 10 Jul 1952; Lt Col Newton P. Littleton, 18 Sep 1952 (temp); Col Andrew J. Bing, 22 Oct 1952; Col James W. Bennett, 6 Apr 1953; Col Albert F. Law, 1 Dec 1954; Col Herbert C. Hartwig, 26 Jul 1956; Col Maurice R. Lemon, 11 Dec 1959; Col Earl E. Batten, 9 Feb 1962 (temp); Col Maurice R. Lemon, c. Mar 1962; Col Robert J. Mason, 15 Jul 1962; Col Frank X. Krebs, 28 Jul 1963; Col James M. Vande Hey, 24 Jul 1965; Col Henry F. Butler, 25 Aug 1966; Col Michael J. Stublarec, c. 5 Oct 1966; Col Jules X. Junker III, 31 Aug 1968; Col Marvin F. Ewing, c. 28 May 1971; Col William H. Luke, 1 Jul 1971; Col Arthur R. Burke, 29 Nov 1972; Col Harold E. Grant, 1 Aug 1973; Col Attilio Pedroli, 12 Oct 1974; Col Jerry L. Welch, 2 Sep 1975; Col Robert B. Plowden, 11 Aug 1977; Col Ronald L. Barker, 24 Apr 1978; Col Keith N. Hall, 12 Mar 1979; Col George W. Acree II, 4 Jan 1980; Col Noah E. Loy, 29 Jul 1981; Lt Col W. David Kauffman, 20 Feb 1982 (temp); Col John L. Borling, 27 Feb 1982–.

Major Off-Base and Detached Installations: * Ramstein Admn Anx, 5

---

*Unless otherwise indicated, all installations are located in the Federal Republic of Germany.

mi W of Kaiserslautern, 1 Apr 1951−; Kaiserslautern Fam Hsg Anx #4, Kaiserslautern, 21 Jun 1951 (actvd)−; Landstuhl Fam Hsg Anx #3, Landstuhl, 25 Jun 1951 (asgnd)−; Kaiserslautern Stor Anx, 6 mi W of Kaiserslautern, 10 Jul 1951 (actvd)−unk; Baumholder RRS, 10 mi S of Idar-Oberstein, 15 Sep 1951 (asgnd)−unk; Kaiserslautern Fam Hsg Anx #3, Kaiserslautern, 1 Mar 1952−unk; Freising Chapel Anx, Freising, 5 Apr 1952 (asgnd)−31 Oct 1959 (dspd); Freising Small Arms Rg Anx, Freising, 5 Apr 1952−31 Oct 1959 dspd); Freising Stor Anx, Freising, 5 Apr 1952−Dec 1960 (inactvd); Landstuhl Labor Svc Unit Camp (Landstuhl Labor Svc Hsg Anx), 15 Apr 1952 (actvd)−unk; Bamberger-Hof RR Anx (Bamberger-Hof RRS), 1 May 1952 (actvd)−unk; Landstuhl/Kaiserslautern Bcn Anx, 15 Jun 1952 (asgnd)−; Ramstein Maint Anx, Kaiserslautern-Einsiedlerhof, 1 Aug 1952 (actvd)−unk; Ramstein Admn Anx #1, 5 mi W of Kaiserslautern, 5 Aug 1952 (actvd)−unk; Regensburg Radar Site, Regensburg, 15 Oct 1952 (asgnd)−unk; Mausdorf Radar Site, Herzogenaurach, 15 Nov 1952 (actvd)−unk; Kaiserslautern Water Sys Anx, 6 mi W of Kaiserslautern, 1 Jan 1953 (actvd)−unk; Huttenkopf Relay Anx, Huttenkopf, 15 May 1953−19 Sep 1956 (inactvd); Kaiserslautern Recrn Anx, 6 mi W of Kaiserslautern, 15 May 1953 (actvd)−unk; Langerkopf Radar Site (rdsgd Langerkopf RRS), Leinen, 15 Oct 1953 (actvd)−unk; Langerkopf Water Point Anx (rdsgd Langerkopf Water Sys Anx), 10 mi NNW of Kaiserslautern, 15 Oct 1953 (actvd)−unk; Pruem Radar Site, Pruem, 16 Oct 1953 (asgnd)−15 Feb 1961 (trsfd to Bitburg AB); Schoenfeld Water Sys Anx, Ormont, 16 Oct 1953 (asgnd)−15 Feb 1961 (trsfd to Bitburg AB); Breitenbach RB Anx, 15 Mar 1954 (actvd)−1 Mar 1966 (inactvd); Bann Comms Fclty #1 (rdsgd Bann Radio Anx #1), 2 mi N of Landstuhl, 12 Aug 1954 (actvd)−unk; Bann AC & W Site (rdsgd Bann Radar Site), 2 mi W of Landstuhl, 15 Aug 1954 (actvd)−unk; Bann Comms Fclty #2 (rdsgd Bann Radio Anx #2), 2 mi W of Landstuhl, 15 Aug 1954 (actvd)−unk; Kindsbach Comms Fclty (rdsgd Kindsbach Comms Anx), 2 mi W of Landstuhl, 15 Aug 1954 (actvd)−1 Jul 1970 (dspd); Pforzheim AC & W Stn (rdsgd Pforzheim RRS), Pforzheim, 20 Oct 1954 (actvd)−30 Sep 1966 (trsfd to Rhein-Main AB); Pforzheim Stor Anx, Pforzheim, 20 Oct 1954 (actvd)−30 Sep 1966 (trsfd to Rhein-Main AB); Pforzheim Water Sys Anx, Pforzheim, 20 Oct 1954 (actvd)−4 Sep 1963 (trsfd to Rhein-Main AB); Pruem Fam Hsg Anx, Pruem, 1 Jan 1955 (actvd)−15 Feb 1961 (trsfd to Bitburg AB); Dueren Radar Site, Kleinhan, 10 Jan 1955 (actvd)−30 Mar 1961 (dspd); Driedorf Msl Site, Driedorf, 26 Jan 1955 (actvd)−1 Oct 1958 (trsfd to Hahn AB); Winterberg Hsg Anx, Winterberg, 15 Jun 1955 (trsfd from Rhein-Main AB)−unk; Landstuhl AB, Landstuhl, 1 Jul 1955 (trsfd from Rhein-Main AB), 28 Feb 1958 (absorbed by Ramstein AB)−; Landstuhl Stor Anx #1, 2 mi SE of Landstuhl, 1 Jul 1955 (actvd)−; Irsch RRS, Oberzerf, 25 Jul 1955 (actvd)–25 May 1964 (trsfd to Bitburg AB); Irsch Water Sys Anx, Oberzerf, 25 Jul 1955 (actvd)–25 May 1964 (trsfd to Bitburg AB); Friolzheim Comms Anx (rdsgd Friolzheim RRS), 14 Feb 1956 (actvd)–1 Oct 1977 (dspd); Pforzheim Fam Hsg Anx, Kieselbronn, 14 Feb 1956 (actvd)–30 Sep 1966 (dspd); Kapaun Adm Anx, Kapaun Barracks, 1 Oct 1956 (actvd)–unk; Stein RRS, Stein, 6 Nov 1956 (actvd)–1 Jul 1962 (inactvd), 11 Nov 1963 (dspd); Heidenheim Comms Fclty, 10 mi E of Weissenburg, 20 Mar 1957 (actvd)–1 Aug 1973 (trsfd to Rhein-Main AB); Freising Admn Ofc, Freising, 15 May 1957 (actvd)–15 Feb 1961 (inactvd); Freising Artillery Kaserne, Freising, 15 May 1957 (actvd)–31 Jul 1957 (inactvd); Freising Radar Site, Freising, 15 May 1957 (actvd)–20 Oct 1959 (dspd); Freising Svc Fclty, Freising, 15 May 1957 (actvd)–15 Feb 1961 (dspd); Freising Fam Hsg Anx, Freising, 29 May 1957 (actvd)–1 Jul 1973 (trsfd to Bitburg AB); Mandern Water Sys Anx, Mandern, 27 Jun 1957 (actvd)–1 Jul 1965 (dspd); Schmarnzell Comms Fclty, Tandern, 18 Jul 1957 (actvd)–1 Nov 1965 (inactvd), 15 Oct 1966 (dspd); Kahren RRS, Kahren, 10 Oct 1957 (asgnd)–18 Nov 1963 (inactvd), 17 Aug 1964 (dspd); Darstadt Water Sys Anx, Darstadt, 15 Oct 1957 (actvd)–1 Jun 1962 (dspd); Breitsol RRS, Esselbach, 22 Feb 1958 (trsfd from Rhein-Main AB)–unk; Giebelstadt AB (rdsgd Giebelstadt Air Aux Fld), Giebelstadt, 28 Feb 1958 (asgnd)–1 Jan 1962 (dspd); Kaiserslautern RB Anx, Kaiserslautern, 28 Feb 1958 (asgnd)–16 Apr 1965 (dspd); Landstuhl Stor Anx #2, Landstuhl, 28 Feb 1958 (asgnd)–14 Dec 1962 (dspd); Pforzheim RRS, Pforzheim, 28 Feb 1958 (asgnd)–30 Sep 1966 (dspd); Pforzheim Stor Anx, Pforzheim, 28 Feb 1958 (asgnd)–30 Sep 1966 (dspd); Pforzheim Water Sys Anx, Pforzheim, 28 Feb 1958 (asgnd)–30 Sep 1966 (dspd); Rothwesten Radar Site, Holzhausen, 28 Feb 1958 (trsfd from Rhein-Main AB)–unk; Siegelbach Comms Stn, Kaiserslautern, 28 Feb 1958 (asgnd)–20 May 1970 (inactvd), 25 May 1971 (dspd); Teufelskopf RRS, Pfeffelbach, 28 Feb 1958 (trsfd from Rhein-Main AB)–20 Jul 1962 (dspd); Wasserkuppe Radar Site, Gersfeld, 28 Feb 1958 (trsfd from Rhein-Main AB)–27 May 1963 (dspd); Hamm Msl Site, Hervern, 1 Oct 1958 (trsfd from Hahn AB)–15 Jul 1962 (inactvd); Brandhof RRS, Elgersdorf, 21 Oct 1958 (asgnd)–1 Jul 1964 (trsfd to Rhein-Main AB); Haindlfing RRS, Freising, 1 Dec 1958 (asgnd on inactive status), 15 Dec 1958 (actvd)–31 Dec 1960 (inactvd); Marktwald RRS, Marktwald, 1 Dec 1958 (asgnd on inactive status), 15 Dec 1958 (actvd)–31 Dec 1960 (inactvd); Tuerkheim Comms Fclty, Tuerkheim, unk–10 Sep 1959 (dspd); Breitenbach RB Anx, Breitenbach, 15 Mar 1959 (actvd)–; Linderhofe Radar Site, Linderhofe, 1 May 1959 (asgnd on inactive status), 1 Mar 1960 (actvd)–1 Oct 1962 (inactvd), 16 Oct 1962 (dspd); St. Andreasberg Comms Fclty, St. Andreasberg, 22 Jul 1959 (actvd)–1 Mar 1960 (inactvd), 30 Jun 1960 (dspd); St. Andreasberg Hsg Anx, St. Andreasberg, 22 Jul 1959 (actvd)–1 Mar 1960 (inactvd), 30 Jun 1960 (dspd); Hof Comms Fclty, Hof,

1 Aug 1959 (asgnd on inactive status)–15 Apr 1961 (trsfd to Rhein-Main AB); Birkenfeld Admn Ofc, Birkenfeld, 1 Sep 1959 (trsfd from Hahn AB)–1 Feb 1963 (trsfd to Hahn AB); Birkenfeld Fam Hsg Site #1, Birkenfeld, 1 Sep 1959 (trsfd from Hahn AB)–1 Feb 1963 (trsfd to Hahn AB); Birkenfeld Fam Hsg Site #2, Birkenfeld, 1 Sep 1959 (trsfd from Hahn AB)–1 Feb 1963 (trsfd to Hahn AB); Pferdsfeld AB, Pferdsfeld, 1 Sep 1959 (trsfd from Hahn AB)–30 Jun 1960 (inactvd), 1 Feb 1963 (trsfd to Hahn AB); Winterberg Comms Fclty #1, Winterberg, 1 Sep 1959 (asgnd)–15 Dec 1961 (trsfd to Rhein-Main AB); Winterberg Comms Fclty #2, Winterberg, 1 Sep 1959 (asgnd in inactive status)–30 Nov 1962 (dspd); Winterberg Comms Fclty #3, Winterberg, 1 Sep 1959 (asgnd in inactive status)–30 Nov 1962 (dspd); Alzey Radar Site (rdsgd Alzey Comms Anx), Orbis, 1 Oct 1959 (trsfd from Sembach AB)–1 Apr 1964 (trsfd to Sembach AB); Erbeskopf RRS, Allenbach, 1 Oct 1959 (asgnd)–1 Feb 1963 (trsfd to Hahn AB); Muehl-Zuesch RRS, Zuesch, 1 Oct 1959 (asgnd)–1 Feb 1963 (trsfd to Hahn AB); Adenau Hsg Anx, Wanderath, 15 Nov 1959 (asgnd)–; Tempelhof Central Aprt, West Berlin, 15 Nov 1959 (trsfd from Weisbaden AB)–1 Jul 1960 (Tempelhof assumed prim instl status); Detmold RRS, Hiddesen, 1 Apr 1960 (actvd)–5 Dec 1961 (dspd); Diepholz Hsg Anx, Steinfeld, 1 Jul 1960 (trsfd from Sembach AB)–22 Aug 1962 (dspd); Marsberg Amn Hsg Anx, Madfeld, 1 Jul 1960 (trsfd from Sembach AB)–unk; Marsberg Msl Site, Madfeld, 1 Jul 1960 (trsfd from Sembach AB)–unk; Marsberg Water Sys Anx, Madfeld, 1 Jul 1960 (trsfd from Sembach AB)–unk; Obernkirchen RRS, Obernkirchen, 17 Oct 1960 (trsfd from Rhein-Main AB)–1 Jul 1964 (trsfd to Rhein-Main AB); Doebra RRS, Doebra, 15 Jul 1961 (actvd)–unk; Reisenbach RRS, Reisenbach, 31 Jul 1961 (trsfd from Sembach AB)–15 May 1967 (inactvd); Koeterberg Hsg Anx, Fuerstenau, 1 Nov 1961 (trsfd from Sembach AB)–1 Jul 1964 (trsfd to Rhein-Main AB); Koeterberg RRS, Fuerstenau, 1 Nov 1961 (trsfd from Sembach AB)–1 Jul 1964 (trsfd to Rhein-Main AB); Gelchsheim Radar Site, Gelchsheim, 6 Nov 1961 (actvd)–15 May 1962 (inactvd), 10 Jan 1963 (dspd); Winterberg Comms Fclty #1, Winterberg, 1 Mar 1962 (trsfd from Rhein-Main AB)–25 Aug 1962 (trsfd to Rhein-Main AB); Kalteneggolsfeld RRS, Kalteneggolsfeld, unk–1 Jul 1964 (trsfd to Rhein-Main AB); Schwarzenborn RRS, Schwarzenborn, unk–1 Jul 1964 (trsfd to Rhein-Main AB); Arft RRS, Arft, 1 Apr 1962 (actvd)–1 Jul 1964 (trsfd to Bitburg AB); Adenau Hsg Anx, Wanderath, 31 Mar 1964 (actvd)–15 Jun 1964 (dspd); Muehl-Zuesch RRS, Zuesch, 1 Jul 1964 (trsfd from Hahn AB)–unk; Wunsdorf Comms Fclty, Klein Heidorn, unk–1 May 1965 (trsfd to Rhein-Main AB); Vogelweh Fam Hsg Anx, Kaiserslautern, 1 Jul 1965 (actvd)–unk; Marktwald RRS, Marktwald, unk–1 Nov 1965 (inactvd), 22 Sep 1966 (dspd); Rimschweiler Water Sys Anx, 1 mi S of Zweibrucken, 29 Aug 1969 (actvd)–1 May 1970 (dspd); Zweibrucken AB, 35 mi SSW of Kaiser-

slautern, 29 Aug 1969 (asgnd)–1 May 1970 (Zweibrucken assumed prim status); Erding Air Stn, Erding, 1 Apr 1971 (asgnd)–1 Jul 1973 (trsfd to Bitburg AB); Rothwesten Fam Hsg Site, Holzhausen, 1 Oct 1972 (trsfd from Rhein-Main AB)–31 Jul 1975 (dspd); Weilerbach Fam Hsg Anx, Weilerbach, 1 Nov 1972 (actvd)–31 Dec 1973 (dspd); Kaiserslautern Fam Hsg Anx #5, Kaiserslautern, 2 Nov 1972 (actvd)–; Kaiserslautern Fam Hsg Anx #1, Kaiserslautern, 1 Dec 1972 (actvd)–; Ramstein Fam Hsg Anx, 10 mi W of Kaiserslautern, 2 Dec 1972 (actvd)–; Kaiserslautern Fam Hsg Anx #2, Kaiserslautern, 23 Dec 1972 (actvd)–; Mackenbach Fam Hsg Anx, 8 mi WNW of Kaiserslautern, 23 Dec 1972 (asgnd), 1 May 1973 (actvd)–; Hauptstuhl Fam Hsg Anx, Hauptstuhl, 1 Jan 1973 (actvd)–30 Jun 1975 (dspd); Landstuhl Fam Hsg Anx, 14 mi W of Kaiserslautern, 15 Jan 1973 (actvd)–; Landstuhl Fam Hsg Anx #2, Landstuhl, 1 Feb 1973 (actvd)–; Kaiserslautern Fam Hsg Anx #2, Kaiserslautern, 1 Mar 1973 (actvd)–; Mackenbach Fam Hsg Anx #2, 8 mi WNW of Kaiserslautern, 14 Mar 1973 (actvd)–; Ramstein Fam Hsg Anx, Ramstein, 15 Mar 1973 (actvd)–; Landstuhl Fam Hsg Anx, Landstuhl, 1 May 1973 (actvd)–; Homburg Fam Hsg Anx, Homburg, 1 Aug 1973 (actvd)–1 Apr 1980 (dspd); Waldmohr Fam Hsg Anx, 5 mi S of Homburg, 20 Jun 1974 (actvd)–28 Feb 1975 (dspd); Hohenecken Fam Hsg Anx, 4 mi WSW of Kaiserslautern, 29 Jul 1974 (actvd)–; Kaiserslautern Fam Hsg Anx #6, Kaiserslautern, 2 Aug 1974 (actvd)–; Baumholder RB Site, Baumholder, 14 Jan 1975 (actvd)–; Eching RB Site, Eching, 17 Jan 1975 (actvd)–; Hohes Moor RB Site, Neuenwalde, 18 Apr 1975 (trsfd from Rhein-Main AB)–30 Jun 1978 (trsfd to Rhein-Main AB); Kaiserslautern Fam Hsg Anx #7, Kaiserslautern, 30 May 1975 (actvd)–; Copenhagen Adm Ofc, Copenhagen, Denmark, 1 Jul 1975 (trsfd from Rhein-Main AB)–30 Apr 1979 (dspd); Copenhagen Sch, Copenhagen, Denmark, 1 Jul 1975 (trsfd from Rhein-Main AB)–30 Jun 1978 (dspd); Oslo Admn Ofc, Oslo, Norway, 1 Jul 1975 (trsfd from Rhein-Main AB)–; Oslo Fam Hsg Site, Oslo, Norway, 1 Jul 1975 (trsfd from Rhein-Main AB)–; Oslo Sch, Bekkestna, Norway, 1 Jul 1975 (trsfd from Rhein-Main AB)–; Hohenecken Fam Hsg Anx, Hohenecken, 1 Oct 1976 (actvd)–; Kaiserslautern Fam Hsg Anx #3, Kaiserslautern, 1 Oct 1976 (actvd)–; Kaiserslautern Fam Hsg Anx #4, Kaiserslautern, 1 Oct 1976 (actvd)–; Kaiserslautern Fam Hsg Anx #5, Kaiserslautern, 1 Oct 1976 (actvd)–; Kaiserslautern Fam Hsg Anx #6, Kaiserslautern, 1 Oct 1976 (actvd)–; Kaiserslautern Fam Hsg Anx #7, Kaiserslautern, 1 Oct 1976 (actvd)–; Kaiserslautern Fam Hsg Anx #8, Kaiserslautern, 1 Oct 1976 (actvd)–31 Mar 1982 (dspd); Kaiserslautern Recrn Anx, Kaiser-slautern, 1 Oct 1976 (actvd)–; Kaiserslautern Stor Anx, Kaiserslautern-Einsiedlerhof, 1 Oct 1976 (actvd)–; Kaiserslautern Water Sys Anx, Kaiser-slautern, 1 Oct 1976 (actvd)–; Landstuhl Fam Hsg Anx #3, Hosp, Land-stuhl, 1 Oct 1976 (actvd)–; Otterbach Fam Hsg Anx, Otterbach, 1 Oct 1976 (actvd)–31 Mar 1977 (inactvd); Ramstein Admn Anx, Kaiserslautern, 1 Oct 1976 (actvd)–; Ramstein Maint Anx, Kaiserslautern-Einsiedlerhof, 1 Oct 1976 (actvd)–; Stelzenberg Fam Hsg Anx, 5 mi S of Kaiserslautern, 1 Oct 1976 (actvd)–; Waldmohr Fam Hsg Anx, Waldmohr, 1 Oct 1976 (actvd)–31 Mar 1982 (dspd); Lahr AB, Lahr, 2 Mar 1977 (trsfd from Hahn AB)–12 Mar 1978 (trsfd to Bitburg AB); Birkenfeld Fam Hsg Site #1, Birkenfeld, 1 Jul 1977 (trsfd from Hahn AB)–1 Mar 1980 (dspd); Birkenfeld Fam Hsg Site #2, Birkenfeld, 1 Jul 1977 (trsfd from Hahn AB)–1 Mar 1980 (dspd); Ramstein Stor Anx, Kaiserslautern-Einsiedlerhof, 1 Nov 1979 (actvd)–; Ramstein Fam Hsg Anx #2, Ramstein-Miesenbach, 1 Dec 1980 (asgnd in inactive status), 15 Jul 1981 (actvd)–; Weilerbach Fam Hsg Anx #2, Weilerbach, 1 Apr 1982 (actvd)–; Kindsbach Stor Site, Kindsbach, 1 Nov 1982 (actvd)–.

Major Changes in Operational Capability: Original tract acquired by French Army and construction work began in Apr 1951; Det 1, 86th Ftr-Bmbr Wg arrived from Neubiberg AB Feb 1952; established as a USAFE base on 5 Aug 1952; operations at Ramstein began 21 Aug 1952; south side of base named Landstuhl AB and the north side (where HQ Twelfth AF was based) named Ramstein; the two sides separated by an autobahn; Ramstein and Landstuhl consolidated on 1 Dec 1957 as Ramstein-Landstuhl AB, a name shortened to Ramstein in 1958; base supported operations of USAF and Allied units as directed by USAFE, Aug 1952–Nov 1968; Ramstein also provided support for HQ Fourth Allied Tac AF, which moved to Ramstein from Trier AB on 10 Nov 1957, and HQ Twelfth AF until 10 Nov 1957, when the advanced echelon of HQ USAFE replaced it; HQ Seventeenth AF, in turn, replaced HQ USAFE at Ramstein on 15 Nov 1959; construction work began on aerial port facilities for MAC, 14 Dec 1970; HQ Seventeenth AF moved to Sembach AB to make room for the expected move of HQ USAFE to Ramstein AB on 31 Jan 1973; HQ USAFE completed its move from Wiesbaden to Ramstein on 14 Mar 1973; HQ Allied AF, Central Europe, established at Ramstein on 28 Jun 1974; Ramstein subsequently provided support for other headquarters, including the 322d Alft Div, which arrived on 23 Jun 1978, and SAC's 7th Air Div, which arrived on 1 Jul 1978; HQ Fourth Allied Tac AF moved from Ramstein to Heidelberg in Aug 1980.

Major Commands to Which Assigned: USAFE, 5 Aug 1952–.

Major Changes in Status: None.

Units Assigned:

	1952		
6 Shoran Bcn Flt		86 Ftr-Bmbr Wg	
(6 Shoran Bcn Sq)	8 Nov 52–1 May 58	(86 Ftr-Intcpr Wg;	
73 Med Mat Sq	2 Feb 52–1 Mar 52	86 Air Div [Def];	
86 AB Gp	3 Sep 52–8 Mar 58	86 Ftr-Intcpr Wg)	21 Aug 52–14 Nov 68
86 Comms Sq	4 Sep 52–8 Mar 58	86 Food Svc Sq	1 Sep 52–11 May 53
		86 Instls Sq	12 Aug 52–8 Mar 58

86 Maint & Sup Gp	30 Dec 52–11 May 53
86 Med Gp	
(86 Tac Hosp)	20 Sep 52–1 May 67
86 MV Sq	
(86 Trnsp Sq)	8 Oct 52–8 Mar 58
86 Sup Sq	30 Dec 52–11 May 53
525 Ftr-Bmbr Sq	
(525 Ftr-Intcpr Sq)	20 Nov 52–12 Feb 57
526 Ftr-Bmbr Sq	
(526 Ftr-Intcpr Sq;	
526 Tac Ftr Sq)	1 Aug 52–
527 Ftr-Day Sq	1 Aug 52–8 Feb 56

1953

1 RR Sq	24 Aug 53–1 Jul 62
2 Air Div	20 Apr 53–1 Mar 54
2 Comms Gp	10 Apr 53–1 Jul 62
15 Comms Sq, AF	16 Apr 53–11 Oct 54
30 WAF Sq	20 Apr 53–8 Jul 54
31 Wea Sq	23 Jul 53–15 Aug 73
86 Maint Sq	5 Feb 53–11 May 53
86 Svcs Sq	
(86 AB Sq)	11 May 53–8 Mar 58
604 Comms Sq, Ops	10 Apr 53–1 Jul 62
7030 HQ Spt Gp	
(7030 Spt Gp;	
7030 AB Wg;	
7030 Cmbt Spt Wg)	6 Apr 53–5 Oct 66
7030 Mat Sq	25 Mar 53–1 May 60
7030 Med Sq	
(7030 USAF Dispy)	16 Jun 53–5 Oct 66
7030 Spt Sq	25 Mar 53–1 May 60
7030 Trnsp Sq	16 Jan 53–5 Oct 66
7420 Comms Flt	
[Radar Siting]	
(7420 Spt Flt	
[Radar Siting];	
7420 Spt Flt	
[Elect Siting	
& Evaluation];	
7420 Spt Sq	
[Elect Siting	
& Evaluation];	
7420 Radar	
Evaluation Sq)	20 May 53–10 Nov 72
Twelfth AF	27 Apr 53–1 Jan 58

1954

19 Comms Const Sq	9 May 54–15 Dec 57
322 Air Div	22 Mar 54–12 Aug 55
440 Ftr-Intcpr Sq	4 Jul 54–17 Feb 56
496 Ftr-Intcpr Sq	4 Jul 54–8 Nov 56
501 Tac Con Gp	17 Nov 54–18 Nov 60
807 Tac Con Sq	13 Nov 54–8 Apr 61
7426 USAF Infmy	
(7426 USAF	
Dispy)	1 May 54–25 Sep 57

1955

2 Air Postal Sq	7 Apr 55–8 Jan 63

526 Tac Con Gp	1 Jul 55–18 Dec 57

1956

53 Ftr-Day Sq	
(53 Tac Ftr Sq)	17 Dec 56–3 Oct 61
461 Ftr-Day Sq	8 Feb 56–2 May 56
7025 Air Postal Gp	2 Jul 56–1 Jan 57

1957

12 Comms Const Sq	31 Oct 57–25 Sep 58
509 Ftr-Bmbr Sq	1 Oct 57–26 Mar 58
1892 AACS Engrg	
& Instls Sq	
(1892 AACS	
Instls Sq)	13 Nov 57–29 Jun 58

1958

457 Ftr-Bmbr Sq	24 Mar 58–16 Aug 58
458 Ftr-Bmbr Sq	16 Aug 58–17 Feb 59
514 Ftr-Intcpr Sq	15 May 58–8 Jan 61
7002 Comms Sq	15 Feb 58–8 Jan 60
7030 Fld Maint Sq	8 May 58–1 May 60
7030 Food Svc Sq	8 Jan 57–1 May 60
7030 Ops Sq	8 Mar 58–1 May 60

1959

417 Tac Ftr Sq	1 Dec 59–1 Jul 68
2874 GEEIA Sq	
(1836 Elect	
Instl Sq)	30 Oct 59–15 Jan 73
Seventeenth AF	15 Nov 59–5 Oct 72

1960

20 Comms Sq, AF	8 Jan 60–1 Jul 62
7030 AB Wg	1 May 60–5 Oct 66

1961

7017 Spt Sq	8 Mar 61–1 Sep 63
HQ, Atlantic	
Air Rscu Cen	
(HQ, Atlantic	
Aerosp Rscu	
& Recovery	
Cen; HQ, 40	
Aerosp Rscu &	
Recovery Wg)	8 Oct 61–30 Jun 73

1962

38 Tac Recon Sq,	
Photo-Jet	
(38 Tac Recon Sq)	26 Jul 62–30 Jan 73
7030 Consold Acft	
Maint Sq	15 Jul 62–5 Oct 66
7030 Mat Sq	15 Jul 62–1 Apr 66

1963

7232 Mun Maint Sq	1 Jul 63–1 Feb 68

1964

50 Flt Line	
Maint Sq	1 Jul 64–15 Dec 65
66 Flt Line	
Maint Sq	1 Jul 64–15 Dec 65
7017 Spt Sq	1 Oct 64–1 Oct 70

1965

7030 CE Sq	8 Apr 65–5 Oct 66

1966

26 AP Sq	
(26 Scty Pol Sq)	5 Oct 66–31 Jan 73
26 Armnt & Elect	
Maint Sq	
(26 Avncs	
Maint Sq)	5 Oct 66–31 Jan 73
26 CE Sq	5 Oct 66–31 Jan 73
26 Cmbt Spt Gp	5 Oct 66–31 Jan 73
26 Fld Maint Sq	5 Oct 66–31 Jan 73
26 Sup Sq	5 Oct 66–31 Jan 73
26 Tac Recon Wg	5 Oct 66–31 Jan 73
26 Trnsp Sq	5 Oct 66–31 Jan 73
7030 Sup Sq	1 Apr 66–5 Oct 66

1967

26 Tac Hosp	1 May 67–15 Jan 73

1968

7 Sp Ops Sq	15 Aug 68–15 Mar 73

1969

26 Recon Tech Sq	1 Jul 69–1 Oct 71

1970

2 Bn, 60 Air Def	
Artillery	12 Aug 70–
326 Mun Maint Sq	1 May 70–7 Oct 72

1971

7002 CE Flt	1 May 71–
USAF Dispy,	
Ramstein	
(USAF Clinic,	
Ramstein)	1 Jul 71–

1972

21 Mun Maint Sq	1 Oct 72–31 Jan 73
26 Orgnzl Maint Sq	1 Feb 72–31 Jan 73
86 Mun Maint Sq	8 Oct 72–31 Jan 79

1973

2 Wea Wg	15 Aug 73–15 Sep 75
86 Avncs Maint Sq	
(86 Component	
Rpr Sq)	31 Jan 73–
86 CE Sq	31 Jan 73–
86 Cmbt Spt Gp	31 Jan 73–
86 Fld Maint Sq	
(86 Equip	
Maint Sq)	31 Jan 73–
86 Orgnzl Maint Sq	
(86 Acft Gnrtn Sq)	31 Jan 73–
86 Scty Pol Sq	31 Jan 73–
86 Sup Sq	31 Jan 73–
86 Tac Ftr Wg	31 Jan 73–

86 Tac Hosp	31 Jan 73–
86 Trnsp Sq	31 Jan 73–
1964 Comms Gp	28 Mar 73–
7055 Ops Sq	31 Mar 73–15 Sep 76
7086 Ops Sq	1 Jun 73–1 Apr 78
7102 Computer	
Svcs Sq	15 Sep 73–
7200 Mgmt Engrg Sq	1 Oct 73–
7260 Spt Sq	15 Feb 73–31 Dec 78
7300 Mat Sq	1 Jun 73–
HQ, USAFE	10 Mar 73–

1974

7000 Mun Spt Sq	1 Apr 74–
7000 Prcmt	
Sq (7000	
Contracting Sq)	1 Feb 74–
7450 Tac	
Intelligence Sq	1 Nov 74–

1975

86 Tac Ftr Gp	22 Sep 75–
European Comms	
Area	31 Dec 75–21 Jun 76

1976

306 Strat Wg	15 Aug 76–30 Jun 78
512 Tac Ftr Sq	15 Nov 76–

1977

58 Mil Alft Sq	1 Sep 77–
608 Mil Alft Spt Sq	1 Jul 77–
7122 Broadcasting Sq	c. 77–
European Air Cmbt	
Ops Staff	1 Nov 77–

1978

7 Air Div	1 Jul 78–
322 Alft Div	23 Jun 78–
417 Tac Ftr Sq	1 Nov 78–

1979

7027 Sch Sq	1 Nov 79–
HQ, Elect Scty,	
Europe	1 Nov 79–

1981

7486 Comptroller	
Sq,	1 Apr 81–
European Audit	
Region	15 Sep 81–

1982

HQ, AF	
Commissary Svc,	
European Region	8 Oct 82–

Rhein-Main Air Base

Location: Located 7 mi WSW of city of Frankfurt am Main, Federal Republic of Germany.

Name: Named after the confluence of the Rhine and Main rivers to the west of Frankfurt am Main and Rhein-Main Air Base, in the Federal Republic of Germany.

Date of Current Name: 15 Sep 1947.

Previous Names: Frankfurt/Rhein-Main Y–73, 26 Apr 1945; Rhein-Main Afld, 14 Nov 1945; Rhein/Main AB, 1 Nov 1946.

Date of Establishment: Established as a German zeppelin port and airfield on 8 Jul 1936; established as a USAAF base on 9 May 1945.

Date Construction Began: Initial construction work undertaken by German government in 1934; USA inaugurated an extensive restoration and construction project at the base on 11 May 1945.

Date of Beneficial Occupancy: 8 Apr 1945.

Base Operating Units: HQ, 826th Engr Avn Bn, 26 Apr 1945; 466th Air Svc Gp, 20 Nov 1945; HQ & Base Svc Sq, 466th Air Svc Gp, 20 Nov 1947; 61st AB Gp, 1 Jul 1948; 60th AB Gp, 2 Jun 1951; 7310th AB Gp, 18 Apr 1955 (rdsgd 7310th Spt Gp, 8 Mar 1958; 7310th AB Wg, 15 May 1960; 7310th AB Gp, 26 Sep 1964; 7310th Tac Alft Wg, 1 Nov 1968); 322d Cmbt Spt Gp, 1 Jan 1970; 435th Cmbt Spt Gp, 1 Jul 1975–.

Base Commanders: Lt Col Walter K. Carroll, 26 Apr 1945; Lt Col Willard E. Leisy, 20 Nov 1945; Col James L. Daniel Jr, c. Jan 1947; Col James B. Davenport, 7 Mar 1947; Maj William B. Furman, 20 May 1947; Lt Col Paul T. Temske, 1 Jul 1948; Col Louis D. Cooper, 21 Nov 1948; Col Frank D. Bostrom, 1 May 1949; Col William A. Stephens, 2 Jun 1951; Col Murl Estes, 21 Feb 1952; Col Andrew J. Bing, 18 Mar 1953; Col Raymond Marshall, 4 Jan 1954; Col Roy N. Hillyer Jr, 7 Dec 1954; Lt Col Leonard T. Geyer, 18 Apr 1955 (temp); Col Clarence B. Hammerle, 18 Jul 1955; Col Henry J. Amen, unk; Col James G. McDonald, 17 Jul 1961; Col Horace A. Crosswell, 8 Jul 1963; Col Robert L. Collie, 23 Aug 1965; Col Norman A. Kriehn, 23 Jun 1966 (temp); Col Richard A. Tiede, 6 Aug 1966; Col Louis L. Leibel, 1 Nov 1968; Col Frank L. Kimbrough, 15 Jun 1969; Lt Col Douglas A. Harrison Jr, 18 Jul 1972; Brig Gen Thomas M. Sadler, 30

Nov 1972; Col Cornelius Nugteren, 12 Feb 1974; Brig Gen Theodore P. Crichton, 1 Jul 1975; Col Robert D. Springer, 23 Jun 1978; Col John D. Sims, 30 Jun 1980; Col Frank J. Kelly, 7 May 1982–.

Major Off-Base and Detached Installations:* Rothwesten Fam Hsg Site, Holzhausen, 26 Apr 1945 (actvd)–1 Oct 1972 (trsfd to Ramstein AB); Rhein-Main/Bremerhaven Pers Processing Stn, Bremerhaven, 15 May 1945 (actvd)–28 Feb 1958 (inactvd); Rhein-Main/Bremerhaven Rifle Rg, Esselbach, 15 May 1945 (actvd)–28 Feb 1958 (inactvd); Rhein-Main/Frankfurt Pers Processing Stn, Frankfurt am Main, 9 Jul 1945 (actvd)–31 May 1956 (inactvd); Wasserkuppe Radar Site, Gersfeld, 20 Jul 1945 (actvd)–28 Feb 1958 (trsfd to Ramstein AB); Rothwesten Radar Site, Holzhausen, 15 Jan 1946 (actvd)–unk; Rhein-Main/Zeppelinheim Hsg Anx (Zeppelinheim Fam Hsg Anx), Sprendlingen, 30 Jun 1946 (asgnd in inactive status), Feb 1947 (actvd)–30 Nov 1959 (inactvd); Schwanheim Comms Anx, Frankfurt/Schwanheim, 1 Jul 1946 (actvd)–31 Oct 1962 (inactvd), 31 May 1963 (dspd); Buchschlag Fam Hsg Anx, 1 mi S of Neu-Isenburg, 31 Aug 1946 (actvd)–unk; Eschborn AB, Frankfurt/Eschborn, 31 Jan 1947–c. 1949; Neu-Isenburg Hsg Anx, Neu-Isenburg, Feb 1947 (actvd)–1 Dec 1962 (dspd); Breitsol RRS, 1 Jul 1947 (actvd)–22 Feb 1958 (trsfd to Ramstein AB); Rhein-Main/Zeppelinheim Air Ammo Dep, Sprendlingen, 15 Sep 1947 (actvd)–unk; Moenchbruch Comms Anx, Moerfelden, 1 Nov 1947 (actvd)–30 Sep 1962 (inactvd), 19 Jun 1968 (dspd); Gateway Gardens Fam Hsg Anx, Frankfurt am Main, 21 Jul 1950 (actvd)–unk; Rhein-Main/Weimar Comms Anx, Zierenberg, 2 Nov 1951 (actvd)–unk; Spieka Comms Stn, Spieka, 22 Jan 1952 (actvd)–unk; Winterberg Hsg Anx, Winterberg, unk–15 Jan 1955 (trsfd to Ramstein AB); Hamm Msl Site, Herbern, Jan 1955 (actvd)–unk (trsfd to Hahn AB); Koeterberg Comms Anx, Fuerstenau, 1 Jan 1955 (actvd)–unk (trsfd to Ramstein AB); Winterberg Bcn Anx (Winterberg RB Site), Winterberg, 15 Jan 1955 (actvd)–1 Mar 1962 (trsfd to Ramstein AB); Driedorf Msl Site, Driedorf, 26 Jan 1955 (actvd)–17 Jun 1958 (trsfd to Ramstein AB); Flensburg Shoran Bcn Site, Nieby, 11 Feb 1955 (actvd)–; Frankfurt Fam Hsg Anx #1, Frankfurt am Main, 26 Jul 1956 (actvd)–31 Jul 1959 (dspd); Frankfurt Fam Hsg Anx #2, Frankfurt am Main, 27 Jul 1956 (actvd)–; Langen Fam Hsg Anx #1, Langen, 21 May 1957 (actvd)–1 Oct 1962 (dspd); Feldberg Comms Stn, 7 mi E of Bad Homburg, 8 Jun 1957 (actvd)–unk (trsfd to Wiesbaden AB); Langerbrand Msl Site, Langerbrand, 15 Jul 1957 (actvd)–5 Aug 1959 (dspd); Langen Fam Hsg Anx #2, Langen, 1 Jan 1958 (actvd)–20 Apr 1963 (dspd); Koeterberg RRS, 6 mi SSW of

---

*Unless otherwise indicated, all installations are located in the Federal Republic of Germany.

Holzminden, 25 Feb 1958 (actvd)-unk (trsfd to Sembach AB); Langen Terrace Fam Hsg Anx, Langen, 4 May 1959 (actvd)-20 Apr 1963 (dspd); Neuenwalde Comms Site (Hohes Moor RB Site), Neuenwalde, 16 Jul 1960 (asgnd)-31 Jul 1972 (dspd); Hof Comms Fclty, Hof, 15 Apr 1961 (trsfd from Ramstein AB)-1 Oct 1962 (trsfd to Hof AS); Winterberg Comms Fclty #1, Winterberg, 15 Dec 1961 (trsfd from Ramstein AB)-1 Mar 1962 (trsfd to Ramstein AB); Winterberg Comms Fclty #1, Winterberg, 25 Aug 1962 (trsfd from Ramstein AB)-30 Nov 1962 (dspd); Pforzheim Water Tower Anx, 4 Sep 1963 (trsfd from Ramstein AB)-unk; Brandhof RRS, Elgersdorf, 1 Jul 1964 (trsfd from Ramstein AB)-; Feldberg RRS, Ober-Reifenberg, 1 Jul 1964 (trsfd from Wiesbaden AB)-; Kalteneggolsfeld RRS, Kalteneggolsfeld, 1 Jul 1964 (trsfd from Ramstein AB)-; Koeterberg Hsg Anx, Fuerstenau, 1 Jul 1964 (trsfd from Ramstein AB)-5 Jul 1966 (inactvd); Koeterberg RRS, Fuerstenau, 1 Jul 1964 (trsfd from Ramstein AB)-; Obernkirchen RRS, Obernkirchen, 1 Jul 1964 (trsfd from Ramstein AB)-30 Nov 1971 (dspd); Schwarzenborn RRS, Schwarzenborn, 1 Jul 1964 (trsfd from Ramstein AB)-15 Dec 1965 (dspd); Pforzheim AC & W Stn, 30 Sep 1966 (trsfd from Ramstein AB)-; Pforzheim Shoran Bcn Anx, 30 Sep 1966 (trsfd from Ramstein AB)-; Oslo Admn Ofc, Fornebu, Norway, 1 Jul 1967 (trsfd from Sembach AB)-1 Jul 1975 (trsfd to Ramstein AB); Oslo Sch, Bekkestna, Norway, 1 Jul 1967 (trsfd from Sembach AB)-1 Jul 1975 (trsfd to Ramstein AB); Oslo Stor Anx [Commissary] (Oslo Stor Site), Oslo, Norway, 1 Jul 1967 (trsfd from Sembach AB)-1 Dec 1972 (trsfd to Wiesbaden AB); Copenhagen Sch, 9 mi NE of Copenhagen, Denmark, 1 Sep 1970 (asgnd)-1 Jul 1975 (trsfd to Ramstein AB); Copenhagen Sch #2, Copenhagen, Denmark, 1 Sep 1970 (asgnd)-1 Jul 1975 (trsfd to Ramstein AB); Oslo Fam Hsg Site, Oslo Norway, 15 Jun 1971 (actvd)-1 Jul 1975 (trsfd to Ramstein AB); Schwanberg RRS, Roedelsee, 1 Jul 1971 (asgnd)-; Kalteneggolsfeld RRS, Kalteneggolsfeld, 1 Jan 1972 (asgnd)-30 Jun 1975 (dspd); Schwarzenborn RRS, 19 mi NW of Bad Herzfeld, 1 Jan 1972 (asgnd)-; Harleshausen Sch, Harleshausen, 1 Oct 1972 (actvd)-; Waldmohr Fam Hsg Anx, 1 Jul 1973 (asgnd)-28 Feb 1975 (dspd); Heidenheim Comms Stn, 1 Aug 1973 (trsfd from Ramstein AB)-; Hohes Moor RB Site, 10 mi SW of Bremerhaven, 31 Jan 1975 (asgnd)-18 Apr 1975 (trsfd to Ramstein AB); Reisenbach Radar Site, Buchen/Odenwald, 1 Mar 1975 (actvd)-; Rothwesten Fam Hsg Site, Holzhausen, 1 Oct 1976 (asgnd)-; Moerfelden Bach Hsg Anx, Wallfelden, 1 Mar 1977 (asgnd)-30 Nov 1978 (dspd); Hohes Moor RB Site, Neuenwalde, 30 Jun 1978 (trsfd from Ramstein AB)-; Nieder-Roden Fam Hsg Anx, Rodgau, 24 May 1979 (asgnd in UC status), 16 May 1980 (actvd)-; Dietzenbach Fam Hsg Anx, Dietzenbach, 18 Sep 1980 (asgnd in UC status), 1 Jun 1982 (actvd)-; Egelsbach Fam Hsg Anx, Egelsbach, 24 May 1982 (asgnd in UC status)-unk.

Major Changes in Operational Capability: In 1909 Count von Zeppelin used area as landing site for his dirigible *Z–II*; planned by Germany to be one of the most important European air terminals, base opened as German commercial field in 1936; northern part of base used as field for airplanes, with extreme southern part near Zeppelinheim serving as a base for rigid airships; that section of Rhein-Main later became port for the *Graf Zeppelin*, its sister ship *LZ–130*, and, until 6 May 1937, for the ill-fated *Hindenburg*; the airships were dismantled and their huge hangars demolished on 6 May 1940 in conversion of base to military use; Luftwaffe engineers subsequently extended the single runway and erected hangars and other facilities for German military aircraft; during World War II the Luftwaffe used field sporadically as fighter base and as experimental station for jet aircraft; U.S. 826th Engr Avn Bn arrived at Rhein-Main in Apr 1945 to begin task of clearing rubble and reconstructing major buildings; Army engineers also built new runways and extended and widened the existing runway, constructed aprons and hardstands as well as taxiways leading to the terminal; new Rhein-Main terminal completed in 1946; air traffic into Rhein-Main increased after the closure of the military passenger terminal at Orly Field, Paris, October 1946; hosted Eastern Air Transport Service in Jan 1947; although envisioned as a bomber base by the Ninth AF, base became a principal European air transport terminal 1947–1959; Rhein-Main was the main western base for the round-the-clock Berlin Airlift operations from Jun 1948 to Sep 1949; USAFE turned over the northern part of the base to the German government for use as *Flughafen* Frankfurt am Main, the chief commercial airport for the greater Frankfurt area, in Apr 1959; rest of the base remained in hands of USAFE as principal aerial port for U.S. Forces in Germany; base assigned to MAC on 1 Jul 1975; under terms of an agreement with the Federal Republic of Germany, only transport aircraft have been stationed at Rhein-Main since 1 May 1975.

Major Commands to Which Assigned: IX Avn Engr Comd, 26 Apr 1945; USAFE, 20 Nov 1945; MAC, 1 Jul 1975–.

Major Changes in Status: None.

Units Assigned:

1945		1946	
362 Ftr Gp	8 Apr 45–30 Apr 45	12 Trp Carr Sq	30 Sep 46–1 Nov 46
377 Ftr Sq	14 Apr 45–2 May 45	1947	
378 Ftr Sq	14 Apr 45–2 May 45	14 Trp Carr Sq	11 Feb 47–21 Jul 50
379 Ftr Sq	c. 8 Apr 45–30 Apr 45	15 Trp Carr Sq	11 Feb 47–21 Jul 50
425 Night Ftr Sq	12 Apr 45–2 May 45	53 Trp Carr Sq	8 Aug 47–20 Jan 48
Co A, 826 Engr		61 Trp Carr Gp	11 Feb 47–21 Jul 50
Avn Bn	26 Apr 45–20 Nov 45	763 AAF BU	
Co B, 826 Engr		[133 AACS Sq]	
Avn Bn	26 Apr 45–20 Nov 45	(763 AF BU	
HQ, 826 Engr		[133 AACS Sq])	10 Sep 47–3 Jun 48
Avn Bn	26 Apr 45–20 Nov 45	831 Engr Avn Bn	16 Dec 47–1 Jul 48

150

884 Air Engrg Sq	9 Apr 47–1 Jul 48
1408 AAF BU	
[Foreign Trpt Sec]	15 Mar 47–3 Jun 48
7907 AF BU	20 Dec 47–1 Jul 48
HQ & Base Svc Sq,	
466 Air Svc Gp	4 Apr 47–1 Jul 48
Rhein-Main BU	
[Prov]	5 Feb 47–20 Dec 47
1948	
12 Trp Carr Sq	20 Jan 48–17 Apr 48
17 Air Ammo Sq	5 May 48–20 Jun 48
20 Trp Carr Sq	1 Jul 48–19 Oct 48
48 Trp Carr Sq	c. 1 Jul 48–Nov 48
53 Trp Carr Sq	22 Apr 48–21 Jul 50
54 Trp Carr Sq	2 Jul 48–26 Sep 48
61 AB Gp	1 Jul 48–2 Jun 51
61 AP Sq	1 Jul 48–2 Jun 51
61 Base Svc Sq,	
Trp Carr	1 Jul 48–2 Jun 51
61 Comms Sq	1 Jul 48–2 Jun 51
61 Food Svc Sq	1 Jul 48–2 Jun 51
61 Instls Sq	1 Jul 48–2 Jun 51
61 Maint & Sup Gp	1 Jul 48–2 Jun 51
61 Maint Sq	1 Jul 48–2 Jun 51
61 MV Sq	1 Jul 48–2 Jun 51
61 Stn Med Gp	
(61 Med Gp)	1 Jul 48–2 Jun 51
61 Sup Sq	1 Jul 48–2 Jun 51
61 Trp Carr Wg	1 Jul 48–2 Jun 51
133 AACS Sq	
(1945 AACS Sq;	
1945 Comms Sq;	
1945 Comms Gp)	1 Jun 48–
313 Trp Carr Gp	9 Nov 48–
330 Trp Carr Sq	19 Nov 48–16 Oct 49
331 Trp Carr Sq	19 Nov 48–16 Oct 49
332 Trp Carr Sq	19 Nov 48–16 Oct 49
333 Trp Carr Sq	19 Nov 48–20 Dec 48
513 Trp Carr Gp	19 Nov 48–16 Oct 49
1420 Air Trpt Gp	
[Prov]	48–23 Nov 48
1421 Maint Sq	
[Prov]	48–1 Dec 48
1422 Air Trpt Gp	
[Prov]	1 Aug 48–1 Dec 48
7370 AF Flt Svc Sq	1 Jul 48–27 Nov 53
7371 Base Compl Sq	1 Jul 48–5 Nov 49
7390 AF Engrg Gp	1 Jul 48–4 Apr 49
7915 AF Flt Svc Sq	5 May 48–1 Jul 48
1949	
10 Trp Carr Sq	26 Sep 49–20 Oct 49
11 Trp Carr Sq	26 Sep 49–23 Sep 55
12 Trp Carr Sq	26 Sep 49–20 Oct 49
60 AB Gp	10 Feb 49–26 May 49
60 AP Sq	10 Feb 49–26 May 49
60 Base Svc Sq	10 Feb 49–26 May 49
60 Comms Sq	10 Feb 49–26 May 49

60 Food Svc Sq	10 Feb 49–26 May 49
60 Instls Sq	10 Feb 49–26 May 49
60 Maint & Sup Gp	10 Feb 49–26 May 49
60 Maint Sq	10 Feb 49–26 May 49
60 MV Sq	10 Feb 49–26 May 49
60 Sup Sq	10 Feb 49–26 May 49
60 Trp Carr Gp	26 Sep 49–23 Sep 55
333 Trp Carr Sq	26 Sep 49–16 Oct 49
7497 Alft Wg	20 Jan 49–10 Jul 49
1950	
10 Trp Carr Sq	5 Jul 50–23 Sep 55
12 Trp Carr Sq	7 Jul 50–13 Sep 55
1951	
1 Med Air Evac Sq	
(1 Aeromed Evac	
Flt; 1 Aeromed	
Evac Sq)	11 Jun 51–8 Aug 58
60 AB Gp	2 Jun 51–1 Oct 55
60 AP Sq	2 Jun 51–1 Oct 55
60 Comms Sq	2 Jun 51–1 Oct 55
60 Fld Maint Sq	2 Jun 51–13 Oct 55
60 Food Svc Sq	2 Jun 51–1 Oct 55
60 Instls Sq	2 Jun 51–1 Oct 55
60 Maint & Sup Gp	2 Jun 51–1 Oct 55
60 MV Sq	2 Jun 51–1 Oct 55
60 Sup Sq	2 Jun 51–1 Oct 55
60 Trp Carr Wg	2 Jun 51–20 Jul 51
67 Trp Carr Sq	6 Aug 51–14 Jul 52
68 Trp Carr Sq	6 Aug 51–14 Jul 52
69 Trp Carr Sq	6 Aug 51–14 Jul 52
433 AB Gp	5 Aug 51–14 Jul 52
433 Comms Sq	5 Aug 51–14 Jul 52
433 Food Svc Sq	5 Aug 51–14 Jul 52
433 Instls Sq	5 Aug 51–14 Jul 52
433 Maint & Sup Gp	5 Aug 51–14 Jul 52
433 Maint Sq	5 Aug 51–14 Jul 52
433 Med Gp	5 Aug 51–14 Jul 52
433 MV Sq	5 Aug 51–14 Jul 52
433 Sup Sq	8 Aug 51–14 Jul 52
433 Trp Carr Gp	5 Aug 51–14 Jul 52
433 Trp Carr Wg	5 Aug 51–14 Jul 52
7000 Base Compl Sq	16 Jul 51–16 Sep 52
1952	
39 Trp Carr Sq	14 Jul 52–23 Mar 53
40 Trp Carr Sq	14 Jul 52–15 May 53
41 Trp Carr Sq	14 Jul 52–23 Mar 53
86 Air Trpt Sq	20 Jul 52–19 May 54
317 AB Gp	14 Jul 52–17 Mar 53
317 AP Sq	14 Jul 52–23 Mar 53
317 Comms Sq	14 Jul 52–17 Mar 53
317 Food Svc Sq	14 Jul 52–23 Mar 53
317 Instls Sq	14 Jul 52–17 Mar 53
317 Maint & Sup Gp	14 Jul 52–19 Mar 53
317 Maint Sq	14 Jul 52–17 Mar 53
317 MV Sq	14 Jul 52–19 Mar 53
317 Sup Sq	14 Jul 52–17 Mar 53
317 Trp Carr Gp	14 Jul 52–23 Mar 53

317 Trp Carr Wg	14 Jul 52–17 Mar 53
	1953
7050 Air Intelligence Svc Wg (7000 Spt Wg; 7113 Sp Activities Gp)	3 Apr 53–1 Nov 72
7167 Sp Air Missions Sq (7167 Air Trnsp Sq, Med [Sp Missions])	3 Apr 53–1 Jul 64
7493 IG Sp Investigations Wg (7493 Sp Investigations Wg)	28 May 53–20 Jul 57
	1954
84 Air Rscu Sq	14 Aug 54–8 May 56
776 Trp Carr Sq	25 Oct 54–1 May 55
7228 Comps Sq (7228 Sp Activities Sq)	19 Jul 54–1 Nov 56
7310 USAF Hosp (7310 USAF Dispy)	1 May 54–1 Jan 70
7417 Aeromed Flt [Casualty Staging] (7417 Casualty Staging Flt)	1 Jul 54–8 Apr 57
	1955
778 Trp Carr Sq	26 Apr 55–4 Nov 55
7063 Sp Activities Sq	1 Jul 55–1 Nov 56
7310 AB Gp (7310 Spt Gp; 7310 AB Wg; 7310 AB Gp; 7310 Tac Alft Wg)	18 Apr 55–1 Jan 70
7310 Mat Sq	18 Apr 55–1 Nov 66
7310 MV Sq (7310 Trnsp Sq)	18 Apr 55–1 Nov 56
7310 Spt Sq	18 Apr 55–5 Aug 62
7366 Radar Eval Sq	27 Sep 55–16 Dec 57
7406 Spt Sq (7406 Ops Sq)	10 May 55–30 Jun 74
7407 Spt Sq	10 May 55–30 Jun 74
	1956
7050 Air Intelligence Svc Gp	1 Nov 56–19 May 58
7145 Spt Gp	1 Nov 56–19 May 58
	1958
2 Aeromed Evac Gp (2 Aeromed Evac Sq)	15 Sep 58–
6937 Scty Flt (6937 Comms Flt)	1 Feb 58–23 Jun 58
	1960
6916 Radio Sq, Mobile (6916 Scty Sq)	1 Jan 60–30 Jun 73
	1961
Prov Spt Gp, 2	28 Apr 61–8 May 61
	1963
7001 Spt Sq	1 Oct 63–1 Jul 64
7004 Spt Sq	1 Oct 63–1 Jul 64
	1964
7310 Consold Acft Maint Sq	1 Oct 64–1 Jul 66
	1966
55 Mil Alft Sq (55 Aeromed Alft Sq)	8 Jan 66–
439 Air Trml Sq (439 Aerl Port Sq)	8 Jan 66–24 Dec 68
7310 AP Sq (7310 Scty Pol Sq)	1 Nov 66–1 Jan 70
7310 CE Sq	1 Nov 66–1 Jan 70
	1968
58 Aeromed Evac Sq	24 Dec 68–1 Jul 72
630 Mil Alft Spt Sq	24 Dec 68–30 Jun 75
7310 CE Sq	1 Nov 68–1 Jan 70
7310 Cmbt Spt Gp	1 Nov 68–1 Jan 70
7310 Consold Acft Maint Sq	1 Nov 68–1 Jan 70
7310 Sup Sq	1 Nov 68–1 Jan 70
7310 Trnsp Sq	1 Nov 68–1 Jan 70
	1969
435 Mil Alft Spt Wg (435 Tac Alft Wg)	1 Jul 69–
	1970
322 CE Sq	1 Jan 70–30 Jun 75
322 Cmbt Spt Gp	1 Jan 70–30 Jun 75
322 Consold Acft Maint Sq (322 Fld Maint Sq)	1 Jan 70–30 Jun 75
322 Scty Pol Sq	1 Jan 70–30 Jun 75
322 Sup Sq	1 Jan 70–30 Jun 75
322 Tac Alft Wg	1 Jan 70–30 Jun 75
322 Trnsp Sq	1 Jan 70–30 Jun 75
	1971
USAF Dispy, Rhein-Main (USAF Clinic, Rhein-Main)	1 Jul 71–
	1972
322 Orgnzl Maint Sq	1 Jul 72–30 Jun 75
6911 Scty Sq	

[Mobile]	1 Jul 72–25 Jul 75	435 Trnsp Sq	1 Jul 75–
7111 Spt Flt		7405 Ops Sq	31 Dec 75–
(7111 Ops Flt)	1 Feb 72–1 Feb 75		1976
	1973	1868 Fclty	
7 Sp Ops Sq	15 Mar 73–	Checking Sq	1 Jan 76–
	1975	7025 Air Postal Sq	1 Jul 76–
31 Wea Sq	1 Oct 75–1 Aug 82		1977
435 Aerl Port Sq	1 Jul 75–	37 Tac Alft Sq	1 Oct 77–
435 CE Sq	1 Jul 75–	7575 Ops Gp	1 Jul 77–
435 Cmbt Spt Gp	1 Jul 75–		1978
435 Fld Maint Sq	1 Jul 75–	435 Tac Alft Gp	15 Sep 78–1 Jun 80
435 Orgnzl Maint Sq	1 Jul 75–		1981
435 Scty Pol Sq	1 Jul 75–	435 Svcs Sq	1 Oct 81–

San Vito dei Normanni Air Station

Location: Located c. 7 mi NNW of Brindisi, Puglie, between the port of Brindisi and the town of San Vito dei Normanni, Italy.

Name: Named after a town in Italy.

Date of Current Name: 17 Jul 1961.

Previous Names: San Vito dei Normanni Comms Stn, 1 Nov 1960.

Date of Establishment: 1 Nov 1960.

Date Construction Began: 16 Jul 1959.

Date of Beneficial Occupancy: 10 Aug 1960.

Base Operating Units: 6917th Radio Sq, Mobile (rdsgd 6917th Radio Gp, Mobile, 1 Jul 1961; 6917th Scty Gp, 1 Jul 1963), 1 Nov 1960; 6917th AB Sq, 1 Jul 1974; 7275th AB Sq, 1 Oct 1978–.

Base Commanders: Capt Sylvester L. Blakely, 1 Nov 1960; Maj John J. Frost, 9 Nov 1960; Col Nicholas J. Rifkin, 8 Dec 1960; Col John A. McVey, 24 Jan 1961; Col Thomas J. Hanley III, 12 Jan 1963; Col Robert O. Brooks, 5 Sep 1964; Col Orin H. Erickson, 29 Jul 1966; Col William L. Rice, 10 Jul 1968; Col Joseph W. Lewandoski, 22 May 1970; Col Floyd E. Cross, 16 Jul 1971; Col William B. Barnes, 16 May 1972; Col Bryan W. Brunzell, 6 Jun 1974; Col Donald L. Moore, 13 Dec 1976; Col Gary E. Spohn, 25 Oct 1978; Col George F. Houck Jr, 11 Jul 1981–.

Major Off-Base and Detached Installations: San Vito dei Normanni Comms Anx, 1 Mar 1961 (actvd)–5 Dec 1969 (inactvd); Martina Franca RRS, Martina Franca, 15 Apr 1981–; Martina Franca Water Sys Anx, Martina Franca, 15 Apr 1981–.

Major Changes in Operational Capability: San Vito dei Normanni AS, without an airfield, began as an off-base installation of Aviano AB with support personnel and equipment furnished by the 6900th Scty Wg in 1960; a primary installation since 1 Mar 1961; base operated from its activation by the United States Air Force Security Service (USAFSS); on 1 Oct 1978 base reverted to HQ Sixteenth AF (USAFE), hosting the 6917th Elect Scty Gp and other assigned U.S. and Allied units and organizations.

Major Commands to Which Assigned: USAFSS, 1 Nov 1960; USAFE, 1 Oct 1978–.

Major Changes in Status: Off-base installation of Aviano AB, 1 Nov 1960; primary installation, 1 Mar 1961.

Units Assigned:

1960

7208 USAF Dispy   1 Nov 60–30 Jun 71

1961

6917 Radio Gp,
Mobile
(6917 Scty Gp)   1 Jul 61–1 Oct 78

1971

USAF Disp,
San Vito
dei Normanni
(USAF Hosp,
San Vito
dei Normanni;

USAF Clinic,
San Vito
dei Normanni)   1 Jul 71–

1974

6917 AB Sq   1 Jul 74–1 Oct 78

6917 Scty Sq
(6917 Elect
Scty Gp)   1 Jul 74–

1978

7275 AB Gp   1 Oct 78–

1979

2113 Comms Sq   1 Feb 79–

1982

7275 CE Sq   1 Apr 82–

Sembach Air Base

Location: Located 3/4 mi SSE of Sembach, 10 mi NE of Kaiserslautern, Federal Republic of Germany.

Name: Named after a village in the Federal Republic of Germany.

Date of Current Name: 15 Apr 1953.

Previous Names: *Flughafen* Sembach, 1939; Sembach Air Aux Fld, 1 Sep 1952.

Date of Establishment: Established as French occupation airfield, 1919; German Luftwaffe base, 1939; USAF installation, 1 Sep 1952.

Date Construction Began: Original construction accomplished by French in 1919; German construction initiated in 1938; French construction for USAF began in 1951; USAF construction undertaken 1952.

Date of Beneficial Occupancy: 5 Apr 1953.

Base Operating Units: 7355th AB Sq, 5 Apr 1953; 66th AB Gp, 7 Jul 1953; 7127th Spt Gp, 18 Jun 1958; 38th AB Gp, 1 Sep 1959; 603d AB Wg, 25 Sep 1966; 601st Cmbt Spt Gp, 1 Jul 1968; 7400th AB Gp, 1 Jun 1973; 601st Cmbt Spt Gp, 1 Jan 1976–.

Base Commanders: Unk, 5 Apr–7 Jul 1953; Col Clarence C. Ailes, 8 Jul 1953; Col John E. Murray, 6 Sep 1955; Col George A. Simeral, 18 Jun 1958; Lt Col Robert B. Alexander, 22 Nov 1959; Col Daniel C. Brawner, 29 Feb 1960; Lt Col James M. Wyse, 2 Mar 1962; Col Roger W. Page, 30 Jul 1962; Col Roswell W. Ard, c. 1964; Col Bertram A. Kibler Jr, 25 Sep 1966; Col William Y. Smith, 28 Jul 1967; Col Arval J. Roberson, 15 Jun 1968; Col Donald J. Perry, 13 Jul 1970; Col David H. Doughty, 9 Jul 1971; Col James O. Gassman, 1 Apr 1974; Col Louis D. Braun Jr, 1 Jan 1976; Col James L. Thompson, 1 Apr 1976; Col Vernon L. Frye, 30 Jul 1977; Col Donald E. Smith, 19 May 1979; Col George E. Daniels, 30 Jul 1981–.

Major Off-Base and Detached Installations:* Gruenstadt Anx, Gruenstadt, 1 Sep 1952 (asgnd)–1955 (inactvd); Hochspeyer Anx, 3 mi ESE of Kaiserslautern, 1 Sep 1952 (asgnd)–1954 (inactvd); Donnersburg/Dan-

---

*Unless otherwise indicated, all installations are located in the Federal Republic of Germany.

nenfels RR Anx (Dannenfels RR Anx), Dannenfels, 15 Apr 1953 (actvd)–unk; Enkenbach Water Sys Anx, 6 mi SW of Kaiserslautern, 15 Apr 1953 (actvd)–unk; Neuhemsbach Inland Petrol Sys, 6 mi SW of Kaiserslautern, 15 Apr 1953 (actvd)–unk; Rohrbach Waste Anx, 5 mi SW of Kaiserslautern, 15 Apr 1953 (actvd)–unk; Sembach Admn Anx, 6 mi SW of Kaiserslautern, 15 Apr 1953 (actvd)–; Finthen Radar Anx, Wackernheim, 15 May 1953 (actvd)–; Reisenbach Comms Anx (Reisenbach Msl Site), 4 mi E of Ederbach, 4 May 1955 (actvd)–31 Jul 1961 (trsfd to Ramstein AB); Hochspeyer Ammo Stor Anx (Hochspeyer Msl Site), 3 mi ESE of Kaiserslautern, 4 Jun 1956 (actvd)–unk; Mehlingen Msl Site, 3 mi WSW of Kaiserslautern, 4 Jun 1956 (actvd)–unk; Alzey Comms Anx, Orbis, 11 Oct 1956 (asgnd in UC status), 13 Jul 1957 (actvd)–1 Oct 1959 (trsfd to Ramstein AB); Dannenfels RR Anx, Dannenfels, 1 Jan 1958 (asgnd)–1 Jul 1961 (dspd); Enkenbach Water Plant Anx, 6 mi SW of Kaiserslautern, 1 Jan 1958 (asgnd)–unk; Fischbach Msl Anx, Fischbach, 1 Jan 1958 (asgnd)–1 Apr 1972 (inactvd), 13 Apr 1977 (dspd); Gruenstadt Anx (Gruenstadt Comms Stn), Gruenstadt, 1 Jan 1958 (asgnd)–1 Feb 1974 (dspd); Hochspeyer Msl Anx, 1 Jan 1958 (asgnd)–1 Feb 1974 (dspd); Kerzenheim Bcn Anx, Kerzenheim, 1 Jan 1958 (asgnd)–17 Feb 1965 (dspd); Mehlingen Anx, Mehlingen, 1 Jan 1958 (asgnd)–31 Aug 1973 (inactvd); Neuhemsbach POL Pumping Anx, 1 Jan 1958 (asgnd)–unk; Rohrbach Sewage Plant Anx, 1 Jan 1958 (asgnd)–unk; Sembach UHF/DF Anx (Sembach Radar Site), Baalborn, 1 Jan 1958 (asgnd)–20 Dec 1961 (dspd); Diepholz Hsg Anx, Steinfeld, 1 Sep 1959 (trsfd from Hahn AB)–1 Jul 1960 (trsfd to Ramstein AB); Diepholz Msl Site, Damme, 1 Sep 1959 (trsfd from Hahn AB)–1 Jul 1960 (trsfd to Ramstein AB); Driedorf Msl Site, Driedorf, 1 Sep 1959 (trsfd from Hahn AB)–1 Apr 1960 (inactvd), 28 Feb 1961 (dspd); Driedorf Water Sys Anx, Driedorf, 1 Sep 1959 (trsfd from Hahn AB)–1 Apr 1960 (inactvd), 28 Feb 1961 (dspd); Gelchsheim Msl Site, Gelchsheim, 1 Sep 1959 (trsfd from Hahn AB)–1 Dec 1961 (trsfd to Ramstein AB); Ilmspan Msl Site, Ilmspan, 1 Sep 1959 (trsfd from Hahn AB)–unk; Koeterberg Hsg Anx, Fuerstenau, 1 Sep 1959 (trsfd from Hahn AB)–1 Nov 1961 (trsfd to Ramstein AB); Koeterberg Msl Site, Fuerstenau, 1 Sep 1959 (trsfd from Hahn AB)–1 Nov 1961 (trsfd to Ramstein AB); Marsberg Amn Hsg Anx, Madfeld, 1 Sep 1959 (trsfd from Hahn AB)–1 Jul 1960 (trsfd to Ramstein AB); Marsberg Msl Site, Madfeld, 1 Sep 1959 (trsfd from Hahn AB)–1 Jul 1960 (trsfd to Ramstein AB); Marsberg Water Sys Anx, Madfeld, 1 Sep 1959 (trsfd from Hahn AB)–1 Jul 1960 (trsfd to Ramstein AB); Reisenbach Msl Site, Reisenbach, 1 Sep 1959 (trsfd from Hahn AB)–1 Apr 1960 (inactvd); Reisenbach Radar Site, Reisenbach, 1 Sep 1959 (trsfd from Hahn AB)–1 Apr 1960 (inactvd); Sackenbach Msl Site, Sackenbach, 1 Sep 1959 (trsfd from Hahn AB)–1 Mar 1960 (inactvd); Hahnerhof Anx [Transformer], 6 mi SW of Kaiserslautern, 1 Apr 1961 (actvd)–1 Feb 1974 (dspd); Mertesheim Water Sys Anx, Mertesheim, 1 Apr 1961 (actvd)–1 Feb 1974 (dspd); Neukirchen Water Sys Anx, Neukirchen, 1 Apr 1961 (actvd)–; Niedermehlingerhof Water Sys Anx, 6 mi SW of Kaiserslautern, 1 Apr 1961 (actvd)–unk; Alzey Comms Anx, Orbis, 1 Apr 1962 (trsfd from Ramstein AB)–1 Feb 1964 (trsfd to Ramstein AB); Oslo Admn Ofc, Fornebu, Norway, 1 Aug 1962 (actvd)–1 Jul 1967 (trsfd to Rhein-Main AB); Oslo Sch, Bekkestna, Norway, 1 Aug 1962 (actvd)–1 Jul 1967 (trsfd to Rhein-Main AB); Oslo Stor Anx [Commissary], Oslo, Norway, 1 Aug 1962 (actvd)–1 Jul 1967 (trsfd to Rhein-Main AB); Alzey Comms Anx, Orbis, 1 Jul 1964 (trsfd from Ramstein AB)–1 Jul 1973 (trsfd to Wiesbaden AB); Mehlingen Anx, Mehlingen, 1 May 1975 (actvd)–; Bad Muender Comms Anx, 14 mi NE of Hameln, 5 Feb 1976 (actvd)–; Hessisch-Oldendorf AS, Hessisch-Oldendorf, 5 Feb 1976 (asgnd)–; Alzey Comms Anx, Orbis, 1 Mar 1976 (trsfd from Wiesbaden AB)–; Schwelentrup Comms Anx, Schwelentrup, 18 May 1976 (asgnd)–; Lindsey AS, Wiesbaden, 1 Jul 1976 (trsfd from Wiesbaden AB)–; Reisenbach Comms Anx, Reisenbach, 1 Jul 1976 (trsfd from Wiesbaden AB)–; Schierstein Admn Ofc, Wiesbaden, 1 Jul 1976 (trsfd from Wiesbaden AB)–; Wiesbaden Hosp, Wiesbaden, 1 Jul 1976 (trsfd from Wiesbaden AB)–1 Apr 1978 (trsfd to Lindsey AS); Hessisch-Oldendorf Fam Hsg Anx #1, Hessisch-Oldendorf, 1 Nov 1976 (asgnd)–; Kalkar Comms Anx, Kalkar, 1 Jan 1977 (asgnd)–; Kalkar Recrn Anx (Kalkar Fam Hsg Anx), Kalkar, 1 Jan 1977 (asgnd)–; Neuhemsbach Petrol Prods Stor Anx (Neuhemsbach POL Retail Distr Stn), Neuhemsbach, 1 Jan 1977 (asgnd)–; Hessisch-Oldendorf Stor Anx, Hessisch-Oldendorf, 1 Oct 1977 (asgnd)–31 Mar 1982 (dspd); Bremerhaven Comms Anx, Bremerhaven, 1 Dec 1977–; Tuerkheim Anx, Tuerkheim, 14 Feb 1978 (asgnd)–; Tuerkheim Comms Anx, Tuerkheim, 14 Feb 1978 (asgnd)–; Niedermoermter Sch, Kalkar-Niedermoermter, 1 Aug 1978 (actvd)–; Basdahl Comms Anx, Basdahl, 15 Mar 1982 (actvd)–; Hessisch-Oldendorf Stor Anx #1, Hessisch-Oldendorf, 1 Mar 1982 (actvd)–; Hessisch-Oldendorf Stor Anx #2, Hessisch-Oldendorf, 1 Apr 1982 (actvd)–; Wanna Comms Anx, Westerwanna, 1 Aug 1982 (asgnd)–.

Major Changes in Operational Capability: French occupation forces surveyed and prepared the first airfield at Sembach in 1919; field served as French flying field until about 1930; thereafter land returned to German agricultural use; Luftwaffe began construction at the site in early 1940, but French defeated before Sembach construction had been completed; base returned to agricultural use in Jun 1940; after World War II French again assumed control over the area and began construction of hangars, hardstands, taxiways, tower, and other facilities required for an operational air base; 8,500-ft concrete runway poured Jun 1951 and other structures completed by the end of that year; base intended for U.S. use and acquired by USAFE in 1953; base supported RB–26 and RF–80 reconnaissance operations, 8 Jul 1953; Sembach became a Matador (later, Mace) missile base on 2 Jun 1956; aircraft operations declined in 1958–1959; the 38th Tac Msl Wg arrived from Hahn AB, making Sembach the Air Force's primary missile base in Europe on 1 Sep 1959; flying mission resumed with the assignment of the 7th Air Commando Sq in Jul 1964; missile function terminated with activation of the 603d AB Wg as host unit at Sembach on 25 Sep 1966; HQ Seventeenth AF moved from Ramstein to Sembach in Oct 1972; since Jun 1973 the base has supported HQ Seventeenth AF, the 601st Wg, and numerous assigned and tenant organizations; new base sewage plant constructed, airmen's dormitories renovated, and base dining hall completed, 1973–1975; dependents' school enlarged, and bachelor officers' quarters and a new base fire alarm system added, 1975–1976; the Hochspeyer munitions storage facility, with 21 earth-covered storage igloo structures, completed and the base runways resurfaced, 1978–1979; major base facilities hardened, a bowling center built, and a new NATO-sponsored lighting system installed, 1981–1982.

Major Commands to Which Assigned: USAFE, 1 Sep 1952–.

Major Changes in Status: None.

Units Assigned:

1953		
12 Air Rscu Gp	21 Sep 53–18 Feb 58	
30 Tac Recon Sq	7 Jul 53–8 Jan 58	
66 AB Gp	7 Jul 53–18 Jun 58	
66 AP Sq	7 Jul 53–18 Jun 58	
66 Comms Sq	7 Jul 53–1 Jul 62	
66 Food Svc Sq	7 Jul 53–18 Jun 58	
66 Instls Sq	7 Jul 53–18 Jun 58	
66 Maint & Sup Gp	7 Jul 53–8 Dec 57	
66 Maint Sq		
(66 Fld Maint Sq)	7 Jul 53–18 Jul 58	
66 MV Sq		
(66 Trnsp Sq)	7 Jul 53–18 Jun 58	
66 Recon Tech Sq	7 Jul 53–13 Aug 53	
66 Sup Sq	7 Jul 53–18 Jun 58	
66 Tac Recon Gp	7 Jul 53–8 Dec 57	
66 Tac Recon Wg	7 Jul 53–9 Jul 58	
81 Air Rscu Sq	25 Sep 53–8 Dec 57	
86 Air Svc Sq		
(86 Mat Sq)	11 May 53–8 Mar 58	
302 Tac Recon Sq	17 Jul 53–25 Aug 58	
303 Tac Recon Sq	7 Jul 53–31 Aug 58	
7355 AB Sq	5 Apr 53–7 Aug 53	
1954		
85 Radio Sq, Mobile	2 May 54–8 May 55	
7233 Air Mun Gp	1 Aug 54–1 Feb 68	
7427 USAF Infmy		
(7427 USAF Hosp)	1 May 54–25 Sep 57	
1955		
6914 Radio Sq, Mobile		

(6910 Radio		
Gp, Mobile)	8 May 55–15 May 61	
1956		
11 Tac Msl Sq	1 Jul 56–1 Oct 82	
587 Spt Sq	15 Sep 56–8 Jan 61	
1958		
512 Ftr-Intcpr Sq	28 Mar 58–1 Jul 59	
822 Tac Msl Sq	18 Jun 58–	
7127 AP Sq	18 Jan 58–1 Sep 59	
7127 Comms Sq	18 Jan 58–1 Sep 59	
7127 Fld Maint Sq	18 Jan 58–1 Sep 59	
7127 Food Svc Sq	18 Jan 58–1 Sep 59	
7127 Instls Sq	18 Jan 58–1 Sep 59	
7127 Sup Sq	18 Jan 58–1 Sep 59	
7127 Spt Gp	18 Jan 58–1 Sep 59	
7127 Trnsp Sq	18 Jan 58–1 Sep 59	
7127 USAF Hosp	18 Jan 58–1 Sep 59	
1959		
38 AB Gp		
(38 Cmbt Spt Gp)	1 Sep 59–25 Sep 66	
38 AB Sq	1 Sep 59–25 Sep 62	
38 AP Sq	1 Sep 59–25 Sep 62	
38 Fld Maint Sq	1 Sep 59–25 Sep 62	
38 Mat Sq	1 Sep 59–25 Sep 62	
38 Tac Msl Wg	20 Aug 59–25 Sep 66	
1962		
6 Tac Dep Sq		
(306 Mun		
Maint Sq)	6 Feb 62–1 Oct 64	
38 CE Sq	25 Sep 62–25 Sep 66	
38 Msl Maint Sq	25 Sep 62–1 Dec 66	
38 Sup Sq	25 Sep 62–25 Sep 66	

38 Trnsp Sq	25 Sep 62–25 Sep 66
823 Tac Msl Sq	25 Sep 62–
887 Tac Msl Sq	25 Sep 62–25 Sep 66
2134 Comms Sq	1 Jul 62–

1963

2 Mobile Comms Gp	1 Aug 63–1 Jun 73
601 Tac Con Sq	25 Mar 63–1 Jun 73

1964

7 Air Commando Sq, Comps (7 Sp Ops Sq)	1 Jul 64–15 Aug 68

1965

601 Direct Air Spt Sq	15 Feb 65–1 Jun 73
601 Tac Con Gp	15 Feb 65–1 Jul 68
601 Tac Con Maint Sq	15 Feb 65–1 Jun 73

1966

603 AB Wg	25 Sep 66–1 Jul 68
603 AP Sq (603 Scty Pol Sq)	25 Sep 66–1 Jul 68
603 CE Sq	25 Sep 66–1 Jul 68
603 Mat Sq	25 Sep 66–1 Jul 68

1968

601 CE Sq	1 Jul 68–1 Jun 73
601 Cmbt Spt Gp	1 Jul 68–1 Jun 73
601 Scty Pol Sq	1 Jul 68–1 Jun 73
601 Sup Sq	1 Jul 68–1 Jun 73
601 Trnsp Sq	1 Jul 68–1 Jun 73

1971

USAF Disp, Sembach (USAF Clinic, Sembach)	1 Jul 71–

1972

Seventeenth AF	5 Oct 72–

1973

601 Tac Air Con Cen Sq	1 Jul 73–15 Sep 73
603 Tac Con Sq	5 Oct 73–30 Jul 78
686 AF Band	1 Oct 73–14 Mar 79
7400 AB Gp	1 Jun 73–31 Dec 75
7400 CE Sq	1 Jun 73–31 Dec 75
7400 Mat Sq	1 Jun 73–31 Dec 75
7400 SP Sq	1 Jun 73–31 Dec 75

1975

601 Tac Con Gp	15 Nov 75–30 May 78

1976

20 Tac Air Spt Sq	1 Jan 76–
601 CE Sq	1 Jan 76–
601 Cmbt Spt Gp	1 Jan 76–
601 Consold Acft Maint Sq	1 Jan 76–30 Apr 79
601 Scty Pol Sq	1 Jan 76–
601 Sup Sq	1 Jan 76–
601 Tac Air Spt Sq	1 Jan 76–
601 Trnsp Sq	1 Jan 76–
704 Tac Air Spt Sq	4 Jul 76–

1979

601 Acft Gnrtn Sq	30 Apr 79–
601 Component Rpr Sq	30 Apr 79–
603 Tac Con Sq	1 Apr 79–

1980

6918 Elect Scty Sq	1 Feb 80–

1982

31 Wea Sq	1 Aug 82–
2005 Comms Gp	1 Oct 82–
Numbered AF Cmbt Ops Staff [Seventeenth AF]	15 Jan 82–

Sondrestrom Air Base

Location: Located 60 mi N of Arctic Circle, 90 mi from the NE end of Sondre Stromfjord, $1\frac{1}{2}$ mi WNW of Ravneklippen, and 70 mi W of Holsteinsborg, Greenland.

Name: Named after Sondre Stromfjord on the west coast of Greenland.

Date of Current Name: 10 Jan 1952.

Previous Names: Bluie West 8, 20 Oct 1941; Sondrestromfjord AAB, 1945; Sondrestromfjord AB, 25 Oct 1947.

Date of Establishment: 20 Oct 1941.

Date Construction Began: Original construction undertaken 7 Oct 1941; later construction began in 1947.

Date of Beneficial Occupancy: 26 Sep 1942.

Base Operating Units: 417th Base HQ & AB Sq, 26 Sep 1942; 1385th AAF BU, 1 Oct 1945; 1004th AB Sq (rdsgd 1234th AB Sq, 1 Oct 1948), 1 Jun 1948; Greenland Base Comd, 21 Jun 1949–9 Oct 1950. 6621st AB Sq, 20 Jul 1951; 6621st AB Gp, 25 Sep 1955; 4084th AB Gp, 1 Apr 1957; 4684th AB Gp, 1 Jul 1960–.

Base Commanders: Capt Bernt Balchen, 7 Oct 1941–c. Aug 1943; Lt Col Walter T. Bogart, c. Aug 1943–unk; Capt Henry R. Olson, Oct 1943–unk; Lt Col Walter T. Bogart, c. Nov 1943–unk; Maj Brown, c. Mar–22 Aug 1945; unk, 23 Aug 1945–30 Jun 1946; 2d Lt John M. Kennedy, 1 Jul 1946; Lt Byron A. Campbell, Nov 1946–unk; Lt Col Warren A. Fackenthall, Dec 1946; Lt Col Maurice S. Dillingham, 26 Feb 1947–unk; Lt Col Warren A. Fackenthall, unk–unk; Lt Col Theodore H. Gorton, 1 Jul 1947; Capt Paul G. Murphy, Nov 1947–unk; Maj Lloyd F. Abbotts, c. 15 Jan 1948–unk; Lt Col William H. Hancock Jr, 17 May 1948; Lt Col Luther W. Burns, 12–24 Mar 1949; Maj Reginald J. Horseman, unk–Apr 1949; Capt Lawrence E. Freligh, unk–c. 2 Aug 1949; Capt John E. Morrow, c. 15 Jan 1951–unk; Capt Samuel G. Taylor Jr, c. 31 Mar 1951–unk; Lt Col Walter W. Thompson, 11 Jun 1951; Lt Col Alfred H. Dehle, 17 Oct 1951–unk; Col Richard Arnold Jr, 19 Jan 1952; Col William L. Herblin, 1953; Col Vernon L. Stintzi, Aug 1953; Col Norman C. Spencer Jr, c. 19 Aug 1954; Col Ronald A. Johnston, Aug 1955; Lt Col Samuel A.

Mitchell, 17 Jul 1956; Col William J. Jowdy, 1 Aug 1956; Col William A. Tope, 29 Dec 1956; Col William J. Jowdy, 18 Jan 1957; Col Byron B. Webb, 15 Jul 1957; Lt Col Vincent P. Hannley, 17 Sep 1957; Col Byron B. Webb, 24 Sep 1957; Lt Col Vincent P. Hannley, 9 Oct 1957; Col Byron B. Webb, 6 Nov 1957; Lt Col Vincent P. Hannley, 8 Jan 1958; Col Byron B. Webb, 28 Jan 1958; Col George Gould, 24 Jun 1958; Lt Col Paul M. Skinner, 11 Nov 1958; Col George W. Haney, 19 Nov 1958; Col Martin B. Schofield, 15 Jul 1959; Col James C. Stewart, 24 Jun 1960; Col Houston W. Longino Jr, 2 Jun 1961; Col Charles A. Stevens, 25 May 1962; Col Herbert L. Phillips, 7 Jul 1962; Col John Y. C. Roth, 2 Jul 1963; Col Bryant Y. Anderson, 19 Aug 1964; Col Richard G. Mendrop, 29 Oct 1964; Col Robert L. Harriger, 10 Dec 1964; Col Reynold C. Dorman, 17 Jun 1965; Col William H. Moore, 14 Jul 1965; Col Leo J. Moffatt, 8 Sep 1965; Col Norman G. Niersbach, 27 Jul 1966; Col Clay D. Albright Jr, 11 Jul 1967; Col Leo J. Moffatt, 18 Mar 1968; Lt Col Lee M. Trowbridge, 22 May 1968 (temp); Lt Col Robert E. Prince, 12 Jun 1968; Lt Col Patrick L. Doran, 20 Apr 1969; Col William J. Daly, 3 May 1969; Col Joe Orell, 15 Jul 1969; Col Jack A. Blacker, 29 May 1970; Col Arval J. Roberson, c. Jun 1971; Col Clarence E. Wilson, 9 Jul 1971; Col Harrison M. Ward Jr, 4 May 1973; Col James W. Stanley, 22 Apr 1974; Lt Col James H. West, 14 Apr 1975; Col Luther E. Millsap, 9 May 1976; Col William D. Hinds, 7 May 1977; Col Carrol D. Buford, 24 May 1977; Col James R. Galloway, 19 May 1978; Col Daniel J. Birmingham Jr, 8 Mar 1979; Col Conway G. Snipes, 9 May 1980; Col Jackie P. Leathers, 8 May 1981; Lt Col Donald W. Molter, 11 May 1982; Col Hamilton W. Kennedy, 11 Jun 1982–.

Major Off-Base and Detached Installations: Cruncher Isl (rdsgd Sondrestrom AB Anx), Simiutak Isl, Greenland, 31 Mar 1958–.

Major Changes in Operational Capability: Ferrying Command, U.S. Army Air Corps, laid plans for establishing field on west coast of Greenland to facilitate movement of aircraft across North Atlantic, to and from Britain; Capt Bernt Balchen, famed arctic flyer, arrived with contingent of men at head of Sondre Stromfjord to prepare initial airstrip and facilities, 7 Oct 1941; base (Bluie West 8, or BW-8) accommodated a weather reporting station and support organizations for North Atlantic route, Ferrying Command; (BW-8 was second base constructed by the U.S. in Greenland, the base at Narsarssuak (BW-1) being the first); radio station at BW-8 began operations while construction workers completed additional living quarters and related facilities, 20 Oct 1941; first small base hospital opened 10 Dec 1941; winter weather hampered base construction and operations each year between November and late May; winter runways were prepared at BW-8 by Feb 1942, and first aircraft landed en route to North America 7 Mar 1942; base transmitted regular weather reports to Ferrying Command throughout World War II, and supported

BOLERO operations, B–17 missions of weather and pathfinder aircraft, the latter supported also by the radio range station on Simiutak (Cruncher) Island, near BW–1; BW–8 boasted a 5,000-by 300-foot asphalt runway by early 1943 and a large, heated steel hangar by Aug 1943; weather forecasting operations ceased as base prepared to phase down 10 May 1945; base shipped excess food stocks to BW–1, sending its surplus equipment and materiel by ship to the U.S.; changed from auxiliary airfield to emergency field 15 Aug 1945, and BW–1 assumed control of Sondrestrom as an outpost of Greenland Base Command 23 Aug 1945; engineer aviation units arrived at BW–8 to repair, restore, and resurface the runway, to construct water lines and central power plant, and to resurface base roads in Jun 1947; further work winterized shops and living quarters in 1948–1949; base assumed standby status Jun 1950 and returned to control of Danish government on 9 Oct 1950; an air base detachment from BW–1 arrived early in Mar 1951 to rehabilitate base and furnish support for Operation BLUE JAY, the development of Thule AB; U.S. units again manned Sondrestrom on 20 Jul 1951, operational control transferred from the Danish government in Sep 1951; contract workers constructed a new hangar, installed runway lights, rehabilitated barracks, built a ground control installation and modern refueling facilities, strengthened the runway, and built taxiways, hardstands, fuel and petroleum storage areas, airmen's barracks, a consolidated mess hall, and bachelor officers' quarters between 1952 and 1954; base supported the Army-Air Force airborne operation WIND CHILL in 1954; became a SAC base, providing refueling, maintenance, billeting, messing and services for aircrews and passengers of SAC aircraft, those of other USAF commands, and of Danish and other Allied nations, including occasionally the Scandinavian Airways System (SAS), 1 Apr 1957; Danske-ESSO began refueling and servicing of commercial aircraft and refueling of military aircraft at the terminal, 1 Dec 1959; base facilities enlarged and improved to support SAC reflex operations 1957–1959; became part of North American Air Defense Command network under ADC 1 Jul 1960, but, upon the inactivation of ADC, 1 Dec 1979, Sondrestrom again became a SAC installation.

Major Commands to Which Assigned: U.S. First Army, 15 Jan 1941; Eastern Def Comd, 12 Dec 1942; Air Trpt Comd, 1 Jan 1946; Mil Air Trpt Comd, 16 Sep 1959; Northeast Air Comd, 1–9 Oct 1950.* Northeast Air Comd, 20 Jul 1951; SAC, 1 Apr 1957; ADC (rdsgd Aerospace Def Comd, 15 Jan 1968), 1 Jul 1960; SAC, 1 Dec 1979–.

Major Changes in Status: Under construction, 15 Jan–20 Oct 1941; active auxiliary airfield and weather reporting station, 20 Oct 1941; emer-

---

*From 9 Oct 1950 to Sep 1951, the Danish Government controlled the base.

gency landing field, 15 Aug 1945; standby status, Jun 1950–20 Jul 1951, base being controlled Jun 1950–Sep 1951 by Danish government; active USAF AB, 20 Jul 1951–.

Units Assigned:

1942	
417 Base HQ & AB Sq	26 Sep 42–30 Sep 45
1947	
Co C, 817 Engr Avn Bn	22 Jun 47–27 Oct 47
1948	
1004 AB Sq (1234 AB Sq, 1 Oct 1948)	1 Jun 48–20 Nov 49
Co A, 817 Engr Avn Bn	13 Jul 48–4 Nov 48
Co B, 817 Engr Avn Bn	13 Jul 48–4 Nov 48
1951	
6621 AB Sq	20 Jul 51–1 Apr 57
1952	
2004 AACS Sq (2004 Comms Sq)	1 Jul 52–
1955	
6621 AB Gp	25 Sep 55–1 Apr 57

6621 Instls Sq	25 Sep 55–1 Apr 57
6621 Mat Sq	25 Sep 55–1 Apr 57
6621 USAF Infmy (6621 USAF Dispy)	1 Jan 55–1 Apr 57
1956	
Sondrestrom Task Force, Prov	1 Jul 56–Unk
1957	
4084 AB Gp	1 Apr 57–1 Jul 60
4084 Instls Sq	1 Apr 57–1 Jul 60
4084 Ops Sq	1 Apr 57–1 Jul 57
4084 Sup Sq	1 Apr 57–1 Jul 60
4084 Trnsp Sq	1 Apr 57–1 Jul 60
4084 USAF Dispy	1 Apr 57–1 Jul 60
1960	
4684 AB Gp	1 Jul 60–
4684 AB Sq	1 Oct 60–1 Apr 62
4684 CE Sq	1 Oct 60–1 Jan 65
4684 Mat Sq	1 Oct 60–1 Apr 62
4684 Sup Sq	1 Jul 60–1 Oct 60

Spangdahlem Air Base

Location: Located 1 mi NW of Spangdahlem, 20 mi N of Trier/Mosel, and 10 mi E of Bitburg AB, Federal Republic of Germany.

Name: Named after a town in the Federal Republic of Germany.

Date of Current Name: 1 Sep 1952.

Previous Names: None.

Date of Establishment: 1 Sep 1952.

Date Construction Began: French initiated original construction, spring 1951; USAF began construction in 1952.

Date of Beneficial Occupancy: 1 Sep 1952.

Base Operating Units: 7352d AB Sq, 1 Sep 1952; 10th AB Gp, 8 May 1953; 49th AB Gp (rdsgd 49th Cmbt Spt Gp, 8 Sep 1962), 25 Aug 1959; 7149th AB Gp, 1 Jul 1968; 36th Cmbt Spt Gp, 15 Sep 1969; 52d Cmbt Spt Gp, 1 Jan 1972–.

Base Commanders: Lt Col John L. Schroeder, 1 Sep 1952; Col Howard J. Withycombe, 8 May 1953; Col William J. Jones, Jun 1954 (temp); Col Milford D. Wissler, 8 Jul 1954; Col Bryan W. Brown Jr, 15 Dec 1955; Col Henry S. Taylor, 7 May 1958; Col John L. Turner, 25 Aug 1959; Col James L. Tucker, 1 Feb 1960; Col Peter P. Dawson, 1 Jul 1962; Col Carleton W. Rogers, 22 Jun 1964; Col Robert W. McDermott, c. Jun 1966; Lt Col John R. Robinson, 1 Jul 1968; Col Eugene J. Budnik, 15 Sep 1969;* Col Roberts L. Underwood, 23 Feb 1970; Col John P. Moore, 3 Jul 1970; Col John J. Gaudion, 1 Jan 1972; Col Dwayne E. Kelley, 27 Oct 1972; Col Robert M. Pfeiffer, 1 Sep 1974; Col Keith P. Watts, 3 Aug 1977; Col Lewis G. Vale, 23 May 1979; Lt Col James W. Spradling, 5 Jun 1980; Col David L. Wagner, 3 Jul 1980; Col Howard K. Carroll, 23 Aug 1982–.

Major Off-Base and Detached Installations:[†] Spangdahlem/ Niederkail Water Pumping Anx (rdsgd Niederkail Water Plant Anx), Niederkail, 15 Feb 1953 (actvd)–; Spangdahlem/Phillipsheim POL Stor

---

*Between 15 Sep 1969 and 1 Jan 1972 Spangdahlem was controlled by Bitburg AB, and the commanders of Bitburg were also commanders of Spangdahlem.

[†]Unless otherwise indicated, all installations are located in the Federal Republic of Germany.

Anx (rdsgd Phillipsheim POL Pumping Anx), Phillipsheim, 15 Apr 1953 (actvd)−; Spangdahlem Waste Anx (rdsgd Spangdahlem Sewage Plant Anx; Spangdahlem Sewage Anx), 15 Apr 1953 (actvd)−; Spangdahlem/Grosslittgen RB Anx (rdsgd Grosslittgen Stor Anx), Grosslittgen, 29 Jun 1953 (actvd)−; Spangdahlem/Schoenfeld AC & W Stn, Pruem, 29 Aug 1953 (actvd)−1 Jul 1955 (inactvd); Spangdahlem/Bitburg Railhead Anx, 20 Oct 1954 (actvd)−; Spangdahlem/Schoenfeld/Dueren/ Kleinham Comms Anx, 10 Jan 1955 (actvd)−; Grosslittgen Water Sys Anx (rdsgd Grosslittgen Water Plant Anx), Grosslittgen, 10 Jul 1956 (actvd)−; Lanfeld Tacan Site, Lanfeld, 11 Apr 1958 (asgnd in UC status)−10 Oct 1961 (inactvd), 11 May 1962 (dspd); Pickliessem RB Anx, Pickliessem, 1 Oct 1958 (trsfd from Bitburg AB)−1 May 1963 (inactvd), 5 Aug 1963 (dspd); Kleine Brogel AB, Kleine-Brogel, Belgium, 1 Jul 1976−; Memmingen AB, Memmingen, 1 Jul 1976; Lechfeld AB, Lechfeld, 6 Sep 1976−; Trier Hsg Anx (rdsgd Trier Fam Hsg Anx), Pfalzel, 1 Oct 1977 (trsfd from Bitburg AB)−; Landsberg AB, Penzing, 1 Feb 1978−; Karup AB, Karup, Denmark, 18 Apr 1978−; Herforst Fam Hsg Anx, Herforst, 25 Apr 1979 (asgnd in UC status)−1 May 1981 (actvd)−; Speicher Fam Hsg Anx, Speicher, 25 Apr 1979−; Dudeldorf Stor Anx, Dudeldorf, 12 Dec 1979 (asgnd)−; Homburg Fam Hsg Anx, Homburg, unk−1 Apr 1980 (dspd); Speicher Stor Anx, Speicher, 15 Nov 1981−; Trier-Olewig Stor Anx, Olewig, 1 Oct 1982−.

Major Changes in Operational Capability: Following French construction at Spangdahlem in 1951, USAFE assumed control of the base on 1 Sep 1952; the 7352d AB Sq made initial U.S. preparations for the arrival of tactical aircraft from Toul AB, France; first to arrive was the 10th Tac Recon Wg on 8 May 1953; compound constructed for 83d Air Rscu Sq and all-base fire alarm system installed, 1953; runways lengthened and reinforced, shoulders widened, and temporary runway arresting barriers erected, 1957; base heating plant renovated, Victor Alert compound and water sewage disposal plants built, 1960−1961; extensive repairs and partial reinforcing of runways completed, MA−1A runway arresting barrier installed, 1963; base runways resealed, munitions storage facilities built, and intruder alarm system installed, 1964−1965; when the 49th Tac Ftr Wg moved from Germany to Holloman AFB, 1 Jul 1968, USAFE organized the 7149th AB Gp to handle base support and host responsibilities at Spangdahlem, particularly for the 7149th Tac Ftr Wg; the 36th Cmbt Spt Gp at Bitburg AB assumed control over Spangdahlem as part of USAFE's only two-wing, "twin-base" organization on 15 Sep 1969; 20 aircraft parking pads with revetments, a taxiway, and four maintenance shelters constructed, and runways reinforced, 1971; base again acquired primary or independent base status when host and support responsibilities at Spangdahlem were assumed by the 52d Cmbt Spt Gp on 1 Jan 1972; a 10,000-barrel POL tank and four fire truck shelters built, 1972−1973; 48 TAB

VEE aircraft shelters erected, warning systems for 44 aircraft shelters and a light/klaxon console installed, 1974; Aerospace Ground Equipment (AGE) pads in 44 TAB VEE aircraft shelters, three jet fuel storage tanks, two regular fuel storage tanks, three hot refueling stands, two squadron operations facilities, and a ready crew facility constructed, 1974–1975; extensive renovation on three airmen's dormitories and a BOQ completed, five POL truck shelters constructed, and 34 TAB VEE shelters upgraded, 1975–1976; major resurfacing work required closure of runways, 5 Jul–31 Aug 1977; runway lighting and aircraft arresting systems repaired, 1977–1978; an explosive ordnance disposal facility built and an instrument landing system installed, 1979; Spangdahlem Elementary School reconstructed and enlarged, airfield paving resealed, avionics facility, liquid oxygen storage facility, and chemical warfare protection building constructed, 1980–1981; 300 new family housing units constructed, 1980–1982.

Major Commands to Which Assigned: USAFE, 1 Sep 1952–.

Major Changes in Status: Primary installation, 1 Sep 1952; off-base installation as half of the "twin-bases" of Spangdahlem and Bitburg Air Bases (controlled by Bitburg), 15 Sep 1969; primary installation, 1 Jan 1972–.

Units Assigned:

	1952	1237 AACS Sq	
7352 AB Sq	1 Sep 52–9 May 53	(2137 Comms Sq)	1 Nov 54–
	1953		1955
1 Tac Recon Sq	8 May 53–25 Aug 59	7428 USAF Infmy	
10 AB Gp	8 May 53–25 Aug 59	(7428 USAF	
10 AP Sq	8 May 53–25 Aug 59	Dispy)	16 May 55–25 Sep 57
10 Comms Sq	8 May 53–25 Aug 59		1958
10 Food Svc Sq	8 May 53–25 Aug 59	10 Armnt & Elect	
10 Instls Sq	8 May 53–25 Aug 59	Maint Sq	15 Sep 58–25 Aug 59
10 Maint & Sup Gp	8 May 53–8 Dec 57	30 Tac Recon Sq	8 Jan 58–25 Aug 59
10 Maint Sq			1959
(10 Fld Maint Sq;		7 Tac Ftr Sq	25 Aug 59–1 Jul 68
10 Consold Acft		8 Tac Ftr Sq	25 Aug 59–1 Jul 68
Maint Sq)	8 May 53–25 Aug 59	9 Tac Ftr Sq	25 Aug 59–1 Jul 68
10 MV Sq		19 Tac Recon Sq	10 Jan 59–25 Aug 59
(10 Trnsp Sq)	8 May 53–25 Aug 59	49 AB Gp	
10 Recon Tech Sq	11 Aug 53–8 Feb 59	(49 Cmbt Spt Gp)	25 Aug 59–1 Jul 68
10 Sup Sq	8 May 53–25 Aug 59	49 AP Sq	
10 Tac Recon Gp	8 May 53–8 Dec 57	(49 Scty Pol Sq)	25 Aug 59–1 Jul 68
10 Tac Recon Wg	8 May 53–25 Aug 59	49 Armnt & Elect	
32 Tac Recon Sq	17 May 53–31 Jul 57	Maint Sq	25 Aug 59–8 Sep 62
38 Tac Recon Sq	4 May 53–1 Aug 57	49 Comms Sq	25 Aug 59–1 Jul 62
83 Air Rscu Sq	1 Aug 53–8 Dec 57	49 Consold Acft	
526 Tac Con Gp	1 Nov 53–30 Jun 54	Maint Sq	
619 Tac Con Sq	1 Nov 53–30 Jun 54	(49 Fld Maint Sq)	25 Aug 59–1 Jul 68
944 Forward Air		49 Food Svc Sq	25 Aug 59–8 Sep 62
Con Sq	1 Apr 53–18 Mar 54	49 Instls Sq	
	1954	(49 CE Sq)	25 Aug 59–1 Jul 68
562 Ftr-Bmbr Sq	12 Dec 54–17 Sep 55	49 Sup Sq	25 Aug 59–1 Jul 68
		49 Tac Ftr Wg	25 Aug 59–1 Jul 68

49 Tac Hosp	25 Aug 59–1 Jul 68	52 Avncs Maint Sq	
49 Trnsp Sq	25 Aug 59–1 Jul 68	(52 Component	
	1961	Rpr Sq)	31 Dec 71–
309 Tac Ftr Sq	10 Oct 61–21 Nov 61	52 CE Sq	31 Dec 71–
	1964	52 Fld Maint Sq	
49 Armnt & Elect		(52 Equip	
Maint Sq	1 Jul 64–1 Jul 68	Maint Sq)	31 Dec 71–
49 Orgnzl Maint Sq	1 Jul 64–1 Jan 66	52 Scty Pol Sq	31 Dec 71–
349 Mun Maint Sq	1 Jul 64–1 Jul 68	52 Sup Sq	31 Dec 71–
	1968	52 Tac Ftr Wg	31 Dec 71–
7149 Armnt &		52 Trnsp Sq	31 Dec 71–
Elect Maint Sq		352 Mun Maint Sq	31 Dec 71–7 Oct 72
(7149 Avncs			1972
Maint Sq)	1 Jul 68–15 Sep 69	52 Cmbt Spt Gp	1 Mar 72–
7149 CE Sq	1 Jul 68–15 Sep 69	52 Orgnzl Maint Sq	
7149 Cmbt Spt Gp	1 Jul 68–15 Sep 69	(52 Acft Gnrtn Sq)	1 Feb 72–
7149 Fld Maint Sq	1 Jul 68–15 Sep 69	7007 Explosive	
7149 Scty Pol Sq	1 Jul 68–15 Sep 69	Ord Dspl Flt	1 Jul 72–
7149 Sup Sq	1 Jul 68–15 Sep 69	USAF Dispy,	
7149 Tac Ftr Wg	1 Jul 68–15 Sep 69	Spangdahlem	
7149 Trnsp Sq	1 Jul 68–15 Sep 69	(USAF Clinic,	
7149 USAF Hosp	1 Jul 68–15 Sep 69	Spangdahlem)	31 Dec 72–
7349 Muns			1973
Maint Sq	1 Jul 68–15 Sep 69	81 Tac Ftr Sq	15 Jan 73–
	1969		1976
39 Tac Elect		480 Tac Ftr Sq	15 Nov 76–
Warfare Sq	1 Apr 69–1 Jan 73		1982
	1971	52 Svcs Sq	1 Feb 82–
23 Tac Ftr Sq	31 Dec 71–		

Suwon Air Base

Location: Located 4 mi S of the city of Suwon, about 20 mi S of Seoul, 26 mi SE of Inchon, and 8 mi E of the western coast of the Republic of Korea.

Name: Named after a city in the Republic of Korea.

Date of Current Name: 26 Dec 1968.

Previous Names: Unk, late 1930s–24 Sep 1950; Suwon Aux AB (K–13), 25 Sep 1950; Suwon Aux Afld, 30 Jun 1957; Suwon Liaison Anx, 12 Jun 1963.

Date of Establishment: 25 Sep 1950.

Date Construction Began: First construction work undertaken by Japanese Army Air Force in late 1930s; USAF construction initiated Jun 1950.

Date of Beneficial Occupancy: 8 Oct 1950.

Base Operating Units: 6131st AB Gp, 8 Oct 1950; 8th AB Gp, 20 Aug 1951; Det 2, 6146th AB Sq, 20 Oct 1954; 6172d AB Sq, 1 Nov 1954; Det 2, 6146th AF Advisory Gp, 15 Sep 1955–30 Jun 1957. 6170th AB Sq, 3 Feb 1968; 152d Cmbt Spt Sq, 24 Mar 1968; 6170th Cmbt Spt Sq, 1 May 1969–30 Sep 1972. 6170th Cmbt Spt Sq, 1 Oct 1981–.

Base Commanders: Lt Col Louis C. Adams Jr, 8 Oct 1950; Col E. G. Finnell, 20 Mar 1951; Maj Robert S. Russell, 8 Jul 1951 (temp); Col Cecil H. Scott, 20 Aug 1951; Lt Col William B. Gillingham, 26 Sep 1951 (temp); Col Cecil H. Scott, c. 5 Oct 1951; Col Alonzo S. Penniston, 2 Mar 1952; Col Emory W. Cofield, 14 Feb 1953; Col James H. Hancock, 1 Jan 1954; Lt Col Dale C. L. Honeycutt, 1 Jun 1954; Lt Col Savell L. Sharp, 10 Jul 1954; Lt Col Victor L. Savage, 25 Jul 1954; Col Charles S. Marshall, 4 Aug 1954; Lt Col Clark O. Thornton, 19 Oct 1954; Lt Col John L. Beck, 1955–unk; Lt Col Horace A. Templeton, 1 Apr–30 Jun 1957. Lt Col Arthur B. Carroll, 3 Feb 1968; Lt Col Warney L. Crosby, 9 Feb 1968; Lt Col Arthur P. Webb, 24 Mar 1968; Lt Col Curt R. Finck, 1 Nov 1968; Col Cecil N. Liles, 10 Mar 1969; Maj David M. Clowers, 24 Mar 1969; Col Robert C. Shaw, 1 May 1969; Col Robert J. Yentz, 15 Jul 1970; Col James H. Hiley, 7 Aug 1971; Maj Marion F. Hagan Jr, 5 Feb 1972 (temp); Col James H. Hiley, 6 Mar 1972; Lt Col Edward J. Murphy, 1–30 Sep 1972. Col Eben Jones, 8 Feb 1981; Lt Col Kenneth W. Keasey, Oct 1981–.

Major Off-Base and Detached Installations: None.

Major Changes in Operational Capability: Base constructed by the Japanese Army Air Force in the late 1930s and served as a Japanese landing strip during World War II; liberated by U.S. Armed Forces in Aug 1945, Americans retained control of Suwon under a United Nations mandate until establishment of the Republic of Korea in Aug 1948; activated as a USAF installation on 25 Sep 1950, and played a significant role in Korean conflict; served as forward fueling point for U.S. and Allied fighters that halted incursions of Communist air units in the Seoul-Inchon area during the Allied evacuation; control of Suwon assumed by the Republic of Korea Air Force (ROKAF) on 18 Mar 1955, U.S. units supported the ROKAF 10th Ftr-Bmbr Wg and provided advisory assistance until USAF inactivated its part of the base on 30 Jun 1957; a detachment (later an OL) of the 6146th AF Advisory Gp remained at Suwon to assist ROKAF units, including aid during the reconstruction of the runway in 1963; American units constructed bunkers and barracks, enlarged dining halls, widened and repaired existing roads, constructed revetments, and built additional hardstands when USAF activated base in 1968; supported a detachment of the 82d Ftr-Intcpr Sq, several federally activated Air National Guard reconnaissance and fighter units, and regular USAF units involved in the air defense of Korea, 30 Jan 1968–18 Mar 1971; RED HORSE troops erected thirteen steel-arch aircraft shelters, constructed dikes around fuel storage sites, and improved the helicopter shelter during 1969; base inactivated on 30 Sep 1972, with official transfer to ROKAF on 22 Nov 1972; Suwon AB activated as a major USAF installation hosting A–10A Thunderbolts on 1 Oct 1981.

Major Commands to Which Assigned: FEAF, 8 Oct 1950–30 Jun 1957. PACAF, 3 Feb 1968–30 Sep 1972. PACAF, 1 Oct 1981–.

Major Changes in Status: Activated 8 Oct 1950 as off-base installation of Osan AB; major base operations transferred to ROKAF on 18 Mar 1955; inactivated on 30 Jun 1957. Activated on 3 Feb 1968; assigned to Osan AB as an off-base installation, 26 Dec 1968; inactivated 30 Sep 1972. Activated as primary installation of PACAF on 1 Oct 1981.

Units Assigned:

	1950		
		18 Sup Sq	1 Dec 50–9 Dec 50
8 Ftr Gp	8 Oct 50–20 Nov 50	35 Ftr-Bmbr Sq	8 Oct 50–27 Oct 50
12 Ftr-Bmbr Sq	1 Dec 50–9 Dec 50	36 Ftr-Bmbr Sq	5 Oct 50–27 Oct 50
18 AB Gp	1 Dec 50–9 Dec 50	67 Ftr-Bmbr Sq	1 Dec 50–9 Dec 50
18 AP Sq	1 Dec 50–9 Dec 50	6131 AB Gp	8 Oct 50–27 Nov 50
18 Comms Sq	1 Dec 50–9 Dec 50	6131 AP Sq	8 Oct 50–27 Nov 50
18 Ftr-Bmbr Gp	1 Dec 50–9 Dec 50	6131 Comms Sq	8 Oct 50–27 Nov 50
18 Ftr-Bmbr Wg	1 Dec 50–9 Dec 50	6131 Food Svc Sq	8 Oct 50–27 Nov 50
18 Food Svc Sq	1 Dec 50–9 Dec 50	6131 Instls Sq	8 Oct 50–27 Nov 50
18 Instls Sq	1 Dec 50–9 Dec 50	6131 Maint & Sup Gp	8 Oct 50–27 Nov 50
18 Maint Sq	1 Dec 50–9 Dec 50	6131 Maint Sq	8 Oct 50–27 Nov 50
18 MV Sq	1 Dec 50–9 Dec 50	6131 Med Gp	8 Oct 50–27 Nov 50

6131 MV Sq	8 Oct 50–27 Nov 50	334 Ftr-Intcpr Sq	15 Mar 51–1 May 51
6131 Sup Sq	8 Oct 50–27 Nov 50	335 Ftr-Intcpr Sq	1 May 51–24 Aug 51
6401 Fld Maint Unit	15 Oct 50–1 Jan 51	336 Ftr-Intcpr Sq	23 Apr 51–27 Jun 51
	1951	802 Engr Avn Bn	17 Apr 51–2 Oct 53
4 AB Gp	20 Mar 51–20 Aug 51	919 Engr Maint	
4 AP Sq	20 Mar 51–20 Aug 51	Co (Avn)	28 Apr 51–12 Mar 54
4 Comms Sq	20 Mar 51–7 May 51	931 Engr Avn Gp	22 Apr 51–10 May 52
4 Ftr-Intcpr Wg	7 May 51–24 Aug 51	Co A, 802 Engr	
4 Food Svc Sq	20 Mar 51–20 Aug 51	Avn Bn	17 Apr 51–27 Sep 53
4 Instls Sq	20 Mar 51–20 Aug 51	Co B, 802 Engr	
4 MV Sq	16 Apr 51–24 Aug 51	Avn Bn	17 Apr 51–2 Oct 53
8 AB Gp	20 Aug 51–19 Oct 54	Co C, 802 Engr	
8 AP Sq	20 Aug 51–19 Oct 54	Avn Bn	17 Apr 51–27 Sep 53
8 Comms Sq	20 Aug 51–19 Oct 54		1952
8 Ftr-Bmbr Gp	25 Jun 51–19 Oct 54	39 Ftr-Intcpr Sq	1 Jun 52–17 Jul 54
8 Ftr-Bmbr Wg	23 Aug 51–19 Oct 54	319 Ftr-Intcpr Sq	10 Mar 52–17 Aug 54
8 Food Svc Sq	20 Aug 51–19 Oct 54	622 Engr Maint	
8 Instls Sq	20 Aug 51–19 Oct 54	Co (Avn)	8 Sep 52–18 Jan 55
8 Maint & Sup Gp	25 Aug 51–19 Oct 54		1954
8 Maint Sq	3 Sep 51–19 Oct 54	51 Maint Sq	20 Jun 54–26 Jul 54
8 MV Sq	23 Aug 51–19 Oct 54	51 Sup Sq	20 Jun 54–26 Jul 54
8 Sup Sq	25 Aug 51–19 Oct 54	6172 AB Sq	1 Nov 54–14 Sep 55
16 Ftr-Intcpr Sq	27 Jul 51–1 Aug 54	6182 Mobile Dispy	2 Dec 54–13 Jul 55
25 Ftr-Intcpr Sq	27 Jul 51–26 Jul 54		1968
35 Ftr-Bmbr Sq	24 Aug 51–19 Oct 54	152 Cmbt Spt Sq	1 Aug 68–1 May 69
36 Ftr-Bmbr Sq	24 Aug 51–19 Oct 54	6170 AB Sq	3 Feb 68–1 Aug 68
51 AB Gp	1 Oct 51–26 Jul 54	Comms Sq,	
51 AP Sq	1 Oct 51–26 Jul 54	Prov 2070	19 Feb 68–1 Oct 68
51 Comms Sq	1 Oct 51–26 Jul 54		1969
51 Ftr-Intcpr Gp	27 Jul 51–26 Jul 54	6170 Cmbt Spt Sq	1 May 69–30 Sep 72
51 Ftr-Intcpr Wg	1 Oct 51–26 Jul 54	6170 USAF Dispy	1 May 69–17 May 71
51 Food Svc Sq	1 Oct 51–26 Jul 54		1971
51 Instls Sq	1 Oct 51–26 Jul 54	6305 Tac Con Flt	31 Dec 71–30 Sep 72
51 Maint & Sup Gp	1 Oct 51–21 Oct 52		1981
51 Maint Sq	1 Oct 51–21 Oct 52	25 Tac Ftr Sq	1 Feb 81–
51 MV Sq	1 Oct 51–26 Jul 54	6151 Consold Acft	
51 Sup Sq	1 Oct 51–21 Oct 52	Maint Sq	1 Oct 81–
80 Ftr-Bmbr Sq	24 Aug 51–21 Oct 54	6170 Cmbt Spt Sq	1 Oct 81–

Taegu Air Base

Location: Located 60 mi NNW of Pusan, 2 mi NNE of Taegu, Republic of Korea.

Name: Named after Taegu, third largest city in the Republic of Korea.

Date of Current Name: 8 Jul 1965.

Previous Names: Unk, 1937–11 Jul 1950; Taegu Aux Afld, 12 Jul 1950; Taegu AB (K–2), 5 Sep 1950; Taegu Aux Afld, East, 18 Sep 1956.

Date of Establishment: 1 Jul 1950.

Date Construction Began: Initial airfield construction by the Japanese Army Air Forces, 1937; USAF construction began 18 Jul 1950.

Date of Beneficial Occupancy: 10 Jul 1950.

Base Operating Units: 6149th AB Unit, 6 Aug 1950; 6149th AB Gp, 5 Sep 1950; 49th AB Gp, 1 Dec 1950; 58th AB Gp, 1 Apr 1953; 6152d AB Sq, 1 Mar 1955–19 Apr 1956.* 6168th Spt Sq (rdsgd 6168th AB Sq, 15 Jan 1968), 8 Jul 1965; 150th Cmbt Spt Sq, 1 Aug 1968; 6168th Cmbt Spt Sq, 1 May 1969; 6168th AB Sq (rdsgd 6168th Cmbt Spt Sq, 1 Jan 1978), 1 Jun 1974–.

Base Commanders: Unk, 1 Jul–5 Aug 1950; Maj Vincent J. Graves, 5 Sep 1950; Col Aaron W. Tyer, 1 Dec 1950; Col Kenneth W. Northemer, 20 Apr 1951; Col Aaron W. Tyer, 27 May 1951; Col Joe L. Mason, 1 Sep 1951; Col David T. McKnight, 1 Feb 1952; Col Robert J. Rogers, c. 19 Aug 1952; Col Joseph Davis Jr, 16 Mar 1953; Col Arthur C. Agan Jr, 8 Aug 1953; Col Earl E. Bates, c. Jul 1954; Maj David O. Camp, 1 Mar 1955–19 Apr 1956. Maj Frederick J. Gavin, 8 Jul 1965; Lt Col Charles E. Massey, 20 Sep 1965; Lt Col Thomas J. Skiffington, 30 Mar 1967; Maj Earl L. Babcock, 21 Nov 1967; Col Charles M. Lamb, c. Dec 1967; Lt Col James E. Maraist, 3 Jul 1968; Lt Col John E. Young, 1 Aug 1968; Lt Col Arthur P. Webb, 6 Nov 1968; Lt Col Vincent H. Anderson, 19 Nov 1968; Lt Col Robert H. Rieck, 1 Mar 1969; Col Jesse C. McIntire, 1 Sep 1969; Col William S. Neighbors, 7 Jul 1971; Lt Col Paul J. Gilmore, 25 Jul 1972; Col

---

*Between 19 Apr 1956 and 8 Jul 1965 the Republic of Korea Air Force operated Taegu Air Base, and the USAF had only a few detachments stationed at the site.

Karl S. Park, 29 May 1973; Col Billie B. Mills, 16 Feb 1974; Lt Col John M. Hammar, 15 Apr 1975; Lt Col Paul Y. Thompson, 16 Jan 1976; Lt Col Thomas H. Turner, 7 May 1977; Lt Col Peter C. Christopolis, 4 May 1978; Col Edward B. White, 27 Nov 1978; Col Charles D. Brown, 7 Feb 1979; Col Robert M. Wilshire, 22 Jan 1980; Lt Col John M. Sanderman, Jan 1981; Lt Col John A. Reedy, Jr, Dec 1981–.

Major Off-Base and Detached Installations: None.

Major Changes in Operational Capability: After constructing a 3,800-ft clay and gravel runway and a few buildings in 1937, the Japanese Army Air Forces continued to operate Taegu airfield as a fighter base until 1945; liberated by U.S. troops in 1945, base was turned over to the new Republic of Korea Air Force (ROKAF) in 1948; the Communist invasion of South Korea in Jun 1950 prompted a rapid buildup of U.S. forces in the Far East; new construction, which began at Taegu with the arrival of the 822d Engr Avn Bn, included hardstands, hangars, water lines, electrical layouts, barracks, and maintenance facilities, and a 5,000-ft pierced-steel-plank (PSP) runway adjacent to the old Japanese airstrip, which became operational on 7 Aug 1950; F–86 units began to operate from Taegu Feb 1951; the PSP runway, pounded by 10,000 weekly landings and takeoffs, became inoperable on 20 May 1951, requiring major airfield construction work; HQ Fifth AF closed at Taegu and opened at Seoul on 14 Jun 1951; a 9,000-ft reinforced concrete runway completed on 28 Jun 1952; Taegu hosted both ROKAF and USAF fighter and fighter-bomber units, chiefly F–84 and F–86 units, until the close of the Korean conflict; USAF and ROKAF officials signed an agreement for the joint use of Taegu AB on 2 Jan 1956, the ROKAF assumed sole control of the base on 19 Apr 1956; a USAF advisory staff and a communications detachment remained until 8 Jul 1965 when the U.S. began a gradual buildup of forces in the Far East; RED HORSE reconstruction work intensified following the *USS Pueblo* crisis of 23 Jan 1968; units transferred to Taegu included the 558th Tac Ftr Sq and air rescue and aerial port detachments, 3 Feb–22 Jul 1968; throughout 1968–1969 Taegu hosted rotating tactical fighters of the 475th Tac Ftr Wg from Misawa AB, Japan; Taegu again strengthened with additional U.S. air units in 1978 and has since been an active USAF base (organized as an off-base installation of Osan AB), owned by the ROKAF.

Major Commands to Which Assigned: PACAF, 1 Jul 1950–.

Major Changes in Status: Activated, 1 Jul 1950 as an off-base installation of Osan AB; off-base installation of Kunsan AB, 5 Sep 1950; off-base installation of Osan AB, 10 Mar 1958; off-base installation of Kunsan AB, 1 Oct 1978; off-base installation of Osan AB, 1 Apr 1982–.

Units Assigned:

	1950	7 Ftr-Bmbr Sq	28 Sep 50–1 Apr 53
5 Comms Sq, Comd	27 Jul 50–14 Oct 50	8 Ftr-Bmbr Sq	1 Oct 50–1 Apr 53

8 Tac Recon Sq	2 Oct 50–26 Jan 51
9 Ftr-Bmbr Sq	1 Oct 50–17 Dec 52
12 Ftr-Bmbr Sq	28 Jul 50–8 Aug 50
18 Ftr-Bmbr Gp	28 Jul 50–8 Aug 50
27 Ftr-Esct Gp	5 Dec 50–15 Aug 51
27 Ftr-Esct Wg	1 Dec 50–12 Dec 50
27 MV Sq	1 Dec 50–9 Dec 50
30 Wea Sq	22 Dec 50–3 Jul 51
45 Tac Recon Sq	27 Dec 50–18 Aug 51
49 AB Gp	1 Dec 50–25 Jan 51
49 AP Sq	1 Dec 50–25 Jan 51
49 Comms Sq	1 Dec 50–1 Apr 53
49 Ftr-Bmbr Gp	1 Oct 50–1 Apr 53
49 Ftr-Bmbr Wg	1 Dec 50–25 Jan 51
49 Instls Sq	1 Dec 50–1 Apr 53
49 Maint & Sup Gp	1 Dec 50–25 Jan 51
49 Maint Sq	1 Dec 50–25 Jan 51
49 Med Gp	1 Dec 50–25 Jan 51
49 MV Sq	1 Dec 50–1 Apr 53
49 Sup Sq	1 Dec 50–1 Apr 53
51 Ftr Sq, Prov	10 Jul 50–5 Aug 50
67 Ftr-Bmbr Sq	28 Jul 50–2 Aug 50
162 Tac Recon Sq	8 Oct 50–26 Jan 51
363 Recon Tech Sq	5 Oct 50–1 Mar 51
502 Tac Con Gp	6 Dec 50–19 Jun 51
522 Ftr-Esct Sq	5 Dec 50–31 Jan 51
523 Ftr-Esct Sq	5 Dec 50–31 Jan 51
524 Ftr-Esct Sq	5 Dec 50–31 Jan 51
543 Tac Spt Gp	29 Sep 50–26 Jan 51
605 Tac Con Sq	28 Aug 50–14 Oct 50
	16 Dec 50–10 Jun 51
934 Sig Bn, Separate, Tac	50–14 Oct 50
	12 Dec 50–4 Jul 51
6132 AC & W Sq	9 Oct 50–2 Nov 51
6132 Tac Air Con Sq (6132 Tac Air Con Gp)	14 Jul 50–10 Oct 50
6143 Air Trpt Unit	26 Jul 50–1 Oct 50
6149 AB Gp	5 Sep 50–1 Dec 50
6149 AB Unit	6 Aug 50–11 Oct 50
6149 AP Sq	5 Sep 50–1 Dec 50
6149 Comms Sq	5 Sep 50–1 Dec 50
6149 Food Svc Sq	5 Sep 50–1 Dec 50
6149 Instls Sq	5 Sep 50–1 Dec 50
6149 Maint & Sup Gp	5 Sep 50–1 Dec 50
6149 Maint Sq	5 Sep 50–1 Dec 50
6149 MV Sq	5 Sep 50–1 Dec 50
6149 Stn Med Gp (6149 Med Gp)	5 Sep 50–1 Dec 50
6149 Sup Sq	5 Sep 50–1 Dec 50
6149 Tac Spt Wg	5 Sep 50–1 Dec 50
6153 AB Unit (6153 AB Sq)	5 Dec 50–1 Jul 51
6154 AB Gp	22 Dec 50–1 Jul 51
6154 Food Svc Sq	22 Dec 50–1 Jul 51
6154 Instls Sq	22 Dec 50–1 Jul 51

6154 MV Sq	22 Dec 50–1 Jul 51
6154 Sup Sq	22 Dec 50–1 Jul 51
6155 AP Sq (6154 AP Sq)	22 Dec 50–1 Oct 53
6164 Tac Con Sq	25 Dec 50–25 Feb 51
6165 RR Sq	25 Dec 50–25 Nov 51
6166 Air Wea Recon Flt	25 Dec 50–26 Jan 51
Co C, 811 Engr Avn Bn	11 Dec 50–15 Jan 51
Fifth AF (Fifth AF in Korea)	24 Jul 50–14 Oct 50
	22 Dec 50–1 Jul 51
Sig Const Co C, 934 Sig Bn, Separate, Tac	50–14 Oct 50
	12 Dec 50–4 Jul 51
Sig HQ Ops Co A, 934 Sig Bn, Separate, Tac	50–14 Oct 50
	12 Dec 50–4 Jul 51
Sig Outpost Ops Co B, 934 Sig Bn, Separate, Tac	50–14 Oct 50
	12 Dec 50–4 Jul 51
1951	
5 Comms Sq, Comd	c. Jan 51–25 Jan 51
7 Comms Sq, Comd (7 Comms Sq, Ops; 607 Comms Sq, Ops)	1 Apr 51–21 Feb 55
12 Tac Recon Sq	15 Mar 51–21 Aug 51
15 Tac Recon Sq	16 Mar 51–26 Aug 51
49 AB Gp	24 Feb 51–1 Apr 53
49 AP Sq	24 Feb 51–1 Apr 53
49 Ftr-Bmbr Wg	24 Feb 51–1 Apr 53
49 Maint & Sup Gp	24 Mar 51–1 Apr 53
49 Maint Sq	24 Mar 51–1 Apr 53
49 Med Gp	24 Feb 51–1 Apr 53
67 AB Gp	25 Jul 51–16 Aug 51
67 Food Svc Sq	28 Jul 51–16 Aug 51
67 Recon Tech Sq	1 Mar 51–22 Aug 51
67 Tac Recon Gp	14 Mar 51–22 Aug 51
67 Tac Recon Wg	21 Mar 51–20 Aug 51
334 Ftr-Intcpr Sq	23 Feb 51–15 Mar 51
336 Ftr-Intcpr Sq	15 Mar 51–23 Apr 51
608 AC & W Sq	2 Nov 51–1 Dec 52
822 Engr Avn Bn	24 Mar 51–17 Jul 54
6151 AB Sq	1 Nov 51–1 Apr 54
6152 AB Sq	1 Jul 51–17 Aug 51
6154 Med Sq	25 May 51–1 Jul 51
6166 Air Wea Recon Flt	15 Mar 51–19 Aug 51
6405 Korean Air Mat Unit	25 May 51–18 Feb 53

Co B, 822 Engr Avn Bn	24 Mar 51–17 Jul 54
Co C, 822 Engr Avn Bn	24 Mar 51–17 Jul 54
Korea Air Mat Unit, Prov	1 Jan 51–25 May 51

1952

2 Mat Recovery Sq	26 Apr 52–23 Mar 53
58 AB Gp	10 Jul 52–15 Mar 55
58 AP Sq	10 Jul 52–15 Mar 55
58 Comms Sq	10 Jul 52–15 Mar 55
58 Food Svc Sq	10 Jul 52–15 Mar 55
58 Ftr-Bmbr Gp	10 Jul 52–15 Mar 55
58 Ftr-Bmbr Wg	10 Jul 52–15 Mar 55
58 Instls Sq	10 Jul 52–15 Mar 55
58 Maint & Sup Gp	10 Jul 52–11 Mar 53
58 Maint Sq	10 Jul 52–11 Mar 53
58 MV Sq	10 Jul 52–15 Mar 55
58 Sup Sq	10 Jul 52–11 Mar 53
69 Ftr-Bmbr Sq	10 Jul 52–9 Mar 55
310 Ftr-Bmbr Sq	10 Jul 52–9 Mar 55
311 Ftr-Bmbr Sq	10 Jul 52–18 Mar 55
417 Engr Avn Brigade	14 May 52–30 May 54
930 Engr Avn Gp	25 Jun 52–10 Oct 52
6149 Hosp Gp	1 Apr 52–1 Aug 52

1953

10 Air Postal Sq	8 May 53–25 Feb 54
428 Ftr-Bmbr Sq	1 Apr 53–22 Nov 54
429 Ftr-Bmbr Sq	1 Apr 53–22 Nov 54
430 Ftr-Bmbr Sq	16 Apr 53–22 Nov 54
474 AB Gp	1 Apr 53–8 Nov 54
474 AP Sq	1 Apr 53–8 Nov 54
474 Comms Sq	1 Apr 53–8 Nov 54
474 Ftr-Bmbr Gp	1 Apr 53–22 Nov 54
474 Ftr-Bmbr Wg	1 Apr 53–8 Nov 54
474 Food Svc Sq	1 Apr 53–8 Nov 54
474 Instls Sq	1 Apr 53–8 Nov 54
474 Maint & Sup Gp	1 Apr 53–8 Nov 54
474 Maint Sq	1 Apr 53–8 Nov 54
474 MV Sq	1 Apr 53–8 Nov 54
474 Sup Sq	1 Apr 53–8 Nov 54
6151 AB Sq	1 Mar 53–1 Jan 54
6156 AB Sq	11 Mar 53–20 Oct 53
6156 Ops Sq	20 Oct 53–8 Nov 54
6157 AB Sq	11 Mar 53–20 Oct 53
6158 AB Sq	11 Mar 53–20 Oct 53

1954

58 Maint & Sup Gp	1 Nov 54–15 Mar 55
58 Maint Sq (58 Fld Maint Sq)	1 Nov 54–15 Mar 55
58 Sup Sq	1 Nov 54–15 Mar 55
6152 AB Sq	10 Jul 54–20 Jan 55
6156 Pilot Tng Sq [Trans-ROKAF] (6156 Fl Tng Sq [Trans-ROKAF])	15 Dec 54–14 Sep 55

1955

6039 Tac Hosp	15 Mar 55–22 Oct 55
6152 AB Sq	1 Mar 55–25 Apr 56

1965

6168 Spt Sq (6168 AB Sq)	8 Jul 65–1 Aug 68

1968

Comms Sq, Prov 2073	24 May 68–1 Oct 68

1969

6168 USAF Dispy	1 May 69–17 May 71

1974

6168 AB Sq (6168 Cmbt Spt Sq)	1 Jun 74–

1978

497 Tac Ftr Sq	1 Oct 78–
USAF Clinic, Taegu	1 Oct 78–1 Apr 80

1979

6497 Consold Acft Maint Sq	1 Apr 79–

Tempelhof Central Airport

Location: Located in the southern suburbs of greater Berlin, about 2 mi from the center of the city; bounded on the north by Columbiadamm, on the west by Mehringdamm, and on the south by the Tempelhof Freight Terminal; about 1/2 mi north of the Teltow Canal, American Sector of West Berlin, Federal Republic of Germany.

Name: Named after the historic Tempelhof parade ground where the airport is now situated, in the Berlin district of Tempelhof.

Date of Current Name: 28 Feb 1958.

Previous Names: Tempelhofer Field, 1721; *Flughafen* Berlin-Tempelhof, 1922; *Zentralflughafen* Tempelhof-Berlin, 1936; Tempelhof AB, 3 Jul 1945; U.S. Army AF Stn, Berlin-Tempelhof, 28 Sep 1945; Tempelhof Army Afld, 14 Nov 1945; Tempelhof Army AB, 19 Sep 1946; Tempelhof AB, 9 Nov 1946.

Date of Establishment: Acquired for use as a Royal Prussian parade and exercise ground by King Frederick William I, 1721; established as a German commercial airfield, 1922; established as a U.S. aerial port, 2 Jul 1945.

Date Construction Began: First airfield buildings constructed in 1922; construction of a modern European international air terminal undertaken in 1934; U.S. reconstruction and expansion work began on 3 Jul 1945.

Date of Beneficial Occupancy: 24 Mar 1945.

Base Operating Units: 473d Air Svc Gp, 2 Jul 1945; 7350th AB Gp (rdsgd 7350th Base Compl Sq, 23 Sep 1949; 7350th AB Sq, 15 Oct 1954; 7350th Spt Sq, 8 Mar 1958; 7350th Spt Gp, 1 Jan 1964; 7350th AB Gp, 1 Jan 1973), 1 Jul 1948–.

Base Commanders: Col William G. Booth, 2 Jul 1945; Col Henry W. Dorr, 15 Sep 1947; Col Carl R. Feldmann, 16 Aug 1948; Lt Col William H. Delacey, 12 Jan 1949; Col John E. Barr, 14 Apr 1949; Col John V. Hart, 24 Jul 1951; Col Roy L. Jones, 1 Mar 1953; Col Wesely H. Vernon, 17 Dec 1954; Col Rex W. Beach, 4 Aug 1956; Col Edward C. Tates, May 1959; Col Kenneth L. Glassburn, 30 Jul 1960; Lt Col Billy G. Greider, 27 Jun 1963 (temp); Col Paul H. Kenney, Aug 1963; Col Joseph D. White, 3 Aug 1965; Col Thomas A. Personett, 1 Jul 1966; Col Clark A. Tate, 12 Jul 1968; Col

Gail S. Halvorsen, 13 Feb 1970; Col Myron G. Smith, 11 Feb 1974; Col Donald W. Lajeunesse, 12 Jul 1976; Col Vernon L. Frye, 29 Jun 1979; Col Gary E. Spohn, 6 Jul 1981–.

Major Off-Base and Detached Installations:* Teufelsberg Comms Fclty (rdsgd Teufelsberg Comms Fclty Anx, 26 Jun 1969), Teufelsberg Chaussee, 3 Jan 1962 (asgnd)–11 Nov 1976 (dspd); Marienfelde Comms Anx (rdsgd Marienfelde Comms Stn, 26 Jun 1968), Marienfelder Allee, 12 Feb 1963–; Tegel Nav Aid Site, Tegel Aprt, 29 Mar 1973 (asgnd)–.

Major Changes in Operational Capability: A Royal Prussian parade ground under Frederick William I in 1721, Tempelhof remained a parade ground until 1918; from 1895–1918 field served also as a demonstration area for balloons, airships, and aircraft, including flights in 1908 by Orville Wright and his Wright Flyer; Germans used the field for commercial aviation in 1922; Ernst Sagebiel designed Tempelhof's futuristic base facilities and terminal 1934–1936; converted into a major European and international airport, the installation officially opened in 1936, with peak passenger traffic attained in 1938–1939; Germany did not use Tempelhof as a military airfield during World War II, except for occasional emergency landings by fighter aircraft; Americans assumed control of the airport and began restoration 2 Jul 1945; Tempelhof hosted passengers arriving and departing the Potsdam Conference, and served as Berlin center for the European Air Transport Service (EATS) Sep 1945 to Mar 1948; postwar airport also supported the mission of the Office of the High Commissioner of Germany (HICOG), and air-sea rescue operations center when USAFE assumed the direct responsibilities of EATS on 20 Dec 1947; Soviet troops closed off all surface routes into West Berlin on 20 Jun 1948, compelling the Western Allies to establish the greatest military airlift in history, flying millions of tons of fuel, clothing, and food into Tempelhof for the beleaguered West Berliners; engineers constructed a new 6,000-ft runway between Jul and Sep 1948 and another between Sep and Oct 1948 to accommodate the expanding requirements of the airlift; the last airlift transport touched down at Tempelhof on 30 Sep 1949; civil aviation agreement allowed the major airlines to use the airport 22 May 1950; U.S. authorities turned over the northeast corner of the airport to the City of Berlin for recreational purposes 1950; Tempelhof remained the main USAFE terminal for West Berlin from 20 Dec 1947 to 1 Sep 1975, when all civil air traffic was transferred to Tegel Airport in the French Sector of West Berlin; since that time Tempelhof's operations have been confined to U.S. military airlift traffic.

---

*All installations are located in West Berlin.

Major Commands to Which Assigned: USAFE, 2 Jul 1945–.

Major Changes in Status: Active, 2 Jul 1945–; detached installation of Wiesbaden AB (HQ USAFE), 2 Jul 1945; primary installation, 9 Sep 1946; detached installation of Ramstein AB, 15 Nov 1959; primary installation, 1 Jul 1960–.

Units Assigned:

	1945	
301 Trp Carr Sq	4 Jul 45–15 Feb 46	
473 Air Svc Gp	5 Jul 45–31 Dec 46	
715 Air Mat Sq	5 Jul 45–31 Dec 46	
891 Air Engrg Sq	5 Jul 45–31 Jan 46	
1119 MP Co (Avn)	24 Mar 45–1 Jul 48	
	1946	
47 Trp Carr Sq	30 Sep 46–5 May 47	
808 Air Engrg Sq	16 Dec 46–25 Dec 47	
2025 Labor Supervision Co (Avn)	15 Aug 46–8 Apr 48	
4713 Labor Supervision Co	15 Aug 46–8 Apr 48	
	1947	
12 Trp Carr Sq	5 May 47–20 Jan 48	
100 Stn Compl Sq	20 Dec 47–1 Jul 48	
632 Air Mat Sq	7 Apr 47–25 Dec 47	
788 AAF BU [158 AACS Sq] (788 AF BU [158 AACS Sq])	10 Sep 47–3 Jun 48	
7908 AF BU	20 Dec 47–1 Jul 48	
HQ & Base Svcs Sq, 371 Air Svc Gp	7 Apr 47–25 Dec 47	
Tempelhof BU [Prov]	20 Jan 47–20 Dec 47	
	1948	
53 Trp Carr Sq	20 Jan 48–22 Apr 48	
158 AACS Sq (1946 AACS Sq)	1 Jun 48–1 Nov 53	
7350 AB Gp (7350 Base Compl Sq; 7350 AB Sq; 7350 Spt Sq; 7350 Spt Sq [USAFE Representative Berlin]; 7350 Spt Gp [USAFE Representative Berlin]; 7350 AB Gp)	1 Jul 48–	
7351 Maint & Sup Sq	10 Sep 48–23 Sep 49	
7352 AP Sq	5 Sep 48–23 Sep 49	
7353 Instls Sq	5 Sep 48–23 Sep 49	
	1950	
8925 VAR Tng Sq (USAFR)	1 Mar 50–25 Apr 54	
	1954	
1946 AACS Sq (1946 Comms Sq)	1 Nov 54–	
	1959	
6912 Radio Sq, Mobile (6912 Scty Sq; 6912 Electronic Scty Gp)	1 Jul 59–	
	1965	
7350 AP Sq (7350 Scty Pol Sq)	4 May 65–1 Jan 72	

181

Thule Air Base

Location: Located 690 mi N of the Arctic Circle on North Star Bay, 39 mi N of the village of Thule, Greenland.

Name: Named after the Eskimo village of Thule.

Date of Current Name: 15 Jan 1952.

Previous Names: Thule Greenland, 12 Jan 1951; Thule AS, Greenland, 1 Mar 1951.

Date of Establishment: 1 Mar 1951.

Date Construction Began: 12 Jan 1951.

Date of Beneficial Occupancy: 20 Jul 1951.

Base Operating Units: 6622d AB Sq, 20 Jul 1951; 6612th AB Gp, 1 Jan 1952; 6607th AB Wg, 1 Jun 1954; 4083d AB Gp (rdsgd 4083d AB Wg, 1 Jul 1959), 1 Apr 1957; 4683d AD Wg, 1 Jul 1960; 4683d AB Gp, 1 Oct 1960; 12th Msl Warning Gp, 31 Mar 1977–.

Base Commanders: Maj William Garrett, 10 Mar 1951; Capt James W. Altum, Apr 1951; Lt Col Bert R. J. Hassell, May 1951; Col James I. Cornett, 11 Nov 1951; Col Herbert M. West Jr, 15 May 1952; Col Robert W. Humphreys, 19 Aug 1952; Col James W. Holt, 23 May 1953; Col Richard T. Hernlund, 30 May 1953; Col William L. Kimball, 17 May 1954; Col Louis W. Rohr, 11 Mar 1955; Col Frank W. Ellis, 12 Mar 1956; Col William B. Haynes, c. Feb 1957; Col Olbert F. Lassiter, 2 Mar 1957; Lt Col George J. Uhrinak, 1 Apr 1957; Col Malvin R. Schultz, 22 Jul 1957; Col Bryson R. Bailey, 15 Feb 1958; Col William B. Haynes, 19 Jul 1958; Col Bryson R. Bailey, 15 Feb 1958; Col John T. Compton, 17 Feb 1959; Col Chester L. Sluder, 23 Jan 1960; Col Harry B. Allen, 29 Oct 1960; Col Frank A. Hill, 17 Aug 1961; Col David B. Tudor, 20 Jul 1962; Col Frank J. Keller, 19 Jul 1963; Col Richard D. Mendrop, 17 Jul 1964; Col James W. Lancaster, 24 Jul 1964; Col Robert L. Harriger, 16 Jul 1965; Col Gene C. Willms, 7 Dec 1965; Col John Luts, 19 Jul 1966; Col Paul D. Copher, 7 Jul 1967 (temp); Col Cornelius S. Dresser, 28 Jul 1967; Col Nat D. King, 8 Mar 1969; Lt Col Robert B. Hutchinson, 18 Mar 1970 (temp); Col Ralph W. White, 6 Apr 1970 (temp); Col Richard H. Hintermeier, 3 May 1970; Col Robert T. Goetz, 5 Jun 1971; Col Michael Navarro, 16 Dec 1971; Col John W. Yocum, 13 Dec 1972; Col Harry B. Casterlin Jr, 5 Nov 1973; Col James J. Kleckner, 27 Aug 1974; Col Douglas D. Brenner, 21 Aug 1975; Lt

Col Church Watkins Jr, 18 Apr 1976; Col Martin W. Kasischke, 17 Aug 1976; Col Thomas C. Thompson, 9 Aug 1977; Col Clark T. Price, 5 Aug 1978; Col James F. Patton, 20 Jun 1979; Col Joel S. Gill, 20 Jun 1980; Col George S. Cudd, 15 Jan 1981; Col Eugene E. Ross, 15 Sep 1981; Col Gary L. Hicks, 14 Jul 1982–.

Major Off-Base and Detached Installations:* Fletcher's Ice Isl [also known as "Drift Stn Bruno T–3"], 1 Mar 1953 (actvd)–14 May 1954 (evacuated), 1 Jul 1959 (dspd); Radar Site I (N–33), 100 mi N of Thule AB, 24 Oct 1953–20 Nov 1956; Radar Site II (N–34), 200 mi E of Thule AB, 24 Oct 1953–20 Nov 1956; Site N–32 (Pingarssuit Mountain), 20 mi S of Thule AB, unk; Site L–32 (North Mountain), unk; Site Alert (joint U.S.-Canadian wea site), unk; Site Eureka (joint U.S.-Canadian wea site), unk; Site Resolute (joint U.S.-Canadian wea site), unk; Site "B" (emerg airstrip), 12 mi E of Thule AB, unk; Fox Site 30 (emerg airstrip), unk; Site "J," 7 mi S of Thule AB, 1 Oct 1960–.

Major Changes in Operational Capability: Under the code name ROBIN (later, BLUE JAY), the Army Corps of Engineers began constructing a 10,000-ft runway and base support facilities at Thule for the USAF in Jan 1951; served SAC B–36 operations 1952–1953; Thule supported staging and recovery of SAC bombers and tankers participating in major exercises from 1953–1957; also supported ADC fighter-interceptor squadrons and Army air defense batteries 1953–1965; hosted SAC rotational units 1955–1959; supported the North American Air Defense Command early warning radar net for the U.S. and Canada from 1952 to the present; after inactivation of the 322d Ftr-Intcpr Sq on 1 Jul 1965, followed soon thereafter by discontinuation of the Army Nike surface-to-air missile system, Thule provided control for air rescue operations in the northern Greenland area and support for all U.S. and Allied units operating out of Thule AB; the Ballistic Missile Early Warning System (BMEWS) became the principal element supported at Thule AB after 1965.

Major Commands to Which Assigned: Northeast Air Comd, 1 Jul 1951; SAC, 1 Apr 1957; ADC (rdsgd Aerosp Def Comd, 15 Jan 1968), 1 Jul 1960; SAC, 1 Dec 1979–.

Major Changes in Status: None.

Units Assigned:

	1951	(1983 Comms Sq)	1 Jul 52–30 Jun 76
6622 AB Sq	20 Jul 51–1 Jan 52	6612 AB Gp	1 Jan 52–1 Jun 54
	1952	6612 AB Sq	1 Jan 52–1 Jun 54
55 Air Rscu Sq	14 Nov 52–15 Mar 60	6612 Instls Sq	18 Oct 52–1 Jun 54
931 AC & W Sq	8 Nov 52–24 Dec 65	6612 Maint & Sup Sq	1 Jan 52–unk 53
1983 AACS Sq		6612 Med Sq	

---

*All installations are located in Greenland.

(6612 USAF Hosp)	18 Oct 52–1 Jun 54
6612 USAF Hosp	18 Oct 52–1 Jun 54
1953	
318 Ftr-Intcpr Sq	1 Jul 53–5 Aug 54
428 AAA Battery	Jun 53–unk
429 AAA Battery	Jun 53–unk
549 AAA Bn	Jun 53–unk
6612 Maint Sq	53–1 Jun 54
6612 Sup Sq	53–1 Jun 54
1954	
74 Ftr-Intcpr Sq	20 Aug 54–25 Jun 58
568 AF Band Sq	1 Jun 54–c. 56
6607 AB Gp	1 Jun 54–1 Apr 57
6607 AB Sq	1 Jun 54–1 Sep 55
6607 AB Wg	1 Jun 54–1 Apr 57
6607 Acft Maint Sq	1 Jun 54–1 Apr 57
6607 Fld Maint Sq	1 Jun 54–1 Apr 57
6607 Food Svc Sq	1 Jun 54–1 Apr 57
6607 Instls Sq	1 Jun 54–1 Apr 57
6607 Maint & Sup Gp	1 Jun 54–1 Apr 57
6607 MV Sq	
(6607 Trnsp Sq)	1 Jun 54–1 Apr 57
6607 Ops Sq	1 Jun 54–1 Sep 55
6607 Sup Sq	1 Jun 54–1 Apr 57
6607 USAF Hosp	1 Jun 54–1 Apr 57
Thule Task Force,	
Prov	1 Sep 54–unk
1955	
26 Air Rflg Sq	9 Sep 55–2 Nov 55
42 Air Rflg Sq	2 Nov 55–28 Dec 55
71 Air Rflg Sq	29 Dec 55–27 Mar 56
96 Air Rflg Sq	31 Jul 55–14 Sep 55
320 Air Rflg Sq	4 May 55–10 Jun 57
509 Air Rflg Sq	c. 17 Jun 55–c. 3 Aug 55
6607 AP Sq	1 Sep 55–1 Apr 57
1956	
26 Air Rflg Sq	5 Sep 56–15 Dec 56
40 Air Rflg Sq	27 Jun 56–4 Sep 56
340 Air Rflg Sq	29 Oct 56–30 Dec 56
341 Air Rflg Sq	27 Mar 56–26 Jun 56
HQ Battery,	
7 AAA Gp	56–unk
1957	
42 Air Rflg Sq	1 Jan 57–7 Mar 57
4083 AB Gp	
(4083 AB Wg)	1 Apr 57–1 Jul 60
4083 AP Sq	1 Apr 57–1 Jul 60

4083 Consold Acft	
Maint Sq	1 Apr 57–1 Jul 60
4083 Food Svc Sq	1 Apr 57–1 Jul 60
4083 Instls Sq	1 Apr 59–1 Jul 60
4083 Ops Sq	1 Apr 57–1 Jul 60
4083 Strat Wg	1 Apr 57–1 Jul 59
4083 Sup Sq	1 Apr 57–1 Jul 60
4083 Trnsp Sq	1 Apr 57–1 Jul 60
4083 USAF Hosp	1 Apr 57–1 Jul 60
Task Force T–3,	
Prov	11 Feb 57–unk
1958	
11 Avn Dep Sq	15 Jan 58–1 Dec 58
40 Air Rflg Sq	c. 1 Oct 58–9 Jan 59
327 Ftr-Intcpr Sq	3 Jul 58–25 Mar 60
1959	
1628 Spt Sq	1 Jan 59–3 Jan 66
1960	
332 Ftr-Intcpr Sq	1 Sep 60–1 Jul 65
4683 AB Gp	
(4683 Cmbt Spt	
Gp; 4683 AB Gp)	1 Oct 60–31 Mar 77
4683 AB Sq	1 Oct 60–1 Jul 64
4683 AD Wg	1 Jul 60–1 Jul 65
4683 AP Sq	1 Jul 60–1 Oct 60
4683 CE Sq	1 Jul 60–1 Jul 65
4683 Consold Acft	
Maint Sq	1 Jul 60–1 Jul 65
4683 Food Svc Sq	1 Jul 60–1 Oct 60
4683 Ops Sq	1 Jul 60–1 Oct 60
4683 Sup Sq	1 Jul 60–1 Jul 65
4683 Trnsp Sq	1 Jul 60–1 Jul 65
4683 USAF Hosp	1 Jul 60–1 Sep 66
1962	
4683 AP Sq	19 Feb 62–1 Jul 65
1966	
4683 USAF Dispy	
[Class A]	1 Sep 66–8 Oct 70
1967	
12 Msl Warning Sq	
(12 Msl Warning	
Gp)	1 Jan 67–
1977	
1983 Comms Sq	1 Jan 77–
4711 AB Sq	
(4685 AB Sq)	31 Mar 77–31 Mar 81

185

Torrejon Air Base

Location: Located 15 mi NE of Madrid, 5 mi W of Alcala de Henares, and 1 mi NE of Torrejon de Ardoz, Spain.

Name: Named after a town in Spain.

Date of Current Name: 15 Dec 1955.

Previous Names: Aeropuerto de Torrejon, unk.

Date of Establishment: 1 Jun 1957.

Date Construction Began: 27 Sep 1953.

Date of Beneficial Occupancy: 1 Jul 1956.

Base Operating Units: 7600th AB Gp, 1 Jul 1956; 3970th AB Gp (rdsgd 3970th Cmbt Spt Gp, 1 Jun 1959; 3970th Strat Wg, 1 Feb 1964), 1 Jul 1957; 401st Cmbt Spt Gp, 15 Apr 1966–.

Base Commanders: Col Joseph N. Donovan, 1 Jul 1956; Col James M. Smith, 17 May 1958; Col Edmund A. Rafalko, 20 Jul 1959 (temp); Col James M. Smith, 17 Aug 1959; Col Robert T. Calhoun, 19 Jun 1961; Col Raymond E. Buckwalter, 7 Feb 1962; Col George D. Hughes, 11 Jul 1964; Col Harry C. Bayne, 15 Apr 1965; Col Raymond E. Hamlyn Jr, 1 Jun 1966; Col Edward F. Rodriguez, 5 Jul 1967; Col Herman C. Ahrens Jr, 6 Nov 1970; Col Samuel T. Dickens, 15 Nov 1971; Col Kenneth A. Shealy, c. Nov 1972; Col Robert F. C. Winger, 15 Feb 1973; Col William A. Evans Jr, 11 Jul 1973; Col LeRoy J. Salem, 30 Jun 1974; Col Joseph T. Guastella, 27 May 1976; Col Victor B. Rodriguez, 10 Jul 1979; Lt Col Gil Coronado Jr, 14 Jun 1981 (temp); Col James J. Sidletsky, 1 Aug 1981–.

Major Off-Base and Detached Installations:* Getafe Air Aux Afld (rdsgd Getafe Afld; Torrejon Air Aux Afld), Getafe, 1 Nov 1953 (actvd)–5 Nov 1957 (dspd); Madrid Stor Stn (rdsgd Torrejon Stor Anx; Royal Oaks Stor Anx), 7 mi NE of Madrid, 1 Mar 1954 (actvd)–30 Jun 1958 (inactvd), 21 Sep 1959 (dspd); Madrid Cmsy Anx (rdsgd Torrejon Admn Anx #1; Madrid Admn Anx #2; Madrid Community Spt Anx; Madrid City Complex Anx #4081), Madrid, 15 Apr 1954 (actvd)–30 Jun 1958 (inactvd), 13 Jun 1966 (dspd); Madrid Med Anx (rdsgd Madrid Hosp), Madrid, 1 Jun 1954

---

*All installations are located in Spain.

(actvd)–1 May 1958 (inactvd); Torrejon Comms Anx #1, unk, 30 Oct 1954 (actvd)–unk; Madrid Sch Playground Anx (rdsgd Madrid Recrn Anx #2; Torrejon Recrn Anx #2), Madrid, 1 Feb 1955 (actvd)–31 Dec 1962 (dspd); Torrejon Civilian Pers Anx (rdsgd Madrid Admn Anx #4; Madrid City Complex Anx #4081), Madrid, 1 May 1955 (actvd)–30 Apr 1958 (inactvd); Torrejon Petrol Prods Stor Anx (rdsgd Barajas Fuel Stor Anx; Barajas Petrol Prods Stor Anx), Barajas, 15 Nov 1955 (actvd)–1 Sep 1976 (dspd); Madrid Motor Pool Anx (rdsgd Torrejon Motor Pool Anx), Madrid, 1 Mar 1956 (actvd)–30 Jun 1965 (dspd); Madrid Admn Anx #3 (rdsgd Madrid City Complex #4081; Torrejon Admn Anx #2), Madrid, 15 Jun 1956 (actvd)–10 Mar 1960 (inactvd); Torrejon Wea Stn Anx (rdsgd Sonseca Wea Stn Site), Sonseca, 7 Dec 1956 (actvd)–; Loeches Petrol Prods Stor Anx, Loeches, 20 Feb 1957 (actvd)–28 Apr 1980 (dspd); Madrid Pers Processing Stn (rdsgd Madrid Hsg Anx; Madrid City Complex #4081; Torrejon Hsg Anx), Madrid, 15 Mar 1957 (actvd)–30 Jun 1963 (dspd); Inoges Hsg Anx, El Frasno, 25 Mar 1957 (actvd)–1 Jan 1980 (trsfd to Zaragoza AB); Jarama Water Sup Anx, 10 mi E of Madrid, 1 Jun 1957 (actvd)–26 Jul 1966 (inactvd); Villatobas AS (rdsgd Villatobas AC & W Stn), Villatobas, 7 Aug 1957 (actvd)–19 Jan 1959 (dspd); Torrejon Admn Anx #1 (rdsgd Madrid Thtr Anx; Madrid City Complex Anx; Madrid Recrn Anx [Thtr]), Madrid, 10 Sep 1957 (actvd)–13 Jun 1966 (dspd); Torrejon Fam Hsg Anx (rdsgd Madrid Fam Hsg Anx #1; Torrejon Fam Hsg Anx #1), Madrid, 16 Sep 1957 (actvd)–30 Jun 1960 (inactvd); Alcala Comms Anx (rdsgd Torrejon Comms Anx #2), Alcala de Henares, 18 Oct 1957 (actvd)–31 Dec 1963 (inactvd), 1 Jun 1964 (dspd); Torrejon TVOR RB Anx (rdsgd Torrejon ILS Outer Marker Anx), 6 mi S of Alcala de Henares, 28 Oct 1957 (actvd)–24 Oct 1979 (dspd); Torrejon Fam Hsg Anx #2 (rdsgd Royal Oaks Fam Hsg Anx), 7 mi NE of Madrid, 11 Jul 1958 (actvd)–; Torrejon Comms Anx #3, Fuencarrel, 15 Sep 1958 (actvd)–16 Jul 1963 (inactvd), 31 Dec 1964 (dspd); Torrejon Sch #1 (rdsgd Royal Oaks Sch), 7 mi NE of Madrid, 2 Oct 1958 (actvd)–; Torrejon Amn Hsg Anx #1 (rdsgd Alcoy Hsg Anx), Alicante, 29 Oct 1958 (actvd)–1 Dec 1964 (inactvd), 31 Dec 1964 (dspd); Torrejon Svc Anx #1 (rdsgd Alcoy Svc Anx), San Juan, 10 Nov 1958 (actvd)–15 Mar 1959 (inactvd), 31 Jul 1961 (dspd); Torrejon Recrn Anx #3, Madrid, 20 Jan 1959 (actvd)–31 Dec 1963 (inactvd); Torrejon Approach Anx (rdsgd Paracuellos Approach Contr Anx), 8 mi SE of Alcala de Henares, 6 Mar 1959 (actvd)–1 Sep 1976 (dspd); Torrejon AS #2 (rdsgd Alcoy AS), Alcoy, 11 Sep 1959 (actvd)–1 Dec 1964 (inactvd); Torrejon Sch #2 (rdsgd Soller Sch), Palma de Mallorca, 15 Dec 1959 (actvd)–15 Dec 1964 (inactvd & dspd); Torrejon Svc Anx #2 (rdsgd Soller Svc Anx), Palma de Mallorca, 1 Feb 1960 (actvd)–31 Dec 1964 (inactvd & dspd); Soller Hsg Anx, Soller, Mallorca, 7 Apr 1960 (actvd)–1 Jan 1980 (dspd); Soller RRS, 24 mi NE of Palma de Mallorca, 7 Apr 1960 (actvd)–1 Jan 1980 (dspd); Torrejon RRS (rdsgd Humosa RRS), Los Santos de la Humosa, 10 Jun 1960 (actvd)–1 Jan 1980 (dspd); Menorca RRS, Ferrerias, 1 Oct 1964 (actvd)–1 Jan 1980 (trsfd to Zaragoza AB); Torrejon Tacan Anx, Torrejon de Ardoz, 26 Jul 1966 (actvd)–1 Mar 1976 (inactvd), 1 Sep 1976 (dspd); Santiago Tacan Site, 7 mi E of Santiago de Compostella, 7 Oct 1966 (actvd)–30 Nov 1968 (inactvd), 1 Sep 1976 (dspd); Alicante Admn Ofc, Alicante, 1 Jul 1971 (actvd)–; Cadiz Port Anx, Cadiz, 1 Jul 1973 (trsfd from Moron AB)–; Madrid Fam Hsg Site, Madrid, 11 Oct 1977 (actvd)–; Estaca de Vares RRS, Vivero, 6 Jan 1978 (actvd)–; El Arahal Petrol Prods Stor Anx, El Arahal, unk–28 Apr 1980 (dspd); La Muela Petrol Prods Stor Anx, Epila, unk–28 Apr 1980 (dspd); San Fernando Stor Anx, San Fernando de Henares, 1 Mar 1981 (actvd)–; Torrejon Stor Anx, Torrejon de Ardoz, 1 Apr 1982 (actvd)–.

Major Changes in Operational Capability: Base originally home of Spanish National Institute of Aeronautics; following the U.S.-Spanish Defense Agreement of 26 Sep 1953, construction began at Torrejon on a new 13,400-ft concrete runway to replace the existing 4,266-ft grass airstrip and on a massive concrete apron and other necessary maintenance and shelter facilities to accommodate the largest U.S. bombers, supervised by the Joint U.S. Military Group, Air Administration (Spain), and, after 15 Jul 1956, performed largely by the Spanish for the U.S. Navy Bureau of Docks and Yards; though construction was not completed until Jul 1957, base support activities began under the 7600th AB Gp in Madrid in Jul 1956; the Sixteenth AF assumed command of Torrejon on 15 Dec 1956; base activated on 1 Jun 1957; SAC assumed control of Torrejon, replacing the 7600th AB Gp with the 3970th on 1 Jul 1957; HQ Sixteenth AF moved to Torrejon on 1 Feb 1958; base hosted SAC reflex operations from 1 Jul 1958 to 1965; B–47 reflex ceased at Torrejon on 31 Mar 1965; USAFE assumed control on 15 Apr 1966; KC–135s ceased to be stationed at Torrejon when the 98th Strat Wg inactivated on 31 Dec 1976; base has supported fighter aircraft and exercises and functioned as a major terminal for the Military Airlift Command's transatlantic flights since 1956.

Major Commands to Which Assigned: Sixteenth AF, 1 Jul 1956; SAC, 1 Jul 1957; USAFE, 15 Apr 1966–.

Major Changes in Status: Under construction, 27 Sep 1953; activated on 1 Jun 1957.

Units Assigned:

	1957		
21 Wea Sq	15 Sep 57–1 Jul 71	3970 AB Gp	
49 Comms Sq, AF	1 Jul 57–15 Apr 66	(3970 Cmbt Spt Gp;	
65 Air Div	1 Oct 57–1 Jan 65	3970 Strat Wg)	1 Jul 57–25 Jun 66
871 AC & W Sq	8 Jan 57–1 Jan 65	3970 AP Sq	1 Jul 57–1 Jun 59
1989 AACS Sq		3970 Consold Acft	
(1989 Comms Sq;		Maint Sq	1 Jul 57–15 Apr 66
1989 Comms Gp)	4 Oct 57–	3970 Food Svc Sq	1 Jul 57–1 Jun 59
		3970 Instls Sq	

(3970 CE Sq)	1 Jul 57–15 Apr 66
3970 Ops Sq	1 Jul 57–15 Apr 66
3970 Sup Sq	1 Jul 57–15 Apr 66
3970 Trnsp Sq	1 Jul 57–15 Apr 66
3970 USAF Hosp	1 Jul 57–9 Apr 64
3971 Recon Tech Sq	1 Jul 57–1 Dec 59
1958	
1 Avn Dep Sq	
(1 Mun Maint Sq)	1 May 58–30 Apr 65
13 Air Postal Sq	15 Apr 58–8 Jan 63
497 Ftr-Intcpr Sq	21 Jun 58–18 Jun 64
Sixteenth AF	1 Feb 58–
1959	
3970 Spt Sq	
(3970 Svcs Sq)	1 Jun 59–15 Apr 66
1960	
Spanish Comms	
Region	1 Mar 60–7 Jan 71
Torrejon Task	
Force, Prov	3 Jun 60–unk
1961	
3970 Cmbt Def Sq	1 May 61–15 Apr 66
1964	
869 Med Gp	9 Apr 64–15 Apr 66
1966	
98 Strat Wg	25 Jun 66–31 Dec 76
307 Tac Ftr Sq	27 Apr 66–15 Jul 71
353 Tac Ftr Sq	27 Apr 66–15 Jul 71
401 AP Sq	
(401 Scty Pol Sq)	15 Apr 66–
401 Armnt & Elect	
Maint Sq	
(401 Avncs	
Maint Sq;	
401 Component	
Rpr Sq)	27 Apr 66–
401 CE Sq	15 Apr 66–
401 Cmbt Spt Gp	15 Apr 66–
401 Fld Maint Sq	
(401 Equip	

Maint Sq)	27 Apr 66–
401 Mun Maint Sq	27 Apr 66–30 Jun 79
401 Orgnzl Maint Sq	27 Apr 66–1 May 66
401 Sup Sq	15 Apr 66–
401 Tac Ftr Wg	27 Apr 66–
401 Trnsp Sq	15 Apr 66–
401 USAF Hosp	
(401 Tac Hosp)	15 Apr 66–
613 Tac Ftr Sq	27 Apr 66–
625 Mil Alft Spt Sq	8 Jan 66–
1968	
7416 Spt Sq	1 Oct 68–1 Oct 70
1971	
612 Tac Ftr Sq	15 Jul 71–
614 Tac Ftr Sq	15 Jul 71–
Joint Air Con &	
Coordination	
Cen, Spain—	
U.S. Sec	15 Oct 71–
Mediterranean	
Comms Region	8 Jan 71–30 Jun 72
USAF Hosp,	
Torrejon	1 Jul 71–
1972	
401 Orgnzl	
Maint Sq	
(401 Acft	
Gnrtn Sq)	1 Feb 72–
7009 Explosive	
Ord Dspl Flt	1 Jan 72–
1977	
7401 Comptroller	
Svcs Sq	1 Apr 77–31 Dec 77
1981	
7401 Comptroller	
Sq	1 Apr 81–
1982	
Numbered AF	
Cmbt Ops Staff	
[Sixteenth AF]	15 Jan 82–

Yokota Air Base

Location: Located 35 mi N of Tokyo, 1 mi SSW of Fussamachi, 9 mi SW of Tachikawa, and 1 1/2 mi W of Yokota, Tokyo-To Prefecture, Japan.

Name: Named after a city in Japan.

Date of Current Name: 17 Nov 1955.

Previous Names: Seimei Reform Sch, pre-1940; Tama Army Afld [Japanese], Mar 1940; Fussa AAFld, Sep 1945; Yokota AAFld, 23 Sep 1945; Yokota AAB, 15 Aug 1946; Yokota AFB, 26 Sep 1947.

Date of Establishment: 6 Sep 1945.

Date Construction Began: Original construction by Japanese Army prior to 1940; U.S. construction work began Dec 1945.

Date of Beneficial Occupancy: 6 Sep 1945.

Base Operating Units: HQ & Base Svcs Sq, 384th Svc Gp, 23 Sep 1945; 7th Air Svc Gp, 16 Apr 1946; 29th Air Svc Gp, 15 Apr 1947; 3d AB Gp, 18 Aug 1948; 35th AB Gp, 1 Apr 1950; 3d AB Gp, 14 Aug 1950; 6161st AB Wg, 1 Dec 1950; 35th AB Gp, 1 Oct 1954; 6102d AB Wg, 1 Jul 1957; 441st Cmbt Spt Gp, 1 Jan 1964; 347th Cmbt Spt Gp, 15 Jan 1968; 6100th AB Wg, 15 May 1971; 475th AB Wg, 1 Nov 1971–.

Base Commanders:* Maj J. Benjamin Hayes, USA, 7 Sep 1945; Col William J. Bell, U.S. AAF, 16 Sep 1945; Maj Raymond J. Morse, USA, Dec 1945; Col Edwin B. Bobzien, 22 Apr 1946; Lt Col Warner B. Gates, 2 Nov 1946; Lt Col John P. Crocker, c. 3 Feb 1947 (temp); Col Edward H. Underhill, 28 Mar 1947; Col James R. Gunn Jr, 2 Jun 1947; Lt Col Louis C. Adams Jr, 18 Aug 1948; Maj Ralph V. Hench, 1 Apr 1950 (temp); Lt Col Allen P. Forsyth, Jul 1950; Maj Ralph V. Hench, 14 Aug 1950; Col Donald L. Clark, 1 Dec 1950; Col Lloyd H. Tull, 5 Sep 1951; Col James J. O'Shea, 1 Aug 1952 (temp); Col Fred D. Stevers, 14 Aug 1952; Col Robert S. Gunderson, 6 Oct 1954; Lt Col William M. Wilkerson Jr, 19 Dec 1954; Col Roland S. Boughton Jr, 9 Jan 1956; Col Eugene B. Fletcher, c. 1 Jun

---

*Various officers administered the base after World War II, but, until 22 Apr 1946 when Col Edwin B. Bobzien assumed the title, none were called base commander.

1957; Col James E. Johnston, 15 Jun 1957; Col Ray Vandiver, 25 Apr 1959; Col Jack R. Banks, 23 Feb 1960 (temp); Col Dalene E. Bailey, 26 Feb 1960; Col Eric T. de Jonckheere, 15 Jun 1960; Col Lewis P. Boone Jr, 4 Jun 1962 (temp); Col Charles S. Overstreet Jr, 11 Jul 1962; Col Chester B. Wine, 3 Sep 1963; Col Rayburn D. Lancaster, 15 May 1964; Col Ray S. McClung, 8 Jul 1964; Col James H. Phifer Jr, 2 Jul 1966 (temp); Col Thomas M. Carhart, 8 Aug 1966; Col John E. Blake, 18 Sep 1967; Col Hewitt E. Lovelace Jr, 3 Oct 1969; Col Nicholas Arabinko, 1 Aug 1970; Col Harry H. Elmendorf, 22 Oct 1970; Col Nicholas Arabinko, 15 May 1971; Col John C. Reed, 1 Nov 1971; Col Mathias J. Martin, 24 Oct 1975 (temp); Col Sharman R. Stevenson, 11 Nov 1975; Col John T. Abell, 9 Jun 1978; Col Anthony J. Burshnick, 25 May 1979; Col Duane C. Oberg, 27 Jun 1980; Col Barry J. Howard, 28 Jun 1982−.

Major Off-Base and Detached Installations:* Ikego Comms Stn, Zushi, 1 Sep 1945 (actvd)−unk; Sagami Comms Stn, Sagamihara, 1 Sep 1945 (actvd)−unk; Fuchu Comms Stn, Fuchu-Shi, 5 Sep 1945 (actvd)−; Atsugi Comms Stn, 1 mi S of Yamato, 7 Sep 1945 (actvd)−unk; Camp Asaka Comms Stn, Asaka, 7 Sep 1945 (actvd)−unk; Camp Zama Comms Stn, Zama, 7 Sep 1945 (actvd)−unk; Yokohama Comms Stn, Yokohama, 7 Sep 1945 (actvd)−unk; Haneda Svc Anx, Haneda, 26 Sep 1945 (actvd)−unk; Kubasak Sch Anx, 3 mi S of the city of Okinawa, 7 Sep 1945 (actvd)−; Yokosuka Comms Stn, Yokosuka, 30 Sep 1945 (actvd)−; Tokorozawa Tmtr Site, Tokorozawa, 1 Nov 1945 (actvd)−unk; Fukaya Comms Stn, Yokohama, 15 Nov 1945 (actvd)−unk; Komatsu Aux Afld (rdsgd Komatsu Tacan Anx), Komatsu-Shi, 15 Nov 1945 (actvd)−20 Aug 1958 (trsfd to Japanese govt); Kosumaki AB (rdsgd Komaki Tacan Anx), 15 Nov 1945 (actvd)−15 Sep 1958 (trsfd to Johnson AB); Momote Village Fam Hsg Anx, Asaka, Dec 1945 (actvd)−unk; Seburiyama RRS, 11 mi S of Fukuoka, 11 Mar 1946 (actvd)−unk; Kisarazu Comms Site, Kisarazu, 1 May 1946 (actvd)−1 Nov 1958 (trsfd to Tachikawa AB); Yokota Rifle Rg, Hakonegasaki, 1 Jul 1946 (actvd)−; Negishi Comms Stn, Yokohama, 1 Oct 1946 (actvd)−; Hakone Radio Site, Hakone-Machi, 1946 (actvd)−unk; Rokko RRS, Kobe, 28 Oct 1947 (actvd)−unk; Tama Ammo Stor Anx (rdsgd Tama Ammo Dep; Tama Chapel Anx; Tama Svc Anx), Tama, 28 Oct 1947 (actvd)−unk; Johnson AS (rdsgd Johnson Fam Hsg Anx; Johnson Comms Site), Johnson Isl, Jul 1948 (actvd)−; Johnson Comms Anx, Johnson Isl, Jul 1948 (actvd)−1 Dec 1978 (trsfd to Japanese govt); Akasaka Comms Anx, Akasaka, 6 May 1950 (actvd)−; Tama West AAA Rg, Ninomiya, 1 Sep 1950 (actvd)−; Hamura AA Anx (rdsgd Hamura Sch), Hamura-Machi, Sep 1950 (actvd)−15 Jul 1957 (inactvd); Kami Seya Comms Stn, Kashiwa, 1950 (actvd)−; Owada

---

*Unless otherwise indicated, all installations are located in Japan.

Comms Stn, 13 mi N of Asaka-Machi, 1950 (actvd)−; Inamba-Shima Air Rg, 65 mi SSE of Shimoda-Shi, Jul 1952 (actvd)−; Wajima Spec Comms Site (rdsgd Wajima AS), Wajima, 8 Oct 1953 (actvd)−; Yokohama Crash Boat Anx, Yokohama, 5 Nov 1954 (actvd)−; Yuki RRS, Machida, 5 Nov 1954 (actvd)−unk (trsfd to Tachikawa AB); Sakata AS, Sakata, 17 Nov 1955 (actvd)−29 Sep 1956 (inactvd & trsfd to Naval Comms Fclty); Chiran RRS, 15.5 mi SSW of Kagoshima, 8 Nov 1956 (actvd)−1958 (trsfd to Dept of the Army); Dake San RRS, 15 Oct 1960 (trsfd from Johnson AB)−; Hakone RR Anx, Hakone-Machi, 15 Oct 1960 (trsfd from Johnson AB)−1 Mar 1961 (trsfd to Dept of the Army); Komaki Tacan Anx, Komaki, 15 Oct 1960 (trsfd from Johnson AB)−; Mineokayama Liaison Anx, Mineokayama, 15 Oct 1960 (trsfd from Johnson AB)−16 Dec 1969 (trsfd to Japanese govt); Mito Air Rg, Mito, 15 Oct 1960 (trsfd from Johnson AB)−1974 (inactvd); Nagoya Far East Network Stn, Nagoya, 15 Oct 1960 (trsfd from Johnson AB)−31 Jun 1964 (trsfd to Japanese govt); Niigata Loran Bcn Anx, Niigata, 15 Oct 1960 (trsfd from Johnson AB)−15 Apr 1965 (trsfd to Japanese govt); Niigata Tacan Anx, Niigata, 15 Oct 1960 (trsfd from Johnson AB)−15 Apr 1965 (trsfd to Japanese govt); Oyama RR Anx, Oyama, 15 Oct 1960 (trsfd from Johnson AB)−1 Mar 1961 (trsfd to Dept of the Army); Sado Shima Liaison Anx, Sado Shima, 15 Oct 1960 (trsfd from Johnson AB)−10 Feb 1964 (trsfd to Japanese govt); Toyooka Comms Anx, Toyooka, 15 Oct 1960 (trsfd from Johnson AB)−; Wajima Liaison Anx, Wajima, 15 Oct 1960 (trsfd from Johnson AB)−c. 1961 (inactvd); Wajima Liaison Anx, Wajima, 15 Oct 1963 (actvd)−; Tama Svc Anx, 1 mi S of Fuchu-Shi, 1 May 1964 (actvd)−; Iwakuni Comms Stn, Iwakuni, 1 Jul 1964 (actvd)−; Sofu Comms Stn, 6.5 mi SW of Iwakuni, 1 Jul 1964 (actvd)−; Tsushima Comms Stn, Izuhara, 1 Jul 1964 (actvd)−; Tokorozawa Radar Site (rdsgd Tokorozawa Tmtr Site), Tokorozawa, 15 Aug 1966 (actvd)−unk (trsfd to Tachikawa AB); Atsugi Comms Stn, 1 mi S of Yamato, 30 Jun 1970 (trsfd from Tachikawa AB)−; Camp Asaka Comms Stn, Asaka, 30 Jun 1970 (trsfd from Tachikawa AB)−; Camp Oji Comms Stn, 30 Jun 1970 (trsfd from Tachikawa AB)−25 Aug 1971 (trsfd to Japanese govt); Camp Zama Comms Stn, Zama, 30 Jun 1970 (trsfd from Tachikawa AB)−; Fuchinobe Comms Stn, Fuchinobe, 30 Jun 1970 (trsfd from Tachikawa AB)−30 Nov 1974 (trsfd to Japanese govt); Fuchu AS (rdsgd Fuchu Comms Anx), Fuchu-Shi, 30 Jun 1970 (trsfd from Fuchu AS)−15 Nov 1974 (part containing basing for U.S. Forces Japan and HQ Fifth AF trsfd to Japanese govt); Fukaya Comms Stn, Yokohama, 30 Jun 1970 (trsfd from Tachikawa AB)−; Grant Heights Fam Hsg Anx, 30 Jun 1970 (trsfd from Tachikawa AB)−30 Sep 1973 (trsfd to Japanese govt); Green Park Fam Hsg Anx, Musahino, 30 Jun 1970 (trsfd from Tachikawa AB)−25 Jan 1973 (trsfd to Japanese govt); Hakone RRS, Hakone-Machi, 30 Jun 1970 (trsfd from Tachikawa AB)−; Haneda Svc Anx, Haneda, 30

Jun 1970 (trsfd from Tachikawa AB)–20 May 1978 (trsfd to Japanese govt); Hiyoshi Comms Stn, Hiyoshi, 30 Jun 1970 (trsfd from Tachikawa AB)–22 Sep 1975 (trsfd to Japanese govt); Ikego Comms Stn, Zushi, 30 Jun 1970 (trsfd from Tachikawa AB)–27 Jun 1978 (trsfd to Japanese govt); Kami Seya Comms Stn, Yokohama, 30 Jun 1970 (trsfd from Tachikawa AB)–; Kanto Mura Fam Hsg Anx, Kanto Mura, 30 Jun 1970 (trsfd from Tachikawa AB)–10 Dec 1974 (trsfd to Japanese govt); Kashiwa Comms Stn, Kashiwa, 30 Jun 1970 (trsfd from Tachikawa AB)–1 Feb 1976 (inactvd), 30 Sep 1977 (trsfd in part to USN and in part to Japanese govt); Kisarazu Comms Stn, Kisarazu, 30 Jun 1970 (trsfd from Tachikawa AB)–20 Jun 1975 (trsfd to Japanese govt); Kishine Comms Stn, Kishine, 30 Jun 1970 (trsfd from Tachikawa AB)–7 Mar 1972 (trsfd to Japanese govt); Momote Village Fam Hsg Anx (rdsgd Momote Svc Anx), Asaka, 30 Jun 1970 (trsfd from Tachikawa AB)–10 Jul 1978 (trsfd to Japanese govt); Nagai Comms Stn, Yokosuka, 30 Jun 1970 (trsfd from Tachikawa AB)–; Negishi Comms Stn, Yokohama, 30 Jun 1970 (trsfd from Tachikawa AB)–; Owada Comms Stn, Tanashi, 30 Jun 1970 (trsfd from Tachikawa AB)–; Rokko RRS, Kobe, 30 Jun 1970 (trsfd from Tachikawa AB)–; Sagami Comms Stn, Sagamihara, 30 Jun 1970 (trsfd from Tachikawa AB)–; Sendai RRS, Sendai, 30 Jun 1970 (trsfd from Tachikawa AB)–30 Sep 1976 (trsfd to Japanese govt); Tachikawa AB, Tachikawa, 30 Jun 1970 (asgnd)–30 Nov 1977 (trsfd to Japanese govt); Tama Svc Anx, Tama, 30 Jun 1970 (trsfd from Tachikawa AB)–; Tokorozawa Tmtr Site, Tokorozawa, 30 Jun 1970 (trsfd from Tachikawa AB)–; Tokyo Comms Stn, Tokyo, 30 Jun 1970 (trsfd from Tachikawa AB)–1 Aug 1973 (trsfd to Japanese govt); Yamato AS, 30 Jun 1970 (trsfd from Tachikawa AB)–30 Jun 1973 (trsfd to Japanese govt); Yokohama Comms Stn (rdsgd Yokohama Admn Anx), Yokohama, 30 Jun 1970 (trsfd from Tachikawa AB–; Yokohama Exchange Anx, Yokohama, 30 Jun 1970 (trsfd from Tachikawa AB)–1 Sep 1977 (inactvd), 7 Apr 1978 (trsfd to Japanese govt); Yokosuka Comms Stn, Yokosuka, 30 Jun 1970 (trsfd from Tachikawa AB)–; Yuki RRS, Machida, 30 Jun 1970 (trsfd from Tachikawa AB)–unk (inactvd); Akasaka Admn Anx, Akasaka, 4 Jul 1973 (asgnd)–; Chitose AS, Chitose, 1 Apr 1976 (asgnd)–; Sasebo Anx, Sasebo, 1 Sep 1977 (asgnd)–; Narita Air Terminal, Narita, 20 May 1978 (actvd)–; Yuki RRS, Machida, 9 Jun 1978 (actvd)–.

Major Changes in Operational Capability: During World War II Yokota became the center of Japanese Army Air Forces flight test activities and the site of the first meeting between Japanese and Italian wartime allies; a detachment of the American 1st Cavalry Div arrived at the base on 4 Sep 1945; base supported C–46 airlift operations from Sep to Dec 1945, when the old runway deteriorated under heavy usage; the runway was repaired and Yokota supported operations of the 3d Bomb Gp by Aug 1946; since that time base has provided support for fighter, bomber, and military airlift operations, hosting B–26, B–29, P–51, KB–50, F–84, B–57, RB–57, RB–29, C–54, F–86D, F–102, F–4D, F–100, F–105, C–5, C–141, and C–130 units; the first C–141 Starlifter touched down at Yokota to begin extensive SEA cargo and medical evacuation operations in 1965; the 347th Tac Ftr Wg became principal operating unit 1970–71, when USAF operations at Yokota diminished in keeping with the U.S. Forces Japan and Japanese government joint agreement; became primarily a support base for MAC passenger and cargo operations on 1 Jul 1972; Yokota remains one of the largest airlift support bases in the Northwest Pacific.

Major Commands to Which Assigned: 1st Cavalry Div, USA Forces Pacific, 7 Sep 1945; FEAF, 16 Sep 1945 (rdsgd Pacific Air Comd, USA, 6 Dec 1945; FEAF, 1 Jan 1947; PACAF, 1 Jul 1957)–.

Major Changes in Status: None, base continuously active since 1945.

Units Assigned:

1945		1948	
5 Cmbt Crgo Sq	Sep 45–15 Jan 46	3 AB Gp	18 Aug 48–1 Apr 50
6 Cmbt Crgo Sq	Sep 45–15 Jan 46	3 AP Sq	18 Aug 48–1 Apr 50
7 Cmbt Crgo Sq	Sep 45–15 Jan 46	3 Base Svc Sq	18 Aug 48–10 Feb 50
8 Cmbt Crgo Sq	Sep 45–15 Jan 46	3 Bomb Wg	10 Aug 48–1 Apr 50
17 Recon Sq	26 Oct 45–27 Apr 46	3 Comms Sq	18 Aug 48–1 Apr 50
20 Recon Sq	27 Oct 45–20 Jun 46	3 Food Svc Sq	18 Aug 48–1 Apr 50
336 Adrm Sq	45–1 Feb 46	3 Maint & Sup Gp	18 Aug 48–1 Apr 50
337 Adrm Sq	45–1 Feb 46	3 Maint Sq, Bomb	18 Aug 48–1 Apr 50
338 Adrm Sq	45–1 Feb 46	3 MV Sq, Bomb	
339 Adrm Sq	45–20 Feb 46	(3 MV Sq)	18 Aug 48–1 Apr 50
600 Engrg Sq		3 Sup Sq	18 Aug 48–1 Apr 50
(600 Air		71 Tac Recon Gp	c. 1 Nov 48–1 Apr 49
Engrg Sq)	17 Oct 45–20 Aug 48	1949	
608 Air Mat Sq	18 Oct 45–17 May 46	8 Tac Recon Sq,	
HQ & Base Svcs Sq,		Night Photo	
384 Svc Gp	23 Sep 45–20 Feb 46	(8 Tac Recon Sq,	
1946		Photo-Jet)	25 Mar 49–9 Jul 50
3 Bomb Gp	15 Aug 46–1 Apr 50	23 Recon Sq,	
6 Night Ftr Sq	1 Sep 46–20 Feb 47	VLR, Photo	16 Mar 49–2 May 49
7 Air Svc Gp	16 Apr 46–unk	2079 Recon Sq	
	1 Sep 46–20 Aug 48	[Prov]	1 Jul 49–1 Dec 49
7 Cmbt Crgo Sq	5 Jan 46–15 Jan 46	6114 Tow Target	
8 Bomb Sq	1 Sep 46–1 Apr 50	Unit	13 Dec 49–1 Apr 50
8 Cmbt Crgo Sq	5 Jan 46–15 Jan 46	1950	
9 Recon Sq	20 Jun 46–20 Oct 47	3 AB Gp	14 Aug 50–1 Dec 50
90 Bomb Sq	c. 10 Oct 46–1 Oct 49	3 AP Sq	14 Aug 50–1 Dec 50
608 Air Mat Sq	6 Sep 46–20 Aug 48	3 Bomb Gp	14 Aug 50–1 Dec 50
1947		3 Bomb Wg	14 Aug 50–1 Dec 50
3 Emerg Rscu Sq		3 Comms Sq	14 Aug 50–1 Dec 50
(3 Rscu Sq)	15 Jul 47–1 Apr 50	3 Food Svc Sq	14 Aug 50–1 Dec 50
29 Air Svc Gp	15 Apr 47–25 Sep 47	3 Instls Sq	14 Aug 50–1 Dec 50
31 Recon Sq	20 Oct 47–16 Mar 49	3 Maint & Sup Gp	14 Aug 50–1 Dec 50
65 Air Engrg Sq	15 Jan 47–20 Aug 48	3 Maint Sq	14 Aug 50–1 Dec 50
82 Tac Recon Sq		3 MV Sq	14 Aug 50–1 Dec 50
(82 Recon Sq;		3 Sup Sq	14 Aug 50–1 Dec 50
82 Tac Recon Sq)	1 Feb 47–25 Mar 49	8 Bomb Sq	14 Aug 50–1 Dec 50
548 Recon Tech Sq	15 Sep 47–8 Mar 60	13 Bomb Sq	14 Aug 50–1 Dec 50

31 Strat Recon Sq	c. 12 Jul 50–14 Aug 50
35 AB Gp	1 Apr 50–14 Aug 50
35 AP Sq	1 Apr 50–14 Aug 50
35 Comms Sq	1 Apr 50–14 Aug 50
35 Ftr Gp	1 Apr 50–14 Aug 50
35 Ftr-Intcpr Wg	1 Apr 50–14 Aug 50
35 Food Svc Sq	14 Aug 50–1 Dec 50
35 Instls Sq	1 Apr 50–14 Aug 50
35 Maint & Sup Gp	1 Apr 50–14 Aug 50
35 Maint Sq	14 Aug 50–1 Dec 50
35 Med Gp	1 Apr 50–14 Aug 50
35 MV Sq, Ftr, SE (35 MV Sq)	1 Apr 50–14 Aug 50
39 Ftr-Intcpr Sq	1 Apr 50–8 Jul 50
40 Ftr Sq (40 Ftr-Intcpr Sq)	13 Mar 50–7 Jul 50
41 Ftr-Intcpr Sq	c. 25 Mar 50–14 Aug 50
91 Strat Recon Sq, Medium, Photo (91 Strat Recon Sq, Ftr)	19 Dec 50–20 Dec 54
325 Bomb Sq	9 Jul 50–29 Oct 50
326 Bomb Sq	9 Jul 50–26 Oct 50
327 Bomb Sq	9 Jul 50–27 Oct 50
339 Ftr Sq (339 Ftr-All Wea Sq)	1 Apr 50–4 Aug 50
343 Bomb Sq	5 Aug 50–25 Jul 54
344 Bomb Sq	5 Aug 50–24 Jul 54
345 Bomb Sq	5 Aug 50–24 Jul 54
512 Bomb Sq	27 Jan 50–14 Aug 50
528 AC & W Gp	1 Apr 50–14 Aug 50
6114 Tow Target Sq	14 Apr 50–12 Sep 51
6161 AB Gp	1 Dec 50–1 Feb 53
6161 AB Wg	1 Dec 50–1 Oct 54
6161 AP Sq	1 Dec 50–1 Feb 53
6161 Comms Sq	1 Dec 50–1 Oct 54
6161 Food Svc Sq	1 Dec 50–1 Oct 54
6161 Instls Sq	1 Dec 50–1 Oct 54
6161 Maint & Sup Gp	1 Dec 50–1 Feb 53
6161 Maint Sq (6161 Fld Maint Sq)	1 Dec 50–1 Oct 54
6161 Med Gp	1 Dec 50–1 Feb 53
6161 MV Sq	1 Dec 50–1 Oct 54
6161 Sup Sq	1 Dec 50–1 Oct 54
FEAF Bmbr Comd, Prov	8 Jul 50–18 Jun 54
1951	
56 Strat Recon Sq (56 Wea Recon Sq)	15 Sep 51–15 Jan 72
1952	
2 Photo Sq	24 Jul 52–8 Jun 54
10 Radar Calibration Sq	21 Mar 52–18 Mar 54
98 Armnt & Elect Maint Sq	25 Jul 52–22 Jul 54
98 Fld Maint Sq	25 Jul 52–22 Jul 54
98 Prdc Maint Sq	25 Jul 52–22 Jul 54
343 Bomb Sq	25 Jul 52–22 Jul 54
344 Bomb Sq	25 Jul 52–22 Jul 54
345 Bomb Sq	25 Jul 52–22 Jul 54
1953	
35 Med Gp (35 Tac Hosp)	1 Feb 53–1 Oct 57
421 Air Rflg Sq	8 Jul 53–18 Feb 65
6091 Recon Flt (6091 Recon Sq)	1 Dec 53–1 Jul 58
1954	
35 AB Gp	1 Oct 54–1 Oct 57
35 AP Sq	1 Oct 54–1 Oct 57
35 Comms Sq	1 Oct 54–1 Oct 57
35 Ftr-Intcpr Gp	14 Aug 54–1 Oct 57
35 Ftr-Intcpr Wg	1 Oct 54–1 Oct 57
35 Food Svc Sq	1 Oct 54–1 Oct 57
35 Instls Sq	1 Oct 54–1 Oct 57
35 Maint & Sup Gp	1 Oct 54–1 Oct 57
35 Maint Sq (35 Fld Maint Sq)	1 Oct 54–1 Oct 57
35 Sup Sq	1 Oct 54–1 Oct 57
37 Air Rscu Sq	23 Jul 54–8 May 55
39 Ftr-Intcpr Sq	31 Jul 54–26 Aug 55
40 Ftr-Intcpr Sq	13 Aug 54–
41 Ftr-Intcpr Sq	13 Aug 54–c. 5 Aug 56
6007 Comps Recon Gp (6007 Recon Gp [Comps])	11 Aug 54–9 Aug 57
6021 Photo Mapping Flt [Tac Recon] (6021 Recon Sq [Comps])	15 Dec 54–29 Jun 57
6023 Radar Evaluation Flt	18 Mar 54–3 Jul 56
6034 USAF Dispy (6034 USAF Dispy [Class B])	2 Dec 54–8 Dec 60
1955	
15 Tac Recon Sq	25 Aug 55–18 Aug 56
Yokota Task Force, Prov	1 May 55–unk
1956	
12 Tac Recon Sq	13 Aug 56–8 Mar 60
67 Tac Recon Gp	13 Aug 56–1 Oct 57
1957	
11 Tac Recon Sq	15 Jul 57–8 Mar 60
67 AB Gp	1 Jul 57–1 Oct 57
67 AP Sq	1 Jul 57–1 Oct 57
67 Comms Sq	1 Jul 57–1 Oct 57

67 Fld Maint Sq	1 Jul 57–8 Nov 60
67 Food Svc Sq	1 Jul 57–1 Oct 57
67 Instls Sq	1 Jul 57–1 Oct 57
67 Maint & Sup Gp	1 Jul 57–1 Oct 57
67 Recon Tech Sq	1 Jul 57–8 Feb 71
67 Sup Sq	1 Jul 57–1 Oct 57
67 Tac Recon Wg	1 Jul 57–8 Dec 60
67 Trnsp Sq	1 Jul 57–1 Oct 57
6067 Armnt & Elect Maint Sq	1 Jul 57–15 May 59
6067 Prdc Maint Sq	1 Jul 57–8 Mar 60
6102 AB Wg	1 Jul 57–8 Jan 64
6102 AP Sq	1 Jul 57–8 Jan 64
6102 Instls Sq (6102 CE Sq)	1 Jul 57–8 Jan 64
6102 Ops Sq	1 Jul 57–8 Jan 64
6102 Sup Sq	1 Jul 57–8 Jan 64
6102 Spt Sq	1 Jul 57–8 Jan 64
6102 Trnsp Sq	1 Jul 57–8 Jan 64
1959	
67 Armnt & Elect Maint Sq	15 May 59–8 Dec 60
1960	
3 Armnt & Elect Maint Sq	18 Nov 60–8 Jan 64
3 Bomb Wg	18 Nov 60–8 Jan 64
3 Fld Maint Sq	18 Nov 60–8 Jan 64
8 Bomb Sq	18 Nov 60–24 Apr 64
13 Bomb Sq	17 Nov 60–24 Apr 64
90 Bomb Sq	18 Nov 60–9 Jun 64
1962	
3 Orgnzl Maint Sq	8 Sep 62–8 Jan 64
41 Air Div	28 Jun 62–15 Jan 68
Orgnzl Maint Sq, Prov 6033	1 Mar 62–8 Sep 62
1963	
403 Mun Maint Sq	8 Apr 63–8 Jun 64
6988 Radio Sq, Mobile (6988 Scty Sq)	1 Feb 63–30 Jun 72
1964	
35 Tac Ftr Sq	24 May 64–15 Mar 71
36 Tac Ftr Sq	24 May 64–15 May 71
80 Tac Ftr Sq	24 May 64–15 Feb 71
441 AP Sq (441 Scty Pol Sq)	8 Jan 64–15 Jan 68
441 Armnt & Elect Maint Sq	8 Jan 64–15 Jan 68
441 CE Sq	8 Jan 64–15 Jan 68
441 Cmbt Spt Gp	8 Jan 64–15 Jan 68
441 Fld Maint Sq	8 Jan 64–15 Jan 68
441 Mun Maint Sq	8 Jan 64–15 Jan 68
441 Orgnzl Maint Sq	8 Jan 64–8 Jun 66
441 Svcs Sq	8 Jan 64–15 Jan 68
441 Sup Sq	8 Jan 64–15 Jan 68
441 Trnsp Sq	8 Jan 64–15 Jan 68

6141 Mat Sq	12 Jun 64–1 Apr 65
1965	
6220 Consold Acft Maint Sq	1 Apr 65–15 Nov 66
1966	
610 Mil Alft Spt Sq	8 Apr 66–1 Oct 78
6034 USAF Dispy	5 Jan 66–15 Jan 68
6141 Mat Sq	15 Nov 66–15 Jan 68
1967	
56 Aeromed Evac Sq	28 Apr 67–1 Aug 72
65 Mil Alft Gp (65 Mil Alft Spt Gp)	14 Aug 67–1 Jan 72
1968	
34 Aeromed Evac Sq	15 Oct 68–1 Jun 69
347 Armnt & Elect Maint Sq (347 Avncs Maint Sq)	15 Jan 68–17 May 71
347 CE Sq	15 Jan 68–15 May 71
347 Cmbt Spt Gp	15 Jan 68–15 May 71
347 Fld Maint Sq	15 Jan 68–15 May 71
347 Mun Maint Sq	15 Jan 68–15 May 71
347 Scty Pol Sq	15 Jan 68–15 May 71
347 Svcs Sq	15 Jan 68–15 May 71
347 Sup Sq	15 Jan 68–15 May 71
347 Tac Ftr Wg	15 Jan 68–15 May 71
347 Trnsp Sq	15 Jan 68–15 May 71
556 Recon Sq	1 Jul 68–30 Jun 72
1971	
475 AB Wg	1 Nov 71–
475 CE Sq	1 Nov 71–
475 Consold Acft Maint Sq	1 Nov 71–31 Aug 75
475 Scty Pol Sq	1 Nov 71–
475 Svcs Sq	1 Nov 71–28 Feb 75
475 Sup Sq	1 Nov 71–
475 Trnsp Sq	1 Nov 71–
6100 AB Wg	15 May 71–1 Nov 71
6100 CE Sq	15 May 71–1 Nov 71
6100 Fld Maint Sq	15 May 71–1 Nov 71
6100 Orgnzl Maint Sq	15 May 71–1 Nov 71
6100 Scty Pol Sq	15 May 71–1 Nov 71
6100 Svcs Sq	15 May 71–1 Nov 71
6100 Sup Sq	15 May 71–1 Nov 71
6100 Trnsp Sq	15 May 71–1 Nov 71
1972	
36 Aerosp Rscu & Recovery Sq	11 Nov 72–30 Nov 72
1974	
1956 Comms Gp	30 Sep 74–
Fifth AF	11 Nov 74–
345 Tac Alft Sq	1 Sep 75–
1867 Fclty	

Checking Sq	8 Sep 75–	316 Tac Alft Gp	1 Oct 78–
1976		6204 Broadcasting	
655 Tac Hosp	1 Apr 76–	Sq (AF Pacific	
USAF Hosp,		Broadcasting Sq)	26 Apr 78–
Yokota	1 Apr 76–	1980	
1978		1837 Elect Instl Sq	1 Jul 80–
316 Aerl Port Sq	1 Oct 78–	Numbered AF	
316 Fld Maint Sq	1 Oct 78–	Cmbt Ops Staff	
316 Orgnzl		[Fifth AF]	15 Jul 80–
Maint Sq	1 Oct 78–		

Zaragoza Air Base

Location: Located 10 mi W of Zaragoza, 168 mi W of Barcelona, and 163 mi NE of Madrid, Spain.

Name: Named after a city in Spain.

Date of Current Name: 15 Feb 1956.

Previous Names: Zaragoza AS, Sep 1954.

Date of Establishment: 15 Feb 1955.

Date Construction Began: U.S. construction began in Sep 1954.

Date of Beneficial Occupancy: 9 Jan 1956.

Base Operating Units: 7603d AB Sq (rdsgd 3974th AB Sq, 1 Jul 1957), 9 Jan 1956; 3974th AB Gp (rdsgd 3974th Cmbt Spt Gp, 1 Jan 1959), 1 May 1958; 3972d AB Sq (rdsgd 7472d Cmbt Spt Sq, 15 Apr 1966), 1 Jun 1964; 406th Cmbt Spt Sq, 1 Jul 1970; 406th Cmbt Spt Gp, 15 Jul 1972–.

Base Commanders: Lt Col Richard C. Harris,* 15 Feb 1955; Col William L. Welch, 9 Jan 1956; Col Lloyd W. Preston, 25 May 1958; Lt Col George H. McKee, 8 May 1961; Col Neil W. Wemple, 11 Jul 1961; Col George H. McKee, 6 Jul 1962; Col Joseph J. McLachlan, 8 Jul 1963 (temp); Col Homer C. Bell Jr, 9 Jul 1963 (temp); Col James N. McFadden, 25 Jul 1963; Col Homer C. Bell Jr, 20 Oct 1963; Maj Gerald W. Nash, 25 Jun 1964; Lt Col John P. Persons Jr, 2 Jul 1964; Lt Col Andrew Sereg, 17 Nov 1965; Col Robert Sullivan, 7 Dec 1965; Lt Col John C. Peck, 19 Jan 1966; Col Francis J. Coleman, 9 Feb 1967; Col John D. Pace, 27 Oct 1967; Col Dale R. Funk, 14 Jul 1969; Col Robert H. Sayre, 26 Jul 1971; Lt Col Cecil B. Juanarena, 4 Aug 1972; Col William T. Roy, 20 Nov 1972; Col George B. Stackhouse III, c. Sep 1975; Col B. Conn Anderson Jr, 6 Sep 1977; Col John C. Price, 27 Aug 1979; Col Wayne C. Pittman Jr, 18 Jul 1980–.

Major Off-Base and Detached Installations:[†] Zaragoza Liaison Anx (rdsgd Zaragoza Admn Anx; Zaragoza Admn Anx #1), Zaragoza, 15 Jan 1955 (actvd)–15 Mar 1956 (inactvd); Zaragoza Admn Anx, Zaragoza, 15

---

*Although Col Harris commanded the American construction activity and basing liaison units, including U.S. Navy representatives, the title base commander began on 9 Jan 1956.

[†]All installations are located in Spain.

Feb 1955 (actvd)–15 Mar 1956 (inactvd); Zaragoza Joint U.S. Military Group (JUSMG) Complex (rdsgd Zaragoza Liaison Anx), Zaragoza, 15 Feb 1955 (actvd)–; Zaragoza Med Anx (rdsgd Zaragoza Hosp), Zaragoza, 2 Jan 1956 (actvd)–30 Apr 1958 (inactvd); Barcelona Petrol Stor Anx, Barcelona, 21 Jan 1956 (actvd)–23 Oct 1956 (inactvd & dspd); Muntados Fuel Stor Anx (rdsgd Muntados Fuel Stor Stn; Zaragoza Petrol Prods Stor Anx), Zaragoza, 21 Jan 1956 (actvd)–23 Oct 1956 (inactvd); Zaragoza Admn Anx #2 (rdsgd Barcelona Admn Ofc), Barcelona, 21 Jan 1956 (actvd)–c. 1965 (inactvd); Zaragoza Med Anx, 10 mi W of Zaragoza, 1 Feb 1956–unk; Zaragoza Admn Anx #1, Zaragoza, 20 Dec 1956 (actvd)–29 Feb 1964 (inactvd & dspd); Inoges AS (rdsgd Zaragoza AS #1), Inoges, 25 Mar 1957 (actvd)–; Zaragoza Depnt Sch Anx (rdsgd Zaragoza Sch #1), Zaragoza, 1 Jul 1957 (actvd)–31 Aug 1960 (inactvd); Zaragoza Stor Stn (rdsgd Zaragoza Stor Anx), Zaragoza, 18 Jul 1957 (actvd)–30 Jun 1961 (inactvd & dspd); Zaragoza RRS, Zaragoza, 27 Sep 1957 (asgnd)–unk; Zaragoza Svc Anx #1, Zaragoza, 1 Nov 1957 (actvd)–30 Sep 1960 (inactvd & dspd); Zaragoza Fam Hsg Anx, Zaragoza, 12 Aug 1958 (actvd)–31 Jul 1964 (inactvd); Barcelona Petrol Stor Anx, Barcelona, 23 Oct 1958 (asgnd)–5 Aug 1974 (dspd); Zaragoza Hsg Anx #1, Zaragoza, 30 Apr 1959 (asgnd)–; Zaragoza Sch #2, Castelldefels, 1 Sep 1959 (actvd)–30 Jan 1960 (inactvd); Zaragoza Svc Anx #2, Barcelona, 2 Oct 1959 (asgnd)–16 Sep 1960 (inactvd); Zaragoza Svc Anx #3 (rdsgd Elizondo Svc Anx), Elizondo, 1 Dec 1959 (asgnd)–14 Dec 1960 (trsfd to Elizondo AS); Elizondo Hsg Anx (rdsgd Zaragoza Amn Hsg Anx #3), Elizondo, 30 Dec 1959 (asgnd)–; Zaragoza Amn Hsg Anx #2, Rosas, 30 Dec 1959 (actvd)–; Zaragoza AS #3, Elizondo, 30 Dec 1959 (asgnd)–31 Dec 1964 (dspd); Zaragoza RRS (rdsgd Elizondo RRS), Elizondo, 2 Oct 1961 (actvd)–5 Oct 1974 (dspd); La Muela Petrol Prods Stor Anx, La Muela, 1 Apr 1971 (actvd)–28 Apr 1980 (dspd); Bardenas Reales Wpns Rg, Arguedas, 21 Sep 1976 (actvd)–; Humosa RRS, Los Santos de la Humosa, 1 Jan 1980 (trsfd from Torrejon AB)–; Inoges Hsg Anx, El Frasno, 1 Jan 1980 (trsfd from Torrejon AB)–; Inoges RRS, Inoges, 1 Jan 1980 (trsfd from Torrejon AB)–; Menoka RRS, Ferrerias, Menorka, 1 Jan 1980 (trsfd from Torrejon AB)–; Soller Hsg Anx, Soller, Mallorca, 1 Jan 1980 (trsfd from Torrejon AB)–; Soller RRS, Soller, Mallorca, 1 Jan 1980 (trsfd from Torrejon AB)–.

Major Changes in Operational Capability: The construction work for enlargement and improvement of the existing Spanish Air Force Base near Zaragoza began in Sep 1954 under supervision of U.S. Navy engineers; installation initially designed for temporary or intermediate use as a war standby base; first U.S. construction project included strengthening the existing 9,921-ft runway and adding 1,000-ft overruns at each end; work on a new concrete runway, 200 ft by 12,200 ft, with 1,000-ft overruns at each end began in 1956 and was completed in 1958; base transferred from the control of the Joint U.S. Military Group (JUSMG), Sixteenth AF, to SAC on 1 Jul 1957; base then furnished operational support for SAC alert force dispersal; with the arrival of the 531st Ftr-Intcpr Sq from Wheelus AB on 5 Sep 1958, Zaragoza hosted not only SAC bomber forces but also fighter-interceptor units; this support continued until 1 Jul 1964, when Zaragoza AB was placed on standby status; reduced to modified caretaker status on 1 Jan 1966 and reassigned to USAFE on 15 Apr 1966; with the closure of Wheelus AB in Libya, Zaragoza returned to active status on 19 Feb 1970; the first aircraft arrived on 9 Mar 1970; base subsequently supported F–102, F–4, and KC–135 operations; Project CREEK STEP, which began in Feb 1970, called for the buildup of Zaragoza AB as a USAFE weapons training site; actual use of the Bardenas Reales Air-to-Ground Bombing and Runnery Range (c. 45 mi NW of the base) began in Mar 1970; base supported DART TOW air-to-air gunnery missions to train detachments of USAFE and Spanish Air Force units, beginning on 1 Apr 1971.

Major Commands to Which Assigned: JUSMG, 15 Feb 1955; SAC, 1 Jul 1957; USAFE, 15 Apr 1966–.

Major Changes in Status: Construction status, 15 Feb 1955; active, 9 Jan 1956; standby status, 1 Jul 1964; modified caretaker status, 1 Jan 1966; active status, 19 Feb 1970–.

Units Assigned:

1956

7603 AB Sq	
(3974 AB Sq;	
3974 Spt Sq)	9 Jan 56–30 Jun 64
7603 USAF Hosp	
(7603 USAF	
Dispy; 7603	
USAF Hosp;	
3974 USAF Hosp)	1 Feb 56–30 Jun 64

1957

Zaragoza Task	
Force, Prov	1 Jul 57–unk

1958

13 Avn Dep Sq	
(13 Mun	
Maint Sq)	12 Mar 58–30 Jun 64
431 Ftr-Intcpr Sq	6 Sep 58–18 May 64
3974 AB Gp	
(3974 Cmbt	
Spt Gp)	1 May 58–30 Jun 64
3974 Instls Sq	
(3974 CE Sq)	1 May 58–30 Jun 64
3974 Mat Sq	1 May 58–1 Jan 62

1959

874 AC & W Sq	5 Jan 59–1 Jan 65

3974 Ops Sq	1 Jun 59–30 Jun 64

1960

3977 Trnsp Sq	1 Mar 60–1 Jan 62
7602 Spt Wg	
(3977 Spt Wg;	
3977 Spt Gp)	1 Mar 60–1 Jul 60

1961

3974 Cmbt Def Sq	1 May 61–30 Jun 64
3974 Consold Acft	
Maint Sq	1 May 61–30 Jun 64
3974 Sup Sq	1 May 61–30 Jun 64
3974 Trnsp Sq	1 May 61–30 Jun 64

1964

3972 AB Sq	
(7472 Cmbt	
Spt Sq)	1 Jun 64–30 Jun 70

1970

406 Cmbt Spt Sq	1 Jul 70–14 Jul 72
406 Mat Sq	1 Jul 70–15 Nov 76

1971

1986 Comms Sq	1 Jan 71–
USAF Dispy,	
Zaragoza	
(USAF Hosp,	
Zaragoza;	
USAF Clinic,	
Zaragoza)	1 Jul 71–

	1972	406 Consold Acft	
406 Cmbt Spt Gp	15 Jul 72–	Maint Sq	15 Nov 76–
406 Tac Ftr			1978
Tng Wg	15 Jul 72–	34 Strat Sq	1 Aug 78–
	1976		

Zweibrucken Air Base

Location: Located 35 mi SSW of Kaiserslautern, 2 mi SE of Zweibrucken, Federal Republic of Germany.

Name: Named after a city in the Federal Republic of Germany.

Date of Current Name: 20 Aug 1969.

Previous Names: Royal Canadian Air Force (RCAF) Stn Zweibrucken, 6 Jan 1953.

Date of Establishment: RCAF establishment, 6 Jan 1953; USAF establishment, 29 Aug 1969.

Date Construction Began: Construction initiated by French Army engineers and German contractors in 1950; construction undertaken by USAF in Aug 1969.

Date of Beneficial Occupancy: Base occupied by RCAF, 6 Jan 1953; USAF occupancy, 20 Aug 1969.

Base Operating Units: 7181st Cmbt Spt Sq, 20 Aug 1969; 86th Cmbt Spt Gp, 1 Nov 1969; 26th Cmbt Spt Gp, 31 Jan 1973-.

Base Commanders: Col Howard A. Jones, 20 Aug 1969; Col Stanley N. Ratto, 23 Nov 1970; Col Arthur R. Burke, 29 Nov 1972; Col Stanley N. Ratto, 31 Jan 1973; Col Ellis C. Vander Pyl Jr, 6 Aug 1973; Col John K. Murtagh, 22 Apr 1974; Col Robert W. Sewall, 1 Aug 1975; Lt Col Charles H. Murphy, 2 Sep 1976; Col George J. Vehrs, 26 Oct 1976; Lt Col Charles G. Luse, 6 Jun 1978; Col Charles W. Bartholomew, 26 Jun 1978; Lt Col Joseph E. Entsminger, 20 Jun 1979; Col George L. Howard III, 23 Jul 1979; Lt Col James T. Billingsley III, 6 Feb 1980; Lt Col Normand G. Lezy, 7 Jul 1981; Col John P. Kelly, 28 Dec 1981-.

Major Off-Base and Detached Installations:* Rimschweiler Water Sys Anx, Rimschweiler, 1 May 1970 (trsfd from Ramstein AB)-; Bliekastel Stor Anx, Bliekastel, 1 Jul 1970 (actvd)-30 Apr 1972 (dspd); Zweibrucken Fam Hsg Anx, Zweibrucken, 1 Jul 1970 (actvd)-unk; Zweibrucken Stor Anx, Zweibrucken, 1 Jan 1972 (actvd)-30 Apr 1982 (dspd); Zweibrucken Fam Hsg Anx #2, Zweibrucken, 12 Jan 1973 (asgnd & actvd)-; Homburg

---

*All installations are located in the Federal Republic of Germany.

Fam Hsg Anx, Homburg, 15 Oct 1974 (asgnd & actvd)–; Grossteinhausen Fam Hsg Anx, Grossteinhausen, 16 Jul 1975 (actvd)–1 Dec 1978 (dspd); Contwig Fam Hsg Anx, Contwig, 1 Aug 1975 (actvd)–30 Oct 1980 (dspd); Zweibrucken Bach Hsg Anx, Zweibrucken, 3 Oct 1977 (actvd)–; Zweibrucken Stor Anx #2, Zweibrucken, 3 Oct 1977 (actvd)–; Zweibrucken Fam Hsg Anx #3, Zweibrucken, 11 Oct 1977 (actvd)–; Zweibrucken Fam Hsg Anx #4, Zweibrucken, 11 Oct 1977 (actvd)–; Erding AB, Erding, 12 May 1978 (trsfd from Bitburg AB)–; Battweiler Fam Hsg Anx, Battweiler, 22 Dec 1978 (actvd)–31 Dec 1981 (dspd); Contwig POL Distr Stn, Contwig, 20 Jun 1980 (actvd)–21 Apr 1981 (dspd); Ingolstadt AB, Manching, 15 Sep 1980 (asgnd & actvd)–; Zweibrucken Hosp, Zweibrucken, 14 Sep 1981 (actvd)–.

Major Changes in Operational Capability: Zweibrucken AB is situated on a section of the former Siegfried Line; base originally designed in 1952 by French engineers and completed by German contractors; the 3d Wg, RCAF assumed control of Zweibrucken AB on 6 Jan 1953 and operated it as a fighter base for 16 years; the RCAF departed on 27 Aug 1969, relinquishing control to the Sixteenth AF, USAFE; USAFE either renovated or enlarged all base facilities, and procured off-base housing for most base personnel upon assuming control of Zweibrucken AB in 1969; two fuel storage facilities and BLSS–500 aircraft-arresting barriers erected in 1969, and BAK–12 midfield aircraft-arresting barriers completed in 1970; family, bachelor officers', and enlisted housing construction undertaken between 1969 and 1972; TAB VEE shelters, reinforced ramps, revetments, medical, repair and aerial port facilities built during 1970–1971; Zweibrucken served as host base for the 86th Tac Ftr Wg from Nov 1969 to 31 Jan 1973, when replaced by the 26th Tac Recon Wg; from 5 Apr to 7 Jul 1979 the base also hosted the 86th Wg while Ramstein AB's runways were closed for extensive repairs.

Major Commands to Which Assigned: RCAF, 6 Jan 1953; USAFE, 29 Aug 1969–.

Major Changes in Status: Activated as a RCAF base, 6 Jan 1953; control assigned to USAFE as an off-base installation of Ramstein AB 29 Aug 1969; assumed primary installation status on 1 May 1970–.

Units Assigned:

1955			
6901 Sp Comms Gp	1 Aug 55–31 Mar 68	86 Tac Ftr Wg	1 Nov 69–31 Jan 73
6905 Comms Sq	1 Oct 55–1 Oct 57	86 Tac Hosp	1 Nov 69–30 Jun 71
1969		86 Trnsp Sq	1 Nov 69–31 Jan 73
17 Tac Recon Sq	1 Nov 69–1 Jan 79	2143 Comms Sq	1 Dec 69–
86 Avncs Maint Sq	1 Nov 69–31 Jan 73	7181 Cmbt Spt Sq	20 Aug 69–1 Nov 69
86 CE Sq	1 Nov 69–31 Jan 73	1971	
86 Cmbt Spt Gp	1 Nov 69–31 Jan 73	81 Tac Ftr Sq	15 Jul 71–15 Jan 73
86 Fld Maint Sq	1 Nov 69–31 Jan 73	USAF Dispy,	
86 Scty Pol Sq	1 Nov 69–31 Jan 73	Zweibrucken	
86 Sup Sq	1 Nov 69–31 Jan 73	(USAF Clinic,	

Zweibrucken)	1 Jul 71–	26 Orgnzl Maint Sq	
	1972	(26 Acft Gnrtn Sq)	31 Jan 73–
86 Orgnzl Maint Sq	1 Feb 72–31 Jan 73	26 Scty Pol Sq	31 Jan 73–
	1973	26 Sup Sq	31 Jan 73–
26 Avncs Maint Sq		26 Tac Recon Wg	31 Jan 73–
(26 Component		26 Trnsp Sq	31 Jan 73–
Rpr Sq)	31 Jan 73–	38 Tac Recon Sq	30 Jan 73–
26 CE Sq	31 Jan 73–		1978
26 Cmbt Spt Gp	31 Jan 73–	417 Tac Ftr Sq	1 Oct 78–1 Nov 78
26 Fld Maint Sq			1979
(26 Equip Maint Sq)	31 Jan 73–	26 Tac Hosp	22 Oct 79–

Appendix 1

Air Bases by Major Command
(As of 17 Sep 1982)

Military Airlift Command
Lajes Fld   Rhein-Main AB

Pacific Air Forces
Clark AB	Kwang Ju AB	Suwon AB
Kadena AB	Misawa AB	Taegu AB
Kunsan AB	Osan AB	Yokota AB

Strategic Air Command
Andersen AFB   Sondrestrom AB   Thule AB

Tactical Air Command
Howard AB   Keflavik Aprt

United States Air Forces in Europe
Ankara AS	Izmir AS	RAF Woodbridge
Aviano AB	Lindsey AS	Ramstein AB
Bitburg AB	RAF Alconbury	San Vito dei Normanni AS
Camp New Amsterdam	RAF Bentwaters	Sembach AB
Hahn AB	RAF Chicksands	Spangdahlem AB
Hellenikon AB	RAF Fairford	Tempelhof Central Aprt
Hessisch-Oldendorf AS	RAF Greenham Common	Torrejon AB
Incirlik AB	RAF Lakenheath	Zaragoza AB
Iraklion AS	RAF Mildenhall	Zweibrucken AB
	RAF Upper Heyford	

Appendix 2

Air Bases by Country
(As of 17 Sep 1982)

Federal Republic of Germany

Bitburg AB	Lindsey AS	Spangdahlem AB
Hahn AB	Ramstein AB	Tempelhof Central Aprt
Hessisch-Oldendorf AS	Rhein-Main AB	Zweibrucken AB
	Sembach AB	

Hellenic Republic

Hellenikon AB   Iraklion AS (Crete)

Italian Republic

Aviano AB   San Vito dei Normanni AS

Japan

Kadena AB (Okinawa)	Misawa AB	Yokota AB
	Osan AB	

Kingdom of Denmark (Greenland)

Sondrestrom AB   Thule AB

Kingdom of the Netherlands

Camp New Amsterdam

Republic of Iceland

Keflavik Aprt

AIR FORCE BASES OVERSEAS

Republic of Korea

Kunsan AB Kwang Ju AB Taegu AB
Suwon AB

Republic of Panama
Howard AB

Republic of the Philippines
Clark AB

Republic of Portugal
Lajes Fld (Azores)

Republic of Turkey
Ankara AS Incirlik AB Izmir AS

Spanish State
Torrejon AB Zaragoza AB

United Kingdom of Great Britain and Northern Ireland

RAF Alconbury RAF Fairford RAF Mildenhall
RAF Bentwaters RAF Greenham Common RAF Upper Heyford
RAF Chicksands RAF Lakenheath RAF Woodbridge

United States of America (Guam)
Andersen AFB

Note on Sources

Most of the data appearing in this volume came from the narrative histories prepared by unit historians at the squadron, group, wing, division, and command level. These records, deposited in the Air Force Historical Research Agency at Maxwell AFB, Alabama, contained not only the story of the base operating units and their particular missions, but also useful appendices and supporting documents. Among the supporting documents are to be found general and special orders, station lists, personnel rosters, morning reports, movement orders, operations orders, letters, newspaper accounts, and photographs. Many histories also included maps, schematics, and sketches of the bases concerned, which often revealed new or recent construction projects.

Information concerning the establishment, activation, transfer, discontinuance, and disposal of installations was gleaned for the most part from the file of 17,000 Engineer Installation Characteristics Reports (AF Form 1192). Data from earlier periods was often found in the index card file known as "Historical Data—Post, Camp, Station or Airfield File," which included data from 11,000 active and inactive bases and provided useful information about the status of the installations. These materials, all held by the Real Property Division of the USAF Director of Engineering and Services, Bolling AFB, DC, were made available to the Air Force Historical Research Agency.

General and special orders issued by the War Department and the air arms of the War Department, and, later, by the United States Air Force and its major commands, provided key information about basing, base housing, off-base and detached installations, location of installations, activation, inactivation, transfer of installations, and names and dates of base commanders. Generally speaking, these orders are on file in the holdings of the Air Force Historical Research Agency. Some orders, however, were found in the collections of the Air Force Reference Branch of the National Personnel Records Center in St. Louis, Missouri, or in the Military Archives Division of the National Archives and Records Administration in Washington, DC.

Army and Air Force station lists and Air Force organizational directories located in the Air Force Historical Research Agency provided excellent background material for base operating units, units assigned, and base commanders. Information was then verified through general or special orders or other official records. Likewise, the Air Force Directory of Key Personnel proved useful in pinpointing the names of commanders of major base operating units, although these did not provide specific dates of assignment. In terms of units assigned and other definitive data on operating units and units assigned, the most valuable source was the collection of organizational record cards on file in the Research Division of the Air Force Historical Research Agency, a working collection constantly updated to reflect the current disposition of Air Force units worldwide. More than 30,000 cards of active, inactive, and disbanded units resolved hundreds of questions concerning locations, activation, inactivation, and assignments.

Finally, while reviewing the manuscript—or on request—many base and unit historians furnished valuable information not found elsewhere. These data contributed materially, making this a more accurate and useful reference work.

Glossary

AAA	antiaircraft artillery
AAB	Army Air Base
AACS	Airways and Air Communications Service
AAF	Army Air Forces
AAFld	Army Air Field
AB	Air Base
abn	airborne
ACW, AC & W	aircraft control and warning
acft	aircraft
actvd	activated
acty	activity
ACWS	aircraft control and warning squadron
AD	air defense
ADC	Air Defense Command
admn	administration
admntv	administrative
adrm	airdrome
ADVON	advanced echelon
aerl	aerial
aeromed	aeromedical
aerosp	aerospace
AF	Air Force
AFB	Air Force Base
Afld	Airfield
AFSS	Air Force Security System
aka	also known as
alft	airlift
ammo	ammunition
amn	airman; airmen
anx	annex
AP	Air Police
aprt	airport
armnt	armament
AS	Air Station
asgn(d)	assign(ed)

atchd	attached
aux	auxiliary
avn	aviation
avncs	avionics
AW	automatic weapons
bach	bachelor
BC	bomber command
bcn	beacon
bmbr	bomber
bn	battalion
bomb	bombardment
BOQ	bachelor officers' quarters
Brig Gen	Brigadier General
BU	base unit
c.	circa (about)
CAA	Civil Aeronautics Administration
Capt	Captain
carr	carrier
CE	civil engineering
cen	center
CG	commanding general
chgd	changed
cmbt	combat
cmsy	commissary
Col	Colonel
comd	command
comdr	commander
comm(s)	communication(s)
compl	complement
comps	composite
con	control
consold	consolidated
const	construction
CONUS	continental United States
crgo	cargo
def	defense
dep	depot
depnt	dependent
dept	department
det	detachment
detchd	detached
DF	direction finding
discd	discontinued

dispy	dispensary
distr	distribution
div	division
dsgd	designated
dspd	disposed
dspl	disposal
ECM	electronic counter measure(s)
elect(s)	electronic(s)
EM	enlisted man(men)
emerg	emergency
engr	engineer
engrg	engineering
equip	equipment
esct	escort
EUCOM	European Command (also USEUCOM)
evac	evacuation
fam	family
fclty (fclts)	facility (facilities)
FEAF	Far East Air Forces
fl	flying
fld	field
flt(s)	flight(s)
FRG	Federal Republic of Germany
ft	foot; feet
Ft	fort
ftr	fighter
ftr-intcpr	fighter-interceptor
FY	fiscal year
GEEIA	Ground Equipment Engineering and Installation Agency
Gen	General
GLOBECOM	Global Communications System (USAF)
gnd	ground
gnrtn	generation
gnry	gunnery
gp	group
gym	gymnasium
hosp	hospital
HQ	headquarters
hsg	housing
IG	Inspector General

215

ILS	instrument landing system
inactvd	inactivated
inf	infantry
infmy	infirmary
instl(s)	installation(s)
intcpr	interceptor
intl	international
IRBM	intermediate range ballistic missile
isl(s)	island(s)
JASDF	Japanese Air Self-Defense Force
JUSMG	Joint United States Military Group
lab	laboratory
LF	low frequency
ln	liaison
log(s)	logistic(s)
Lt	Lieutenant
Lt Col	Lieutenant Colonel
Lt Gen	Lieutenant General
MAC	Military Airlift Command
maint	maintenance
Maj	Major
MAJCOM	major command
mat	materiel
MATS	Military Air Transport Service
med	medical
mgmt	management
mi	mile(s)
mil	military
MP	military police
msl(s)	missile(s)
mun	munitions
MV	motor vehicle
NATO	North American Treaty Organization
nav	navigation(al)
NCO	noncommissioned officer
obs	observation
ofc	office
off	officer
OL(s)	operating location(s)
op(s)	operation(s)
ord	ordnance

orgnzl	organizational
PACAF	Pacific Air Forces
perm	permanent
pers	personnel
petrol	petroleum
plt	pilot
POL	petroleum, oil, and lubricants
pol	police
prcmt	procurement
prdc	periodic
prim	primary
prods	products
prov	provisional
pur	pursuit
qm	quartermaster
qtrs	quarters
RAF	Royal Air Force (British)
RB	radio beacon
rcvr	receiver
rdsgd	redesignated
recon	reconnaissance
recrn	recreation
regt(s)	regiment(s)
repl	replacement
rflg	refueling
rg(s)	range(s)
RNAF	Royal Netherland Air Force
ROK	Republic of Korea
ROKAF	Republic of Korea Air Force
rpr	repair
RR	radio relay
RRS	radio relay site
rsch	research
rscu	rescue
SAC	Strategic Air Command
sch	school
scty	security
SEA	Southeast Asia
SE	single engine
sec	section
sig	signal
sp	special

spt(d)	support(ed)
sq	squadron
stat	statistical
stn	station
stor	storage
strat	strategic
sup	supply
svc(s)	service(s)
sys	system(s)
TAB VEE	specially hardened shelters approved by the Theater Air Base Vulnerability Study Group
thtr	theater
TAC	Tactical Air Command
tac	tactical
tacan	Tactical Air Navigation
TCC	Troop Carrier Command
tech	technical
temp	temporary
tmtr	transmitter
tng	training
trml	terminal
trnsp	transportation
trnst	transient
trp	troop
trpt	transport
trsf(d)	transfer(red)
trsmn	transmission
TVOR	terminal VHF omnirange
UC	under construction
UK, U.K.	United Kingdom
unk	unknown
US, U.S.	United States (of America)
USA	United States (or U.S.) Army
USAAF	United States Army Air Forces
USAF	United States Air Force
USAFE	United States Air Forces in Europe
USAFSS	United States Air Force Security Service (later, Electronic Security Command)
USEUCOM	United States European Command
USMC	United States Marine Corps
USN	United States Navy
VAR	Volunteer Air Reserve

218

VLR	very long range
VOQ	visiting officers' quarters
VOR	VHF Omnirange
VORTAC	VHF Omnirange Tactical Air Navigation
VR	vehicle repair
WAF	Women in the Air Force
WD	War Department
wea	weather
wg	wing
whse	warehouse
wpns	weapons